After the Hector

*The Scottish Pioneers of Nova Scotia
and Cape Breton 1773–1852*

After the Hector

The Scottish Pioneers of Nova Scotia and Cape Breton 1773–1852

LUCILLE H. CAMPEY

NATURAL HERITAGE BOOKS
TORONTO

Published by Natural Heritage / Natural History Inc.
PO Box 95, Station O, Toronto, ON, Canada M4A 2M8
www.naturalheritagebooks.com

Cover illustration: *Town of Pictou*, by William Kitchin, 1822, *courtesy of Art Gallery of Nova Scotia, 1985.45, gift of Phyllis Ross, Moncton, New Brunswick, in memory of her brother, W.T.D. Ross, 1985.* Back cover: Mabou Pioneer Cemetary of Indian Point in West Mabou. It is dedicated to the first Catholic Highlanders who settled in the area from the early 1800s. *Photograph by Geoff Campey.*

Design by Blanche Hamill, Norton Hamill Design
Edited by Jane Gibson
Printed and bound in Canada by Hignell Book Printing, Winnipeg, Manitoba

The text in this book was set in a typeface named Granjon.

National Library of Canada Cataloguing in Publication

Campey, Lucille H
    After the Hector : the Scottish pioneers of Nova Scotia and Cape Breton, 1773–1852 /
Lucille H. Campey.

Includes bibliographical references and index.
ISBN 1-896219-95-0

    1. Scots—Nova Scotia—History—18th century. 2. Scots—Nova Scotia—History—
19th century. 3. Scotland—Emigration and immigration—History.
4. Nova Scotia—Emigration and immigration—History. I. Title.

FC2350.S3C35 2004 971.6'0049163   C2004-901495-1

Natural Heritage / Natural History Inc. acknowledges the financial support of the Canada Council for the Arts and the Ontario Arts Council for its publishing program. It acknowledges the support of the Government of Ontario through the Ontario Media Development Corporation's Ontario Book Initiative. It also acknowledges the financial support of the Government of Canada through the Book Publishing Industry Development Program (BPIDP) and the Association for the Export of Canadian Books.

I dedicate this book to the memory of my late father, William James Thomson, who was born in Pictou. My great-great-grandfather William Thomson, described as William, "Pioneer," emigrated from Morayshire in North East Scotland in the early 1800s. He was one of the Scottish pioneers of West River, Antigonish.

CONTENTS

Tables and Figures   IX

Acknowledgements   XI

Preface   XIII

Abbreviations   XVII

1   THE NEW WORLD BECKONS   3

2   THE *Hector* ARRIVES IN 1773   18

3   THE LOYALIST EMIGRANTS   34

4   CREATING A NEW SCOTLAND   56

5   THE ATTRACTIONS OF THE TIMBER TRADE   83

6   CAPE BRETON'S GROWING POPULARITY   109

7   NOVA SCOTIA'S LINGERING APPEAL   125

8   POOR BUT DEFIANT: CAPE BRETON'S PIONEER SCOTS   144

9   SHIPS AND ATLANTIC CROSSINGS   164

10 THE SCOTTISH LEGACY   182

    APPENDIX I   Extant Passenger Lists for Ship Crossings   193
                  from Scotland to Nova Scotia and
                  Cape Breton

    APPENDIX II   Emigrant Ship Crossings from Scotland to   234
                  Nova Scotia and Cape Breton, 1773 to 1852

CONTENTS

APPENDIX III   The Ships which took Emigrant Scots to   278
                Nova Scotia and Cape Breton, 1773–1852
APPENDIX IV   Sir Edward Mortimer's Debtors, c. 1819   299
Notes   304
Bibliography   339
Index   349
About the Author   375

TABLES & FIGURES

TABLES

1 Men from the disbanded 82nd Regiment who settled at   46
   Fischer's Grant (between Pictou and Merigomish Harbours)
   from 1784.

2 Men from the disbanded 84th Regiment who settled   51
   on the East River, Pictou in 1784.

3 Highlanders, including men from the disbanded   52
   84th Regiment, who settled on the East River,
   Pictou in 1797.

4 List of passengers who lately came from Scotland   69
   to the Province of Nova Scotia c. 1802.

5 List of emigrant Scots who were residing in   93
   the Pictou District by the Spring of 1816.

FIGURES

1 Predominant areas of Scotland from which the Nova Scotia   20
   and Cape Breton emigrants originated, 1773–1852.

2 Concentrations of Scots in Pictou County, 1773–1816.   28

3 Locations of Loyalist settlers in the Maritime region, 1784. 36

4 Predominant ethnic groups in Nova Scotia 45
   and Cape Breton, 1871.

5 Concentrations of Scottish settlement 59
   in eastern Nova Scotia, 1773–1850.

6 Roman Catholic and Presbyterian affiliations of Scots 60
   in Nova Scotia and Cape Breton, 1871.

7 Concentrations of Scots in the eastern Maritimes 61
   by the mid- 19th century.

8 Scottish settlements in Cape Breton. 100

ACKNOWLEDGEMENTS

I AM INDEBTED TO MANY people. I wish to thank Garry Schutlak, archivist at the Nova Scotia Archives and Records Management, in Halifax, for his help and guidance. A special treat was my visit to the Gaelic College of Celtic Arts and Crafts in St. Anns, in Cape Breton. I arrived on a morning in August to see a fiddling class taking place in the open air and hear the stirring sound of the bagpipes coming from the other side of the lawn. Classes in Gaelic were in progress. What a wonderful place! I am grateful to Peggy MacAskill and Helen MacLeod for their time and trouble in showing me around parts of the College and in providing me with one of my illustrations. I also appreciated my discussion with Donald Morrison. I wish also to thank Mary Beth Carty at the Antigonish Heritage Museum for introducing me to *The Casket* newspaper and making me aware of John MacLean's Gaelic poetry.

Thanks are due to the staff at the National Archives of Canada, the National Library of Scotland and the National Archives of Scotland. I also wish to particularly thank the staff at the Toronto Reference Library and the Aberdeen University Library.

I am very grateful, as well, to the people who have helped me obtain illustrations. I thank Lord Strathnaver for the photograph of the statue of the first Duke of Sutherland and photographs of the portraits of the first and second Dukes of Sutherland. I thank Richard Kindersley who very kindly gave me a photograph of the Emigration Stone at Cromarty, which he designed and carved. I am grateful to Dr. Dianne O'Neill and

ACKNOWLEDGEMENTS

Troy Wagner of the Art Gallery of Nova Scotia for their help in obtaining illustrations and I also thank Marven Moore of the Maritime Museum of the Atlantic, in Halifax.

I thank my good friend Jean Lucas for her comments on the initial manuscript and her wonderful company during our recent trip to the Maritimes. Most of all I thank my husband Geoff for his support and practical help. Without him the book could not have been written.

PREFACE

THE PROVINCE OF NOVA SCOTIA is justifiably proud of its rich Scottish heritage. Thousands of Scots, who came mainly from the Highlands and Islands of Scotland, settled in the province during the late eighteenth century and the first half of the nineteenth century. As a consequence, large tracts of mainland Nova Scotia and what was formerly the separate Island of Cape Breton became great bastions of Scottish culture. The very first to arrive were the nearly 200 people who sailed on the *Hector* in 1773. After landing in Pictou they sparked off one of the greatest ever migrations of Scots to the New World. As the first Scottish immigrants they had no way of appreciating the long-term importance of their pioneering achievements. They certainly could never have imagined that people today would continue to celebrate their arrival with such fervour and pageantry. Why does this one event have such lasting significance? Why were the *Hector* settlers followed by thousands more Scots? Why did so many Scots choose to settle in the province? How was the creation of Canada's New Scotland actually achieved?

These are some of the questions which I attempt to answer in this book. I have built on D.F. Campbell and R.A. MacLean's *Beyond the Atlantic Roar: A Study of the Nova Scotia Scots,* written some thirty years ago, which was the first major, comprehensive study of the subject. In considering the factors which drove and directed the Scottish influx, they concentrated much of their attention on the various social and economic developments in Scotland which may have caused people to leave.

I have extended their work by looking more closely at the reasons why the province attracted pioneer Scots. One of the crucial factors which influenced them was the prospect of owning their own land and achieving better living standards. The region's rapidly expanding timber trade with Britain was the key to this better life.

In fact, the timber trade acted like an enormous magnet. The Scots, who came in the late eighteenth and early nineteenth centuries, were initially drawn to the major timber-producing regions on the east side of the province. Being the earliest to arrive, pioneer Scots established themselves in the most favourable locations close to timber collecting bays and along the rivers which flowed into them. Developed with Scottish capital and business acumen, the timber trade provided the ships which took emigrant Scots to the province and it underpinned the region's economy. Thus the progress of Scottish settlements and the timber trade were inextricably linked.

To appreciate the full extent of the Scottish influx to Nova Scotia and Cape Breton it has been necessary to delve into shipping records. When we do this we see how the two-way traffic in people and timber actually worked and we gain a far clearer impression of the geographical origins of the emigrant Scots who came to the province. After leaving their home ports, ships would call at Highland and Island ports like Fort William, Tobermory, Stornoway and Cromarty to collect emigrants before heading west across the Atlantic to Pictou or Sydney. Once the passengers disembarked, timber was collected from the region and cargoes were loaded on the ships returning to Scotland. The process depended on the accessibility and affordability of passing timber ships and the Highlander's enthusiasm for emigration. Covered in this book are three hundred and thirty-one Atlantic ship crossings, which together account for some thirty thousand Scots. Very few names are known but their presence as passengers on timber ships can be deduced from surviving customs records and newspaper shipping reports.

Two recurring themes in the book are the importance which Scots placed on their culture and on religion. Being mainly Highlanders, they emigrated in large groups. Follow-on emigration usually came from the areas of Scotland which had fostered the original settlement footholds, thus creating highly distinctive Scottish communities. Presbyterians and Roman Catholics expanded their territories quite separately, leaving mainland Nova Scotia and Cape Breton with their clear religious demarcations. The clergymen sent out from Scotland were a valuable religious and cultural lifeline. I have used their extensive accounts of visits to the various Scottish settlements to identify the progress of Scottish colonization. They were on-the-spot observers and through their reports we can distinguish between long-established settlements and those which were in the process of being formed when the clergymen first arrived.

Initially much of the influx was to mainland Nova Scotia but, by the 1820s, Cape Breton soared ahead in popularity. With the collapse of the Hebridean economy, Cape Breton increasingly became a refuge for poverty-stricken Highlanders. Their allegiance to Cape Breton was quite phenomenal. Upper Canada had far better land and employment prospects but, in spite of this, a great many Hebridean emigrants preferred to go to Cape Breton. At the height of the famine in 1847 the Lieutenant Governor of the province actually had to intervene to stop them from coming to Cape Breton. These emigrants clearly placed a far higher value on living close to fellow Scots, who shared their culture and values, than on the financial benefits they might gain from emigrating.

Having identified a total of two hundred and thirteen different ships as having carried emigrant Scots to the province, I then pursued another line of enquiry. I wondered whether they were good ships or rickety old barges. The *Lloyd's Shipping Register*, still in use today, remains the authoritative source on a ship's age, condition and quality of construction. Because of limitations in the shipping data I was only able to obtain data from the *Register* for one hundred and thirty-four ships. Nevertheless this is a substantial sample. Sixty percent of the ones which could be identified in the *Register* were of the highest quality while most of the remaining ships were classed as seaworthy, with only minor defects. The popular perception that emigrants travelled on the worse ships is simply not born out by the evidence. The data clearly shows that a good standard of shipping was on offer.

It seems that history is sometimes a matter of fashion. When Alexander MacKenzie, editor of the *Celtic Magazine,* gave the first written account of the *Hector* crossing in 1773, he embellished it by suggesting that brutal landlords had driven the emigrants from their homes. Writing one hundred and ten years after the event, he conveniently ignored the fact that people had left Scotland in 1773 in the face of fierce opposition. Landlords regarded emigration as a threat and sought to hold on to their tenantry. Sadly, he and later commentators have helped to create a lasting pioneer mythology which requires victims and scapegoats. Passions about the Highland Clearances of the 1840s and 1850s understandably run high. They caused considerable turmoil and suffering. This was the one period when some people were forced to emigrate but they were a tiny minority of the total who emigrated to the New World.

The fact remains that most emigration was voluntary and self-financed. Emigration became an unstoppable force. This combination of push and pull factors brought thousands of Scots to the province. They laid down a rich and deep seam of Scottish culture which continues to flourish in eastern Nova Scotia and Cape Breton to this day.

ABBREVIATIONS

ACA	Aberdeen City Archives
AH	*Aberdeen Herald*
AJ	*Aberdeen Journal*
AR	*Acadian Recorder*
DC	*Dundee Courier*
DCA	Dundee City Archives
DGC	*Dumfries and Galloway Courier*
DWJ	*Dumfries Weekly Journal*
DCB	*Dictionary of Canadian Biography*
EA	*Edinburgh Advertiser*
GA	*Greenock Advertiser*
IC	*Inverness Courier*
IJ	*Inverness Journal*
JJ	*John O'Groat Journal*
LSR	*Lloyd's Shipping Register*
NAS	National Archives of Scotland
NLS	National Library of Scotland
NSARM	Nova Scotia Archives & Records Management
PAPEI	Public Archives of Prince Edward Island

ABBREVIATIONS

PC	*Perthshire Courier*
PRO	Public Record Office
PP	*Parliamentary Papers*
QG	*Quebec Gazette*
QM	*Quebec Mercury*
SM	*Scots Magazine*
SRA	Strathclyde Regional Archives

After the Hector

*The Scottish Pioneers of Nova Scotia
and Cape Breton 1773–1852*

THE NEW WORLD BECKONS

A spirit of emigration hath seized the people and the murmurs of discontent and painful distress are everywhere echoed from the mouths of the poor, who groan beneath a weight of penury.[1]

LAMENTING THE LOSS OF so many people to the New World, the *Edinburgh Advertiser* called for something to be done to stem the outflow of Scots. But even by this early date, in 1773, the exodus had developed an unstoppable momentum. High rents and oppressive landlords in Scotland, coupled with the positive reports of the better life to be had in North America, had led many people to opt for emigration. Having been amongst those who succumbed to the so-called "spirit of emigration," some one hundred and ninety Scots had sailed to Pictou on the *Hector* in the very month and year of the newspaper's pronouncement. Like the others who had gone before, they had made a deliberate choice to emigrate and were certainly not victims of any expulsions. Quite the contrary. They left against a backdrop of feverish opposition.

At this time emigration was seen as being highly detrimental to Scotland's interests. Men were being lost who would otherwise serve in its workforce or armed forces. Some Highland landlords, fearing the loss of tenants from their estates, tried to halt the exodus, but to no avail. Our *Hector* arrivals had essentially defied Scottish public opinion and,

The Highlander statue in Pictou. The inscription reads "In proud commemoration of the courage, faith and endurance of the gallant pioneer passengers in the ship *Hector*." *Photograph by Geoff Campey.*

as they stepped from their ship after a dreadful crossing, their immediate prospects looked bleak. It was not an easy beginning.

A larger-than-life bronze statue of a Highlander in full regimental dress now stands watch on a hillside above the *Hector*'s landing place. From his vantage point he overlooks the modern-day replica which is now moored at the Hector Heritage Quay on the Pictou waterfront. Two hundred and thirty years ago a seagull perched on this same site would have witnessed the real thing – the historic landing of Nova Scotia's first Scottish pioneers. It must have seemed deeply ironic to these founders of "New Scotland" that the people who came forward to greet them were New Englanders. This was already an English colony. The Nova Scotia which they saw before them was Scottish in name only.[2]

The region had attracted the attention of Sir William Alexander, Earl of Stirling, some one hundred and fifty years earlier. Having acquired colonization rights over "New Scotland" (or Nova Scotia, as it was designated in a Latin charter), he attempted to found a Scottish colony but his efforts came to nothing. Scottish lairds were happy to buy land but they had little interest in recruiting settlers.[3] Lord Ochiltree came close to establishing a small colony in Cape Breton in 1629, but he and his settlers were sent packing by the French when he tried to extract tax revenue from local fishermen.[4] When this property developers' charade ended, the French settlements, which were mainly concentrated in the Acadian heartland around the Bay of Fundy, took on a new lease of life. While French-speaking Acadians were fast becoming a sizeable minority at this stage, they were greatly outnumbered by the Native inhabitants who were mainly Mi'kmaq.[5]

However, the situation changed drastically when France surrendered Acadia (peninsular Nova Scotia) to the British in 1713. The die was now cast. Britain bolstered her hold over Nova Scotia by exchanging its indigenous population for immigrants who could be relied upon to support her interests. The Native Peoples were systematically marginalized and thousands of Acadians were forcibly removed.[6] After the Acadian deportation of 1755, some 8,000 American colonists of English ancestry arrived to take their place.[7] These were the New England "Planters" who were brought, at government expense, to the Minas Basin region between 1759 and 1762.[8]

Nevertheless, in spite of this policy of expulsion, some Acadians remained in the region. Many had, in fact, escaped deportation in 1755

The ship *Hector*, a reconstruction. This replica of the original ship, which took nearly a decade to complete, is moored at the Hector Heritage Quay on the Pictou waterfront. *Photograph by Geoff Campey.*

by fleeing to Ile Royale (Cape Breton) and Ile Saint Jean (Prince Edward Island), where they re-established themselves as settlers. But, once again, they were forced to surrender their lands. Another round of deportations took place in 1758 when British control was extended over these Islands.[9] With the ending of hostilities in 1763, many Acadians later returned to the eastern Maritimes although they were confined to mainly remote areas and to relatively poor land.[10] Thus, when the *Hector* arrived in 1773, Nova Scotia's European population was largely of English descent. The *Hector* settlers would plant some settlement footholds but the dawning of their New Scotland was still a distant dream.

The Highlander statue which overlooks Pictou Harbour deserves a closer look. This is a confident-looking young man, in full military dress, who holds his settler's axe over his left shoulder and a musket in his right hand – appropriately enough, for a decade after the *Hector*'s arrival at Pictou a good many Highlanders would come to the area as ex-soldiers. When the American War of Independence ended in defeat for Britain in 1784, the government relocated many ex-servicemen, at public expense, to areas such as Pictou, which it wished to protect.[11] Thus, much needed military muscle and direction came to Pictou at a crucial time in its development. However, there was something particularly significant about these military settlers and their families. Most came from east Inverness-shire, in the northeast Highlands, – the place of origin of many of the *Hector* settlers. Lord Selkirk, one of the few high-ranking Scots to support emigration, saw for himself, during his travels through North America, why it was that "the same district of Scotland gathered round the same neighbourhood in the colonies." The success of those who had gone before, in this case the *Hector* settlers, had been "a sufficient motive" to draw further people from their part of Scotland.[12] Early links were being reinforced. This was the catalyst which would cause east Inverness-shire to lose so many of its people to Pictou.

The overall Scottish exodus was being fuelled by other factors as well. The disruption being caused by the introduction of large sheep farms, from the late eighteenth century, and a worsening economic situation were contributing to growing surges in emigration. Religious persecu-

tion lay behind the departure, in the early 1770s, of many hundreds of
Catholic Highlanders, from parts of the Western Isles and mainland
west Inverness-shire. They initially chose Prince Edward Island but, by
1791, they had also established settlements on the other side of the
Northumberland Strait at Arisaig, in peninsular Nova Scotia. Catholic
Highlanders were also to be found in Cape Breton, in spite of government regulations which were meant to keep them out. Wishing to protect
its coal mining interests on the Island, the government had made Cape
Breton as inaccessible as it possibly could to settlers. Legally binding
restraining orders had been issued but Scottish colonizers took no notice
of them. From 1790 they slipped across from Prince Edward Island and
mainland Nova Scotia to the Western Shore of Cape Breton and helped
themselves to the best land.

The fact that there were two, quite separate, concentrations of Scots,
one Presbyterian and the other Catholic, can be attributed to Father
Angus MacEachern (later Bishop). Based at the time at Prince Edward
Island, he feared the loss of Catholic newcomers to Pictou's growing
Presbyterian congregation. Unless he intervened there was a real danger
that Reverend James MacGregor, Pictou's first Presbyterian Minister,
would win them over as converts. So he devised a plan. As emigrant
Scots disembarked from their ships, he effectively held up a signpost
pointing Presbyterians towards Pictou and Catholics towards Arisaig
and Cape Breton.[13] By doing this, Catholic Highlanders were encompassed in a neat triangle on the east, which he could access by boat, and
both they and the Presbyterians could expand their territories separately
as they preferred to do.

The Scottish exodus from the Highlands and Islands grew rapidly
because it offered people an escape from poverty and oppression. It held
out the prospect of land ownership and a better standard of living. And
it had another advantage as well. Highlanders could have opted for the
good employment opportunities to be had in the manufacturing industries of the Scottish Lowlands. But this would come at a price. They
would lose their cultural identity once they had become absorbed within
the melting pot of an urban society. However, by emigrating to British

America in large groups, they could transplant their communities intact and continue with their traditional way of life. Faced with these two alternatives, it is little wonder that so many Highlanders chose to emigrate. But thus far we have dwelt only on the factors which caused people to leave Scotland. We have still to consider why so many Scots chose to go to the eastern Maritimes.

One obvious reason was proximity to Scotland. Having a relatively short sailing time from Scotland, ports like Pictou were cheaper to get to, an important consideration for emigrants who had to struggle to find the money for their fares. Secondly, for many Scots the development of the eastern Maritimes' burgeoning timber trade was another important factor. The *Hector* settlers had begun to export timber to Britain from as early as 1775, just two years after their arrival. And by 1803 when our roving reporter, Lord Selkirk, arrived on the scene "about twenty vessels at 400 tons on average" were loading up each year at Pictou Harbour.[14] By 1805 the number had rocketed to fifty ships a year. And as greater numbers of ships arrived from Scottish ports to collect timber, many would come with a fresh batch of emigrant Scots in their holds.

As was the case elsewhere in the eastern Maritimes, Scottish merchants had been quick to spot the economic potential of the timber trade. By the early nineteenth century they were providing the region with a great deal of its early economic impetus and capital investment. Scots effectively controlled the region's economic life. The Scottish-born timber merchant, Edward Mortimer, whose wealth and influence earned him the title of "King of Pictou," was the lynch pin of Pictou's economy.[15] By offering Scottish settlers credit he gave them a stake in Pictou's timber trade. Thus the timber trade provided emigrants both with the means of transport and with great economic benefits, once they became established as settlers. Having been the first Europeans to arrive in eastern Nova Scotia and Cape Breton, they could choose the best coastline and river locations. They could profit most from the sale of their own cut timber and enjoy the overall benefits of living in a region with a rapidly expanding economy. And Mortimer's preference for only doing business with his own people, ensured that Scots would always get the best opportunities.

To sum up, there were strong forces which caused people to leave Scotland, while the timber trade was the magnet which drew them to the eastern Maritimes. These "push and pull" factors together, with the early success of the *Hector* settlers, and those who followed them, fuelled a growing Scottish influx, which was dominated by Highlanders and Islanders. But their success was hardly a foregone conclusion. These people originated from areas of Scotland with few trees and limited agriculture – hardly the best qualifications for clearing an outback in North America. Yet they had other qualities which made them ideal pioneers:

"The habits, employments and customs of the Highlander seem to fit him for the American forest, which he penetrates without feeling the gloom and melancholy, experienced by those who have been brought up in towns and amidst the fertile fields of highly cultivated districts. Scottish emigrants are hardy, industrious and cheerful – and experience has fully proved that no people meet the first difficulties of settling wild lands with greater patience and fortitude."[16]

Highlanders did succeed, not due to any practical skills which they brought with them, but because of their toughness and ability to cope with isolation and extreme hardships. When it came to harsh conditions and remoteness there was no better training ground than the Highlands and Islands of Scotland.

By using a wide range of documentary sources, including newspaper shipping records, customs records, passenger lists and the reports of visiting clergymen, the actual size of the influx can be estimated, although the inadequacies of the available data mean that the results are incomplete. It can be shown that, during the forty year period from the *Hector*'s arrival in 1773 to 1815, a minimum of 6,500 emigrant Scots arrived in eastern Nova Scotia, and Cape Breton while at least 4,000 Scots went to Prince Edward Island.[17] The exact numbers of those who arrived shall never be known since the relevant data was not systematically listed in British and Colonial records. Because there are large gaps in these records, it is highly probable that the actual figures were much higher.

9

But, in spite of their limitations, these estimated figures are capable of revealing the broad picture. They demonstrate the popularity of the eastern Maritimes. Just under seventy percent of the total numbers leaving Scotland for British North America during this period chose this region.[18]

However, when these figures are put into the context of the overall population of peninsular Nova Scotia, which, in 1806, was around 65,000, the 6,500 Scots who went to it and Cape Breton seem but a drop in the ocean.[19] Due to the economic downturn which followed the ending of the Napoleonic Wars in 1815, the Scottish influx grew substantially. The customs records, which become more reliable from this stage, show that between 1815 and 1838 some 24,000 Scots entered Nova Scotia and Cape Breton, along with 13,000 Irish and 2,000 English immigrants.[20] But here again, if this is put into the context of Nova Scotia's overall population, which in 1831 stood at about 140,000, the Scottish component seems insignificant. A further 8,300 Scots arrived in the period from 1839 to 1851, at which point the flow of emigrants declined sharply.[21] But the truly amazing statistic is not the relative numbers, but the actual numbers. These figures show that a minimum of just under 40,000 Scots came to Nova Scotia and Cape Breton in the eighty years which followed the *Hector*'s arrival. The actual numbers were probably much higher. The large depopulated areas, which can be seen today in the north of Scotland, especially in inland areas of Sutherland and Inverness-shire and in the Western Isles, stand witness to this staggering loss of Scots to the eastern Maritimes.

Unlike mainland Nova Scotia, where they were only ever a substantial minority, Scots came to dominate the overall population of Cape Breton. Here, too, there are great difficulties in computing the actual numbers. Not only are there gaps in the official records, but the fact that most of the emigrant Scots who arrived at Cape Breton before 1817 probably entered the Maritimes at either Pictou, Halifax or Charlottetown must be acknowledged. Because of the restrictions placed in their way by the government, Scots would have found it almost impossible to find a ship which would take them directly to Cape Breton. There was one notable exception which is duly commemorated at Sydney Harbour:

The cairn and plaque at Sydney Harbour, commemorating the 340
emigrant Scots who sailed on the *Northern Friends* of Clyde in 1802.
They were the first arrivals from Scotland to sail directly to Cape
Breton. *Photograph by Geoff Campey.*

"Arrival of *Northern Friends* of Clyde in 1802 at Sydney – This
marked the first emigration directly from Scotland to Cape Breton
and formed the vanguard of the great migration which gave the
Island its Scottish character."[22]

Cape Breton's Scottish population grew rapidly. The five-fold increase in its population from around 8,000, in 1817, to nearly 38,000, in 1838, can be attributed mainly to the large influx of Hebridean emigrants which occurred in this period.[23] Scots were the predominant ethnic group by the early 1820s. And by 1871 people of Scottish descent actually outnumbered the rest of the population by two to one.[24]

Having been a squatters' paradise during its earliest phases of colonization,[25] Cape Breton's immigration figures are extremely difficult to quantify. Customs officials later had to admit that "no record whatever has been taken" of passenger arrivals on the Island from 1790 to 1820. And while there were recorded figures which showed that 6,500 Scots had entered the port of Sydney, from 1821 to 1830, they were only a fraction of the true numbers:

"In addition to the number returned, several vessels arrive annually and land their passengers on the Western Shore of this Island, the masters [of ships] neglecting to make any report of the number in consequence of an officer not being stationed at Ship Harbour."[26]

D.C. Harvey estimates that 20,000 Scots arrived in the period from 1815 to 1838. A total of 10,000 Scots can be computed from official customs records and newspaper shipping reports but Harvey suggests that the true figure is double this total.[27] Given that the Sydney emigrant arrivals went unrecorded until 1821 and that the Island offered limitless, unsupervised landing places for emigrant ships, this estimate seems highly probable.

However, in spite of the deficiencies of the data, these figures demonstrate the continuing pulling power of Cape Breton. Its attraction to Hebridean Islanders was quite phenomenal. Upper Canada, with its much better land and conditions, emerged by the mid-1820s as the clear favourite of most emigrants, Scots included. However, Hebridean emigrants remained impervious to Upper Canada's obvious benefits. Cape Breton continued to attract considerable numbers of them. Some 7,000 Hebridean settlers came to Cape Breton during the five year period from

1839 to 1843, at which time the influx came to an abrupt end.[28] If ever there was a demonstration of the great importance placed by Scots on preserving their identity it was this. Cape Breton was soon to have the largest Gaelic-speaking population in the world, outside of Scotland.

Much of the previous research carried out on Scottish emigration has been preoccupied with the poverty of the emigrants and the forces which drove them from their homelands. Little thought has been given to the factors which attracted them to their destinations. The immense importance of the timber trade in shaping settlement patterns has been completely overlooked. The doubling of the already high duties on European timber in 1811 had the effect of pricing it out of the market.[29] This made North American timber far cheaper, in spite of the greater distance to North America, and, as a consequence, Maritime timber exports soared. As the trade grew more ships crossed the Atlantic and shipowners actively sought emigrants to take on their ships' westward journeys. Competition brought down fares and transatlantic crossings became regular occurrences. The timber trade was the sole reason why ships left in such numbers from Scottish ports and without those ships the early Scottish takeover of the eastern Maritimes could not have happened.

The trade forged new shipping routes from Scotland to the timber-producing areas of the eastern Maritimes. Being the earliest major group of immigrants to arrive in eastern Nova Scotia and Cape Breton, emigrant Scots found the most favourable locations close to the timber collecting bays and along the rivers which flowed into them. They felled timber and cleared land along these coastal and river frontages, creating distinct pockets of settlement. Thus the timber trade and colonization were not separate developments but were inextricably linked. The striking division of Nova Scotia into a Scottish east and an English (mainly New Englander) west, as revealed by the 1871 Census, is a consequence of the timber trade. It was responsible for the large concentrations of Scots to be found in Pictou, Colchester, Antigonish and Guysborough counties in mainland Nova Scotia and throughout most of Cape Breton.

These overall patterns tell us, in broad terms, where Scots were concentrated, but they are a composite picture only. They say nothing of the individual Scottish communities within these areas. When emigrant Scots came to live in eastern Nova Scotia and Cape Breton they carefully selected their locations. It was not some random leap into the dark. Documentary sources, such as customs records and passenger lists reveal where they came from in Scotland while land grant records, contemporary histories and genealogical studies identify their chosen locations in the Maritimes. Through an analysis of these sources the potency of family and community ties can be demonstrated by observing how people who originated from particular parts of Scotland banded together in the same parts of Nova Scotia or Cape Breton. That Scots had an incredibly strong desire to preserve and share a common culture is equally demonstrated. This desire was what drove later arrivals to their particular Maritime locations. The high value which they placed on their cultural identity helped them to succeed as pioneers and it also left parts of Nova Scotia and Cape Breton with their highly distinctive Scottish communities.

Of course, religion was very important to Scots and here again there are cultural connotations. The Presbyterian missionaries, who were sent across by the Church of Scotland to establish congregations stood no chance at all unless they could speak Gaelic.[30] After preaching to some 150 people, who were of "a respectable class" at Broad Cove, Cape Breton, Reverend James Frazer then fought his way "through a dreary forest eleven miles broad, which occupied us for 8 hours" to get to the Middle River settlements.[31] This was all in a day's work for an itinerant missionary. By bringing Presbyterianism to scattered communities in the wilds of Cape Breton, he reinforced Scottish values and traditions. But Reverend Frazer, and others like him, would not have been in Cape Breton in the first place had it not been for the campaigning zeal of Mrs. Isabella MacKay, a most remarkable Edinburgh lady. Although she had never been to Cape Breton, she dedicated her life to raising funds for its Presbyterian congregations. Founding the Edinburgh Ladies Association in 1831, which did the fundraising, and recruiting missionaries and schoolteachers herself, she brought religion and education to every corner of Cape Breton.

Unlike the pioneer Scots of Belfast, Prince Edward Island, who were assisted by the wealthy Lord Selkirk, the Scots who came to Nova Scotia and Cape Breton had to fend for themselves.[32] No one from outside their communities provided any financial help or leadership. And as Lord Selkirk observed, emigrants left to their own devices could waste considerable time and money:

"They found that they were at no great distance from some relations who had formerly settled in Nova Scotia. Having found every new situation better than the former and concluding that their friends must have chosen best of all they determined to join them. They proceeded therefore with their families and baggage to that settlement, where they found that all the best situations were taken up. They would willingly have returned but had incurred so much expense as well as loss of time that they were under the necessity of remaining upon inferior land, with diminished resources."[33]

Because Selkirk employed a surveyor and was directly involved in the process of allocating land holdings, his colonists were spared such disappointments.

But Cape Breton did have one very forceful leader. The Reverend Norman McLeod, a fire and brimstone preacher, led his band of followers, in 1820, from Assynt, in northwest Sutherland, first to Pictou and then to St. Anns, Cape Breton. He stamped his indomitable spirit, moral certainty and discipline on his people, and they prospered. And although he and many of his followers later moved on to New Zealand, sizeable numbers stayed. The Gaelic College of Celtic Arts and Crafts, which was built on Norman MacLeod's land, now perpetuates their memory.

Popular imaginings would have us believe that Scots were forced to leave their country and that those who emigrated were always destitute and helpless. While some emigrants were often very poor, particularly the later arrivals, few were ever forced to emigrate. Because of the strong opposition to it initially, early emigration has to be seen as an act of defiance. It was only when the Scottish economy went into a sharp decline in 1815, with the ending of the Napoleonic Wars, that attitudes changed. Afterwards, emigration increasingly came to be regarded as a cure-all

The monument to Reverend Norman McLeod at the Gaelic College
of Celtic Arts and Crafts, St. Anns, Cape Breton. *Photograph by Geoff
Campey.*

for the nation's social ills. Highland landlords, who had formerly fought
to retain their tenants, swung around in favour of emigration schemes.
But this change of attitude did not happen until the 1820s, some fifty
years after the *Hector* settlers had first arrived at Pictou. Throughout
this period and beyond, most emigrants paid their own way across the
Atlantic and carefully chose where they would settle.[34] Thus the more
representative stereotype is of self-funded, and positively motivated people
who sought the better standard of life which the New World offered.

The collapse of traditional kelp markets,[35] bad harvests and a general
industrial depression brought huge changes to the Highlands from the
late 1830s, the most traumatic being the large-scale removal of people to
make way for sheep farms. With the passing of the 1845 Poor Law
Amendment Act, which, for the first time, made landlords liable for
poor tenants on their estates, landlords looked to emigration as the obvious

way of ridding themselves of their unwanted tenantry. And as the story moves into the dark days of the Highland Famine Years, from 1846 to 1856, occasional instances of forced or determinedly executed evictions linked with emigration can be found but these were the exception. These events still command considerable public attention but they should not be allowed to distort one's understanding of what drove Scots to emigrate. The reality is that when one looks back over the eighty-year influx of Scots to Nova Scotia and Cape Breton, it can be seen that people were strongly motivated by positive factors – both in their decision to emigrate and in their choice of destination. Far from deserving pity, these emigrant Scots should be admired for readily achieving their ultimate goal of becoming self-sufficient landowners in the New World:

"The settlers around our shores [Cape Breton] in their adopted land could still boast of their physical surroundings, beauty of landscape, and mountain scenery as well as the uniqueness of its lakes. These people, although they did not make fortunes, made comfortable homes, provided with all the necessities, but few of the luxuries of life. One thing they prized – they owned their own land."[36]

So this emigration saga eventually had a happy ending. Inevitably it was the first steps which were the most difficult and important. The key happening was the decision taken by many of the *Hector* settlers to stay put in Pictou and found their settlements even though, at the time, they faced appalling difficulties and obstacles. Men like Alexander Cameron who, with his family, went the short distance across the Harbour to found Loch Broom were certainly in the "vanguard of that army of Scottish immigrants whose intellectual ideals, moral worth and material achievement have contributed greatly to the good government and upbuilding of Canada."[37] To this can be added that through their immense courage, determination and resilience they actually founded Canada's New Scotland.

THE *HECTOR* ARRIVES IN 1773

At Loch Broom, Alexander Cameron, Sr., aged 103, who came to Nova Scotia in 1773. He left to mourn an aged widow and eight children, 63 grand and 21 great grand-children. He named the settlement after his native place in Ross-shire, Scotland.[1]

A LEXANDER CAMERON WAS ONE OF the one hundred and ninety or so people who had sailed to Pictou on the *Hector* in 1773. Aged 44 at the time of his arrival, he would take the memories of a harrowing voyage and the grim experiences of the early years to his grave. He and his wife, Janet Ross, and their two children settled on the northern end of the peninsula which divides the West and Middle rivers at Pictou Harbour. As was the case with many of the others who had sailed on the *Hector,* the Cameron family prospered. Raising eight children in all, they left a long line of descendants and transferred the name of their home parish in the northwest of Scotland to Pictou. The Loch Broom name survives in Pictou to this day. A replica log church, dedicated to the early pioneers, reminds visitors of the first settlers, "lest we forget their toils, their hardships and their faith in God."[2]

The *Hector* arrivals originated from three distinct areas of the Highlands. One contingent came from the Coigach Peninsula near Loch Broom, in Wester Ross. The Cameron family were part of this group which consisted of six families and twelve single men. Ten families and two single men formed the group from east Inverness-shire while four-teen families and six single men formed the third contingent, which came from Sutherland.[3] Many of the Inverness-shire emigrants came from the Beauly area. While information on parish origins is sketchy, later evidence suggests that most of them originated from Kirkhill, Kiltarlity and Kilmorack parishes.[4] Many in the Sutherland contingent were from Assynt. Reports of emigration, in the early 1770s, from the Sutherland parishes of Creich, Durness and Farr would indicate that they too had lost people to the 1773 exodus to Pictou. Also included among the passengers were one family from Banff, another from Dunfermline and five single men and one family, of unknown geographical origins, who boarded ship at Glasgow (see Figure 1).[5]

Because no passenger list was compiled at the time of the *Hector*'s departure, there is some doubt and confusion over the number of people who actually sailed. Robert Pagan, son of John Pagan who owned the *Hector,* stated in 1808 that the passengers were comprised of seventy-two families consisting of 190 people.[6] William Mackay, a passenger on the *Hector*, produced a list in around 1820, some fifty years later, naming 179 people who boarded ship at Loch Broom (Ullapool) and ten people

A replica of the log church at Loch Broom, Pictou. The original church, measuring 30 by 40 feet was built in 1787. *Photograph by Geoff Campey.*

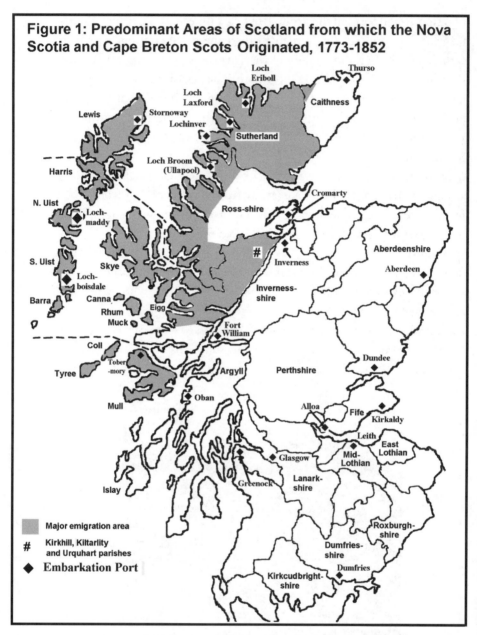

Figure 1: Predominant Areas of Scotland from which the Nova Scotia and Cape Breton Scots Originated, 1773-1852

who left from Glasgow (see Appendix I).[7] A similar 1837 list compiled by fellow passenger William MacKenzie, nearly 70 years after the crossing, corroborates William MacKay's list. It distinguishes between heads of families and single men and gives geographical origins. While recording that thirty-three families and twenty-five single men had sailed on the *Hector,* it fails to state the total number of people this represented.[8] The three sources taken together would suggest that the ship had around 190 passengers. What is certain is that the *Hector* came to Loch Broom on the 10th of July, from the Clyde, with a small number of passengers already on board. She then collected most of her passengers at Loch Broom and sailed for Pictou, arriving on the 15th of September.[9]

It was a long and miserable crossing. The ship's hull was so rotten that "the passengers could pick the wood out of her sides with their fingers." Smallpox and dysentery claimed the lives of eighteen children who were buried at sea. Severe gales off Newfoundland blew the ship off course and added fourteen days to the journey time. Food supplies became scarce and the water was foul. The oatcakes which the emigrants had brought with them had become so mouldy that many had been thrown away early in the crossing. However, as their supplies became depleted in the final days of their voyage, mouldy oatcakes did not seem so unpalatable. Fortunately, Hugh Macleod had gathered them up and was later able to offer his fellow passengers a much needed extra store of food, probably saving many lives.[10] And after surviving this gruesome and heart-rending voyage, the emigrants were confronted with the awesome sight of huge and dense forests as they approached Pictou Harbour. Rising to the occasion, a piper on board ship "blew up his pipes with might and main, its thrilling tones, for the first time startling the denizens of the endless forest and its echoes resounding through the wild solitude."[11]

They had come to settle on land in the so-called Philadelphia plantation, a vast 200,000 acres of wilderness, which was owned by the Philadelphia Land Company.[12] The company's offer of good and accessible land on easy terms seemed very promising back in Scotland. Although the boundaries of the Philadelphia grant were later redrawn to include some of the shore line of Pictou Harbour, most of it was inland of the coast. The *Hector* arrivals thought they were coming to a place with "about twenty miles of sea coast...bounded by two rivers on each side that run into it."[13]

It had all seemed so promising. But their land was not on the coast, as they had been led to believe. It was deep into the interior:

"They were landed without the provisions promised them and without shelter of any kind, and were only able, by the aid of those few who were there before them, to erect camps of the rudest and most primitive description to shelter their wives and children from the elements. Their feelings were most bitter when they compared the actual facts with the free farms and comfort promised them by the lying emigration agent. Many of them sat down in the forest and wept bitterly; hardly any provisions were possessed by the few who went before them and what there was among them was soon devoured, making all old and newcomers – almost destitute. To make matters worse they were sent some three miles into the forest so that they could not even take advantage, with some ease, of any fish that might be caught in the harbour."[14]

The *Hector* passengers landing at Pictou Harbour in 1773, from John Murray, *Scots in Canada* (London: 1911). *Courtesy of the National Library of Canada, NLC 22627.*

Having arrived in September, it was far too late to put down crops for the coming year. The settlers had little or no experience of felling trees. Those people who came from treeless, coastal areas must have been quite dumbfounded by the very sight of large trees. This was all too much to bear. James Grant and family moved to Kings County, while Donald Munroe went to Halifax. John Sutherland and Angus MacKenzie moved to Windsor in Hants County, while Kenneth Fraser, William Matheson, James Murray and David Urquhart, together with their families, moved to Londonderry. Others relocated themselves in nearby Truro and Onslow. They worked as labourers and servants in already-settled areas, this being far preferable to chopping down trees in a primeval forest. Two-thirds of the original group drifted away leaving only about seventy-eight people at Pictou.[15]

The *Hector* settlers had every reason to feel angry with the Philadelphia Land Company, and with John Ross, the man employed by the company to recruit them. They had been completely misled by the company's assurances and promises. It was, after all, owned by men who sought to profit from land sales. The welfare of any settlers they might attract was of little consequence. The company owed its origins to Alexander McNutt, an Ulsterman who, in 1760, had persuaded several hundred people from Northern Ireland to settle in Nova Scotia.[16] Having insufficient resources, his venture was fraught with problems and, fearing the growing depopulation of Ulster, the government halted the exodus in 1762. But McNutt persevered and through his associations with various land companies acquired more land. One of the companies with which he was associated was the Philadelphia Land Company. Initially it had fourteen Scottish proprietors, all influential lawyers and merchants who lived in Philadelphia. In June 1765, Alexander McNutt obtained 200,000 acres in Pictou and Colchester from the British government on the company's behalf. But in doing so, he secured the best water frontage for himself, including much of the coastline of the later town of Pictou.[17]

Initially the company had great difficulty in finding colonists for its Pictou grant. People in the Highlands and Islands showed a marked preference for North Carolina, where they had friends and family who had already established themselves in settlements.[18] After much effort the company managed to locate only six families, who originated from Pennsylvania and Maryland, for their 1767 crossing to Pictou.[19] Among the passengers were Dr. John Harris, the company's agent and legal representative, and Robert Patterson, the company's surveyor. Both men would play a prominent role in later events. The families managed to grow some crops and to attract some people from the outlying areas. However, by the end of 1769 the company had only one hundred and twenty inhabitants at its Pictou settlement. This was far short of the numbers which should have been present to comply with the terms of their grant.[20]

By 1770 the company had come under the control of two Scots – the Rev. Dr. John Witherspoon, a Presbyterian minister from Paisley, near Glasgow, and John Pagan, a Glasgow merchant and shipowner. Both wished to promote Highland emigration to North America. They acquired controlling shares in the Philadelphia Company and began a systematic search for Scottish settlers in real earnest.[21] Their first newspaper advertisement, in the September 1772 edition of the *Edinburgh Advertiser,* was addressed to "all farmers and others in Scotland who are inclined to settle on easy terms in the province of Nova Scotia." Pagan and Witherspoon offered 150 acres of land, at the low rate of sixpence per acre, to the first twenty families who came forward and less advantageous rates for any remaining families who would get the same quantity of land. John Pagan would supply the ship and charge the "easy rate of three pounds five shillings" for each full passenger, the money "to be paid before the ship leaves Scotland."[22]

Pagan and Witherspoon chose badly in selecting their Highland agents. There was Provost James Campbell at Inveraray (Argyll), Archibald Gray at Maryburgh (near Fort William), James MacDonald at Portree in Skye, Dougald Stewart at Fort Augustus (Inverness-shire) and Baillie Alexander Shaw at Inverness. Shaw immediately took great exception to the advertisement and issued a press announcement stating that he had not given his consent to act as agent for the partners.[23] Further hostile comment followed. Writing in the *Edinburgh Advertiser*, "a well-wisher to Old Scotland" wondered how "a dreary tract of an uninhabited and uncultivated wilderness" could be "of the smallest use" and concluded that "this scheme will prove certain ruin to poor people." He also questioned John Witherspoon's motives. "Some ignorant persons may perhaps imagine that he lives near that place; but that Reverend Doctor is Principal of the College of New Jersey, where he resides, and which is at least 1000 miles distant."[24] Following wide-ranging criticism, Witherspoon sought to defend his actions publicly in the *Scots Magazine* but, being opposed to emigration, the editor declined to print his lengthy letter.[25]

An etching of Reverend Dr. John Witherspoon, the Scottish Presbyterian minister who became President of Princeton College, New Jersey. He and John Pagan, a Glasgow merchant, were in charge of the 1773 Pictou venture. *Courtesy of Princeton University Library, University Archives, Department of Rare Books and Special Collections.*

On the face of it, John Witherspoon's involvement in this colonization scheme seems odd. A prominent figure in the Church of Scotland, he came to the notice of Princeton College when it was seeking a new President. Accepting the post in 1766 and moving to New Jersey from Paisley, he immediately made a name for himself. He introduced the new educational ideas which were sweeping through Scotland at the time to the College, encouraged free thinking and promoted libertarian ideals. He openly supported American independence and, in 1776, would be one of the signatories of the Declaration of American Independence.[26] This was a man who believed in giving power to the common people. Thus a venture which enabled poor Scots to throw off their feudal shackles appealed to his libertarian instincts. Having become aware of the Philadelphia Land Company through the alumni and trustees at the College, he approached Pagan. Together they purchased almost 40,000 acres of the Philadelphia Grant for £225. From the outset, Witherspoon wanted assurances from Pagan that emigrants would not be over-charged for their land and upper limits on payments were agreed.[27] Thus Witherspoon had a conscience about his involvement in the colonization scheme but Pagan, who would be supplying the ship, had fewer scruples.

Having failed in their first attempt, Witherspoon and Pagan had much greater success when they appointed John Ross as their agent. He achieved amazing results almost immediately. Being both a merchant in Dingwall, Easter Ross, and a manager of a linen station in Loch Broom for the Forfeited Estates Commissioners, Ross had first-hand knowledge of large stretches of the Northern Highlands.[28] He had worked for Pagan and Witherspoon once before, in 1770, when he had led a group from Scotland to Boston on the *Hector*. Thus he was particularly well-qualified to soothe anxieties over crossing the Atlantic Ocean in this particular ship, and could describe the uncertainties which lay ahead from personal experience. And with a promise that he would accompany emigrants and manage their relocation, any lingering doubts would have vanished. In just a few months Ross recruited sufficient numbers to fill the *Hector*. His recruits originated from Wester Ross, west and north Sutherland and east Inverness-shire – those regions where he had extensive business contacts. For his part Ross was to receive 20,000 acres of land. In return he had to accompany the settlers that year and remain behind with them to direct their colonization efforts.[29]

For those who had remained behind in Pictou, the immediate concern was not the solid mass of forest but the prospect of imminent starvation. Some of the settlers, who had sailed to Pictou on the *Betsey* in 1767, offered help but their food resources were barely enough to sustain themselves. The Philadelphia Company had built a store at Brown Point in Pictou Harbour, which had provisions, but its meagre supplies were insufficient even to meet the most basic of needs. Relief was at hand when the *Hector* arrived back a few weeks later from Boston with supplies. However John Ross refused to let the newcomers have this, their first year's provisioning, as had been promised, because of their refusal to settle on company lands. A heated quarrel erupted and Ross resigned his position as leader, abandoning the settlers to their fate. Having been "driven to extremity" the Highlanders seized control of the company store by force:

"They seized the [company] agents, tied them, took their guns from them, which they hid at a distance; told them that they must have the food for their families, but that they were quite willing and determined to pay for them, if ever they were able to do so. They then carefully weighed, or measured the various articles, took account of what each man had received and left, except one powerful and determined fellow who was left behind to release the two agents. This he did, after allowing sufficient time for his friends to get to a safe distance, and he informed the prisoners where they could find their guns."[30]

This was hardly the best of beginnings, but these drastic measures helped the Highlanders to survive their first winter at Pictou. The two company agents, John Harris and Robert Patterson, who had been attacked by the settlers, understandably sought redress but no action was taken. And, according to Robert Patterson, they eventually paid "every farthing" back to the company. "In the following Spring they set to work and soon improved their position." By 1774 they had produced "269 bushels of wheat, 13 of rye, 56 of peas, 36 of barley, 100 of oats and 340 pounds of flax." They had acquired farm stock consisting of "13 oxen, 13 cows, 15 young neat [bovine] cattle, 26 sheep and one pig" and learned "to hunt the moose."[31] While most of the emigrants were undoubtedly of very modest means, the acquisition of so much livestock, only a year after arriving, would indicate that some of them had come to Pictou with spare capital.[32] Robert Innes, from Inverness, had an uncle who was a Mid Lothian banker, while John Patterson, originating from near Paisley, was a house builder with several properties to his name. Thus there were some in the group who would have been able to make sizeable purchases.[33]

However at this stage the population was small and the settlement was struggling. By the Autumn of 1774 there were only seventy-eight people left at Pictou Harbour, of whom some were earlier American arrivals. In all a population of some twenty-three men, fourteen women, twenty-one boys and twenty girls were living in dwellings stretching from Brown Point to Lyons Brook near to the mouth of the West River

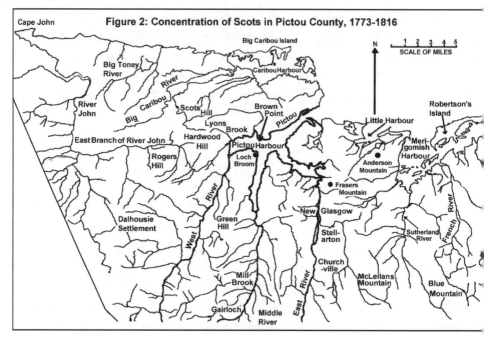

Figure 2: Concentration of Scots in Pictou County, 1773-1816

(see Figure 2). Only two of the thirty-three families and three of the twenty-five bachelors who had sailed on the *Hector* can be identified in the Census which was taken at the time.[34] Both families, one headed by Alexander Ross, the other by Colin MacKenzie, originated from Ross-shire, as did William MacKenzie, one of the single men, although he later moved on to Londonderry.[35] However, many more of the *Hector* passengers were present during the following year when yet another Census was taken. This shows that by November 1775, the population had nearly doubled. Twenty-four men, from the *Hector,* either with families or living on their own, were now living at Pictou. Now that a major foothold was established, others would follow.[36]

In the following year, they managed to attract fellow Scots from Dumfries-shire and Kirkcudbrightshire, whose plight was even worse than theirs. Having landed at Three Rivers in Prince Edward Island in two separate crossings, in 1774 and 1775, they had lost their crops and "experienced all the miseries of a famine."[37] Hearing that there was food to be had in Pictou, fifteen families immediately left Prince Edward Island and relocated themselves in Pictou. Although they fared little better initially, their circumstances soon improved to the point where "thousands of their grandchildren" were later said to be "living in comfort and plenty."[38]

The settlers quickly realized that their best option was to "inhabit the rich lands bordering the three rivers" where they could fish and use the rivers as "the primary means of transportation."[39] An added benefit of being close to river frontages were the "large tracts of intervale" land which were to be found in the floodplains. Once the rivers subsided these naturally occurring water meadows provided settlers with abundant quantities of good farmland.[40] River frontages, up to a distance of several miles from Pictou Harbour, were selected as prime colonization sites and were taken by squatting. The Highlanders immediately sought government grants for this land. Having been owned by Alexander McNutt and later reverting to the Crown, the land would eventually be theirs in a legal sense; but the necessary paperwork would take up to eight years to materialize. They soon began to cut timber and, in 1775, sent their first cargo from Pictou, "the first of a trade very profitably and extensively carried on ever since."[41] Thus did they lay the foundations of Pictou's important timber trade which would eventually come to dominate eastern Nova Scotia's economy. By 1805 some fifty ships a year would be needed to carry Pictou's exports of squared timber to Britain.

Once the Highlanders had cleared their lands along the three river frontages, the Pictou settlement began to take shape. Four of the Inverness-shire arrivals, William (later Squire) MacKay, Colin MacKay, Roderick Mackay and Donald Cameron went to East River. And later, as conditions improved, two other Inverness-shire men, James Grant, who had gone to Kings County, and Donald Munroe, who had moved to Halifax, joined them at East River. Apart from Hugh Fraser, the Kiltarlity weaver who settled at West River, Donald MacDonald, a second Hugh Fraser, Colin Douglas and Alexander Fraser, who were the remaining Inverness-shire family heads, all located themselves at Middle River (see Figure 2).[42] Their initial concentration along the East and Middle rivers reveals a single community transplanting itself to Pictou. These were clearly extended families and friends who, sharing a common identity and culture, wished to settle as one community. But the wide dispersal of the Ross-shire and Sutherland settlers suggests a totally different pattern. They were probably small groups from quite different areas.

The Ross-shire settlers were to be found at all three river frontages and at places further afield. Alexander Cameron went to the peninsula opposite Pictou Harbour, naming it Loch Broom after his place of birth. He and his family were joined later by the Ross-shire-born William MacKenzie, who had initially gone to live in Liverpool (Queens County). William McLellan settled at the West River, while John McLellan gave his name to McLellans Brook near to the East River. Alexander MacLean, Donald MacKay and Colin MacKenzie and family established themselves at East River, while Alexander Ross took his family to Middle

The memorial at Loch Broom, Pictou, commemorating the arrival of Alexander Cameron (1728–1831). It is also dedicated to other emigrant Scots who settled in North America in the 18th and 19th centuries. *Photograph by Geoff Campey.*

River. Alexander Falconer settled near Hopewell, further to the south of McLellans Brook, while Robert Sim moved to New Brunswick after living in Pictou for a few years. But a good many of the Ross-shire emigrants, especially the single men, simply left the area without trace.

The same was true for the Sutherland settlers. Many Sutherland families, and men travelling on their own, left Pictou soon after their arrival and apparently did not return. James MacLeod was one of those who stayed behind, claiming land on the Middle River. Kenneth Fraser and family, having first settled at Londonderry, returned later to Middle River. John Sutherland, having moved initially to Windsor, returned and gave his name to the Sutherland River settlement, to the south of Merigomish. Hugh MacLeod and his children settled on the West River, while William Matheson and family returned from their place at Londonderry to relocate themselves at Rogers Hill, near the West River. However, James Murray and David Urquhart, having settled with their families at Londonderry, never returned to Pictou.[43]

Although some of the original *Hector* arrivals were lost to the Pictou settlements, sufficient numbers remained to lay down the foundations of what would become a bastion of Scottish society and culture. It was a remarkable achievement given the obstacles and harrowing problems which the settlers had to overcome. The ship crossing had been awful. John Pagan had sent people off to Pictou in a leaky old ship, classified by *Lloyd's* as being only suitable for short voyages within Europe. The *Hector*'s hull was in poor condition and her equipment was of substandard quality.[44] She was not sea-worthy. However, this made little difference to John Pagan. Because fares had to be paid in advance, he was guaranteed his financial reward as the ship's owner before she even sailed. John Ross also stood to benefit. He was due to get 20,000 acres of land out of the episode. Pagan and Ross clearly had no scruples. They were in the business of recruiting emigrants solely to make money.

But what about John Witherspoon? He was in cahoots with two rascals and, like them, must have hoped to get some financial payback from his investment in the Philadelphia Land Company. As the President of Princeton College in New Jersey, he was meant to be the respectable and honest face of the company. He gave his good name to the Pictou undertaking on condition that land prices should be fair and carefully controlled. Somehow the company's promotional literature, which misleadingly described the Philadelphia Grant as having coastal and river frontages, escaped his notice. Although Witherspoon believed passionately in the advantages that the New World had to offer emigrant Scots and had humanitarian concerns for their well-being, he failed to keep a watchful eye on them. As the settlers would soon realize, no one associated with the company actually cared about their welfare or felt the need to help them find suitable locations on which to settle.

The Philadelphia Company's policy of restricting land grants to Protestants would have been pursued with even greater vigour when John Witherspoon became associated with the company. A prominent member of the Presbyterian Church in Scotland, he was also a powerful voice for North American Presbyterianism. Predictably nearly all of those who came to Pictou in 1773 were Presbyterians. The only exception was Donald Cameron and his family, who were Roman Catholics.[45] Thus Pictou had the rudiments of a Presbyterian congregation from the first day it was founded. Presbyterianism took root in Pictou and strengthened even further when Reverend James MacGregor came to Pictou in 1786. It remained the dominant religion in spite of the large influx of Roman Catholic Highlanders to the region from 1791 to 1803. The new arrivals stayed clear of Pictou and segregated themselves within separate Catholic territories in Antigonish and Cape Breton.[46]

Through their hard work, determination and great courage, the *Hector* settlers made history. They founded Nova Scotia's first Highland settlement and prompted one of the greatest ever surges in emigration from Scotland to British North America. They defied the land speculators and took over the prime river frontages near Pictou Harbour. Theirs was a collective triumph, but they had their heroes and leaders to see them through some very testing times. Hugh MacLeod had been instrumental in saving lives during the final stages of the sea crossing. He lost his wife tragically just as the *Hector* arrived at Pictou. Settling with his children at West River, he later married the widow of Alexander

MacLeod who was drowned at Shubenacadie. Then there was William MacKay, who lived to the ripe old age of 97. He was "a leading man among his countrymen," someone whose "house was always open and his table welcome to travellers and neighbours."[47] Lord Selkirk met "Squire MacKay, so called from his being a Justice of the Peace," during his travels through Nova Scotia, in 1803. He observed "a mere countryman," yet a man who had "the manners of a true Highlander."[48]

In 1826, when Hugh Fraser, the weaver from Kiltarlity, died aged 86, there were "twelve of the *Hector* passengers [left], several of whom followed his funeral on foot to the cemetery."[49] People in the cortege would have reflected on the early years. Success was far from guaranteed. They had struggled to clear their land and build their settlements. A major factor in their success, oddly enough, was the outcome of the American War of Independence, which began in 1773, the year of their arrival in Pictou. Having lost the war, the British government relocated large numbers of ex-servicemen to the Pictou area when the war ended. As William MacKay explained to Lord Selkirk, initially the war had "put a check to the settlement" but from 1784 "a great number of soldiers were settled and from that time the settlement advanced rapidly."[50]

3

THE LOYALIST EMIGRANTS

Timber of the best quality abounded and American vessels came in, which supplied them with necessaries, in exchange for staves, shingles, etc. And they were beginning to surmount their difficulties, when the American Revolutionary War broke out, and this branch of trade being stopped, they were cut off from all supplies from abroad. Even salt could not be obtained except by boiling down sea water, and in summer the settlers might be seen in fine weather, spending days at the shore preparing their winter's supply.[1]

FOR THE DURATION OF THE American War of Independence, from 1775 to 1783, Scots at Pictou experienced food shortages and disruption to their general trade, although they were not themselves directly involved in the conflict. As far as the war was concerned, they "were decided Loyalists, while those who came from Philadelphia and most of the inhabitants of Truro and the adjacent settlements had a very warm sympathy with the Americans."[2] Given that the Pictou people included men like Alexander Fraser who, as a boy, had actually witnessed the bloody and savage defeat of Highlanders at the Battle of Culloden in 1745–46, their loyalty to the British side seems odd. Yet Scottish Highlanders were particularly well-known for their loyalty to the old enemy. Not wishing to become Americanized, they had a strong desire to preserve their clan and country links. Because of this attachment most were almost invariably Loyalist.[3]

At the beginning of the War, when a muster roll had been taken "of the inhabitants of Pictou or Tinmouth [Teignmouth] capable to bear arms" on the British side the names of sixty-five men were listed, of whom only a third had come to Pictou on the *Hector*.[4] At that time most of the *Hector* settlers were still residing on the west side of the province, although many would return later to the Pictou area. Those people who had moved west would be joined in the mid-1780s by large numbers of Loyalists. Some 40,000 people fled from the American colonies following the British defeat in the American War of Independence. Civilian refugees came in 1784, a year after the war ended, and they were soon followed by Loyalist ex-soldiers and their families. Around 35,000 of the 40,000 Loyalists who flooded into British North America would settle in the Maritime region, with most going either to the mouth of the St. John River and its fertile river valley or to Port Roseway (later Shelburne) at the southern end of Nova Scotia (see Figure 3).[5]

From the time of the Conquest, the British government's colonization policies had been guided by its defence interests. Loyal British emigrants could be useful to the Crown not just as settlers, but as guardians and protectors of territory. The government's policy was to offer inducements to emigrants to settle in areas which were considered most vulnerable to attack. It is therefore no accident that a large proportion of the earliest immigrants to British North America were former British officers and soldiers. After serving in one or more of the North American military campaigns, they and their families were given free grants of land, which were usually located in militarily strategic areas along boundaries and major rivers and bays.

The practice of settling loyal people in carefully chosen areas had already been tried and tested by the time the government was faced with prospect of relocating the large numbers of Loyalists who came to British America in the mid-1780s. Most of the 35,000 exiles who came to the Maritime region were granted land in the militarily important areas around the Bay of Fundy. Around half of them were civilian refugees. The remainder were officers and soldiers from disbanded British regiments and provincial Loyalist units, such as the Royal North

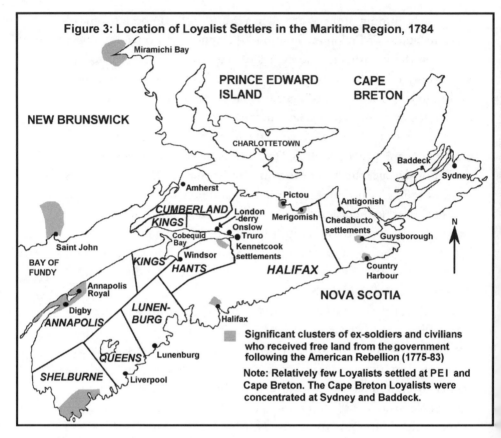

Figure 3: Location of Loyalist Settlers in the Maritime Region, 1784

Significant clusters of ex-soldiers and civilians who received free land from the government following the American Rebellion (1775-83)

Note: Relatively few Loyalists settled at PEI and Cape Breton. The Cape Breton Loyalists were concentrated at Sydney and Baddeck.

Carolina Regiment, the King's Carolina Rangers and the Loyal Nova Scotia Volunteers.[6] In addition to being provided with free land they could also claim provisions and other help from the government. Former soldiers were granted land according to their rank, with the usual amount ranging from 1,000 acres for officers to 100 acres for privates. Civilians normally got 100 acres for each head of family and 50 additional acres for every person belonging to the family.

Men who had seen action in earlier military campaigns, once resettled, could provide some form of military backup should the need arise. But the policy of moving large numbers of loyal settlers into areas judged by the government to have military importance had its drawbacks. A soldier's training and experience did not necessarily prepare him and his family for the rigours of pioneer farming. Having to farm land chosen for its military value, not its soil quality, also had its perils. Inferior land created dissatisfaction and discouraged settlers from staying, although some Loyalists clearly found good land and prospered. When this happened, they often attracted fresh bands of emigrants to their settlements.[7] But the majority of Nova Scotia Loyalists had to contend with poorly administered land grant procedures and some cold-shouldering from local people who felt resentful over their provisioning and other advantages. Greatly disillusioned, many simply gave up. By the late 1780s many thousands would be returning to the United States.[8]

However, it was a very different matter for the small number of Scottish ex-soldiers and their families who were allocated land in the Pictou

Banner of the Nova Scotia Loyalists, 1789, artist unknown. *Courtesy of the National Archives of Canada, C-001527.*

area. Originating mainly from Urquhart and other east Inverness-shire parishes, they came to live along Pictou's East River in 1784. The first-wave *Hector* colonizers, who had arrived ten years earlier would have been there to meet them. And because some of the *Hector* arrivals had also originated from east Inverness-shire, both groups could identify with the same part of Scotland. These Loyalist settlers remained and contributed to the area's strong sense of community, which had its roots in a shared homeland. This was one of the few instances where the government's relocation efforts actually coincided with settler preferences.

Pictou was a popular destination for Scots. It had many advantages. It was relatively close to Scotland. Although the extra distance was not all that great when compared with an ocean crossing, Pictou was nearer than ports on the west of the province, an important factor for emigrants of limited means. It was also becoming a major timber trade centre. Its timber exports quickly attracted large numbers of ships from the Clyde, giving emigrant Scots affordable fares for their Atlantic crossings. Thus, Pictou with its long-established communities, its timber trade and relative proximity to Scotland was fast becoming a Scottish stronghold.

But back in 1784, the many Loyalists, who arrived in the Maritime provinces, whatever their destinations, must have come with high hopes of a better future. These streams of people from the south brought a sudden and huge rise in the region's population. Around 19,000 people came to the Nova Scotia peninsula, of whom 2,000 were disbanded British soldiers and their families and 1,000 were ex-soldiers from Georgia and the Carolinas. A full ten percent were Black Loyalists, who fared badly in spite of the varied skills which they brought with them.[9] New Brunswick, which was divided from the peninsula as a separate colony in 1784, suddenly acquired some fifteen thousand or so Loyalists.[10] Located as they were on both sides of the Bay of Fundy, Loyalist settlers, taken together, doubled the population of peninsular Nova Scotia and swelled the population count, to the north of the bay, by fivefold.[11]

Thus the major influx was to mainland Nova Scotia and New Brunswick, with Prince Edward Island and Cape Breton acquiring relatively few Loyalists. Several hundred Loyalists obtained land on the

Island of St. John (later Prince Edward Island), but few remained because of its chaotic system of land ownership, which led to considerable confusion over land titles and encouraged tenancies rather than freeholds. In all, only about four hundred Loyalists moved to Cape Breton, with most settling in Sydney and Baddeck.[12] Anxious to protect its coal mining interests there, the government had little desire to colonize it with settlers and later made Cape Breton as inaccessible as possible to emigrants. It introduced restraining orders which restricted freehold grants to Loyalists and fish merchants. Although Cape Breton acquired very few Loyalists, emigrant Scots later came to its shores in their thousands. Ignoring government regulations, they first arrived in 1790 and took their land by squatting. Quickly establishing successful Scottish communities, they would attract many others to follow them, transforming Cape Breton into a major Scottish enclave by the early 1800s.[13]

Most of the Loyalists who settled in Nova Scotia in 1784 originated from the middle colonies of New York and New Jersey, but a substantial number also came from North and South Carolina. A marked characteristic of these southern colonies was their large intake of Scottish Highlanders from as early as the mid-eighteenth century.[14] One of the first major migrations was in 1739 when 350 people from Argyll went to North Carolina. They were joined in the 1760s and 1770s by many more emigrants from the islands of Arran, Jura, Islay and Gigha.[15] Some 1,600 of them arrived in the three year period from 1768 to 1770. Rough estimates suggest that by 1775 North Carolina had acquired around 12,000 Highlanders. The number of Loyalist Scots who left North Carolina at the end of the war cannot be quantified, but the reports of "great numbers" suggest that there had been a substantial exodus. Most would have gone to Nova Scotia.[16]

Although there is little quantitative data, it can safely be said that Scots were well represented amongst the Loyalists who came to Nova Scotia.[17] Anyone touring Nova Scotia in the mid-1780s would have realized that, as was the case with the most other Loyalists, Scots had been settling, in large numbers, on the southwest side of the peninsula. Visiting Nova Scotia in 1795, ten years after the Loyalists had arrived, the

Reverend James Munro had been struck by the number of Scots he encountered. At Jordan River, to the north of Shelburne, there had been "25 families, mostly Presbyterians, who live by fishing and farming, lumber having greatly failed."[18] And in Digby he noted that though the Loyalists "came from the States a good many of them are Scotch people."[19] Visitors to the south side of Cobequid Bay also would have noticed the various Scottish settlement clusters which had become established to the east of Windsor (see Figure 3). This was mainly a military population formed by the families of the ex-soldiers who had served with the Royal Highland Emigrants Regiment (the 84th) in the American War.

The 84th Regiment, which was raised at the beginning of the American War in 1775, acquired its recruits mainly from Highland emigrants, loyal to the British side, who were living at the time in North America. The Regiment eventually had two battalions which were to see action "until the present unnatural rebellion be suppressed."[20] Discharged veterans of the Seven Years War, who formed the nucleus of the new Regiment, included former members of the Royal Highland Regiment (42nd) as well as the Fraser (78th) and Montgomerie Highlanders (77th). "Their uniform was the full Highland garb, with purses made of racoons' instead of badgers' skins. The officers wore the broad sword and dirk, and the men a half basket sword."[21] After the British defeat, men who had served with the 84th Regiment, came to the Cobequid Bay region to take up their land grants.

At the time of being recruited, most of these Highlanders were living on land which they had previously acquired from the government as a result of their military service in earlier campaigns. Many were enlisted in North Carolina and New York while others had been recruited in Nova Scotia, the Island of St. John and Newfoundland. In the end, most of the men who signed up to join the Royal Highland Emigrants Regiment came from either New York or Nova Scotia.[22]

Many Highlanders rushed forward to join in great numbers but some were coerced. Fear of losing men to the American side and a strong sense of urgency that men needed to be found for the new regiment very quickly led the army to resort to strong-arm tactics. It was a case of enlisting men "partly by threats and partly by persuasion."[23] Emigrant ships from Scotland were often boarded to find men who wished to "volunteer" for His Majesty's service. Targeted were indentured servants who would have little choice but to accept. By joining the regiment they could get money and free land and be released from their indentures; but if they refused they would have to go to jail to pay off their debts.[24] So it was a choice between going to war or going to prison and, when they went to war, their conditions were often appalling. Men from the second battalion of the 84th Regiment "made a horrid and scandalous appearance on duty" and were "despised by the soldiers of the other corps."[25] But while their time in the Regiment may have been grim, these men could claim their reward when the war was over – free land in Nova Scotia.[26]

When the war ended, over seven hundred ex-soldiers from the disbanded 84th Regiment were allotted 81,000 acres in a vast tract of land extending roughly from the Kennetcook River to the Shubenacadie River.[27] This placed them in an area to the east of Windsor (Douglas township) in Hants County. Two settlements, Gore and Kennetcook, were to be founded by men from the disbanded regiment:

> "Of the extensive tract examined, the lands on both sides of the Nine Mile River and on the Kinetcoot [Kennetcook] have been preferred and a grant for them alone is taken out, being 81,000 acres which at 100 acres /private; 500 [acres] to a subaltern, 750 [acres] to Captains; 1,000 [acres] to field officers, is the quantity necessary for the Regiment."[28]

However, the officer in charge of mustering soon realized that few would stay and farm their allotted lands. Almost from the beginning, men were selling their provisions to the already-established settlers and looking for work. A major problem was that much of the best land had already been taken up by absentee proprietors. Lands along the coast "from Minas Basin to the embouchure [mouth] of the Shubenacadie [River] and all along its banks had been granted away from time ago except a few farms here and there."[29] Large tracts of lands along both sides of the Nine Mile River, which were considered "the best in our grant by far" and stretches along the Kennetcook River had already been claimed by another regiment.

Officers like Murdoch MacLean, a Captain in the 84th Regiment who had served "in the war ending in 1763 and in the late war," clearly intended to take up their land entitlements. He requested and probably obtained 2000 acres of land in the Minas Basin, a further 1000 acres "on River Kenetcook" as well as an additional 2000 acres of land in Annapolis County, much further to the west.[30] But the ordinary ex-soldier had to make difficult choices. Faced with the prospect of accepting inferior land or working for others, many opted for the latter alternative. The failure of local surveyors to assist people in getting on their land was an added difficulty. In the end many ex-servicemen abandoned any attempt to farm their own land and instead worked as labourers and servants in the surrounding community.[31] Reverend John Sprott, the Presbyterian minister, who visited the area in 1826, found little cheer when he saw the "settlers [who] are sunk in ignorance and depravity.... There is scarcely a family in the County of Hants who has a copy of the Holy Scriptures.... Needy emigrants have to contend with hard and unsubdued forests and it is long before they turn their attention to the temples of religion."[32]

Most of the 19,000 Loyalists who had come to live in peninsular Nova Scotia after the American War ended, could be found in several distinct areas. Halifax had around 1,200 Loyalists and beyond the capital city there were around 2,000 Loyalists in the Annapolis Valley and approximately 1,300 in Digby, while Shelburne had 10,000 Loyalists, making it the fourth largest town in North America (after Philadelphia, New York and Boston).[33] These Loyalist concentrations were all on the west side of the province. The most remarkable thing about this influx was the speed and extent of the exodus which followed it. When Reverend Munro visited the region in 1795, he found that the town of Shelburne had only 150 families and that there were fewer that 2,000 people in the vicinity. When William Black, a Methodist minister, visited Shelburne in 1804 he noticed that its population was one-tenth its former size.[34] In 1815, Joshua Marsden, a Methodist preacher, found Shelburne "almost deserted," a description confirmed by Reverend Gavin Lang, a Presbyterian missionary who saw it nearly fifteen years later:

"The harbour of Shelburne is well-known in America as being one of the most beautiful and secure which it contains....When viewed in the distance Shelburne looks somewhat considerable, but alas, on closer inspection, desolation and decay manifest themselves all around. Shelburne has fallen, I am afraid, never more to rise, for the few who remain neither possess wealth nor influence, and are in our mind strongly contrasted with the active and highly polished sons of Caledonia."[35]

The town of Digby also experienced a drop in its population and, as was the case at Shelburne, this decline was blamed largely on confusion and delays over land allocations. Some three hundred families were to be accommodated around St. Marys Bay and the Sissibou River, but more than one third never got to their lands and by 1795 only sixty-eight families remained.[36] By 1802 a consortium had been formed to market Digby properties to the outside world.[37] Digby's Loyalist residents were selling up and moving on:

"as it is probable that the peace which has lately taken place, may occasion many military and other transient persons to look for settlements in these provinces and some such may incline towards Digby...several gentlemen of that place [Digby] have associated for the purpose of removing...such difficulties as are most likely to oppose themselves to new settlers...they have selected and secured a number of commodious house lots...a proportion of these adjoining the water are adapted to trading persons – others are calculated for mechanics – and a few more for such as are only concerned in having an agreeable spot for a house, and room for a garden. The first applicant will have the first choice, and so on with other applicants in succession, until the whole are sold at the prices fixed."[38]

Digby and St. Marys Bay, an extract from Purdy's *Map of Cabotia, comprehending the Provinces of Upper and Lower Canada, New-Brunswick and Nova-Scotia, with Breton Island, Newfoundland etc.* (London: Richard H. Laurie, 1825). *Courtesy of Toronto Reference Library, Map Collection, 912.71 P79.*

Discontent over the government's failure to administer land grants, dissatisfaction with their land and the antagonism diverted towards them from surrounding non-Loyalists communities led many Loyalists to leave the towns which they had initially attempted to create.[39] Some went to other areas of Nova Scotia or other parts of British America, a few returned back to Britain but the majority went back to the United States. Probably only a small fraction of the people actually stayed in the areas allocated to them. Thus land grants to Loyalist ex-soldiers and civilians had not led to great cycles of further emigration as the government had hoped. Land speculators did well but not the settlers.[40] However, some Loyalists did remain on the lands they were allocated on the west side of the province. Later census data would show that when this happened, it was mainly the English and Irish who remained and not the Scots.

Loyalist Scots differed from their English and Irish counterparts in showing a much stronger preference for the eastern Maritimes. The descendants of English and Irish Loyalists were far more inclined to remain in the western counties of Nova Scotia than were the descendants of Scottish Loyalists (see Figure 4).[41] Thus, in spite of having come in such large numbers as Loyalists to the west of the province, most Scots eventually became concentrated along the bays and rivers of eastern Nova Scotia and Cape Breton. Pictou was the initial attraction. The *Hector* settlers had claimed an early foothold at its Harbour and along its river frontages. Their colonization efforts were given a boost, a decade later, with the arrival of ex-soldiers from two disbanded Scottish Regiments: the Duke of Hamilton's Regiment (82nd) and the Royal Highland Emigrants Regiment (the 84th).

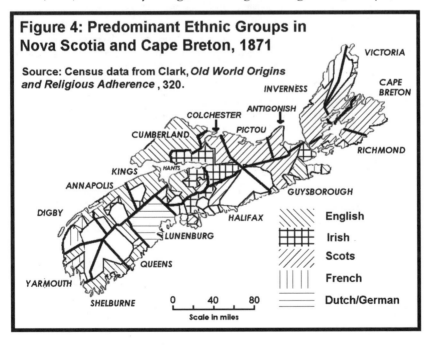

Figure 4: Predominant Ethnic Groups in Nova Scotia and Cape Breton, 1871

Source: Census data from Clark, *Old World Origins and Religious Adherence*, 320.

TABLE 1

Men from the disbanded 82nd Regiment (Duke of Hamilton's Regiment) who settled at Fisher's Grant (between Pictou and Merigomish harbours) from 1784*

Officers

1 COL. ALEX. ROBERTSON. Obtained the big island of Merigomish as his share, hence sometimes known as Robertson's Island. Never lived on it himself, but some relatives of the name settled upon it. Employed an agent, who built a large house on it, which he called Struan House. At his death, his property in this county descended to his nephew, Oliphant, of Gask.

2 CAPT. JOHN FRASER. Lived at Frasers Point, appointed a magistrate October 15th, 1784. His wife and two sons followed him from Scotland. One of the latter, John, being afterward known as Collector Fraser, the other, Simon, called also Major, and sometimes Colonel Fraser, afterward employed in bringing out passengers.

3 ALEX. McDONALD. Unknown.

4 COLIN McDONALD. Believe the same known as Cole McDonald, who lived on the Big Island, near what is still known as Coles Brook.

5 DONNET FENUCANE. His land located to the west of Frasers Point, but his history unknown.

These last three received each 500 acres.

6 JOHN McNEIL. Received 300 acres, but history unknown.

Non-Commissioned Officers Receiving Each 200 Acres

7 CHARLES ARBUCKLES. A native of Falkirk, moved afterward to the Ponds. Married to a daughter of B. McGee. His descendants numerous.

8 DAVID BALLANTYNE. Removed to Cape George, where his descendants are numerous.

9 GEORGE BROWN. Settled on Frasers Mountain.

10 JOHN BROWNFIELD. A native of Derry, in Ireland, and a Presbyterian, died near French River, where his descendants still are.

11 JAMES CARMICHAEL. A native of Perthshire. His descendants well known.

12 ROBERT DUNN. A native of Glasgow, settled on property now owned and occupied by his sons.

13 JOHN FRASER. A Highlander from Inverness. One of 18 who survived out of a detachment of 111 men, employed in the Southern States during the war, the rest having been cut off by fever. He lived at Fishers Grant, where he was one of the first elders of the Pictou congregation. Afterwards removed to French River, where his descendants still are.

14 DEFFEY GILLIES. Believe the same as James Gillies, who lived where R. S. Copeland now resides, afterward removed to Big Island, where his descendants still are.

* From George Patterson, *History of the County of Pictou, Nova Scotia* (Montreal: Dawson Bros., 1877) 458–61.

15 JAMES PEACOCK. Lived near Chance Harbour, but do not know what became of him.

16 JOHN ROBSON. From being able to bleed, and his skill otherwise, he was usually known as Dr. Robson. His descendants still there.

17 CHARLES ROBINSON, PROPERLY ROBERTSON. Was a son of the proprietor of the estate of Lude, at the foot of the Grampians. Was a student attending College when he enlisted. One daughter, married to Robert Patterson (Black).

18 JOHN SCOTT. Sold out to John Fraser, 1785.

19 ROBERT SMITH. His lot where the Merigomish church now stands. His descendants still there.

20 DAVID SIMPSON. Had been a student at College, but he and some others having indulged in "a spree," some eighteen of them found themselves in the morning with the King's Shilling in their pockets. The professors endeavoured to obtain their discharge, but without success. From his education, he obtained some office in the regiment. His lot, on which his descendants still live, the farthest up in Merigomish, in the grant. He was afterward employed as a schoolmaster in several parts of the county.

21 ROBERT STEWART. Usually known as Smashem, from this being a favorite expression in describing battle scenes. He acted as agent for Col. Robertson, and lived on the Big Island, at a point which has since received the name of Smashems Head.

22 ROBERT MILLER, Gerrard Cullen, heirs of John Eves, John Fowler, John Foot, Thomas Loggan, Archibald Long, Alexander McKinnon, John McNeil, George Oswald, James Robertson, Alexander Stewart, James Struthers, William McVie, William West, Archibald Wilson. History unknown.

Receiving 150 Acres Each

23 JOHN BAILLIE. A native of Sutherlandshire; afterward took up land at the mouth of Baillies Brook, which received its name from him.

24 ARCHIBALD CAMERON. History unknown.

Privates Receiving 100 Acres Each

25 ANDREW ANDERSON. A native of East Lothian, and the first settler on Andersons Mountain. Died 3rd August, 1845.

26 JOHN BRADAW, PROPERLY BRADY. Sold out.

27 DAVID BOGGEY. Died at Fishers Grant, leaving no family.

28 DUNCAN CHISHOLM. Removed to Baillies Brook, where his descendants still are.

29 WILLIAM CAMPIN OF CAMPDEN. Sold out and removed to Truro.

30 JOHN COLLY. Suppose the same who afterward settled on Middle River, where his descendants still are. A native of Elgin.

31 JAMES DANSEY OR DEMPSEY. An Irishman; settled at French River Bridge, his descendants still there.

32 BRITISH FREEDOM. Strange as this name is, there is in the Registrar's office in Pictou a deed from him of his lot, under this inspiring name. Hence I presume that he moved away.

33 HARDY FERDINAND. A very stout, well-made Irishman, who afterward enlisted in Governor Wentworth's Regiment.

34 THOMAS FLEMMING OR FLEEMAN. Sold out and removed away.

35 ROBERT FERRET, PROPERLY GERRARD. An Irishman, afterward removed to Rogers Hill.

36 ALEXANDER GORDON. "Died at Fishers Grant on the 18th inst., after an illness of eight days, which he bore with resignation to the divine will, for which he has always been exemplary, Mr. Alexander Gordon, aged 80 years, leaving a circle of relatives and friends to mourn their loss. He was of the old 82nd Regiment, and one of the earliest settlers in the district of Pictou." – *Bee*, August 31st, 1836.

37 JOHN IVES. A native of Nottingham, England, but married in the North of Ireland. Died in Halifax, and his children, the eldest, the late George Ives, Elder, then 12 years of age, came to take possession of their lot at Fishers Grant. His descendants well known.

38 WILLIAM KIRK. Afterwards removed to St. Mary's, where his descendants are numerous. A grandson in the Dominion legislature.

39 ANDREW MUIRHEAD. A lowland Scotchman; first settled at the Ponds. His descendants at Little Harbour and other places.

40 HUGH McCARTHY. A tailor. Sold out and removed to Truro.

41 JOHN McDOUGALL. Blacksmith in the Regiment. Lived at Fishers Grant. The ferrymen, Donald and William, his sons.

42 ANGUS McQUEEN. A native of the Isle of Skye; settled at Little Harbour; a number of his descendants still in that neighbourhood. Donald McDonald (Lochaber), Donald McDonald (Bann), Angus McDonald. These four the first settlers in Little Harbour.

43 CHARLES McKINNON. From the Isle of Barra. Moved to Baillies Brook where his descendants still are.

44 JOHN McNEIL, DONALD McNEIL, MURDOCH McNEIL, MATTHEW McNEIL, JOHN McNEIL, JUN. Isle of Barra men, most of whom removed to Antigonish County.

45 JOHN AND JAMES McPHERSON. Settled at Fishers Grant; John dead in 1785. James at his death described as a native of Badenoch. Their descendants still there.

46 WILLIAM ROBINSON. A Scotchman. His descendants settled there.

47 WILLIAM SHARP. Died at the Beaches.

48 WILLIAM SYMPTOM. Married to Ives' widow, lived at lower part of Fishers Grant.

49 JOHN SMALL. Afterward the Elder, belonged to the Grenadier company. One of the 18 saved from the wreck of the Transport. For some time in an American prison, but with fifteen others made his escape; and passing through the American lines reached a British man-of-war. But afterward drowned near his own house, at a part of the harbour of which it was said that he knew every foot as well as his own farm.

50 JAMES TRUESTATE, PROPERLY TRUESDALE. Sold out and removed to Truro.

The first to arrive in 1784 were the former members of the 82nd Regiment who were granted 26,000 acres of land extending from the southeast side of Pictou Harbour to Merigomish Harbour – an area which came to be known as Fisher's Grant.[42] Two hundred men were to be allocated land on the East River at Pictou and at Merigomish, with grants ranging from 100 acres for Privates to 1500 acres for a Lieutenant Colonel.[43] According to government sources, there was "exceeding good arable" land near Pictou and Merigomish harbours, particularly along the rivers which flowed into them.[44] However, "the habits of the army ill-fitted them for the work of clearing the forest, or of any employment requiring industry and perseverance."[45] As was the case with men from the disbanded 84th Regiment, who were allocated land in the Cobequid Bay region, many of these ex-soldiers simply sold their land on to established settlers. Nevertheless, around 50 of them are believed to have actually taken up their land allocations and settled in the area with their families. (see Table 1).

Colonel Alexander Robertson "obtained the big island of Merigomish as his share, hence sometimes known as Robertson's Island. [He] never lived on it himself, but some relatives of the name settled on it." Captain John Fraser "lived at Frasers Point," while George Brown "settled on Fraser Mountain." John Baillie, "a native of Sutherlandshire afterward took up land at the mouth of Baillies Brook, which received its name from him" (see Figure 2). Andrew Anderson "a native of East Lothian" became the first settler on Anderson Mountain. Angus McQueen from Skye "settled at Little Harbour," while Charles McKinnon "from the Isle of Barra moved to Baillies Brook where his descendants still are."[46] Included among those who left the Pictou area were five McNeils (John, Donald, Murdoch, Matthew, John Junior), all Roman Catholics from Barra, who later re-established themselves at Antigonish.[47]

The next to arrive in the Pictou area were sixteen families headed by men who had served with the Royal Highland Emigrants Regiment (the 84th). Most men from this regiment had obtained their land grants in Hants County. However some of these ex-soldiers were able to claim land on the upper reaches of the East River at Pictou.[48] Having become "steady, industrious settlers," they quickly established farms for themselves on their allocated lands. They included Donald Cameron "with his brothers, Finlay and Samuel" who were "natives of the parish of Urquhart," James Fraser "a native of Strathglass" and John Chisholm, a Roman Catholic who also originated from Strathglass (see Table 2).[49] These Highlanders were joined in the summer of 1784 by eight more families from the Beauly area who also settled on the East River.[50] By 1797 an additional twenty-five men, believed to be mainly veterans of the 84th Regiment, also came to the East River. John Robertson settled at Churchville, John Fraser at Springville, while Alexander MacLean took up land "opposite Stellarton, part of it still occupied by his descendants"[51] (see Table 3). These men and their families had come mainly from Urquhart parish, to the south of Beauly, the former home of many of the *Hector* settlers (see Figure 1). Thus, successive waves of colonizers had reinforced Pictou's early links with east Inverness-shire Scots.

While much smaller in size, there were also Loyalist population clusters in Antigonish and Guysborough, although the initial Scottish presence in these districts was far less pronounced than was the case in Pictou.[52] After the American War ended, the Antigonish area acquired many disbanded troops from the Nova Scotia Volunteers.[53] Timothy Hierlihy, their former Commander, led around eighty-six officers and men to Antigonish Harbour where they established a settlement at Town Point, renamed Dorchester.[54] Gradually the community moved up river to the present site of Antigonish. Many of Hierlihy's men had Irish names and judging from a local priest's observations in 1787 that "there could be large [Roman Catholic] congregations formed," Antigonish had a significant Roman Catholic population at this time.[55] The relocation of so many Irish Loyalists, who were mainly Catholics, to Antigonish may have been a factor in its later popularity with Catholic Highlanders. They came in very large numbers from 1791 and would soon turn the whole of Sydney County (later Antigonish and Guysborough counties) into another Scottish stronghold.

TABLE 2

Men from the disbanded 84th Regiment who settled on
the East River, Pictou in 1784*

On the East Side of the River

1 DONALD CAMERON. 150 acres. With his brothers, Finlay and Samuel, afterward mentioned, were natives of the parish of Urquhart. Served 8 years and 4 months. His son, Duncan, long the elder, was a drummer boy in the regiment, having served two years, and being fifteen years of age at his discharge.

2 ALEX. CAMERON. 100 acres.

3 ROBT. CLARK. 100 acres.

4 FINLAY CAMERON. 400 acres. Enlisted in Canada with the view of joining his friends in Nova Scotia. Returned thither to bring his family at the peace. Was drowned shortly after his arrival, along with John Chisholm at the Narrows.

5 SAMUEL CAMERON, JR. 100 acres.

6 JAMES FRASER (BIG). 350 acres. A native of Strathglass. Settled where his grandson, Donald, lives, a little below St. Pauls.

7 PETER GRANT. The first elder in this settlement.

8 JAMES MCDONALD. Long the elder; said to have been the strongest man in the Regiment. Removed to the London district of Ontario. Hon. James McDonald his grandson.

9 HUGH MCDONALD. 100 acres.

On the West Side

10 JAMES FRASER, 2ND. Usually known as Culloden; 100 acres; farthest-up settler on that side. His descendants there still. Rev. James W. Fraser descended from him.

11 DUNCAN MCDONALD. 100 acres.

12 JOHN MCDONALD. 250 acres. Brother of James.

13 SAMUEL CAMERON. 300 acres; brother of Donald and Finlay, already mentioned.

14 JOHN CAMERON, SEN. 300 acres. A Roman Catholic from Strathglass; drowned with F. Cameron, as mentioned; father of Mrs. John McKenzie, Sen., West River.

15 JOHN CHISHOLM, JUN. 200 acres. Son of the last.

16 JOHN MCDONALD, 2ND. 250 acres.

---

* From George Patterson, *History of the County of Pictou, Nova Scotia* (Montreal: Dawson Bros., 1877) 462–3.

TABLE 3

Highlanders, including men from the disbanded 84th Regiment, who settled on the East River, Pictou in 1797*

1	WILLIAM FRASER	350 acres	From Inverness, land situated at Big Brook, now owned by his grandchildren.
2	JOHN McKAY	300 acres	
3	JOHN ROBERTSON	450 acres	At Churchville.
4	WM. ROBERTSON	200 acres	Son of the last, also near Churchville.
5	JOHN FRASER	300 acres	From Inverness, Springville, now occupied by Holmes and others.
6	THOS. FRASER	200 acres	From Inverness. An elder and noted for piety. His lot was at the head of the west Branch.
7	THOS. McKENZIE	100 acres	Settled near Fish Pools.
8	DAVID McLEAN	500 acres	A sergeant in the army, or as some say a petty officer in the navy. Was captured by the Spaniards, and afterward exchanged as a prisoner. He was a better scholar than usually found among the settlers, was a surveyor, a magistrate, an elder in the church, and a leading man in that section of the county.
9	ALEX. CAMERON	300 acres	
10	HECTOR McLEAN	400 acres	From Inverness. Land still occupied by his descendants.
11	JOHN FORBES	400 acres	From Inverness. Land on East Branch River.
12	ALEX. McLEAN	500 acres	Brother of Hector. Land opposite Stellarton, part of it still occupied by his descendants.
13	THOS. FRASER, JR.	100 acres	
14	JAS. McLELLAN	500 acres	From Inverness. Land above the Fish Pools, on the opposite side of the river, occupied by his descendants.
15	DONALD CHISHOLM	350 acres	From Strathglass, originally a Catholic, but became a Presbyterian. St. Columbas church built on part of his farm.

* From George Patterson, *History of the County of Pictou, Nova Scotia* (Montreal: Dawson Bros. 1877) 463-4.

16	ROBT. DUNBAR	450 acres	Three brothers from Inverness. All we believe in the 84th. Their land still occupied by their descendants.
17	ALEX. DUNBAR	200 acres	
18	WM. DUNBAR	300 acres	
19	JAMES CAMERON	300 acres	Of the 84th. Land still occupied by his descendants.
20	JOHN McDOUGALL	250 acres	In the Registrar's book, "J.M. Douglass."
21	JOHN CHISHOLM	300 acres	
22	DONALD CHISHOLM, JUN	400 acres	From Inverness. Land occupied by his grandsons.
23	ROBERT CLARK	150 acres	Of the 84th, but moved away. Land now occupied by Mr. Thomas Fraser.
24	DONALD SHAW	300 acres	From Inverness. Land occupied by his grandsons.
25	ALEXANDER McINTOSH	500 acres	From Inverness. His land now partly occupied by Hopewell village.
26	JOHN McLELLAN	100 acres	From Inverness. Land occupied by D.H. McLean and James Fraser.

The most of those marked as from Inverness were from the parish of Urquhart, in that county, and served in the 84th. In the record of the grant, dated 1st April 1793, there are the additional names of Colin Robinson, William Robinson, William McKenzie, William Robertson, heirs of John Forbes, Hugh Dunoon, and Thomas Fraser, but Hector McLean's is omitted.

The Guysborough area's Loyalists were concentrated at Guysborough itself, along Chedabucto Bay, and at Country Harbour to the southwest of it. Guysborough's initial settlers were men from the Duke of Cumberland's Regiment, who were joined by men from the 71st Regiment (Fraser Highlanders) and various other groups. The Country Harbour intake came from the disbanded Royal North Carolina Regiment, the South Carolina Royalists and the King's Carolina Rangers.[56] Although the Scottish influx into Antigonish County would eventually be very large, to the point of spilling over into the western stretches of Guysborough County, this growth in numbers would have had little to do with the efforts of these Loyalist settlers. They failed to attract many followers. As was the case elsewhere, most ex-soldiers, lacking farming experience, simply moved on after selling their land. However, a few Scottish Loyalists did remain. In 1837, a visiting Presbyterian missionary, from the Glasgow Colonial Society, discovered "that scattered through the county" were "the descendants of Scotchmen who served in the 71st Regiment [Fraser Highlanders], which many years since was disbanded."[57] Having fought with the Royal Highland Emigrants Regiment in the American War, many had taken up land along Chedabucto Bay.[58]

With Reverend James MacGregor's arrival in 1786, Pictou acquired a Presbyterian minister who could preach the Gospel in Gaelic. As news of this development filtered back to Scotland, Pictou would have seemed more attractive than ever. By the early 1800s hundreds of emigrant Scots would be streaming into Pictou. This was in stark contrast to the west of the province which would, in later years, lose many of its already-established Scottish settlers and would attract very few new arrivals from Scotland. A decade after the arrival of the *Hector,* more than five hundred, mainly Scottish settlers, could be found living around Pictou Harbour or along the frontages of the three rivers, in clearings stretching up to ten miles and more. They were also progressing along the County's eastern shoreline towards Barneys River at Merigomish Harbour.[59]

It must have seemed ironic to the British government that, having invested so much money and effort in moving Nova Scotia Loyalists into the west of the province, the greatest population growth would later take place in the east. When only a relatively small band of Scottish ex-soldiers were granted land along the eastern shore, they had an enormous impact on settlement growth. But the majority, who had been placed on the west, left far fewer traces behind. The primary attraction of the east to Scots was Pictou's timber trade. Having quickly established themselves in the industrial life of the area, they created an enormous magnet for Scottish colonization. The lumber industry was developed with Scottish capital by Scottish-born merchants and located in an area which had established distinctive Scottish enclaves from the late eighteenth century. It is therefore hardly surprising that these areas proved so irresistible. The combined effect of the clannish favouritism shown by close-knit Scottish business communities for Scottish recruits, the ready availability of transatlantic shipping from the Clyde, Aberdeen and Leith, and the presence of early Scottish settlement footholds thus became a potent force which drew considerable numbers from Scotland to the Maritime forests over many decades.

A man, who would become the first principal emigration agent for the Highlands, had arrived with his family in 1784 when the men of the disbanded 82nd Regiment came to Pictou. Simon Fraser, son of Captain John Fraser, who was "called Major and sometimes Colonel Fraser," would become quite notorious within the upper echelons of Scottish society.[60] The Scottish establishment would castigate Fraser for being an irresponsible rogue. He persuaded unsuspecting and vulnerable people to emigrate, took their money and profited from their foolishness and misfortune. The emigrants, who sailed on his ships, would leave under a cloud of negative and victim prone propaganda. However comforting this portrayal was to the many people back in Scotland who disapproved of emigration, it was a travesty of what was actually taking place. The feverish growth in the numbers wishing to emigrate was being stimulated by the considerable success of emigrant Scots and the growing realization that Nova Scotia and Cape Breton offered potentially great advantages to enterprising people.

4
CREATING A NEW SCOTLAND

*Major Simon Fraser, called Nova Scotia in this country for his
zealous endeavours to people that Province by a traffic in emigrants
for many years past, is on his return to these parts [Fort William,
Scotland] for a cargo.*[1]

AJOR SIMON FRASER'S INVOLVEMENT IN taking large numbers of Highlanders and Islanders to Nova Scotia brought
him great notoriety. His ships ran so regularly to Pictou that
he earned the nickname of "Nova Scotia" and was credited with having
single-handedly "peopled" Nova Scotia with the emigrant Scots who
sailed on his ships. Much of the growing exodus had been fuelled by
the upheaval caused by the new and more productive farming methods
which were being introduced in the Highlands and Islands from the
late eighteenth century. Large commercial sheep farms were being established, causing estate tenants to be evicted to make way for sheep. Tenants
were forced to relocate somewhere else within their landlords' estates
and, for good measure, their rents were raised. In the kelping districts
of the Hebrides and on the west coast mainland the opposite trend was
happening. Here land was being sub-divided into ever smaller lots to
accommodate the growing population of people who were employed
in the task of extracting kelp from seaweed.[2] While the manufacture
of kelp proved extremely profitable for landlords it was not so good for

their tenantry who became increasingly dissatisfied with their payments and conditions.

Thus, a large-scale displacement of people and worsening economic conditions were causing many people to leave the Highlands and Islands. Some took on factory jobs in the manufacturing Lowlands, but this required them to surrender their cultural roots. A better way out for many was emigration. People could transplant their Highland customs by emigrating and preserve their traditions in New World communities. This consideration together with the favourable reports from Scots already settled in North America gave people particularly strong and positive incentives to emigrate. Those who fretted about the harm being done to Scotland by the loss of so many people could not halt the exodus, try as they did. Emigration had become an unstoppable force by the late eighteenth century.

With his many business interests in Pictou and in Fort William, on the northwest coast of Scotland, Simon Fraser was particularly well placed to run an emigration agency.[3] Through his contacts with various influential tacksmen,[4] who held large leaseholds on Highland estates, he knew where the zeal to emigrate was particularly strong. Having come with his parents in 1784, to live at Fraser's Point near Pictou, he knew about pioneer life and could describe conditions in Nova Scotia from personal experience. He personally supervised shipping and embarkation arrangements and, on some occasions, actually accompanied emigrants across the Atlantic and to their final destinations, always in Nova Scotia.[5]

Reported to have "made a trade of the business since 1790," Simon Fraser first rose to prominence in 1791 when he brought a group of mainly Western Isle Roman Catholics from the Clanranald estate to Pictou. A total of six hundred and fifty people were taken in two ships, one of which was the *Dunkenfield* (or *Dunkeld*). But they arrived "in a wretched condition – the greatest part at this time are in want of sustenance and that number will daily increase."[6] Fearing that they might move on to South Carolina, the Lieutenant Governor, of Nova Scotia John Parr, took them under his wing and paid for their provisions himself. "My heart bleeds for the poor wretches and I am distressed to know what to do with them. If they are not assisted they must inevitably perish upon the beach where they are now hutted; humanity says that cannot be the case in a Christian country."[7] Parr gave them food to survive the winter and, when Father Angus MacEachern (later Bishop) who was based in Prince Edward Island at the time, learned of their plight, he hurried across to Pictou to provide them with spiritual as well as practical help.[8]

Predictably, anti-emigration campaigners in Scotland seized on news of their suffering to focus attention on the perils and hazards of pioneer life. Agents like Simon Fraser were attacked in the *Caledonian Mercury* and *Edinburgh Advertiser* for their greed and duplicity.[9] But the fact remains that these emigrants were successful. A decade after their arrival a visiting priest found them to be living "comfortably if they have been in any ways industrious."[10]

Reverend Angus Bernard MacEachern, first Bishop of Charlottetown, artist unknown. *Courtesy of the Diocese of Charlottetown, PEI Public Archives and Records Office, 2320/70–3.*

With Father MacEachern's help most of them had found land in the Antigonish area. However, some Eigg families and six Kennedy brothers from Canna chose to go to Parrsboro (Cumberland County), the Eigg families having acquired land from two brothers, "both Frasers," who were local land agents.[11] And another dozen Eigg families settled at Cape d'Or, a little to the west of Parrsboro (see Figure 5). But as was the case with most Scots who went initially to the Minas Basin region, they did not stay. After remaining in Cumberland County for nine to ten years, most moved to the Antigonish area where they rejoined other members of the

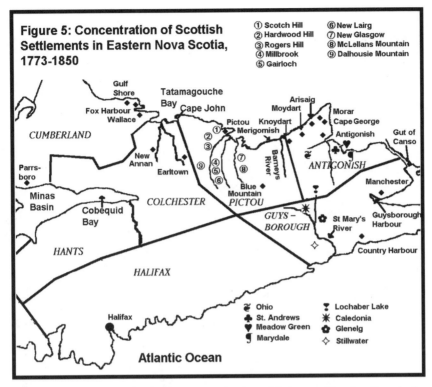

Figure 5: Concentration of Scottish Settlements in Eastern Nova Scotia, 1773-1850

① Scotch Hill
② Hardwood Hill
③ Rogers Hill
④ Millbrook
⑤ Gairloch
⑥ New Lairg
⑦ New Glasgow
⑧ McLellans Mountain
⑨ Dalhousie Mountain

Clanranald group who had gone to Antigonish immediately after their arrival in 1791.

Their compelling reason for moving on was to be nearer churches "where they could practise their Catholic religion."[12] Living on the west side of the province, they had to walk some 150 miles to Arisaig if they wished "to fulfil their Easter duty" once a year. This strong allegiance to their religious beliefs proved to be a major factor in determining where Scots would settle. Most Scottish colonists segregated themselves sharply by religion. As if by common consent, they established separate Protestant or Catholic territories within the vast stretches of the eastern Maritimes which they eventually came to dominate. The 1871 *Census Returns,* the first to give ethnic origins, reveal those locations where Scots were concentrated and the segregation by religion which occurred (see Figure 6).[13] Although the end-product was a single concentration of Scots, we are actually looking at separate communities, from different

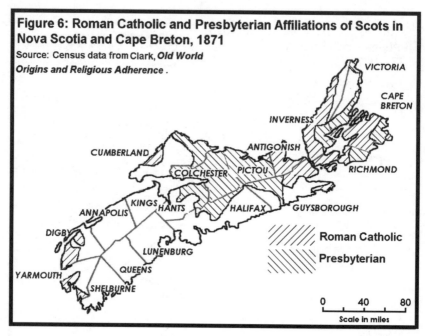

Figure 6: Roman Catholic and Presbyterian Affiliations of Scots in Nova Scotia and Cape Breton, 1871

Source: Census data from Clark, *Old World Origins and Religious Adherence*.

parts of Scotland, who established themselves at different times. Having laid claim to Pictou from 1773, Presbyterian Scots soon occupied much of Pictou County, then moved into the neighbouring counties of Cumberland and Colchester and later into Cape Breton. The Catholic Highlanders, who had come in such large numbers from 1791, settled in Antigonish County and afterwards extended their territory southward to Guysborough County as well as to Cape Breton.[14]

The Catholic Highlanders who found themselves in Antigonish by the early 1790s were actually following on the heels of others from the Clanranald estate who had come to the area some twenty years earlier. The driving force then had been religious persecution. In 1769, tenants on the Clanranald estate in South Uist had been ordered by their landlord to convert to Presbyterianism on pain of losing their lands. Rather than do this some two hundred and fourteen people from the Clanranald estates in South Uist, Barra, Eigg and mainland west Inverness-shire had emigrated in 1772 to Prince Edward Island. They established themselves at Scotchfort on the east side of the island, under the leadership of John MacDonald of Glenaladale, a prominent tacksman, who purchased land with the assistance of the Catholic Church. Then, with the ending of the American Revolution in 1783, even greater numbers came from the Clanranald estate to Prince Edward Island in 1790.[15] Thus, in going to Pictou in 1791, the Clanranald settlers were effectively creating additional footholds in Nova Scotia on the other side of the Northumberland Strait. By 1793 large numbers of them were to be found at Arisaig, in Antigonish County, a short distance across from the southeastern end of Prince Edward Island (see Figure 7).

The sudden arrival of so many Catholic Highlanders in Arisaig can be attributed to the behind-the-scenes manoeuvrings of the vigilant

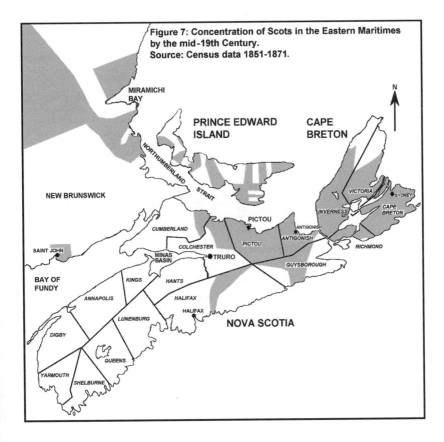

Figure 7: Concentration of Scots in the Eastern Maritimes by the mid-19th Century.
Source: Census data 1851-1871.

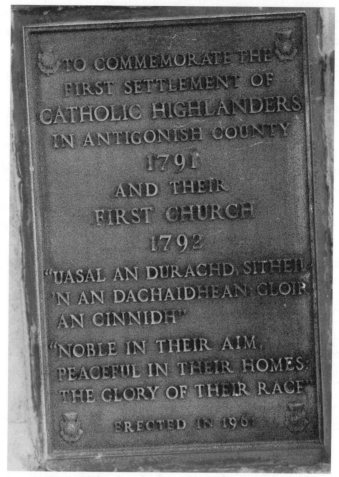

The plaque at Arisaig Harbour "To commemorate the first settlement of Catholic Highlanders in Antigonish County, in 1791, and their first church in 1792." The first church was a log chapel, built on a site near the present Arisaig Pier, and was named after St. Margaret, Queen of Scotland. *Photograph by Geoff Campey.*

Father MacEachern. Worried that his new Catholic arrivals might be lost to the missionary endeavours of Reverend James MacGregor, the Pictou Presbyterian minister, he persuaded them to settle in Antigonish County or Cape Breton. By 1792 they had built Antigonish County's first Roman Catholic Church at Arisaig.[16] Father MacEachern's foresight in directing Catholics to these particular areas meant that Scottish Catholics were effectively concentrated in one single region. By 1807 he had taken charge of a sprawling parish which encompassed the east side of Prince Edward Island, the eastern end of the Nova Scotia mainland and the western shore of Cape Breton.[17] It was a vast area to cover. The Arisaig mission alone extended some 70 to 80 miles. But "Father MacEachern possessed the true missionary spirit. He used to visit our county once a year."[18] Making these incredibly long trips to a scattered population, he saw their initial poverty but also offered an immensely important spiritual lifeline.

By 1801 the Eigg families, who settled initially in Cumberland County, were being re-united in Antigonish with the other Clanranald people with whom they had sailed in 1791. According to Father MacEachern, there were more than 1,050 Catholic families "between Merigomish and around to Antigonish"[19] at this time. However, the numbers would soon mushroom even beyond this as the growing exodus from the Highlands and Islands continued unabated. The large numbers of Roman Catholics from the Western Isles and west mainland, who came in 1791, were joined by hundreds more in 1801 and 1802. And Presbyterians also arrived in their hundreds in 1802 and 1803. Edward Fraser of Reelig, the customs collector at Inverness, claimed that "during the peace after the American Wars, Major Simon Fraser and others carried out 4000" emigrants.[20] If anything this is probably an underestimate. Data on known ship crossings shows that exceedingly large numbers of Highlanders came to Nova Scotia and Cape Breton in this short period between 1801 and 1803, with Catholics and Presbyterians coming in roughly equal numbers (see Appendix II).

Six vessels carried large numbers of Catholic Highlanders from the west coast of Scotland to Pictou in 1801. The *Hope* of Lossie (100 passengers), left from Isle Martin (Ullapool), while the *Nora* (500 passengers) the *Golden Text* of Aberdeen (numbers unknown), the *Dove* of Aberdeen (219 passengers), *Sarah* of Liverpool (350 passengers) and *Alexander* (numbers unknown) all left from Fort William.[21] The *Nora* took sixteen weeks to get to Pictou. Smallpox broke out on the crossing and some sixty-five children under the age of five had died. Some seventy-five years later, Margaret Chisholm could "tell of the horrors of that long, long voyage. How that at the starting nought could be heard but the laughter and frolic and crying of children, how that one by one their tiny bodies were consigned to the angry deep, until at last the laughter and frolic and crying were hushed, and the hearts of the mothers were filled with anguish."[22] Yet, the *Nora's* problems seemingly went unnoticed. Attention was focused instead on Hugh Dunoon's ships.

Having come from Killearnan (Ross-shire) to live on the East River of Pictou in 1784 and later in Merigomish, Hugh Dunoon quickly established himself as a prominent local figure with an office close to the town centre of Pictou.[23] As a collector of customs and a local merchant, he was ideally placed to offer his services to emigrant Scots. But his efforts in organizing ships for emigrant Scots proved to be calamitous. They earned him great notoriety in Scotland and contributed to passenger legislation which was later introduced to protect passengers from ill-treatment. However, when he began looking for passengers in the Highlands large numbers came forward to buy places on his ships. Duncan Grant, factor to Sir James Grant, an Inverness-shire laird, witnessed this growing exodus and wondered about its implications for the estate:

"I am at a loss what to say.... A spirit of emigration to America is creeping in amongst the lower classes of the people in this country. Several families are preparing to emigrate against May 1st along with a Mr. [Hugh] Denoon, [Dunoon] a brother of David Denoon [Dunoon], Minister of Killearnan, who came lately from America and who proposes to return in May. I hear he brings several families from the Aird [near Beauly], Strathglass and Glen Moriston also. Unluckily it is not the very poorest he brings with him."[24]

Dunoon offered three vessels. There was the tiny, 72 ton sloop, the *Hope* of Lossie, the larger *Dove* of Aberdeen (186 tons) and the much larger *Sarah* of Liverpool (372 tons). Surviving passenger lists reveal that Dunoon found many of his passengers from Kilmorack, Kiltarlity and Urquhart in east

The Roman Catholic Church at Arisaig, which was built in 1878, still retains the name St. Margaret of Scotland. *Photograph by Geoff Campey.*

Inverness-shire, parishes which had previously lost people to the Pictou area as a result of the *Hector* crossing in 1773 and the Loyalists influx of 1784. His ships also carried large numbers from the predominantly Catholic districts of Moidart, Knoydart and Morar in west Inverness-shire.[25]

His two principal ships, the *Dove* and *Sarah,* carried 569 passengers from Fort William to Pictou.[26] As smallpox swept through one of his ships, thirty-nine children under ten died. Thirty-six of the *Sarah*'s young and most able male passengers were nearly pressed into the British Navy off Newfoundland; but by convincing the Navy men that he was a government agent, Hugh Dunoon won their freedom.[27] Upon arrival, the passengers were quarantined and afterwards assisted by the local Scots who took them into their homes during their first winter in Pictou. The Presbyterians remained in the area, settling at Mount

Thom, McLellans Mountain and East River, while the Catholic arrivals dispersed to Antigonish and Cape Breton.[28]

Dunoon's ship crossings were highly controversial. The crucial issue was the formula he used in counting the number of passengers who were under the age of 16. He agreed on a formula with the customs officials at the time which allowed him to compute each child as a fraction of an adult. It was agreed that he would total the ages of those under sixteen and divide by sixteen to get the final total. Based on this formula the *Dove* (186 tons) was cleared as having 180.5 full passengers and the *Sarah* (372 tons) as having 258, although the *Dove* actually carried 219 souls and the *Sarah* 350.[29]

After examining passenger numbers and allegations that further people had boarded ship after customs clearance, the Highland Society of Edinburgh concluded that there had been severe overcrowding on the *Dove* and *Sarah*. Based on their calculations, his space allocations were worse than the conditions on slave ships. His formula enabled him to take more passengers than would have been allowed under slave trade regulations. This was a devastating criticism of one man and his two ships. In the end the Society's arguments were a major factor in convincing the government to introduce tougher passenger legislation. By 1803 when the Passenger Act was in force, emigrants were to have a minimum space allocation which allowed one person for every two tons burthen.[30] However, the immediate effect of the Act was to cause fares to nearly double and thus greatly limit the numbers of people who could afford to emigrate.[31]

When new arrivals from Scotland came to Pictou in 1815, they had a particularly difficult time owing to the "scarcity of provisions and the consequent poverty of their friends already settled in the county."[32] Yet it was Hugh Dunoon whom they turned to the following year when they submitted their petition to the Nova Scotia government asking for help. So it seems that Dunoon's reputation in Pictou had not been tarnished by the controversy which surrounded the *Dove* and *Sarah*. Dunoon immersed himself once more in his business activities and public duties but had nothing further to do with emigrant shipping. By contrast,

Simon Fraser's emigration agency was taking on more work in 1802 and 1803. The exodus was spreading to many parts of the Highlands and Islands causing an unprecedented number of emigrants to look for ship crossings to Pictou.

In 1802, Simon Fraser's ship, the *Aurora* of Greenock, took one hundred and twenty-eight people, who originated from east and west Inverness-shire, from Fort William to Pictou.[33] Once again the Presbyterian arrivals settled in the Pictou area and the Catholics dispersed to Antigonish and Cape Breton. According to Hector MacLean of Fort William, Fraser was promising another crossing in 1803:

"We set sail tomorrow [15th December 1802] for Nova Scotia. Our ship can't call in any harbour in Mull for emigrants as she is cleared for Customs House direct for Pictou. If there are any of the people that wishes to go to America...you will have the goodness to inform them that my brother-in-law [Simon Fraser] will have a ship early in the Spring going out if they wish to go with him. Let them address to him, Major Fraser, care of James Skinner, writer, Parliament Square, Edinburgh."[34]

However Fraser's *Aurora* was just one of many ships which had arrived in Pictou in 1802. Around nine hundred Catholic emigrants, who originated from Barra and South Uist, came to Pictou that year (see Appendix II). Included in this number were three hundred and seventy people who had sailed from Lochboisdale in South Uist:

"In the month of August, 370 landed, natives of the Island of Barra, and all Roman Catholics. As they had been accustomed to the fisheries, Governor Wentworth located them for a time on Pictou island and the shores adjacent but they all moved away eastward to Antigonish and Cape Breton. A number of Protestants also arrived, who settled in various places, but we are not informed of any settlement informed by them."[35]

They petitioned for land on their arrival:

> "The under-mentioned petitioners who are desirous to be accom-
> modated on the lands on the South Branch of the River Antigonish,
> such unappropriated lands as may be found in the vicinity and on
> the new road leading from Manchester...I have therefore to request
> you will allow these people and lay out their lands in the propor-
> tions attached to their respective names, they finding their own axe
> men and chain bearers."[36]

In the end, 10,025 acres of land in the district which is now St. Andrews, Antigonish, were granted to sixty-eight families, which included many MacDonalds, MacGilvrays and MacEichrons (see Table 4). Many of the families who had sailed on the *Nora* in 1801 also came to the area to take up land on or close to the line of the proposed Manchester Road which ran in a southeasterly direction from Antigonish. Settlements were soon founded at St. Andrews, Marydale and Meadow Green (see Figure 5).[37] However, a few of the Barra people, like Hector MacNeil, later moved on with their families to the north east region of Bras d'Or Lake in Cape Breton.[38]

Although no ships had actually sailed to Cape Breton Island from Scotland, it had already acquired a great many Scottish settlers by the early 1800s. This was in spite of government restrictions which were intended to block colonization efforts on the Island. The British gov-ernment's actions seem odd, given its belief that settlers should be used to bolster population growth in strategic areas such as this. Along with Newfoundland, Cape Breton controlled the access to the Gulf of St. Lawrence. Cape Breton's valuable coal mines were the reason. The gov-ernment wished to have unfettered access to its coal reserves in order to supply the army units based in Halifax and Newfoundland. Addition-ally, it did not wish to have Britain's coal mines competing with Cape Breton mines or see Cape Breton's coal being exported to the United States. Thus for a number of reasons connected with coal, the govern-ment tried to stop all but Loyalists and fish merchants from acquiring freeholds on the Island, a restriction which remained in force until 1817.

TABLE 4

**List of passengers who lately came from Scotland
to the Province of Nova Scotia c. 1802***

Family details	Acres
Donald McDonald, his wife and five children	200
Donald McDonald Jnr., his wife and five children	200
John Smith, his wife and five children	200
Neil McLeod, and his wife	125
Donald McLeod, his wife and four children	200
John McLeod, his wife and five children	200
Ewen McLeod, his wife and two children	175
Hector McNeill, his wife and five children	200
Rory McNeill	100
Hector McKinnon and his wife	125
Donald McKinnon, his wife and one child	150
John McEichron, and his wife	125
Ewen McEichron	100
Neill McEichron	100
Alexander McEichron	100
Margaret McEichron, a widow and one child	100
Angus McDonald	100
Roderick McDonald, his wife and one child	150
Donald McDonald, his wife and two children	175
Alexander McDonald, his wife and four children	200
John McDonald, his wife and four children	200
Donald McDonald, his wife and two children	175
Alex'r McGregor, alias McDonald, his wife and two children	175
John McGilvray, his wife and six children	200
Donald McGilvray, his wife and two children	175
Angus McGilvray, his wife and two children	175
Ewen McDougald, his wife and child	150
Alex'r McGilvray	100
John McGilvray	40
Ewen Gillies, his wife and nine children	200
Donald Gillies	100
Angus McGilvray, his wife and seven children	200
Duncan McGilvray	100

* From: RG1 Vol. 396B ff.81–83, The Letter Book of Instructions of the Surveyor
General Charles Morris to his deputies for surveys and land grants to Loyalists
and others 1800–26.

Family details	Acres
Donald McGilvray, his wife and nine children	200
Angus McGilvray	100
John McDonald, his wife and his mother	150
Alexander McDonald	100
Ewen McDonald, his wife and sister	150
Neil McDonald	100
Donald McDonald and his mother	125
Angus McDonald, his wife and child	150
John McPherson	100
Ewen McKelock and his wife	125
Agnes Patterson	100
John Fraser, his wife and child	150
William Fraser, his wife and three children	200
Alexander McEichron	100
Mary McEichron	25
Katherine McEichron	25
John Steele	100
John Chisholm, his wife and four children	200
Alex'r Chisholm, his wife and child	150
Archibald Chisholm, his wife and child	150
James Chisholm and his wife	125
William Grant, his wife and child	150
Donald McDonald, his wife and sister	150
Donald Fraser, his wife and two children	175
Donald McDonald, his wife and sister	150
Donald Chisholm and four children	200
Andrew Chisholm, his wife and sister	150
Thomas McDonald, his wife and two children	175
Alexander Stewart, his wife and two children	175
Angus McDougall, his mother and three brothers	200
John McPherson, his wife and five children	200
Donald McDonald, his wife and one child	150
John McDonald, his sister and two children	175
Margaret McIsaac, widow and one child	100
Kenneth Chisholm, his wife and two children	175

Acres   **10,025**

However emigrant Scots took no notice of these legal restraints and simply slipped across to Cape Breton.[39] These were pioneer squatters. Some, having settled previously in Prince Edward Island or mainland Nova Scotia, were seeking better locations. Prince Edward Island Scots had great difficulty in acquiring freehold land and were attracted by the prospect of grabbing their own land in Cape Breton. All sought the favourable positions which were to be found along Cape Breton's extensive west and south coastlines and large interior lakes.[40] There were no proprietors on hand to provide capital, organization and leadership. At the end of the eighteenth century, Cape Breton was a sparsely settled and largely undeveloped British colony. Only around 2000 people lived on the island, of whom half were French-speaking Acadians. Most of the rest were Loyalist refugees from the United States. The cod fishery supported most of the Island's economy. Farming operated at a subsistence level only. Agricultural communities consisted of a scattering of farms which were spread over very large areas. There were no roads. No churches had been built. There was no effective local government.[41] Nevertheless Scots came in their hundreds.

There were around three hundred Scots in Cape Breton by 1802, with more than half living in Inverness County (see Figure 8). Some might

View of Sydney in 1799. Painting by John Hames. *Courtesy of the National Archives of Canada, C-024939.*

have been Loyalists, who had taken up their land grants at Sydney and Baddeck in 1784, but the majority were squatters. Thus, Scottish immigration to Cape Breton had its origins in the late nineteenth century in spite of the fact that no emigrants actually sailed to Cape Breton from Scotland at this time. There was one ship crossing to Sydney in 1802 and no further emigrant ossings took place until 1817. Yet from 1802 to 1814 an average of one hundred and fifty Scots a year settled in Cape Breton.[42] By 1814 Cape Breton's population was estimated to be between 4000 and 5000, with Scots making up half the total. This growth relied on a steady migration of Scots from Pictou and Prince Edward Island to Cape Breton which continued until 1820.[43] Nearly all of the earliest arrivals originated from the Catholic areas of Inverness-shire (principally Lochaber, Arisaig and Strathglass) and the Inner and Outer Hebrides.

The extensive land grant records which were produced retrospectively, from 1817, once the legal restraints on land ownership in Cape Breton were removed, allow the exactly locations where these Highlanders and Islanders settled to be pinpointed. They reveal that the earliest arrivals were concentrated on the Western and Southern Shores.[44] The desire to settle amongst fellow Catholics and to be near water frontages had attracted them to these areas.[45] Rather than coping with inland locations, which was all many could find in either Pictou or Prince Edward Island, they opted instead for the extensive water frontages which Cape Breton's vast coastline, rivers and internal lakes had to offer. They still had to fell trees but they were no longer being enveloped completely by the "gloomy forests."[46]

It was said that the Western Shore offered "a more congenial soil and greater facilities for prosecuting the sea fisheries in which they had been engaged in the Western Islands."[47] Margaree, on the Western Shore, had its first Scottish settlers by 1785, while Port Hood was founded a year later.[48] Judique's Catholic parish of St. Andrews was in existence by 1790 and a chapel was built sometime before 1804. And Mabou had also built its first Roman Catholic Church by the early 1800s.[49] Catholic Highlanders were colonizing Broad Cove (Inverness) by 1790, Long Point by 1798, and Low Point at the entrance to the Strait of Canso by 1801. By

St. Andrew's Roman Catholic Church, Judique. The congregation had a resident priest from 1818. *Photograph by Geoff Campey.*

1800 they had also moved further inland to River Inhabitants and to St. Peters on the south side of the island, near the Acadian settlements.[50] And St. George's Channel in the West Bay of Bras d'Or Lake had its first Scots by 1802. But when people from South Uist and Barra discovered Bras d'Or's northeastern stretches, a large number of their fellow countrymen actually sailed out directly from Scotland to join them.

Having arrived in Pictou that year, the nine hundred emigrants from Barra and South Uist went to two different locations. Sixty-eight families went to St. Andrews in Antigonish County while most of the remaining families went to Christmas Island, the Grand Narrows and the Iona peninsula. They found a landscape which reminded them of their beaches back home. It was also a particularly opportune location.[51] They were near the Big Bras d'Or entrance, on the east side of the Island, "the principal opening into the interior sea, being the only channel by which the shipping engaged in the timber trade can be admitted."[52] This would be in one of the first regions near Sydney to be opened up for timber felling and shipbuilding.[53] The settlers would later export the large quantities of fish to be found in Bras d'Or Lake, and large numbers of people from Barra and South Uist would follow, reinforcing these settlements and creating new ones on the south side of Boularderie.[54] Red Islands, on the southeast side of Bras d'Or lake, became another Catholic stronghold, owing its beginnings to the arrival in 1802 of Hector MacNeil from Barra.[55] He was followed between 1807 and 1811 by eighteen families, eleven of whom were Barra MacNeils.

In flagrant breach of the restrictions placed on colonization by the British government official policy, the *Northern Friends* of Clyde carried Highlanders to Cape Breton in 1802, having been first "fitted out from Greenock."[56] She arrived at Sydney with three hundred and forty Catholics from the Clanranald estate in Moidart. General John Despard, Cape Breton's very able Administrator, was pleased to see them. Fearing that they might be tempted to move on "to a foreign county" he persuaded local councillors to lend money, raised from a local liquor tax, to the new arrivals.[57] Married couples were to be loaned (in reality probably given) 40 shillings, each child over twelve 20 shillings and children under twelve were to get 15 shillings.[58] They dispersed to the Catholic strongholds along the Western Shore and Bras d'Or Lake.[59]

The cairn at Christmas Island, on the site of the first church built in 1814 by Catholic Highlanders. *Photograph by Geoff Campey.*

Reverend Duncan Ross, a Presbyterian minister, from J.P. MacPhie, *Pictonians at Home and Abroad*. Born in Ross-shire, he emigrated to Pictou in 1795. Reverend Ross took charge of congregations at West River, Middle River, and Rogers Hill from 1801 until his death in 1834. *Courtesy of The Trustees of the National Library of Scotland.*

Meanwhile, Presbyterian Scots were also coming to Pictou in ever-increasing numbers in 1802 and 1803.[60] John Gerrond, who visited Pictou in 1797, was struck by the number of Scots, who even then lived in the area:

"Many Scotsmen reside along the rivers and gulfs of Pictou, most of whom are from the Highlands…went to one of their meeting houses on the West River…. They performed family worship twice every day. The Minister's names were Mr Ross on the West River and Mr Biggar [MacGregor] on the East River. I could not but remark on the hardiness of these people; for although they came through the snow wet-footed, you would not hear so much as a cough in the whole [prayer] meeting. The Ministers preach English in the forenoon and Gaelic in the afternoon, that the Highlanders may enjoy it in their own way."[61]

By the early 1800s the port of Pictou was having to cope with increasing numbers of Scottish immigrants. According to George Patterson "the notice of the arrival of an emigrant vessel [from Scotland] brought people from all quarters to enquire for relatives on board, whom they took to their homes, or to find acquaintances or persons from their native

75

districts or even strangers, to whom they would freely extend the same hospitalities."[62] However, the arrival of the *Favourite* of Kirkaldy, from Isle Martin in August 1803, attracted more interest than most:

"She [*Favourite*] sailed from Ullapool without a clearance and arrived in Pictou on the 3rd August, having made the passage in 5 weeks and three days, being regarded then and for some time after as the quickest ever made. She had 500 passengers on board, one birth and no deaths taking place on the voyage. But almost immediately after the passengers' goods had been landed she sank in the harbour."[63]

Particularly large numbers had arrived from Strathglass, in east Inverness-shire. This followed the major clearances which were carried out in 1801 by William Chisholm and his wife, Elizabeth Macdonnell, to make way for sheep farms.[64] Hugh Dunoon's *Dove* and *Sarah* had taken large numbers from Strathglass and the surrounding area in 1801, while Simon Fraser had supplied two vessels in 1803. Four more vessels came to Pictou in 1803 from the Moray Firth with 480 Strathglass emigrants, two of the ship crossings having been "organized by a club of Strathglass people."[65] It is not surprising that Pictou attracted such interest:

"It is well irrigated by streams and brooks which, by their union, form several rivers. Of these the East and French Rivers fall into Merigomish, the East Middle and East Rivers flow into the harbour of Pictou and the Big and Little Rivers discharge themselves into Caribou [Harbour], between which and the boundary of the district of Colchester are the rivers Toney and John. The soil is in general of a superior quality and susceptible of a high state of cultivation."[66]

The Scottish population was rapidly growing at Pictou itself and along its East, Middle and West rivers. Settlements had also been founded at River John on the extreme west of Pictou County and at Scots Hill, Hardwood Hill, Rogers Hill, and Green Hill near the West River. There were settlements at Andersons Mountain, Frasers Mountain and McLellans

The monument to the first Duke of Sutherland (1758–1833) erected in 1836 on Ben Bhragaidh, overlooking Dunrobin Castle and Golspie on the east coast of Sutherland. The colossal statue was carved by Joseph Theakston, based on a model by Francis Chantry. The statue became associated with the Sutherland clearances although the first Duke had merely provided the funds for the estate restructuring. Following the clearances, which began in 1807, large numbers emigrated to Nova Scotia and Cape Breton. *Courtesy of Lord Strathnaver.*

Mountain, near to the East River and at Merigomish, as well as along Barneys River which flows into Merigomish Harbour (see Figure 2).

Many of the early emigrants who came to Pictou were the victims of evictions and thus arrived in large groups. The ready availability of land at the time meant that great numbers could settle in one place. A good many people from Sutherland arrived shortly before the major clearances which began in 1807, when seventy families were removed from the parishes of Lairg and Farr.[67] Seventy Sutherland emigrants sailed to Pictou on the *Tweed* of Ullapool in 1802, and a further five hundred came on the *Favourite* of Kirkaldy in 1803.[68] Finding land about twenty miles or so up the Middle River from Pictou Harbour, they founded Mill Brook and New Lairg, the latter named after their native parish.

Sheep farms had also come to the Outer Hebrides. "Several hundred souls" had been removed during the 1790s for the sake of sheep in South Uist and Canna and, in 1793, the whole parish of Uig in Lewis was being advertised as a sheep farm.[69] By 1803 six hundred Lewis emigrants were making their way to Pictou from Stornoway. Three vessels had taken them, one of which was the *Alexander:*

"The captain died on the passage and the owner [Mr. McIvor] who was on board took sick, when the vessel [*Alexander*] was taken charge by Mr. David McGregor, father of John McGregor, afterward M.P. for Glasgow and Secretary to the Board of Trade, but then only a child."[70]

Even so the *Alexander* managed to arrive safely and returned the following year with more Lewis passengers. They too settled together as a group. Most of the Lewis settlers established themselves on the coast at Wallace, a substantial distance to the west of Pictou, in Cumberland County.

When Lord Selkirk toured the Pictou area in September 1803, he found that "Highlanders have since settled up the [East] River for, it is said, 20 miles"[71] and were living well. William [Squire] MacKay, one of the *Hector* arrivals of 1773, had by then:

"built a new stone house, exactly a good comfortable farm house in Scotland.... He keeps 12 cows...has about 100 acres clear – besides farms for several of his sons. The old settled Highlanders, even those of 10 or 12 years date have in general cleared as much as they want and do little more- being not ambitious of making money so much as living comfortably. Many of the older settlers are now building or have got neat framed houses – those [here for] ten or twelve years are mostly living in log houses."[72]

Visiting "the house of a new settler, MacIntosh," who had come to the East River in 1802, Selkirk found that he lives "upon the top of a steep bank, has two or three acres cleared, mostly planted with potatoes…. MacIntosh's house has no chimney yet and is very ill-stuffed between the logs, yet his family passed the winter in it." But "he is now going to build a chimney. The settlement sends out little or no grain, the land being generally laid to grass, except what is requisite for the family…. They raise a good deal of upland hay, the river has little salt marsh…the intervales above the tide are valuable hay grounds."[73]

Going up the West River, Selkirk met emigrants from Dumfriesshire and Kirkcudbrightshire, established there for some thirty years, who had previously lived in Prince Edward Island.[74] Anthony McLellan "came over as an infant, [in 1775] his father having been one of the original settlers.[75] "He has a lot of 500 acres – half a mile front…about 40 acres clear." The others were also progressing well:

"The first two miles along the West River from Pictou Harbour is almost entirely settled by the Galloway Colony, who extend along the river and form a continued scene of cleared land along the Valley…. These people emigrated in 1774 and 1775 and appear to have been very industrious and successful – their houses bear every mark of comfort and their countenances of content. The general appearance of the settlement strongly recalled some scenes in Switzerland. They retain many peculiarities of Galloway, the girls wear hats etc., they will treat you with shortbread and in their Orchards is the Thorle Pippen [apple trees]."[76]

Selkirk came across Mr. MacGilivray about twelve miles further up the West River. He was "a Highlander, settled about fourteen years ago, who has done but little and does not go on clearing here, but has taken up some new land for his son, farther up…. He has a long strip of inter-vale which would be good meadow but is full of stumps. His house is miserable, covered with spruce bark and ill-fitted. However this may be owing to his former house having been burnt, which would force him to build in a hurry. His barn is better and shingled."[77]

Then, as he continued even further, Selkirk encountered some recent arrivals – "Highlanders of the emigration, in 1801" who had "almost as much land in cultivation as MacGilivray. This is their first grain crop. Last year they had potatoes only…but this year's crop will give them abundance of everything."[78] He also met a Perthshire family who orig-inated from Strowan (Struan) in Rannoch near Blair Atholl. Having "been turned out of their farm three years before they emigrated," they now lived on the West River.[79] At the time there were few other Perthshire settlers in the area. However this changed with the arrival, later in 1803, of a Perthshire contingent of seventy, who had sailed on the *Commerce* from Port Glasgow.[80] Their locations are uncertain. They may have gone to Piedmont in Pictou County, just to the south of Lower Barneys River, an area which later attracted many settlers from Blair Atholl.[81]

In his travels Selkirk had met many "Highlanders from Fraser's Country." They were the former tenants of Lord Lovat (Clan Fraser) who would have told him about the evictions and uncertainties they had faced back in Scotland. It was predicted that "sheep farming will occasion the expulsion of three quarters of the present tenantry" of the Lovat estates in east Inverness-shire.[82] It clearly had. They had come in the great influx from 1801 to 1803. Thirty years earlier, Lovat tenants had signed up with John Pagan and come across to Pictou on the *Hector*. This had followed the seizure of the Lovat estates by the Crown, in the post-Culloden aftermath. Disquiet over the high rents being imposed by the Board of Forfeited Estates had caused many tenants to opt for emigration.[83] And when the American War ended in 1783, many ex-soldiers who came from Beauly, Inverness, and the surrounding area, took up their land grants in Pictou. Thus Pictou's early and strong asso-ciations with east Inverness-shire continued to grow.

People from Sutherland were also beginning to make an impression. In the end, they would be the ones who would have the longest-lasting links with eastern Nova Scotia. A Sutherland contingent had come on the *Hector* in 1773 and more Sutherlanders probably came to the area in the Loyalist influx of 1784. They were particularly well-represented in North Carolina as a result of the emigration which had taken place in the early 1770s from the parishes of Tongue, Durness, Farr and Kildonan.[84] Some of the men are likely to have joined the North Carolina Volunteers and become repatriated in Nova Scotia as Loyalist ex-servicemen when the American War of Independence ended. Great numbers of Sutherland emigrants would come to Nova Scotia and Cape Breton in the years ahead, especially during the peak emigration period after the Napoleonic Wars.

Right from the beginning Cape Breton's strongest links were with the Western Isles. Very visible in the early days were the people from Barra – particularly the MacNeils. Donald MacNeil, who had served with the British Army at the siege of Louisburg in 1758, appears to have been one of the initial catalysts. After returning home to Barra and lauding the beauty and riches of the Bras d'Or Lake, he was followed by four more MacNeils (Donald, Eoin, Rory and John). They landed at Pictou in 1799 and, after settling first in Arisaig, moved on in 1801 to Bras d'Or "at the point where the Barra Strait was narrowest."[85] Thus began the great Barra influx to Iona, Grand Narrows and Christmas Island. The Western Isle domination would continue and reach new heights in the 1820s with the collapse of the kelp industry in Scotland.

Emigration levels plummeted with the onset of the Napoleonic Wars in 1803 and the higher fares which resulted from the new regulations laid down in the 1803 Passenger Act.[86] However, the exodus from Scotland resumed with a vengeance when the wars ended in 1815. The severe economic depression which followed, easier and cheaper access to transatlantic shipping services and the continuing good reports from Scots who had already settled brought increasing numbers of Scots to Nova Scotia and Cape Breton.

Until the early 1800s most emigrant Scots boarded ship at west coast ports. Fort William and Isle Martin (Ullapool) in the northwest Highlands were major collecting points and the ships used were often based at the Clyde (see Appendix II). However, that soon changed. The explosive growth in the Maritime region's timber trade completely revolutionized emigrant transport. The doubling of already high duties on European timber in 1811 priced it out of the market and paved the way for the North American timber trade. Maritime timber exports soared and as they did more ships left Scotland for Pictou. The Clyde lost its near monopoly and by 1816 all major Scottish ports were trading with British America and offering space on their vessels to emigrants wishing to cross the Atlantic.

The MacNeil monument, which overlooks Grand Narrows, erected at Iona, August 5, 1983. *Photograph by Geoff Campey.*

∞ 5 ∞

THE ATTRACTIONS OF
THE TIMBER TRADE

Persons still living can recollect when the point above the town
[Pictou], where he [Mortimer] did business, presented every season
a forest of masts. He is said to have loaded 80 vessels in one year,
not, however, all in Pictou Harbour, but many in surrounding
ports, his business extending to Bay Verte and Prince Edward
Island. His book-keeper stated that in one season, in seven succes-
sive weeks, he shipped timber to the value of £35,000, or at the
rate of £5,000 per week.[1]

AVING ARRIVED IN NOVA SCOTIA in the late 1780s, from Keith
in the northeast of Scotland, Edward Mortimer quickly established himself as a prominent player in the Maritime economy.
A man "of commanding presence, tall, broad-shouldered and portly,"
he was said to be "manifestly a born leader of men."[2] Entering into partnerships with William Liddell, a Glasgow merchant, as well as other
timber merchants, he came to dominate Pictou's trade and transatlantic
shipping.[3] By 1813 he had set up a firm with himself as principal, William
Liddell and George Smith, another Scot from Pictou, as his associates.[4]
Through his extensive interests in timber, the fisheries and coal mining,
he accrued a huge fortune said to be worth £100,000. He had a massive
stone mansion (now Sir Edward Mortimer Inn) built in Pictou at a cost

Edward Mortimer (1768–1819), portrait by Robert Field c. 1815. Upon becoming Pictou's leading merchant, he strongly supported his local community giving generously to the Pictou Academy from its founding in 1815. *Courtesy of the Nova Scotia Art Gallery 1977.60. Gift of Janet Johnstone, Halifax, Nova Scotia, 1977.*

of around £17,000, for which he brought out skilled Scottish carpenters and stonemasons. He entered politics, representing Halifax County in the General Assembly for some twenty-one years.[5] Mortimer was quite simply "the chief man of Pictou, wielding so much influence as to be called the King of Pictou."[6]

"By the system of credit which prevailed," Mortimer controlled the economic life of Pictou. "He had almost every inhabitant of the county in his books."[7] Settlers obtained credit and Mortimer took their cut timber as repayment. They paid for equipment and any land purchases through loans advanced by him and clearly remained heavily in debt to him over many years. The many Frasers, MacDonalds, Camerons and MacKenzies in his list of debtors testify to the predominance of Scots and to his desire to do business with his own people. All would have been engaged with him in some aspect of timber cutting or transport. At the time of his death in 1819, there were one hundred and fifty-one debtors, probably all Scots, who together owed him some £10,554 (see Appendix IV).[8]

While he held great influence over the people on his ledger, Mortimer appears not to have abused his position:

"The poor and the friendless were freely helped and ever after retained a grateful recollection of such services. We have conversed

84

frequently with country people, who recollected that period, and their general testimony was that in any difficulty they had only to apply to Mortimer to receive ready help. Though he wished to have people on his books and loved the power that this gave him, yet he was never disposed to deal harshly with them. On the contrary, his inclination was rather to act the Lord Bountiful."[9]

After his death people could see that Mortimer's great wealth was not what it seemed. When his estate came to be settled up, he was actually insolvent.[10] And it was only then that the people on his ledger "felt the evils of the credit system, under which they had become so deeply involved." However, Mortimer's "credit system," with all of its faults, gave ordinary settlers a stake in Pictou's timber trade. It worked because he never called in his debts. He knew that the local economy would collapse if he did.

Thus, Edward Mortimer had advanced much of the capital needed to finance Pictou's fledgling timber industry. He was the middle man in a complex chain of small operators who included storekeepers, brokers, saw millers and the various farmer/lumberers who actually cut the trees.[11] It was a Scottish-dominated cartel run by Mortimer who probably excluded all but Scots from his business dealings. In this way, emigrant Scots were well placed to benefit from Pictou's increasing prosperity. Because the trade depended on regular Atlantic crossings, it also paved the way for further influxes from Scotland. And it influenced settler destinations. As was the case with their predecessors, new arrivals sought favourable locations close to the timber collecting bays in and around Pictou. The town of Pictou grew rapidly in size and, by 1810, the town of New Glasgow, a short distance to the south on the East River, was receiving its first Scottish inhabitants. The earliest arrivals sought the best locations along the coast near to harbours and bays while those who followed progressively colonized river frontages and their tributaries.

As timber felling moved into the more remote areas, timber production came to rely increasingly on large lumbering parties. But in the early days most of the lumbering operations were carried out by small family ventures.[12] While winters may have found some men "deep in the heart of the forest primeval, in a log camp crowded with their mates," most settlers would have combined lumbering activities with farming:

> "They are loggers or lumberers, men not quite of the forest nor quite of the farm. Their summers are occupied by the rude cultivation of some rugged patch, by courtesy called a farm where a few acres of clearing fall apart from the dark shadows of the coniferous woods."[13]

However, these Scots came as colonizers. Few would have been engaged full-time as lumberers. After clearing their land of trees, they sold timber only as a preliminary step to creating their settlements:

> "The cutting, hewing, hauling, rafting and shipping of timber became, for some years, almost the business of the people of Pictou. The farmer not only spent his time in winter in cutting and preparing it, but also much of the spring and summer in rafting and shipping it. As to his fields he thought only of hastily committing his seed to the ground in spring and gathering at harvest time what crop had chosen to grow and paid no attention to manuring, rotation or other improvements.... While, however, lumbering was the business of Pictou, at this time, yet even the partial attention which people gave to their farms brought plentiful returns. The soil was so rich that in many places people took crop after crop of wheat."[14]

And, because they were drawn to the major rivers and tributaries in order to exploit the forests, their settlements became concentrated in the broad belts of land along which the lumbering operations could be carried out.[15]

The Maritime timber trade opened up new shipping routes from Scotland and brought emigrants in their thousands to its timber-producing areas. It had begun as a specialist trade supplying large oak and pine masts to the Navy. But Napoleon's blockade of the Baltic in 1806 turned it into a general trade. When British ships were barred access to

Baltic timber, the government looked to North America. What started as a temporary arrangement became a permanent transfer of trade. The already high duties on European timber were nearly doubled in 1811, thus pricing it out of the market. Greater distance ceased to be an obstacle to profitable trade. By this action Britain's timber purchases were effectively transferred from Europe to North America.[16] Eastern Nova Scotia was one of the earliest regions to be cleared of its timber and Pictou, at the centre of this trade, was the prime beneficiary. By 1805 fifty ships a year were needed to carry 300,000 cubic feet of squared timber from Pictou to Britain, and by then the average annual value of Pictou's timber exports was around £100,000.[17]

The imposition of the duty on Baltic timber had the effect of stimulating an already growing market. Wartime conditions brought a rapid expansion in North American timber exports which soared ahead from 1806. Between 1806 and 1811 exports multiplied by more than eightfold. In 1809, British North America accounted for almost two-thirds of the pine timber imported into Britain. By the early 1800s, even before the punitive tariffs had been introduced, timber represented over half of the value of all goods imported to Scotland from Nova Scotia. By 1812 Nova Scotia's trade had quadrupled.[18]

The trade grew so quickly in the eastern Maritimes that settlers and ship's masters were often caught trying to barter timber and goods with each other privately, in flagrant breach of the customs regulations. In Cape Breton, where Scots were illegally occupying land, there would have been no checks at all. Settlers would have agreed informal deals with ship captains to have their timber collected from the countless locations along the coastline, all of which could be easily accessed by passing timber ships.

As Pictou's timber trade grew, the number of ship crossings between Scotland and the eastern Maritimes mushroomed. The trade was no longer mainly between west coast Scottish ports and Pictou as had been the case before the tariffs were raised. Before 1811 most Highlanders had been collected at Fort William or at Isle Martin (Ullapool) by Clyde-registered ships which had been diverted there to collect them. The

Sir Edward Mortimer Inn in Pictou, Mortimer's former home built
at Norway Point overlooking Pictou's waterfront. *Photograph by
Geoff Campey.*

service was well-suited to west coast Scots, but few on the east side could
get crossings to Pictou from ports near to their homes. However, the
massive rise in duties on Baltic timber forced east coast ports like Aberdeen
and Leith to establish new transatlantic trade links. North American
timber was now a cheaper alternative in spite of the considerable dis-
advantage of ships having to circumnavigate northern Scotland before
they even got to the Atlantic Ocean.

Emigrants with access to Aberdeen and Leith soon had a choice of
crossings as shipowners sought to minimize their costs by carrying passengers. Following the economic downturn in Scotland after the
Napoleonic Wars, both Leith and Aberdeen experienced a great rise in
the numbers departing for either Pictou or Halifax between 1816 and
1819 (see Appendix II).[19] As throngs of poor Lowlanders flooded into
Pictou, concerns were raised over the increasing burden on public finances.
In 1817, it was being predicted that "not less than two thousand five
hundred and eight strangers will arrive amongst us!"[20] And they included
carpenters, weavers, cordwainers and tailors – people with little or no
farming experience. However, their circumstances clearly varied. The
seventy people who arrived from Leith on the *Aurora* in 1816 were

certainly well regarded.[21] Hugh Dunoon, the Customs Collector, thought them to be "of a superior class to those of last year and it is probable that but few of them will remain in the district."[22]

The post-war economic slump had hit industries in the manufacturing Lowlands and the textile districts of the Scottish Borders particularly hard. The *Kelso Mail* began printing advertisements of Leith ship departures for North America from 1817, a sure sign that emigration was claiming people from that part of Roxburgh.[23] Fife was also losing people to Nova Scotia. There was a sufficient rush of Fife people wishing to go to Nova Scotia in 1817 for a Kirkcaldy shipowner to briefly enter the transatlantic passenger trade. That year the *Helen* of Kirkaldy took ninety-three emigrants to Halifax.[24]

The available services developed one stage further when Cromarty came to be used as a central collecting point for the northeast Highlands. Aberdeen ships regularly called at Cromarty for passengers and, by 1816, Leith ships were doing the same.[25] And by then smaller ports like Dumfries, on the southwest coast, developed regular timber trade links with the eastern Maritimes. People from the southwest Borders

Cromarty in the Moray Firth, 1821, engraving by William Daniell. Having an excellent harbour, Cromarty became the main collecting port for emigrants in the North East Highlands. *From the collections of the National Monuments Record of Scotland.*

could now easily get to Pictou from Dumfries. A marked but short-lived exodus from Dumfries-shire to the eastern Maritimes followed, as emigrants took advantage of the new transport opportunities being created by the timber trade.[26]

Dumfries-shire immigrants "were distinguished by steady industry and rigid economy, and they generally not only made a living but saved money."[27] Being relatively late arrivals they had to be content with sites some distance to the west of the earlier Scottish settlements. The Dalhousie settlement near the western end of Pictou County attracted many former hand loom weavers, who would have originated from textile-producing districts in Dumfries-shire.[28] New Annan, in Colchester County, their other settlement, lay seven miles to the south of Tatamagouche Bay. In spite of being near the French River, they had to "trod their seven miles on a Sabbath morning, over hills, through marshes, covered with fallen trees, and across the French River to hear the Gospel"[29] at Tatamagouche. And when the Reverend Mr. Mitchell came out from Tatamagouche to see them, he found that "there was not the semblance of a road about New Annan or even Tatamagouche. He had to travel from the seashore through "blazed paths through the woods." Yet "from their sturdy Scotch industry and frugality these settlers soon attained comparative comfort."[30] Writing in 1877, George Patterson found "many of their descendants" to be "in good circumstances."[31]

With the ending of the Napoleonic Wars in 1815, much of Scotland was gripped by a severe economic depression. Poverty, displacement and unemployment now worked hand in hand in the Highlands and Islands to fuel a growing exodus to Nova Scotia and Cape Breton. East Inverness-shire continued to lose people to Pictou County. Settlers from Glen Urquhart and the Beauly area came to live along the west branch of the French River to the east of McLellans Mountain, which they named Blue Mountain.[32] As if to symbolize the strong links being developed between many parts of the Highlands and Pictou, the *Inverness Journal* carried a large advertisement setting out the land and timber opportunities available at the time. On offer were: a 110 acre estate, "contiguous to the East River of Pictou and fronting on McKay's Cove," a 200 acre woodland at nearby Frasers Mountain, and 600 acres of "valuable good hard woodland on the post road from Halifax to Pictou...about six miles from Pictou and one mile from Rogers [Hill] village."[33]

People arrived at Pictou from many parts of the Highlands, but the predominant intake was increasingly coming from the Sutherland estate. The upheavals and uncertainties caused by the introduction of sheep farms, begun in the early 1800s, led many Sutherland tenants to seek their livelihood abroad.[34] Unfortunately, disaster had struck in 1807. On her crossing from Stromness to Pictou, the *Rambler* of Leith, carrying emigrants from the Sutherland parishes of Farr, Lairg, Creich and Rogart enroute to Pictou, was wrecked near the Bay of Bulls off Newfoundland. Only three of the one hundred and thirty passengers on board survived. The local newspaper found it a very sad loss for "these deluded people...none of whom were under the necessity of leaving their native country.... Most criminal infatuation that can thus lead men to mitigate from their native homes into a state of voluntary banishment."[35] And yet, as the clearances progressed, they continued their "voluntary banishment" to Pictou.

The increasing number of newspaper advertisements describing new sheep farms at Rogart, Dornoch and Golspie reveal the rapid spread of

Portrait of the first Duke of Sutherland (George Granville Leveson-Gower). An English millionaire, he was created first Duke in the year of his death in 1833. His wife, the Countess of Sutherland, had inherited the Earldom of Sutherland in 1766. *Courtesy of Lord Strathnaver*.

the new farming methods, and their impact can be seen in the steady numbers who embarked on ships at Cromarty to go to Pictou.[36] Open conflict had actually erupted at Kildonan and Clyne in 1812 when tenants tried to resist the measures being adopted to dispossess them of their lands. But yet people were being criticized for wanting to emigrate. Alexander Gunn from Rogart, who had arranged one of their crossings, sent a letter to the editor of the *Inverness Journal*, disassociating himself from the "emigration schemes" which were becoming "so controversial in Sutherland."[37] But still they went.

The *Perseverance* of Aberdeen brought an unknown number of Sutherland families from Cromarty to Pictou in 1814, while in the following year the same ship, together with the *Prince William*, apparently brought some three hundred families to the area, some of whom came from the northern parishes of Farr and Eddrachilles and others from parishes in the south. But they may also have included people from Reay in the adjoining parish of Caithness. In their petition for land in Pictou County, the nineteen families, who arrived on the *Prince William* in 1815, wrote of their service in the Local Militia of Scotland, almost certainly the Reay Fencibles (see Appendix I).[38] Many of the 1815 arrivals came "under the agency of a countryman named Logan" and "Lt. Col. Simon Fraser – a gallant and most worthy man."[39] The emigrants had sensibly used shipping agents who were based in Pictou.[40] Once again Simon Fraser had been involved in procuring ships for Highland emigrants.

By 1805 people from Sutherland had established themselves a few miles down from Pictou Harbour on the Middle River in three separate communities – Mill Brook, Gairloch and New Lairg.[41] Because these were prime lumbering and farming locations, they soon filled up and later arrivals were forced further afield. By the time more Sutherland families arrived in 1814–15, a fourth Sutherland community, Earltown, was taking shape in Colchester County. Although it was near two rivers, the Waugh and the River John, which flow into Tatamagouche Bay, neither river could be used for transporting goods beyond the tidewater limits. Thus, early settlers had to establish trails and access their land on foot.[42]

TABLE 5

List of Emigrant Scots who were residing in the Pictou District by the Spring of 1816*

Names	Age Yrs	Marr'd Single or Widow	No. of Children	Trade	Where residing or settled	General Remarks
Neil McLellan	25	married	1	Labourer	Merigomish	poor
his wife						
William Murray	25	single		Farmer	do.	
John Cameron	18	do.		Labourer	Lower Settlement East River	at Service
Marion McLean	70	widow				Maintained by Charity
Angus Cameron	31	single		Labourer		at Service
William Cameron	25	do.		do.		do.
Ann Cameron	60	widow				poor; maintained by her friends
Angus Cameron	30	married	3	do.		poor
his wife						
William Sutherland	56	do.	3	do.	West Branch East River	very poor
his wife						
Robert McKay	35	married	3	do.	Lower Settlement	do. do.
his wife						
Alexander Sutherland	40	married	3	do.	do.	very poor
his wife						
William McKenzie	22	married		Taylor	do.	able to maintain himself.
his wife						
John McKenzie	25	do.	1	Labourer	do.	———
his wife						
John McKay	35	do.	6	do.	do.	very poor
his wife						
James McKay	21	single		Taylor	do.	
Simon Fraser	24	do.		Blacksmith	do.	
John Mathewson	21	do.		Labourer	do.	
Peter McCallum	17	do.		Clerk	do.	
Alexander Munro	22	do.		Carpenter	do.	

From: NSARM RG1 Vol. 227 Doc. 118.

Names	Age Yrs	Marr'd Single or Widow	No. of Children	Trade	Where residing or settled	General Remarks
John McKay his wife	60	married	8	Labourer	Fishers Grant	very poor, the catechists or instructors of the Parish from whence these McKays came.
William Ross his wife	30	married	3	do.	do.	able to work poor.
John McKay his wife	32	married	6	do.	do.	do.
Hugh McKay	22	single		Weaver	do.	
John McKay	20	do.		Labourer	do.	
James McKay	18	single		Labourer	Fishers Grant	
Kenneth McKay his wife	45	married	5	Shoemaker	do.	a very poor man
Catherine McKay	52	widow				
Christian McKay	24	single			Fishers Grant	
Margaret McKay	20	do.			do.	
John McKay his wife	40	married	7	Labourer	do.	a poor family
Catherine McKay	65	single			do.	poor
Mrs. Kirby	40	widow since married	3		Little Harbour	
Donald Ross	22	single		Labourer	Fishers Grant	sick from a falling of a tree; the only support of his family
James Ross his wife	51	married	9	do.	do.	
Robert McKenzie his wife	60	do.	2	do.	do.	
John McKenzie his wife	25	do.	1	do.	Little Harbour	
Donald McKenzie	24	single		do.	do.	
William McKenzie his wife	22	married		Taylor		
John McKay his wife	30	married	1	Labourer	Middle River	very poor indeed

94

Names	Age Yrs	Marr'd Single or Widow	No. of Children	Trade	Where residing or settled	General Remarks
Christian Campbell	38	single			do.	at service
Margaret McKay	30	do.			do.	do.
John Fraser	44	married	5		West River	
his wife				Weaver		very poor
Francis Hendry	30	married	2	shoemaker	do.	
his wife						
Alexander McKay	40	married	5	Labourer	do.	These two families
his wife						very poor indeed
Donald Murray	25	do.	2	do.	do.	having lived
his wife						entirelyupon their
						friends who are ill
						able to help them
Donald McKay	23	single			do.	
William McKay	28	do.			do.	
Alexander Ross	60	married	5	Millwright	do.	poor
his wife						
William Graham	50	married	7	Labourer	do.	very poor but
his wife						industrious
John McKay	25	married		do.	do.	poor
his wife						
Angus Murray	72	married			Rogers Hill	very poor
his wife						
Donald McKay	62	married	1	Labourer	do.	very poor
his wife						
Alexander McKay	30	married		Taylor	do.	
his wife						
William McKay	23	married	2	Labourer	do.	
his wife						
Catherine McDonald	60	widow	1		do.	very poor
William McKay	54	married	3	Labourer	do.	
his wife						
William Douglas	26	married	2	do.	do.	
his wife						
Donald Douglas	24	single		Blacksmith	do.	
Anne Douglas	50	widow	4		do.	
Donald Murray	40	married	5	Labourer	do.	very poor
his wife						

Names	Age Yrs	Marr'd Single or Widow	No. of Children	Trade	Where residing or settled	General Remarks
John Fraser	40	married	6	Weaver	do.	
his wife						
John Ross	70	married	3	Farmer		
his wife						
William Nicol	40	married	4	Labourer	Mount Town	)
his wife						)
Archibald Gunn	21	single		do.	do.	) These are all
Elizabeth Gunn	24	widow	1		do.	) poor Families
James Cameron	23	married	2	Sawmiller	do.	)
his wife						)
James Reid	28	married	4	Labourer	do.	poor but industrious
his wife						
John Simpson	62	married	7	Farmer	do.	3 children able to support themselves
his wife						
John Scot	44	married		Labourer	do.	his family in Scotland
John McKenzie	29	single		Carpenter	do.	
Alexander Sutherland	45	married	4	Labourer	Scots Hill	poor
his wife						
William Sutherland	60	married	2	Farmer	do.	very poor
his wife						
George Munro	36	married	3	Weaver	Caribou	very poor
his wife						
Robert Sutherland	46	married	6	Labourer	do.	do. do.
his wife						
John Sutherland	45	married	4	do.	do,	do. do. supported by his neighbours charity
his wife						
Hugh McIntosh	70	married	1	do.	do.	very poor
his wife						
Alexander Munro	30	married	1	Labourer	Caribou	industrious but no~ very poor
his wife						
Andrew McKenzie	35	married	4	do.	do.	sick since his arriv~ and very poor
his wife						
Kenneth McKenzie	48	married	6	do.	do.	poor
his wife						
James Ferguson	33	married		Mason	Harbour Mouth	poor
his wife						

Names	Age Yrs	Marr'd Single or Widow	No. of Children	Trade	Where residing or settled	General Remarks
Thomas McKay	20	single		Labourer	do.	
Donald Urquhart	27	married		Labourer	Harbourmouth	
his wife						
Catherine McKay	70	widow			do.	very poor
Alice McKay	60	widow	5		do.	frequently sick a great object of charity
James Munro		married	1	Joiner	Pictou Town	
his wife						
John McCallum	45	married	4		do.	
his wife						
James Leaper	46	single		Chainmaker	do.	
Finlay Ross	50	married	7	Shoemaker	do.	an industrious man
his wife						
Donald Ross	60	married	1	Labourer	do.	
his wife						
John Rutty	30	married		Shoemaker	do.	
his wife						
Alexander Ross	35	married	5	Blacksmith	do.	a very industrious man, poor
his wife						
John Thompson	54	married	4	Mason	do.	)
his wife						)
Valentine Laws	29	married	2	house Carpenter	do.	)
his wife						)
George Paterson	36	married	4	ditto	do.	)
his wife						)
John Grant	23	single		ditto	do.	)
William Fraser	29			Schoolmaster	do.	) able to support
William McKay	26			Clerk	do.	) themselves not
Eleanor Sutherland	24			Servant	do.	) needing any
Margaret Sutherland	19			do.	do.	) assistance
Christy Sutherland	36			do.	do.	)
Ann McKay	29			do.	do.	)
Isabella McKenzie	18			do.	do.	)
Margaret McKay	23			do.	do.	)
Flora Gally	17			do.	do.	)
Jean McKay	18			do.	do.	)

Names	Age Yrs	Marr'd Single or Widow	No. of Children	Trade	Where residing or settled	General Remarks
John Sutherland his wife	22	married		Taylor	do.	do.
James Brown	63	single		Mason	Pictou	works at his trade but poor

Total	166 men & women 200 children

Receiving its first settlers in 1813, the population of Earltown grew steadily in spite of its extremely isolated, inland location.[43] Ships carrying people from Rogart, Clyne, Lairg, Dornoch and Golspie – the southern parishes of Sutherland – arrived in a continuous progression from 1814 to 1817 (see Appendix II). According to Donald MacLeod, writing in 1841, the people who came to Pictou at this time left Sutherland "under favourable circumstances" paying the cost of their passages by selling their cattle "which then got extraordinary prices."[44] However, this was not the picture they presented to the authorities on their arrival. The family heads listed in "the emigrants from Great Britain in 1815" were clearly in a bad way (see Table 5). Nearly all were described as "very poor" and one or two were "objects of charity."[45] To add to these difficulties, there was great general distress in the area owing to "the failure of the crops all over the Province" and "the scarcity of provisions."[46] However, in spite of food shortages, the even bleaker economic conditions back in Scotland were stimulating ever greater numbers of people to relocate to Nova Scotia.

New arrivals continued to respect the religious territorial boundaries which had been designated earlier. Presbyterians, sought districts in Pictou and Colchester counties, while Antigonish and Guysborough counties and Cape Breton attracted Roman Catholics. Presbyterian Scots were drawn from many parts of Scotland, both Lowland and Highland, while Catholics mainly originated from the North West Highlands and Western Isles. Antigonish County was the first area of the mainland to attract large numbers of Catholic Highlanders. Having been encouraged by Father MacEachern, they surged into the coastal and river areas from the 1790s. The first colonizers went to Antigonish Harbour. St. Andrews, to the south of the Harbour, acquired its first Highlander settlers by 1802 as did Marydale and Meadow Green, lying a short distance to the east on the Pomquet River.[47] By 1803 Antigonish's Scottish mission, based at Arisaig, had some 3,000 communicants.[48] Ohio on the Ohio Lake was founded by 1805.[49] By 1810 Malcolm McMillan, Hugh McMillan and John Cameron had moved into the southern extremity of the county where they founded Lochaber, naming it in honour of their homeland in West Inverness-shire.[50] They were joined a few years later by a number of settlers from Rannoch (Perthshire) including Alexander, Duncan and John Stewart.

As had happened at Pictou, the timber trade had drawn colonizers to Antigonish's coastline and river frontages. In time, the West River area attracted the attention of settlers from Pictou County who relocated there to take advantage of its lumbering opportunities:

"Induced by the rich intervale land and the valuable timber which lined the banks of the stream, many of the older settlers removed to it [West River], and as it was the part best suited for the timber trade, which was extensively carried on between the years 1812 and 1819, it soon became thickly settled."[51]

Stretches along and near the St. Marys River in Guysborough County also attracted already-established settlers from Pictou County as news spread of "its magnificent timber, extensive intervales, rivers teeming with fish and abundance of game in the forest."[52] The settlements of Glenelg, Caledonia and Stillwater owe their beginnings to families from the Pictou area, especially from Green Hill, who relocated there in the period from 1810 to 1814. As was the case with Lochaber, the Glenelg place name probably denotes the West Inverness-shire origins of many of its early settlers.

Initially, the Nova Scotia mainland attracted many Catholic Highlanders. But Cape Breton's pulling power was stronger and lasted longer. It was

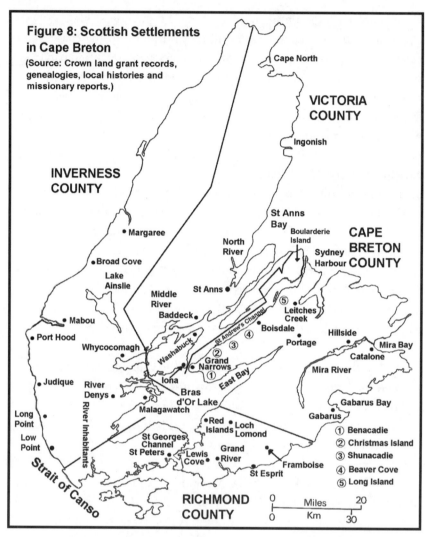

Figure 8: Scottish Settlements in Cape Breton
(Source: Crown land grant records, genealogies, local histories and missionary reports.)

rapidly becoming the favoured choice of the large numbers of Highlanders and Islanders, who arrived in the region after the end of the Napoleonic Wars. The first arrivals had been Roman Catholic squatters who began migrating from Prince Edward Island and mainland Nova Scotia in 1790. They normally came in small numbers, but occasionally large groups arrived. Forty families from McLellans Brook, in east Pictou, came in 1806 together with a "MacMillan" party consisting of ten families.[53] By the early 1800s

immigrant Scots had established a string of settlements along the Western Shore, stretching
from Margaree down to Low Point, and had
created a major settlement foothold in the southwest of the Island at River Inhabitants (see
Figure 8).[54] It is not surprising that settlers
should seek coastal locations. There were no
roads in Cape Breton and water was the only
route for transport. What is significant about
these settlement sites is their proximity to Pictou
and to the routes taken by the ships which came
to the region to collect timber. Ships from Britain
would sail directly past these settlements on
their way to the Northumberland Strait. Thus,
the initial influx had been concentrated on those
areas which were most accessible to the region's
timber trade activities.

The Western Shore settlements grew
steadily. When Bishop Plessis came to Arisaig
in 1812, he found a "new church, 40 feet long
by 26 feet wide, well wainscoted outside, but
perfectly bare within, like the other Scottish
churches."[55] At Port Hood he found a crudely
built chapel enclosing a space of about 40 square
feet, which allowed "rain, wind and hail to
come in without obstacle." The alter frontal
was "an old silk cloth, whose colour can no
longer be recognized, but whose stains are very
visible" and animals could be seen grazing "in
their unfenced cemetery." But there were eight

Tombstone memorial to
Reverend Allan McLean at
Judique. (St. Andrew's
Roman Catholic Cemetery.)
He was the first pastor of St.
Andrew's parish, working
there from 1818 until his
death in 1841. *Photograph
by Geoff Campey.*

hundred families living there. What was significant was the considerable
Scottish population at Port Hood. However untidy these colonists may
have seemed to the Bishop, they could support a priest and they had
already raised a fund of some £600 to recruit additional priests.[56]

The enterprising Scots of the late eighteenth and early nineteenth centuries had shown considerable daring and initiative in grabbing their land. By 1814 some 315 Scottish heads of households had illegally occupied more than 62,000 acres of Crown Land in Cape Breton. Consequently, by 1817, when the land-owning restraints were removed, Cape Breton was fast becoming a Scottish enclave. Having taken advantage of Pictou's relatively early timber trade, they created great settlement magnets first in the west of the Island and later in the northeast when Sydney's timber trade began to develop. And because they were making these strides on their own, and without any official or financial backing, they sensibly came in groups. This contributed to their success. They could act collectively in the interests of their communities and they gave themselves a supportive social environment. The timber trade itself had also helped. Apart from giving them a market for their cut timber, it also concentrated their settlements in specific areas. Settlers would clear forests along a river frontage up to a certain distance from the inlet or cove from which timber could readily be collected. They would then repeat the process along a neighbouring river, thus creating distinct pockets of settlement.

Sydney's timber trade was far slower to develop. Timber exports to Britain only began from 1804, some ten years or so after Pictou's trade had become established.[57] Yet here, too, Scottish colonization appears to have been influenced by the desire to exploit Sydney's timber trade. Cape Breton had to wait until 1802 before it received its first emigrant ships directly from Scotland. The nine hundred Catholics from Barra and South Uist who arrived that year took up locations in Christmas Island, on the east side of the Grand Narrows in Bras d'Or Lake. This was near the only entrance to the Bras d'Or Lake through which timber vessels could pass. Bras d'Or was, in fact, "the principal repository of the timber trade, its shores and inlets furnishing the material and most convenient places for loading."[58] And, as Sydney's timber trade began its upward spiral from around 1811, Scots began colonizing the northern and eastern stretches of Bras d'Or Lake in ever increasing numbers. By 1816 this area was attracting almost as many settlers as the Western Shore.[59] It is apparent that the opportunities to be had from selling timber had a crucial effect on Scottish settlement patterns.

In 1817, some three hundred and two immigrants from Barra arrived at Sydney, aboard the *William Tell* and *Hope,* on what was the first direct sailing from Scotland since 1802.[60] The ships had been procured by Simon Fraser, who had worked behind the scenes to assist the settlers in getting financial assistance. Being canny Scots, they sought to extract what they could from Major-General George Robert Ainslie, Cape Breton's Lieutenant-Governor. They claimed that Simon Fraser had told them to expect "provisions or three years, what land they wanted, and farming and agricultural utensils."[61] Not being in a position to offer any of these items, Governor Ainslie felt that the new arrivals "had been much deceived." He directed them to "go among their countrymen, who are settled on the great island sea, the Bras d'Or," pointing out that their "food crops are most promising."[62] They took this advice, and settled near the Grand Narrows, in northeast Bras d'Or. But, in the end, they received £43. 14s. 6d. from the government to cover the cost of hiring a schooner and for their "provisions of pork, flour and mutton." Their strategy had paid off.[63]

Governor Ainslie clearly had no time for Fraser. Neither did Roderick MacNeil, landlord of the Barra emigrants. MacNeil was absolutely furious with him. According to MacNeil, Fraser had exploited his tenants solely to make money.[64] In signing up people for his ships, "Mr. Fraser acts as a job to get money and his profits would be better in the pockets of the passengers."[65] But Simon Fraser was a much maligned person. He had worked closely with the Colonial Office, in helping the Barra tenants to secure land in Bras d'Or. He had sent them salt from Greenock so that they could preserve meat for their sea crossing from cattle which they would slaughter themselves.[66] His role as an agent had thus extended far beyond the task of just chartering ships.

Iona, Christmas Island and Grand Narrows attracted these Barra people, but new settlements at Washabuck, Benacadie and Shunacadie were taking shape as well. MacNeils from Barra were the earliest colonizers of Red Islands, on the opposite side of Bras d'Or Lake.[67] Following Hector MacNeil's arrival in 1802, other MacNeils soon followed. Eleven of the eighteen families who went to live at Red Islands between 1807 and 1811 were Barra MacNeils.[68] And Barra emigrants had also "settled at Mabou among the Lochaber people there."[69] While large numbers of Barra settlers and West Inverness-shire settlers had come directly to the region from Scotland in 1802, they were the exception. No emigrants had sailed directly to Cape Breton before 1802 and few could have sailed during the Napoleonic War years from 1803 to 1815.[70] However, in spite of these difficulties, the influx of Scots to Cape Breton, which had begun in 1790, continued during this first decade of the nineteenth century and beyond. It came not from Scotland but from the Nova Scotia mainland and Prince Edward Island. These were Catholic Highlanders who had migrated from their earlier settlements to more favourable sites in Cape Breton where they could join their compatriots in establishing their own communities.

As noted, much of the early colonization of Cape Breton had been the work of Catholic Highlanders. However, their domination of the Island was rapidly coming to an end. Cape Breton acquired its first major Scottish Presbyterian community by 1811. It was established by a small group from Wester Ross, who had previously settled in 1803 at Lord Selkirk's Belfast settlements in Prince Edward Island. Reverend Angus MacAulay, one of Lord Selkirk's many agents, had led the initial attempt in 1807, to move "a considerable number of Protestant families" from Belfast to locations on each side of Cape Breton's Middle River (formerly Wagamatcook). But MacAulay failed to execute his plan.[71] Because the Middle River valley had considerable attractions, having good natural meadows and marshes and abundant supplies of good timber, it was not long before a second attempt was made.

Success came in 1811 when Roderick MacKenzie and Kenneth MacLeod promised the Cape Breton Council that they would bring twenty-four "creditable families" to the settlement. By the following year, seven MacLeod families, six MacRae families, two Campbell families, two MacQuarrie families, two MacKenzie families and a Cameron family had established themselves in the Middle River valley on the northwest side of Bras d'Or.[72] Some of the MacRaes and Campbells, had come from Belfast, although they had originated from Applecross in Ross-shire. Coming from Lochalsh, Roderick Mackenzie also had Ross-shire connections and, like many of the others, he had previously lived in Belfast.

A reconstructed log cabin representing the early 1800s, Iona Highland Village. *Photograph by Geoff Campey.*

Having acquired 250 acres of good land at Belfast, from Lord Selkirk, MacKenzie would have had little reason for moving on.[73] But it was not his own interests that he was concerned about. It was becoming increasingly difficult for new arrivals to find good locations in Prince Edward Island. Most of the best sites with water frontages had gone by the early 1800s. Because Cape Breton's colonization had been deliberately held back, it still had many favourable sites to offer settlers, particularly in the intersecting lakes and rivers of Bras d'Or. Thus, Roderick MacKenzie's decision to move to Middle River in 1811 was a crucial move. He spotted a prime location and notified people back home in Scotland. The later influx, beginning in 1820, of Lochalsh, Kintail and Applecross families to the Middle River area was the result.[74] Those who travelled in 1823 probably sailed on the *Atlantic* of Stornoway, which was due to collect emigrants at Lochalsh in the summer of that year.[75]

The worsening economic situation in Scotland and the availability, from 1817, of freehold grants in Cape Breton on generous terms, greatly stimulated the desire to emigrate. Now, along with Catholic Highlanders, Presbyterian Scots were also seeking land in Cape Breton. Because they were relatively late arrivals, many would have had to contend with less favourable locations on the so-called backlands, behind the Western Shore settlements. This was almost certainly the destination of some of

Above left, Tombstone memorials, Middle River Cemetery, Cape Breton: Alexander McRae, born Applecross, Dec. 4, 1803, died Middle River, Oct. 6, 1869 aged 66; wife Mary McLennan, born Applecross March 12, 1809 died Middle River Dec. 13, 1875 aged 66 years; *above right*, Tombstone memorial: Donald McRae born Kintail, Ross-shire, died Middle River Oct. 20, 1881, aged 80 years; his wife Ann McDougall, born Mull, Argyll, died Middle River, Dec. 23, 1888, aged 82 years; *below right*, Tombstone memorial: Angus Campbell born Applecross, Ross-shire, 1795, died Middle River April 1901, aged 106 years; wife Catherine Beaton, born Coll, 1801, died Middle River, Oct. 29, 1886 aged 85 years. *Photographs by Geoff Campey.*

the families who sailed from Tobermory to Pictou in 1816 on the *Tartar* of Perth.[76] Although they went to Long Point, which fronts on the Western Shore, their actual land holdings were almost certainly deep into the interior, many miles from the coast.

Soon the backlands around Lake Ainslie were developing distinct settlements (see Figure 8). Located in the path of Cape Breton's Roman Catholic/Protestant divide, Lake Ainslie had two distinct parts. Its west side, first cleared in 1811 by emigrants from South Uist, Moidart, Arisaig and Lochaber, was Catholic. Its east side, cleared by settlers from Mull, Tyree, Coll and Muck eventually acquired sixty-three Presbyterian families. Loch Lomond, a large lake in the southeastern interior, and nearby Grand River would become major Presbyterian strongholds, drawing their settlers mainly from North Uist and Harris in the Outer Hebrides.

Proximity to Pictou had given the settlements on the west and southwest of the Island a considerable advantage and they were the first to fill up. Proximity to Sydney and to the Bras d'Or entrance channel, on the east of the Island, had concentrated many of the earliest Scottish settlers in the northeastern stretches of Bras d'Or Lake. However, Loch Lomond and Grand River were some of the last areas of the Island to be colonized by Scots. These sites were far away from Pictou and Sydney, they were cut off from Bras d'Or, and often the land was poor. A visiting missionary found "their situation to be so isolated and remote that they can hardly ever expect to share with any other settlement in the labours of a clergymen."[77]

However, even by as late as 1820, some of the coastline on the north east coast of Cape Breton was still relatively untouched. St. Anns, near Sydney, would become Cape Breton's most famous Presbyterian community. Norman MacLeod, a Presbyterian minister from Assynt in Sutherland, had led his followers to Pictou in 1817 and had then taken them on to their great pioneering adventure in St. Anns. They would quickly establish a successful shipbuilding operation and, John Munro, one of their number, would become a prominent figure in Cape Breton's timber trade. This is a far cry from the picture of destitution which Cape Breton later presented to the outside world.

With the collapse of the kelp industry in the Hebrides, from the mid-1820s, Cape Breton increasingly became a refuge for poverty-stricken Scots. A Presbyterian minister observed that "there is not a place in the whole world professing Christianity where there are so many families so near to each other and so utterly destitute as our poor countrymen in this island are."[78] And over the next decade, as impoverished Hebridean emigrants came to Cape Breton in their thousands, this picture of extreme poverty would be reinforced many times over.

6

CAPE BRETON'S
GROWING POPULARITY

Emigrants of late years have not come out in any considerable
numbers, as formerly to Nova Scotia, but they continue to arrive
in Cape Breton principally from the Western Isles of Scotland;
upwards of 500 persons have come out this year from thence at
their own expense. They landed at Sydney, Ship Harbour [Port
Hawkesbury] in the Gut of Canso and other parts of the Island
and disappeared the moment they got on shore to seek their
friends who had previously arrived.[1]

BY THE 1820s CAPE BRETON was rapidly overtaking Nova Scotia as the preferred location of Highland Scots. Most of the favourable sites in mainland Nova Scotia, along the coast or along major rivers, had long since gone to the earliest settlers. However, relative latecomers could still find good locations along Cape Breton's extensive coast lines, river valleys and internal lakes. With the severe economic depression at the end of the Napoleonic Wars and the hardships caused by the collapse of the kelp industry, emigration levels soared. In these changed circumstances the government decided to lift its restraining order on the granting of freehold land in Cape Breton.

Settlers could get freehold grants from 1817, and on very generous terms.[2] The early arrivals had simply ignored the regulations and squatted illegally on Crown land; but now settlers were being welcomed. Those already on the Island could now acquire documentation to legitimize their holdings, while new arrivals could get land grants on the remaining available sites. Although plenty of Crown land was still available after 1820, some of it was of poor quality, the best having been taken up by the first waves of settlers. Even so, the response from the Highlands and Islands was immediate. The influx grew rapidly, peaking in 1828 when a total of 2,413 Scots sailed to Sydney in a single year. A further 1,713 people landed there in 1829–30.[3] Even when allowing for gaps in the customs records, we know that at least 6,245 Scots arrived at Sydney in the decade from 1821 to 1830.[4]

While most of the emigrants who came to the Island during the 1820s originated from the Western Isles, one very notable group arrived from Assynt in Sutherland. Their leader was Reverend Norman McLeod, a charismatic Presbyterian minister, who, having led his people to St. Anns Bay in 1820, would later take them on to New Zealand. He was a larger than life character with uncompromising views and a deep distrust of authority. Having completed his university studies, first at Aberdeen, then Edinburgh, he abandoned his plan to become a minister of the Church of Scotland and established his own religious sect. He became a schoolmaster at Ullapool in 1814, but his unorthodox views and methods soon led him into conflict with the local parish minister.[5] Emigration seemed the best way forward. Because this was a time when people in his native Assynt were being removed from their lands to make way for large sheep farms, Norman readily found others who were willing to join him.[6] To pay for his passage and other costs in getting to Nova Scotia, he took up a job at the fishing station in Wick. In 1817, he and his followers, who then totalled one hundred and thirty-six, sailed from Fort William to Pictou on the *Frances Ann* of Irvine.[7]

After a long and difficult voyage of some nine or ten weeks, in which the *Frances Ann* was caught in a gale and sprang a leak, they finally reached Pictou. Although most of the best sites were taken, they found some unoccupied land on the Middle River, between Alma and Gairloch. After they had quickly established themselves at their new location, McLeod wrote to his friends in Assynt, extolling the fertility of the soil and the good farming opportunities to be had.[8] In the following year, one hundred and fifty Assynt people sailed from Lochinver to Pictou on the *Perseverance* of Aberdeen. However, they were unable to settle near to McLeod, as they had hoped. The land was fully occupied and so they scattered to a number of places. Unhappy with this situation and fearing for the moral well-being of his people, he decided that it was time to leave Pictou. He had heard "profane swearing" at the bridge and forge of West River and there were, in the town, "the loosest and wildest set of young men."[9]

Reverend Norman McLeod, painting by Ernest Munro. (Made available by kind permission of the Gaelic College of Celtic Arts and Crafts, St. Anns, Cape Breton.) *Photograph by Geoff Campey.*

Norman McLeod decided to take up a long-standing invitation from Highlanders in Ohio, in the United States, who wished him to join their settlement. Having persuaded his people to go with him, together they set to work building the *Ark*, the small schooner which would take them to the Gulf of Mexico and up the Mississippi River to their new destination. They left Pictou on September 1819. As they passed Cape North and caught sight of the Cape Breton coastline they edged nearer to take a closer look. After a short deliberation they weighed anchor in what was St. Anns Harbour. The earlier French settlers had long since withdrawn from the site and the bay was teaming with fish. Ohio was quickly forgotten.

By 1820 fifteen families (78 people) were laying the foundations of the St. Anns settlement.[10] More of McLeod's followers left Scotland that year and another group came in 1821, and still more came in the following year.[11] Further emigrants from the Outer Hebridean Island of Harris came to join them.[12] The best coastal locations eventually filled up and later colonization proceeded along the North River, on the north side of St. Anns Harbour.[13] Within ten years time, St. Anns had become a well-settled community. McLeod was minister, schoolmaster and magistrate. Observing the Sabbath was taken to new lengths as he decreed that potatoes for use on a Sunday had to peeled on a Saturday and fresh water drunk on a Sunday had to brought from the well on a Saturday. His forceful sermons in Gaelic lasted two to three hours at a time.[14] He frowned on luxuries, merrymaking and denounced alcohol. His people never received communion since he judged them too unworthy to receive it. They endured his autocratic rule and harangues from the pulpit and, with good reason, became widely known as "the most sober, industrious and orderly" settlers on the Island.[15]

John Munro, one of the original emigrants who went with McLeod to Pictou and later to St. Anns, became a substantial figure in the timber trade and the Labrador fishery. After setting himself up in business in 1825, he constructed his first ship a few years later. Eventually as many as seven of Munro's vessels loaded up each year in his timber yard, for Aberdeen, Glasgow and Greenock. The employment which he provided to the men who cut and hauled his timber transformed the economy of St. Anns. For the first time, local people could purchase both food and manufactured goods at his store.[16] However, in the late 1840s, when McLeod discovered that Munro was smuggling brandy into the settlement, he instructed the local community to boycott his store. This they did, in spite of the near famine conditions which were being experienced. By then McLeod had decided that it was time to move on again. A favourable account, from his son, of life in Australia persuaded him and his followers to go to Adelaide in 1851. Finding it disappointing, he moved on to Melbourne. However the gold rush was not to his taste either and, in 1853, he and his followers left for New Zealand where they settled permanently.[17]

The original pioneers of St. Anns had been moderately affluent, but they were followed by far less fortunate people. Those Sutherlanders, who arrived in the early 1820s, had needed help in raising funds for their fares and basic supplies. This eventually became the pattern for many of the people who landed at Cape Breton. "The poor emigrants, lately from Scotland," who landed at St. Peter's in 1820, were given "Indian

Meal" to meet their immediate needs.[18] By the second half of the 1820s more emigrants would arrive in extreme poverty, sometimes suffering from either smallpox, typhus or cholera.[19] In fact, cholera made a brief but deadly visit to Halifax in 1834, when 284 people died. A Halifax merchant, who originated from Wick in Caithness, reported that "times are here miserably dull. The cholera last summer destroyed all trade; it was really awful."[20] But even when the disease was checked relatively quickly, as in this case, ports like Halifax could not relax their vigilance. Such diseases travelled with the emigrants and therefore stringent quarantine arrangements had to be put in place.

However, the saga of emigrant arrivals at local ports should not be made to sound more harrowing than it actually was. The fact is that most emigrants arrived in good health and without incident. The large numbers of Scots who went to areas just to the southeast of St. Anns came quietly and attracted little attention. "The beautiful and interesting Island of Boularderie," in northeast Bras d'Or, held particular appeal (see Figure 8). As they had done at Lake Ainslie, the earliest settlers divided Boularderie into two distinct Roman Catholic and Presbyterian sections. The south side, the first to be colonized, was a Catholic preserve, drawing many people from Barra and South Uist. By 1820 the north side was set to become a Protestant stronghold, as it acquired its "unbroken line of families...chiefly from the district of Gairloch [Ross-shire] in the Highlands of Scotland." Some forty families in all, they were said to "exhibit those features of industry, sobriety and decorum which peculiarly distinguish emigrants from this district."[21]

A tombstone memorial in the St. Andrew's Roman Catholic Cemetery, Boisdale, erected in the memory of Roderick McNeil, Carpenter, born Barra, died 1882 aged 80 years. *Photograph by Geoff Campey.*

Arrivals from South Uist, during the 1840s, would later replenish the Catholic communities on the south side of Boularderie and would add to the numbers at Boisdale on the opposite side of St. Andrews Channel.[22]

The Middle River settlements at the northwest end of Bras d'Or continued to grow as colonization continued up the river valley. More Ross-shire families, from Kintail, Applecross and Lochalsh, joined earlier groups who came from these same regions, reinforcing the strong Ross-shire presence in this part of Cape Breton. By 1828 Middle River had a large Presbyterian congregation having "upwards of fifty families" who were "pretty compact together, and some in very independent circumstances."[23] Later arrivals from Gairloch in Ross-shire established themselves on high ground to the west of Middle River, naming their settlement Gairloch Mountain after their native parish.[24] Baddeck, just to the west of Middle River, continued to attract emigrant Scots, but it was "not so exclusively Scottish," having acquired a substantial number of English Loyalists in the 1780s.[25] Many of its Scottish inhabitants originated from Harris in the Outer Hebrides. Following worsening economic conditions in Harris during the 1840s, more Harris people would move to Baddeck.[26]

The west side of Bras d'Or also attracted much interest in the early 1820s as emigrant Scots discovered the accessible and favourable locations to be had there. Whycocomagh, on the St. Patrick's Channel, attracted many Tyree, Coll and Mull colonizers while nearby Mull Cove (later Orangedale) was founded a little later.[27] Many families, including a good number of McKenzies, McKinnons and McLellans established themselves at Malagawatch in 1820 and, five years later, "new settlers from various quarters, but especially from the Highlands of Scotland,"[28] were taking up their holdings along the Denys Basin and the River Denys. By 1828 St. George's Channel had acquired "no less than one hundred and fifty Protestant families."[29] This area together with Malagwatch, River Denys and Whycocomagh, would all become major centres of Scottish Presbyterianism.

Cape Breton was quickly becoming a haven for Hebridean Scots. It was attracting Western Isles emigrants directly from Scotland and drawing in already-established settlers from the surrounding area. People

At Whycocamagh, a view of McKinnon Point, the landing place of the first Scottish settlers who arrived May 15, 1821. *Photograph by Geoff Campey.*

like Donald McPhail, and John MacNeil, who had previously gone to live in Prince Edward Island, moved to Cape Breton in the mid-1820s. Coming from Mull, Donald went to Mull Cove, while John, who originated from Colonsay, went to the north side of River Denys. Meanwhile ships were arriving each year with ever more settlers. Three hundred and fifty emigrants from Barra landed at Sydney in 1821, an unknown number from the Island of Muck, came the following year, landing at Plaster Cove (now Port Hastings). And, in 1823, the *Emperor Alexander* of Aberdeen sailed from Tobermory to Sydney with thirty families, many of whom originated from the Island of South Uist and from the mainland parish of Kintail in Ross-shire.[30]

With declining kelp production and the increasing number of sheep farms, landlords in the Highlands and Islands sought the removal of what they saw as their surplus tenantry. This was a reversal of their previous stance in the late eighteenth and early nineteenth centuries when they did everything in their power to prevent the exodus of people from their estates. In the Hebrides, where a large part of the kelp industry had been concentrated, conditions were particularly dire.[31] Inevitably large numbers of job losses take time to absorb, even in a vibrant manufacturing area, but in a weak and narrowly based economy, as was the case in these Islands, alternative prospects were bleak or non-existent. Emigration

A tombstone memorial erected in St. Columba Roman Catholic Cemetery, Iona. The inscription reads: John MacNeil Born Barra, Scotland 1817, emigrated 1823, died Gillis, Prince Edward Island. Wife Katherine born Iona 1832, died 1881. *Photograph by Geoff Campey.*

seemed the obvious answer to deal with the many people living in poverty and squalor. Many people were ready to leave, but most needed help to pay for their removal costs.

As the plight of these poor people became more widely known, the British government came under intense pressure to provide public funds to assist them to emigrate.[32] Requests poured in during the mid-1820s from many of the Islands which had taken the brunt of the deteriorating economic conditions. Four to five hundred Uist and Barra inhabitants asked for the "means to join their friends who were assisted to emigrate to Cape Breton in 1817." Three hundred others "from the Hebrides" wanted "assistance to emigrate to Cape Breton." And a further 1,600 people in Mull, Benbecula, Barra and North Uist wanted "to know if they will receive any aid from the Government to British America this season as they are in great distress."[33] The people of Benbecula had made it clear that they would go only to Cape Breton "and no where else if they can help it." But Duncan Shaw, the Benbecula factor, wanted proprietors to have a say in "selecting the emigrants" – otherwise "the most wealthy and industrious of our population will emigrate and we will be left with the dregs."[34] But, in the end, the government declined to offer any help.

Even though the Emigration Select Committee, which sat in 1826–1827, recommended that aid should be offered to poor emigrants, the government refused. It was convinced that emigrants should remain self-financing. Government thinking had probably been influenced by men like Richard John Uniacke, the Attorney General for Nova Scotia. He told the Select Committee that poor Highlanders had found a way of getting to Cape Breton. By supplying their own provisions and making use of an obliging ship captain, fares to Cape Breton could be reduced to £3 – a sum they could just about scrape together themselves. What was more they could look after themselves when they got there:

"As soon as it was known in Scotland that there was an allotment of land made on the Island of Cape Breton, a number of poor people in the North of Scotland where the customs-house regulations are not so strictly enforced, found the way to embark three or four vessels; and there have in the years 1824 and 1825 upon a moderate calculation at least 300 settlers come from the North of Scotland whose passage did not cost them more than 50 s. or £3; for those people provided for themselves; all that the master of the vessel looks to is to see that they have a pound of oatmeal for every day he calculates the passage to run, from four to five weeks; and every man brings a pound of oatmeal for every day, and half that quantity for a child with perhaps about half a pint of molasses, a little butter and a few eggs; and he provides them with water in the passage, they paying about thirty to thirty five shillings. Those settlers come out there upon their own expense; there was not a mouthful of provisions or anything given to them by government; they settled themselves upon the land that Sir James Kempt [Lt. Governor of Nova Scotia] allotted to them: and I doubt whether there is in Scotland so happy a set of people as those."[35]

He spoke also of the advantages of the Bras d'Or Lake which "abound with oysters." Even in the winter, by cutting a hole in the ice, they can get "as many oysters as they chose to eat, so that there can be no starvation in that country."

So the influx of self-financing emigrants continued. In 1826, the *Northumberland* landed around thirty-one families at St. Andrew's,

A tombstone memorial in St. Margaret of Scotland Roman Catholic Cemetery, Broad Cove. The inscription reads: Donald McLellan Native of Morar, Scotland, died 26 Jan. 1890, aged 84 years. His wife Mary McPherson died 3 Feb. 1894, aged 75 years. *Photograph by Geoff Campey.*

New Brunswick, but "many of the settlers removed later on to Inverness County," Cape Breton. The *Tamlerlane,* which had sailed from Greenock, with settlers from North Morar in Inverness-shire, went to Sydney while the *Cadmus,* which had come from Tobermory, landed her passengers at the Strait of Canso.[36] By this time there were at least "one hundred Protestant families" who lived along "this much frequented sound." On his visit there, Reverend John McLennan found "the great bulk to be poor, but there are some who are well able" but unwilling, to contribute to the support of a minister. Being "the principal inlet to Cape Breton and a sort of thoroughfare for people of all nations," he feared that, without a clergyman, Canso's Presbyterian inhabitants would be subject to unwelcome "encroachments of view."[37]

In late September there were "about four hundred emigrants from the Hebrides, lately arrived at this Island, who are now in the lake" and "two more vessels with an equal number are daily expected."[38] But the newcomers, who landed at McNab's Cove on the south side of Bras D'Or, were "at a loss for land.... No good land being vacant on the Bras d'Or." Thus, by 1826 new arrivals were having to travel inland, south of Bras D'Or. The success of the Lake Ainslie settlements, near the Western Shore, had shown the way. "Lake Ainslie a short time ago was of no moment and although it is quite an interior it is now a considerable settlement."[39] The considerable frontages around Loch Lomond were now being cleared by colonizers from the Outer Hebridean Islands of Harris, North Uist and Berneray (just to the south of Harris). They would also extend their territory inland at Lewis Cove, Grand River, St. Esprit and Framboise further to the south. All of these areas would acquire substantial Presbyterian communities.[40] These were some of the most remote and isolated regions on the island. Before the St. Peter's Canal was built, there was no access to Bras d'Or from the south coast.[41] The only access point was along the channel north of Sydney. So not only were people on the south of the island furthest away from centres of population, they could only get to Bras d'Or by travelling overland.

By the late 1820s, as new Scottish settlements began to develop in the south of the island, the populations of the more long-established Scottish enclaves in northeast Bras d'Or were also augmented. When he visited the region in 1815, Bishop Plessis had found a recently constructed chapel built by the one hundred families who had settled at Christmas Island and in the surrounding area:

"It was night when we reached the place [Christmas Island], and the chapel was chosen immediately as a lodging for the Bishop and his companions. When this chapel is completed it will have two windows, but no place has yet been cut out in the walls for them, although the little sashes have been glazed and are all ready to be put in. Meanwhile there is no light inside except what comes through the door, when it is open and through the open spaces between the logs which make up the body of the chapel."[42]

This was a poor community. When twenty-four families (127 people) arrived at St. Andrew's Channel "in very destitute circumstances and, many of them, under the additional pressure of disease" it was "the poor settlers" of Christmas Island who helped them to survive their first winter.[43] The newcomers were part of a much larger group of six hundred Hebridean settlers from North and South Uist, Benbecula and Barra who had sailed to Cape Breton in 1827 on the *Columbus, George Stevens* and *Stephen Wright* of Newcastle. By now colonization was progressing along the St. Andrews Channel from Christmas Island to Beaver Cove, Boisdale, Long Island and Leitches Creek.[44]

As more poor Scots flocked to Cape Breton, local officials became increasingly concerned over the pitiful state of some of the new arrivals. More than a third of the *Stephen Wright*'s passengers had caught smallpox and other diseases. Three people died during the passage, ten while in port and a further two after landing. The *Harmony* of Whitehaven had arrived that year at Halifax, with two hundred and thirty-six emigrants, thirteen of whom died on the passage, while "twenty-two were cut off after landing on an uninhabited spot by measles, dysentery and starvation." The surgeon who reported these deaths to the Lieutenant Governor had no doubt that the fatalities were due to "the confined, crowded and filthy state of the vessels – the quantity and quality of food in the case of one of them, at least, and the scarcity of water." He had learned from the captains "that a very extensive emigration was contemplated in the ensuing Spring" and "that ten to fifteen vessels, belonging to the owner of the *Stephen Wright,* had been chartered to convey these poor creatures from the Highlands and Islands of Scotland to meet famine, disease and death on the shores of Cape Breton."[45]

The surgeon's dire prediction proved groundless in spite of the record number of new arrivals in 1828.[46] Such was the state of over-crowding on the *Universe* of Aberdeen that six families "were obliged to live in the long boat during the whole voyage."[47] Nevertheless, although conditions were grim, disease was kept at bay. Only one ship, the *Two Sisters* of Pictou, which came from Greenock with one hundred and sixty passengers, had people "under the smallpox." Although one quarter of the total number had succumbed there were no deaths. As a precaution, constables went on board the ship "under a warrant pursuant to law to prevent any persons from leaving the vessel or visiting from the shore."[48] The constables remained for eight days and nights. As was the case with many other emigrants, these passengers were poor and "very much in want of provisions."[49] They were given vegetables, 28 lbs. of rice, 14 1/2 bushels of potatoes, 2 gallons of molasses, lamb and mutton, all of which cost the Council £20.4s.4d.[50]

A staggering six hundred North Uist people and seven hundred Harris people had come to Cape Breton in 1828.[51] While many were miserably poor on arrival, they would soon be assimilated into well-organised and supportive communities. A cairn built "to honour and perpetuate the memory of the pioneers who came to Loch Lomond from the Islands of Harris and Uist," is a lasting reminder of that great influx. Some of the North Uist and Harris families went to Leitches Creek, in northeast Bras d'Or. Here too their arrival is commemorated by a cairn. Others settled along the Mira River valley, further to the east and at nearby Catalone.[52]

In 1841, Duncan Shaw, the Harris and North Uist factor, would tell the Select Committee on Emigration that "the people who then went [in 1828] are doing well at Cape Breton and I believe that a great many of the Harris people are now willing to join them."[53] He would be proved right. Three hundred and fifty of "the poorer class" emigrated from Harris in 1840, while nine hundred and fifty "chiefly poor cottars" emigrated from North Uist between 1840 and 1842.[54] Many came to Cape Breton where they extended long-established communities at Loch Lomond, Grand River and Leitches Creek, but also branched out to new areas such as Cape North at the northern end of the Island.[55]

The Island of Rhum also lost people to Cape Breton in 1828. The landlord, MacNeil of Canna, having decided that he could not maintain his tenantry, had gone to Rhum in 1826 with a plan: He told his tenants that he would write off any arrears owing, give them their cattle and "I will give you £600 over and above, to enable you to remove to America, for I cannot afford the present system." It is doubtful whether all of his tenants "very cheerfully accepted," as was claimed, but the exodus was apparently "conducted under the very best superintendence" and later reports indicated that his former tenants were "most comfortable."[56] Around two hundred sailed to Ship Harbour in 1828, where they "dispersed into the district of Port Hastings and other interior sections" of Cape Breton while a good many others probably moved to Prince Edward Island.[57]

Skye people also left in large numbers at this time, although there is no evidence that they received any financial assistance. A good part of the 1829–1830 exodus was from Lord MacDonald's estate, in northeast Skye, and as was the case with the Rhum exodus, most Skye people headed for either Prince Edward Island or Cape Breton.[58] Donald Murchison's family had decided to emigrate but was not sure where to go:

"The reduction of our circumstances induces us to banish ourselves and families from our native and lovely country to those distant colonies of the Kingdom entirely unknown to us, with the sole view of supporting our numerous offspring."[59]

Families also had to raise money for their passages. In desperation many turned to the government, but most petitions for financial help were rejected. Few landlords in the 1820s and 1830s offered help and most people were left to their own devices. Even so, hundreds of Skye people managed to get to Prince Edward Island and Cape Breton in 1829. To everyone's relief, the passengers who sailed on the *Louisa* had brought "a limited stock of provisions and none of them as far as we can learn will be objects of legislative assistance."[60] And they were also free of any disease. However, the 1830 arrivals were not so fortunate. Owing to "their distressed situation," the forty-nine Skye families (220 people) who sailed on the *Malay* received land "free of charges other than the usual fees" and £100 "from the "King's Casual Revenue."[61] Arriving at Margaree, they moved deep into the interior to the south of Lake Ainslie, where they founded Skye Glen.

Land regulations were once again tightened in 1827, just as emigration levels from Scotland were nearing their peak. Wishing to attract settlers who had capital, the government replaced the previous system of free grants with a regime of land sales by public auction. Few people could afford such payments and most became squatters.[62] However, a more positive development was the massive capital investment in Sydney's coalfield, made by the British-based General Mining Association. The Sydney mines were greatly expanded from 1827 and production rose sharply. Because coal mining was hugely labour intensive, a large workforce was required. Emigrant Scots, who before this had shunned town life, now flocked to Sydney to take up mining jobs. Nearly half of all the South Uist emigrants who arrived in the 1840s settled in the area.[63]

The tombstone memorial in St. Andrew's Roman Catholic Cemetery, Judique. The inscription reads: Isabella McLean, Died 1865, aged 55 years, Daughter of Alexander McLean and Catherine McVarish from Inverness-shire, Scotland. *Photograph by Geoff Campey.*

When Reverend McLennan of Prince Edward Island made his extensive tour of Cape Breton in 1828, he had to journey a distance of about 300 miles to visit fifteen Presbyterian congregations and baptise 520 children.[64] When Bishop MacEachern visited the Western Shore five years earlier he found that:

"All the country from Chetecan [Cheticamp] to Magrie [Margaree] and 5 miles in the interior to a large lake 13 miles long and 6 wide, stretching towards Mabou, Justaucorps, in the rear of Judique and to River Inhabitants is taken up, and mostly settled with our people.... There are no roads fit for horses in most of said district, except on the Judique shore.

There is a church in Broad Cove, one in Mabou, one in Judique, one on River Inhabitants; and the Catholics of Port Hood talk of erecting one in stone. It would be desirable that some person could be got to take some part of Mr MacDonnell's labours off his hands. He is too heavy for snow shoes and no horse can carry him through deep snow."[65]

Since there were so few roads, travelling such distances was a heroic feat. The people wasted no time in constructing their first chapels. Built close to the water's edge, these churches brought scattered communities together. Occasional visits from clergymen gave them a glimpse of the wider world, but for the most part these emigrant Scots lived in extreme isolation. Their primitive log huts and small clearings in the forests would set them on their way to a better life. They had landed as poverty-stricken emigrants, but were fast becoming successful pioneers. Many more Scots would come to Cape Breton during the 1830s and 1840s to further reinforce the island's strong Scottish identity. Times were changing, however.

By the 1830s, the timber trade, once so vital to Pictou's economy, was on the wane. Nevertheless mainland Nova Scotia was increasingly taking on a more settled appearance. The days of basic survival were over, and a more advanced and confident society was slowly emerging.

$$\mathcal{C}\mathcal{O}7\mathcal{O}\mathcal{O}$$

NOVA SCOTIA'S LINGERING APPEAL

Now, I must say something about the far-famed Pictou; it is a small town principally settled by Scotch people who are very kind and hospitable; there is a fine harbour and three rivers, the East, West and Middle which flow into it. The scenery accordingly is very picturesque and beautiful. There are the Albion [coal] mines up the East River (which I suppose you have heard of) and great numbers of vessels come here in the summer season, particularly for coal and besides several steam ships which makes the place very busy.[1]

HELEN CREIGHTON'S DESCRIPTION OF PICTOU in 1837 reveals a thriving Scottish town. The large square-rigged ships which came to Pictou to collect timber cargoes were now less frequent callers, their place being taken, in part, by the small coastal vessels that carried coal. With the opening up of the province's ample coal reserves, mines were in full production and coal exports were rising. The timber trade, which had once dominated Pictou's economic life, was well into its decline as the search for timber progressively favoured New Brunswick and the Saint Lawrence region.[2] Joseph Howe, editor of the *Novascotian,* blamed the downturn on "the scarcity of the article and the decline of prices."[3] There had been a disastrous fall in prices and it was true that Nova Scotia farmers and lumberers had depleted most of its best pine forests. But with its diversified

Pictou, from Mortimer's Point (c. 1834–37). Lithograph by William Eagar, from *Nova Scotia in a Series of Views Taken on the Spot and on Stone. Courtesy of the National Archives of Canada, C-041689 W.H. Coverdale Collection of Canadiana.*

economy, based on coal, shipbuilding, fishing and farming, Pictou's future was secure.

A very dramatic and unexpected impetus to the region's economy came in 1826–27 when the London jewellers Rundell, Bridge and Rundell acquired the rights to virtually all of the province's mineral resources by paying off the Duke of York's debts.[4] Taking its acquisition very seriously, the London jewellers formed the General Mining Association and invested huge amounts of capital in state of the art machinery for what became the Albion Mines, located just to the south of New Glasgow.[5] A skilled workforce was acquired by recruiting experienced miners from Britain, but the coal fields eventually became a major source of local employment. Coal was extracted through the use of steam-driven mining equipment and, by 1830, the province's first railway line was in place to take coal from the pits to Pictou Harbour, from where it could be exported to the United States.[6]

Few emigrants were arriving from Scotland in the late 1830s but, as has been seen, the situation had been quite different earlier. The Scottish influx to mainland Nova Scotia, which began from the late eighteenth century, reached its first peak in the early 1800s, rose again steadily from 1816 when the Napoleonic Wars ended, and peaked again in the early 1830s, when a severe economic depression gripped much of Scotland.

After a lull of a few years, in the late 1830s, adverse economic forces once again stimulated another influx, which began in the early 1840s. Looking back to the very beginning, the earliest arrivals of the late eighteenth and early nineteenth centuries were not just escaping from the poor economic conditions which faced them in Scotland but they were also responding to the positive advantages of the New World. Poverty may indeed have been a factor, but the prospect of self-betterment was an equally powerful force. By being the first people to build up and secure control over eastern Nova Scotia's timber trade, Scottish merchants had created an enormous magnet for their fellow countrymen. Enterprising Scots had the prospect of selling timber as a preliminary step to establishing their farms and they came over in their thousands to benefit from the region's burgeoning timber trade.[7]

To sum up, Scottish settlements grew initially around timber-collecting harbours, along coastlines near harbours and along the major rivers which emptied into them. These "were the scenes of the labours of the early emigrants."[8] The *Hector* arrivals of 1773, the earliest of the Presbyterian colonists, settled near Pictou Harbour and gradually progressed up the East, West and Middle rivers. They were joined a decade later by Scottish Loyalists, many of whom settled in the vicinity of Merigomish Harbour and along Barneys River, which flows into it. Very large numbers of Catholic Highlanders came to the Antigonish area, from the early 1790s, taking up land along the coastline, to the east of Merigomish, establishing footholds at Knoydart, Moydart, Arisaig, Malignant Cove, Cape George and Morristown. They also settled at Antigonish Harbour and along the South and West rivers, which empty into it, and at Pomquet Harbour and along the Pomquet

John Frazer, First Collector of Customs, Pictou. Portrait by Robert Field. *Courtesy of the Nova Scotia Art Gallery 1978.38. Gift of Charles Ritchie, Ottawa, Ontario, 1978.*

A tombstone memorial in Oak River Cemetery, West River, Pictou. The inscription reads: Donald Fraser, died 21 Jan., 1839, aged 72 years, native of Inverness, Scotland, emigrated in 1803. *Photograph by Geoff Campey.*

River. By the early 1800s colonization was progressing from Tatamagouche Bay along the Waugh River, the French River and River John, and from Wallace Harbour further to the west, as successive waves of Presbyterian Scots came to the area in search of land.

The town of Pictou grew quickly, with "no regular plan," each person building a house "just where he pleased."[9] And since the town's streets developed later, they were "blessed with their due proportion of sinuosities." Having its first house in place by 1790, Pictou "progressed in a manner very creditable to the zeal and perseverance of the original settlers and their descendants." By 1830 it had around two hundred buildings and a buoyant local economy. There were increasing job opportunities for craftsmen and tradesmen in the town, but most Scots preferred to settle in rural communities where they could acquire their own land:

"A curious feature in the character of the Highland population, spread over the entire province, is the extravagant desire they cherish to purchase large quantities of land."[10]

By 1828 the quest for land produced a number of scattered Scottish communities along the East River, whose population totalled just over three thousand people. There were other clusters at Merigomish with just under 2,000 residents, at the town of Pictou with around 1,400 people, at Middle River with about the same number, at West River which had a total population of around one thousand, and at River John which had a similar population.[11]

These were solidly Presbyterian communities which organized themselves into compact congregations, served by ministers who travelled considerable distances to get to them. McLellans Mountain and Frasers Mountain, on the East River, had their first congregations by 1817 and had built "two good houses of worship...exclusively pertaining to the Church of Scotland."[12] Reverend Donald Mackintosh, who presided over a string of settlements along the West River, up to Mount Thom, and along the Middle River, up to New Lairg, was being paid "the sum of one hundred and fifty pounds of the current money of Nova Scotia yearly..." to discharge the duties of a minister of religion in the Gaelic and English languages. And, by 1844, Rogers Hill and River John each had a church "regularly built and seated and in good order," having at least 2,000 "persons within the range," while the town of New Glasgow, with its growing population of miners, had a Gaelic preacher who came regularly from Pictou.[13] A common and overriding aim of these early communities was always the preservation of their language and religion."[14] This was applied to temporal matters as well. In 1836, "one hundred and two persons of wealth, respectability and intelligence," who lived at West River, judged the time had come for their district to have its own magistrate who would be "conversant in the Gaelic and English languages."[15]

Scots quickly came to dominate other ethnic groups in Pictou County, much of Colchester County, Antigonish County and large swathes of Guysborough County. By 1829 Antigonish appeared to be "one of the prettiest villages in the eastern section of Nova Scotia," although with a population of nearly, 2,500 it was more like a town. St. Andrews and Arisaig, each had around 1,500 people.[16] In fact, much of the northern half of Antigonish County was being colonized by Catholic Highlanders. While they were a very large component of the early Scottish influx to mainland Nova Scotia, they did not remain so. By the mid-1820s the majority of Scottish arrivals at Pictou were Presbyterians, with a high proportion originating from the County of Sutherland.

An important step forward for emigrants came in 1821 when the government of Nova Scotia established Land Commissioners. Instead of having to walk miles to request land, settlers could apply to their local Boards to get a temporary permit and could join with others later to share the cost of the necessary fees, when they took possession of their land.[17] By then large tracts of good land were only to be found inland, in remote locations, usually with poor accessibility to the outside world. There were two regions which offered good land: one in the Cobequid Hills to the west of Pictou and the other to the east of Pictou, extending south from the Merigomish frontages to St. Marys, in Guysborough County (see Figure 5). A local surveyor knew "from personal survey and observation" that the latter region had land "of excellent quality, well-watered by Barneys River, running into Merigomish Harbour and the branches of the St. Marys [River], running into the Atlantic. The streams are small, this being their source and not fit to float timber."[18]

St. Mary's Roman Catholic Church at Lismore (near Knoydart), Pictou County, built in 1834. *Photograph by Geoff Campey.*

Lowlanders, who boarded ships primarily at Aberdeen, Leith and Greenock, continued to arrive at Pictou and Halifax throughout the first half of the nineteenth century, but the majority of newcomers originated from the Highlands (see Appendix II).[19] The great clearances which took place in Sutherland, from the early 1800s, were to have major repercussions for Nova Scotia. Many of the estate tenants, who were being removed from their holdings to make way for large new sheep farms, decided that emigration was preferable to the alternatives being offered to them. Most would choose Nova Scotia. They were caught up in the most extensive and dramatic of the clearances ever to be carried out in Scotland. Between 1807 and 1821, thousands of people were removed from their holdings. Cleared first, in 1807, were the parishes of Lairg and Farr, followed by Rogart in 1809; the Assynt, Kildonan and Clyne clearances began in 1812 and these were followed, in 1814–15, by the removals in Strathnaver, in the northern part of the estate.[20] The final stage involved the southern parishes of Golspie, Loth and Dornoch, which were cleared from 1819 to 1821.

It was always the intention that these displaced people would move to one of the new coastal communities being established at the time. The Countess of Sutherland wanted to keep her tenantry. It was a case of moving them to other locations and jobs to best suit the needs of the estate. But her tenants saw things differently. William Young could not "account for the emigration from Rogart – there is not a man has been dislocated but with a view to make him better and that in place of having his land in run ridge it may now be in a lot on a nineteen year lease."[21] A great many people quite simply preferred the prospect of becoming independent farmers in Nova Scotia to a continuation of the grinding poverty and subservience which the Sutherland estate had to offer.

From 1813 to 1815 Kildonan parish lost around one hundred and eighty people to Lord Selkirk's Red River Colony.[22] But most Sutherland people opted for Nova Scotia. Sutherland emigrants had been well represented on the *Hector* and word would have filtered back to friends and relatives at home that good land and a better life was theirs for the taking in and around Pictou. Knowing this and realizing that they were about to be evicted, many people emigrated. Sutherland emigrants had created their own distinctive communities at Mill Brook, Gairloch and New Lairg, along Pictou's Middle River, well before the great clearances had actually begun. Sadly, the 1807 contingents from Farr, Lairg and Rogart lost their lives in a terrible shipwreck. But this calamity did not halt the exodus.[23] A steady stream of people continued to make their way to Pictou as huge swathes of Sutherland were being cleared to make way for sheep.

The growing exodus caught Francis Suther's attention by 1817. One of the Sutherland estate managers, he had "no doubt many of the inhabitants, who are to be removed from the interior of this part of the [Strath]naver district of the estate, will, rather than settle on the lots to be offered them on the coast, buy a trip to America if they can possibly raise funds to pay for their passages."[24] But he was not happy with Simon Fraser's involvement:

"There is a person at present by the name of Fraser…I heard yesterday had gone to Strathnaver to endeavour to induce the people to go to America with him. This Fraser is from America and has come to this country for the sole purpose of taking out people."[25]

Once again the indefatigable Simon Fraser was trying to sell places on his ships. But Suther wanted the estate tenants to purchase their fares from someone he knew. He recommended the Leith-based merchant, William Allen, a business acquaintance. Any agent "sent by Mr. Allen would be successful in picking up a cargo early in the Spring."[26] Suther knew that people from Assynt, Farr, Kildonan and Lairg intended to emigrate, but they were having great difficulty in raising funds to pay for their crossings. When he learned that a certain Mr. Dudgeon was trying to help them, Suther suspected the worst:

"An attempt was made to form an association by a Mr. Dudgeon, a farmer from Fearn in Ross-shire, apparently to the relief of the people…to supply them with the means of emigration, but which failed from all the gentlemen whose names he presumed without their sanction to advertise as forming the committee of the association.... He cares less for the people than any man in Scotland...his forwardness in this business was merely to satisfy an old grudge he has to the family."[27]

Thomas Dudgeon, a Ross-shire man, was leading the campaign to assist the hard-pressed Sutherland tenantry.[28] He called a meeting at the Meickle Ferry Inn, in Dornoch in June 1819, just as the Golspie, Loth and Dornoch tenantry were about to be evicted. Suther's men were sent to spy on the meeting and report back:

"upwards of 1,000 persons they say were present from all quarters in expectation of their receiving money." Some had even come from "the most distant parts of Caithness.... He [Dudgeon] got money off them to subscribe to a paper the purpose of which when returning home they did not know and for which subscription each person paid at least 6d to Mr Dudgeon or his buddy in the swindle – Gibson of Tain Academy, a teacher besides Thomson, the third fiddle in the trio who keeps the Public House of the [Meikle] Ferry."[29]

The Sutherland and Transatlantic Friendly Association was duly formed. It was a peoples' movement with the potential to cause great embarrassment. Estate managers had feared that a parliamentary inquiry might be in the offing as a result of the mounting criticism of the Sutherland clearances. Now Dudgeon was using his group to inflame the situation even more. His views on the injustices of the clearances, which were reported in the *Scotsman*, gave added negative publicity. And when Dudgeon asked that his association be consulted in the allocation of the coastal lots which were being offered to tenants who remained on the estate, this was seen as open rebellion. It was a "most impertinent attempt to interfere in the management of private property."[30] Dudgeon had to be stopped.

Estate managers issued orders for notices, signed by a sheriff and two Justices of the Peace, to be displayed on the doors of parish churches. The estate tenantry were told to stay away from Dudgeon's meetings and if they ignored the notices they were to be intercepted and stopped.[31] People were told that Dudgeon had villainous and subversive aims and that his meetings were illegal. He was a menace. After a few months these tactics caused Dudgeon's Transatlantic Friendly Society to be disbanded and his reputation to be in tatters. Dudgeon was even accused of pocketing its funds for his own ends.[32]

However badly Dudgeon may have been treated, his efforts were not in vain. By providing Sutherland people with the means to band together, he enabled them to realize their aim of getting to Nova Scotia. In 1821–22, three hundred and sixty Sutherland people sailed off to Pictou in the *Ossian* of Leith, the *Harmony* of Aberdeen and the *Ruby* of Aberdeen.[33] An unnamed "association at Edinburgh" and unknown sources in Bengal, enabled them to buy the hatchets, spades, pick axes, saws, nails, Gaelic Bibles, yards of tartan and barrels of pork which they would need in their new settlements.[34] Dudgeon's association had brought whole communities together to plan, raise funds and organize their departures. They sought large tracts of good farm land where they could live together in groups and by the time they left Scotland they had already decided where they would settle.

People from the southern parishes of Sutherland (Clyne, Rogart, Dornoch, Golspie, Loth and Lairg) would have been attracted to Mill Brook, Gairloch and New Lairg, places on the Middle River which had already been founded by their compatriots; but they also had their eye on the Cobequid Hills, to the west of Pictou. Having arrived at Pictou, they made their way west, to Tatamagouche Bay.[35] They then travelled through dense forests, going about eight miles into the interior, on foot, until they reached Earltown. There, to meet them were Donald MacIntosh and Angus Sutherland, two compatriots who had been preparing the site since 1813.[36] The Province's Deputy Surveyor, probably had these people in mind when he described emigrant Scots as "the most useful description of settlers that come here [Colchester]...with a determination to settle immediately."[37]

They quickly established their new communities and soon attracted followers from Sutherland, who came in substantial numbers throughout the 1820s.[38] By 1826 Earltown had sixty Sutherland families who greatly impressed a visiting Presbyterian Minister. They were:

"remarkable for their attachment to the Church and their knowledge of the Bible.... The inhabitants of these settlements, having emigrated but a few years ago, are necessarily straitened in circumstances, and consequently are in the situation of those who have the best claims to assistance. They are a religious or more properly speaking a high professing people intimate with the doctrine of our Church and conversant with the usual topics of experimental religion. Consequently none but a sound Evangelical Pastor could give satisfaction or be useful."[39]

Earltown continued to grow. By 1828 Earltown and Tatamagouche, taken together, had 1,211 settlers.[40] In 1832, it had "some one hundred and twenty families from Sutherland" who were still being admired for being "well versed in the prominent doctrines of the Bible." They would require a Minister "of no ordinary qualifications."[41] It seems that Reverend William Sutherland, who came from Rogart, met with their approval. He arrived soon after and ministered to the people of Earltown until his death in 1848.[42] By 1844 "a good church" had been erected which had a congregation of some 1000 people who came from both Earltown and nearby New Annan.[43]

While their spiritual needs were being met, temporal requirements for better roads had been sorely neglected:

"Your petitioners beg leave to state to your Excellency that very little has been done by way of public grants to open up or make said line of road which is not as yet passable for carts or sleds via which access many of your petitioners are compelled to carry their produce to market on their backs and take home their supplies of fish, salt etc., in the same manner."[44]

Earltown had nearly two hundred families by this time. Its population continued to grow until the 1860s, when there was a gradual exodus as people sought better land or employment in towns. Even in its declining years Earltown clung to its Scottish traditions. Gaelic remained in use until at least 1877 and was "more generally spoken in Earltown than in any part of Nova Scotia proper."[45]

Having gone to Earltown in large numbers, Sutherland emigrants were also to be found in other districts. By 1829 New Lairg, "having been settled by emigrants from Sutherland," was reported to have a Presbyterian congregation of "upwards of 500," while at nearby Gairloch, another Sutherland foothold, a congregation of "from 600 to 700 have regularly attended the public ordinances of religion on the Sabbath."[46] Some joined settlements at Wallace, to the northwest of New Annan, which were founded initially, in 1803, by people from the Island of Lewis.[47] Wallace received twenty more Lewis people thirty years later, but beyond this, there is no evidence of any follow-on emigration from Lewis.[48] However, the Wallace area soon attracted large numbers of Highlanders and, by 1829, its settlements were "flourishing and fast increasing and perfectly able now to afford a Gaelic Minister on an annual salary of from £100 to £120 currency."[49]

The nearby settlement of Ramsheg, was also "composed mainly of Highlanders, who have made an offer of £60 as an annual stipend to a minister having Gaelic as well as English"[50] (see Figure 5). Two Presbyterian ministers, who visited the area, preached "for five successive days…at Wallace on Wednesday, at Fox Harbour on Thursday, at the Gulf shore on Friday, at Wallace again on the Sabbath and River John on Monday. Besides preaching Mr. MacKenzie baptized 56 children."[51] This area, too, was fast becoming yet another Highland stronghold:

"In the neighbourhood there is a mixture of French, Dutch, English etc., but on account of their steadiness and industry the Scotch Highlanders are rapidly gaining the ascendancy in point of numbers, influence and independence…and their attachment to the religious institutions of their native country has been unshaken amidst all the difficulties and privations with which they contend in this country for upwards of twenty years; and not withstanding the zeal of emissaries of various persuasions, they continued steadfast in their adherence to the Church of Scotland. There are two stations for preaching about nine miles apart and separated by [channels traversed by] two ferries each [channel] upwards of a mile broad."[52]

While the 1819 to 1822 exodus from Sutherland had been mainly directed at Earltown, some people chose to settle along the upper stretches of Barney's River, which had plentiful supplies of good farming land. Further contingents from Sutherland arrived during the 1830s.[53] John MacLean, the poet, lived briefly on a farm belonging to a Sutherland emigrant at Barneys River, before moving a short distance to the east to Glen Bard, in Antigonish County.[54] By 1834 "the heads of families belonging" to the Barneys River Presbyterian congregation were estimated to be about ninety, and a decade later it was said to have eight hundred people and two Presbyterian churches.[55]

Highlanders were also establishing footholds in the extensive tracts of good land to be found to the south of Antigonish and in Guysborough County. Lochaber Lake had particular appeal:

"The lands on both sides of this lake, particularly towards its upper extremity, rise from it with abruptness to a considerable elevation, but without rocks or precipices. The water is nearly as pure as spring water and of great depth. It is never frozen with the exception of a small piece at its head, until after several weeks of severe frost; and long after all the neighbouring lakes and streams are passable for horses and loaded sleighs, it presents for three or four miles a surface altogether free of ice. Its breadth is from 40 to 120 rods, and its shores are wholly without rocks, and for the most part of beautiful gravel."[56]

Lochaber Lake, Antigonish County, Nova Scotia. The etching and aquatint are by
William Moorson, 1830. *Courtesy of the Art Gallery of Nova Scotia 1998.421. Gift of John
and Norma Oyler, Halifax, Nova Scotia, 1998.*

While its earliest settlers were almost exclusively Roman Catholics,
the post-1820 influx included many Presbyterians. By 1826 two hundred and seventeen Highlanders were looking for "a Gaelic Gospel
minister" to preside over their congregation and were in the final stages
of "completing a meeting house in a centricale part of our settlement."[57]
However, Catholic Highlanders continued to arrive as well. Seven Roman
Catholic families from Inverness-shire came to the area in 1843, settling
at Giant's Lake, just to the east of Lochaber Lake.[58]

Lochaber Lake marked the beginning of the St. Marys district, which
was "specially noted for its magnificent timber, extensive intervales, rivers
teeming with fish and the abundance of game in the forest."[59] Highlanders from Inverness-shire, Perthshire and Sutherland were establishing
themselves here in "thinly scattered" settlements along the St. Marys
River, from the head of Caledonia to its mouth, a distance of about thirty
miles. In addition, they were colonizing the east branch of the same river,
a distance of around fifteen miles, "embracing, in fact, half a county."
By 1838 when Rev. John Campbell, came to attend to his Presbyterian
congregation, he found that roads were "mere footpaths or bridle paths."

Some places had "little more than mere openings, cut in the woods, with a pathway full of holes made by the horses feet.... There was not a wheeled carriage within the whole bounds of the congregation."[60]

The northeast Highlands continued to lose people to Nova Scotia throughout the early 1830s. In April 1833, the Reverend Lewis Rose noticed the "two large vessels just now in Cromarty Bay taking in passengers.... So far, however, as I can ascertain there will not be so many emigrants from this country this season as there have been for several seasons back."[61] Three further ships actually called at Cromarty for emigrants that summer, but by the following year, the numbers leaving this port had declined sharply. A severe economic depression in Scotland had stimulated a rise in emigration during the early 1830s and, although most of the exodus from Scotland was directed at Upper Canada, a substantial number of people who boarded ship at Cromarty went to Nova Scotia.

By this time Pictou would have seemed a lot less welcoming. The people of Nova Scotia had grown weary of having to subsidize the growing numbers of poverty-stricken immigrants who came to their ports. After experiencing a decade of dealing with penniless newcomers, the Nova Scotia legislature decided that it was time to act. In 1832, they introduced a head tax of 5 shillings, payable by each overseas passenger, to raise funds for "the benefit of the poor emigrants arriving in the province."[62] Archibald MacNiven, an emigration agent from Skye, was certain that the tax would be "the cause of stopping emigration entirely" but it failed to do this.[63] While some emigrants endured great hardship to pay the tax, the scheme enabled the province to contain disease at its major ports by using the money raised to build quarantine facilities.

Scottish miners made their first appearance at Pictou in 1829. The Albion Mines recruited some one hundred and fifty-seven men, who sailed from Greenock on the *Hero*, and a decade later a similar number arrived on the *Isabella* of Glasgow.[64] In time, the Pictou coal mines would also attract poor Scots seeking the most basic of labouring jobs. And former estate tenants from Sutherland would continue to arrive. With the passing of the 1845 Poor Law Amendment Act, Scottish lairds were, for the first time, legally responsible for the destitute on their estates. This gave them an added incentive to promote emigration and, to achieve this, many helped their tenantry with their removal costs. The Duke of Sutherland was no exception.[65] He assisted many of his tenants to emigrate to both Nova Scotia and Upper Canada.[66] Those who originated from the parish of Farr were given "very liberal assistance," from £5 to £25 per family, while people from Rogart also "received some help to pay their passages."[67] Between 1840 and 1842 three or four ships a year called at one or more of the North Highland ports – Cromarty, Thurso, Lochinver and Loch Laxford – to take these and other Sutherland families to either Pictou or Quebec (see Appendix II).

An average of about two hundred emigrants, mostly from Sutherland, came to Pictou yearly at this time. Some had succumbed on their voyages to smallpox or other virulent diseases, although they were the exception, rather than the rule. The *Lady Grey* of North Shields arrived at Pictou Harbour in July 1841, with typhus spreading among her passengers. To contain the disease the sick and the healthy were separated, but the fever spread and, by September, six people had died.[68] Disease threatened Pictou once again in 1843 when the *George* of Dundee arrived with "malignant fever and dysentery on board." Health officials found "the stench and heat below decks...almost intolerable."[69] Emigrants were immediately removed from the "floating pest-house" and taken to beaches where they stayed until a temporary building was constructed to accommodate them. Again it was a long time before the quarantine regulations could be relaxed and Pictou could be declared free of disease.

On her approach to Pictou from Glasgow in 1842, the *Isabella* of Glasgow "became entangled in the ice" on the north side of Cape Breton and became "a total wreck" although none of the fifty-four emigrants on board perished.[70] However, most emigrant ships arrived without incident. The "healthy appearance" of the *Lady Emily* of Sunderland's passengers in 1842 impressed the *Pictou Observer*'s reporter while the captain was praised for his kindness and "strict and unremitting attention" to the passengers' "health and comfort during a voyage unusually protracted by calms and contrary winds."[71] The *Superior* of Peterhead, which arrived that same year, also made a very favourable impression.

The *Pictou Observer* had "never seen a healthier or more respectable set of immigrants arrive at our port." The passengers "speak of Captain Manson's urbanity and kindness in the highest terms" during a long passage of some fifty days.[72] Included amongst the passengers were Donald and Janet MacDonald of Kiltarlity, near Beauly, who settled at Black River, a site which was probably located in West Pictou.[73]

The deepening economic crisis in the Highlands and the Great Famine from 1846 to 1856 stimulated further clearances, which once again created rising levels of emigration. Several areas in the western parishes of Assynt and Eddrachilles, in northwest Sutherland, were partially cleared at this time.[74] Having been assisted by the Duke of Sutherland with their travel expenses, one hundred and seventeen people sailed from Thurso to Pictou in 1847 on the *Serius*.[75] Further emigrants from the Sutherland estate, arrived at Pictou in the following year on the *Ellen* of Liverpool, a ship which had been chartered by the Duke.[76] It was a good voyage in which, apparently, the captain, Dugald McLachlan, acted "onto one and all of them more like the head of a family than a shipmaster. No praise that they can bestow upon him can be too great."[77] However, some difficulties arose when six families, who having paid their five shillings head tax on arrival in Pictou, were required to pay it a second time when they went on to Prince Edward Island.[78] The Duke of Sutherland later complained of their "cruel treatment," but he was subsequently chided by the Assembly for sending too many of his impoverished, former tenants to Nova Scotia:

"It may be extremely convenient and beneficial for the Duke of Sutherland and other great landed proprietors...of Scotland, to expatriate a large, and perhaps troublesome, pauper tenantry and they may not hesitate to expend considerable sums to attain so desirable an object. It would, however, be a matter of sincere pleasure to the Colonies...if some funds were also provided by these noblemen and gentlemen to relieve the Provinces from the expense so often entailed...by so large an influx of destitute persons."[79]

Portrait of the second Duke of Sutherland who held the title from 1833 until his death in 1861. *Courtesy of Lord Strathnaver.*

That same year the *Hope* arrived at Pictou from Glasgow with one hundred and thirty-seven passengers, of whom the adult males were colliers intending to work for the Albion Mines in Pictou, but most of the families subsequently moved on to the United States.[80] The *Lulan* also arrived at Pictou in 1848 with her cargo of one hundred and sixty-seven passengers from South Uist. Although most of them were destined for Cape Breton and Prince Edward Island, they included thirty men, with families, who also intended to work as colliers at the Albion Mines. They were Col. John Gordon of Cluny's former tenants. No other landlord, at the time, provoked as much outrage and contempt as this man. As was the case on so many occasions, he had not made suitable arrangements for his people. Having been told to go to the Clyde, the South Uist emigrants boarded a vessel, which was bound for Boston. A passenger "who understood a little of the English language" discovered this "deliberate deception" in time for the passengers to disembark at Glasgow and wait for a ship which would take them to Pictou, but none came and:

> "the poor creatures were obliged to find shelter where they best could, and while some got tolerably well housed, a large number, including women and children, several of the latter being ill with whooping-cough and measles, were obliged for want of funds to bivouack [camp] under the sheds of the Broomielaw [Glasgow]. This homeless group attracted the notice of the authorities and one portion was sheltered and fed in the Anderston Police-Office and the other in the Night Asylum."[81]

When the South Uist emigrants finally arrived in Pictou on the *Lulan,* smallpox was raging below decks. The Board of Health found the passengers to be "very scantily clad" and most of them were "in extreme poverty." Twenty-four people died a few weeks after their arrival, four or five people were still in hospital, while ninety-seven were reported to be "free from disease." Gordon of Cluny had paid their fares but not their "head tax" and, in the end, the Nova Scotian authorities had to find the £470 owed in addition to the onward travel costs of most of the passengers.[82] These South Uist people could not have had a worse beginning.

Emigration was not an easy option. Sutherland people had to plot and scheme for years to obtain the funds and knowledge they needed to transform themselves from feudal tenants to freeholders in Nova Scotia. They soon demonstrated the Highlander's much-admired facility for adapting to the trying conditions of pioneer life. And, their early successes ensured that a steady stream of people followed them. These people showed an unwavering loyalty to their new communities in Nova Scotia, long after Upper Canada had become the favoured choice of most other emigrant Scots. With its better land, climate and employment opportunities, Upper Canada had far more to offer than Nova Scotia. Without the Sutherland emigrants, the pioneering work of the first arrivals would have petered out. The Inverness-shire and Wester Ross settlers, who had come on the *Hector,* attracted followers for a period, but from the mid-1820s, when Upper Canada was opened up, they lost interest in Nova Scotia. Thereafter it drew its primary intake of Scots from the county of Sutherland.

While Nova Scotia's strongest and most enduring links were with the northern stretches of the Highlands, Cape Breton's intake of Scots came almost entirely from the islands on the west side of the country. By the 1830s it was firmly established as the favoured choice of the many thousands of poor people in the Western Isles who were seeking relief from the dire circumstances confronting them at home. Although they were the poorest of the poor, they were independent spirits with a clear view of their own interests and how to achieve them. They experienced some tough times in their new communities, but they overcame the rigours of early pioneer life and quickly established themselves as successful colonizers.

8

POOR BUT DEFIANT:
CAPE BRETON'S PIONEER SCOTS

Many of our people left their country without the means of
paying their passage, the Captain accepting their note of hand for
payments when they could; when they have been here a few years
round comes the Captain's agent for principal and interest. Money
they cannot have – their cow is taken and perhaps their land...
and the unhappy family must begin a new lot in the forest. At this
moment a majority of settlers have not paid for their grants,
which may sink them in ruin again.[1]

IN HIS TOUR OF CAPE BRETON in the mid-1830s, the Reverend John
Stewart, a Presbyterian minister, saw emigrant Scots who were
living in abject poverty. Having been very poor at the outset, many
had lacked the funds to emigrate. Some people obtained help from
family and friends, who were already settled, but others took the more
desperate step of borrowing their passage money, which at the time
amounted to about £3 per person.[2] Being in debt to some captain or
merchant, they faced the risk of losing their holdings and of never being
able to break the cycle of poverty within which they were snared. To
make matters worse, newly arrived settlers had great difficulty in
acquiring land. Unlike their predecessors who could obtain land on
extremely easy terms, these later arrivals had to buy their land on the

basis of its commercial value. Because land purchase was beyond their means, they squatted. By 1837 more than half of Cape Breton's population was thought to be squatting on Crown land.[3]

New arrivals also had to contend with another major difficulty. Because most of the favourable locations had long since been occupied by earlier waves of settlers, they had to accept holdings "behind the front[ages]," in the inferior backlands, where people "are, in general, extremely poor."[4] In such areas colonizers often had to cope with thin and stony soils which either eroded quickly or were too wet to drain. Settling on poor land and having little or no capital, these backland farmers could eke out a basic living, but they were vulnerable to severe destitution when their crops failed. Their prospects would have been so much better had they gone to western Upper Canada. It had plentiful supplies of good land, offered on easy and secure terms, and far better employment opportunities. Yet thousands of Scots preferred a squatter's perilous existence in Cape Breton to the more comfortable life which Upper Canada could offer. This apparent paradox had mystified the *1841* Emigration Select Committee:

[Chairman] "Are you aware whether the people of the Long Island [Outer Hebrides] would have any preference for any particular part of North America?"
[Duncan Shaw, factor of Harris and North Uist estates] "Yes, Cape Breton."
[Chairman] "Do you think that if they were instructed that [Upper] Canada was a better place for them to go, they would not go there?"
[Duncan Shaw] "I think that they might be induced to go there if they were so instructed; but their principal inducement for preferring to go to Cape Breton is that there are a great many of their own countrymen there."[5]

Thus it was the prospect of living in a home away from home, among people they knew, that drew emigrants to Cape Breton. It was a place where they could follow "the mode of living by cultivation and fishing, [which] is like what they are used to at home."[6]

The cairn at St. Mary's Roman Catholic Church at Big Pond, dedicated to the "Scottish Gaels from Barra and other area of the Highlands who settled in Big Pond and vicinity during the 19th century." *Photograph by Geoff Campey.*

Cape Breton had consistently attracted settlers primarily from the North West Highlands and Islands. The first to come had been Roman Catholics from mainland West Inverness-shire and the islands of South Uist, Barra, Eigg and Canna, who began arriving from 1791. Presbyterians, mainly from the islands of Lewis, Harris, North Uist, Skye, Mull, Tyree,

Rhum Coll and Muck, but some from Wester Ross and northwest Sutherland, dominated the later and much larger influx which began from 1816 and continued into the 1840s. Consequently, even though its land prospects were relatively poor, Cape Breton continued to give Highlanders and Islanders the comforting feeling that their way of life could go on. The "flattering accounts," which filtered back home, reflected the high value being placed on kinship ties and a landscape which was reminiscent of home. Far from attracting "the lame" and "the aged," Cape Breton was getting "chiefly people in the very prime of life."[7]

The good agricultural land along the coast, Bras d'Or Lake and the river valleys were the first to be occupied by emigrant Scots.[8] Small and scattered settlements followed:

"as must be the case from the manner in which the land is granted to them. Along the lakes and rivers of the Island the land is parcelled out in lots of 200 acres each. On each of these lots you have a house so that between every house there is an average of one quarter of a mile; consequently when you hear of a settlement you will understand that a great distance lies between the extremes."[9]

Thus, the various Scottish communities were "divided from one another, here and there in small settlements, by large lakes, arms of the sea, mountains and forests."[10]

They were also divided by religion. Catholics had always predominated along the Western Shore and much of the east side of Bras d'Or, particularly along both sides of the St. Andrews Channel and East Bay. Being the later arrivals, those Presbyterians who came to the Western Shore were forced to settle mainly on the backlands. Presbyterian and Catholic Scots lived in close proximity, but in separate enclaves, at Boularderie, Lake Ainslie, Mira and at Sydney, while large concentrations of Presbyterians were to be found in three distinct areas. They had their communities on the west side of Bras d'Or, principally at St. George's Channel, Malagawatch, River Denys, Whycocomagh, Washabuck, on its north side at Baddeck and Middle River, and on the south side of the Island, at Grand River, Loch Lomond and Framboise. They had also been attracted to those few pockets in the northern extremities, at Cape North and Ingonish, where land suitable for agriculture could be found. Meanwhile the followers of the Reverend Norman MacLeod, who practised their unique brand of Presbyterianism, continued to prosper at St. Anns and North River on the northeast coast (see Figure 8).[11]

Later settlers reinforced these distinct communities, thus creating the various Catholic and Presbyterian enclaves which were revealed so clearly by the Census of 1871 (see Figure 6). However, farming was not the only consideration. As was the case at Pictou, Sydney's coalfields were becoming an increasingly important component of its export trade. Coal production had risen sharply from 1827, when the London-based General Mining Association invested huge amounts of capital in local mines.[12] In 1832, Sydney Mines employed one hundred and seventy-four men, rising to three hundred and seventy-two men by 1838. Mining was also developed at nearby Lingan and Bridgeport, but their production levels were far lower. Even so, by 1838 Bridgeport Mines were employing one hundred and forty-three men. Taken together the coal mines were the largest single employer of men on the island.[13] Predictably these new and expanding employment opportunities attracted Scots to the Sydney area, both as skilled miners and as unskilled labourers. By 1850 most of the colliers employed in the area originated from Scotland.[14]

Great importance was placed throughout Cape Breton on respecting religious boundaries between settlements in spite of the shortage of clergymen and churches. Catholic Highlanders had fared far better than their Presbyterian counterparts. Having been long established at Quebec, the Catholic Church sent missionaries and bishops to Cape Breton from the time the first Scottish settlers had arrived.[15] With their help Catholic Highlanders were able to build eight chapels by 1825 and support resident priests at Judique, Margaree and Broad Cove on the Western Shore, at Grand Narrows on Bras d'Or Lake and at Sydney.[16] But, initially, most Presbyterians in Cape Breton had to fend for themselves.

When Reverend Stewart toured in the mid-1830s, he estimated their number to be "upwards of 11,000." Even though many lacked the means

to maintain ministers or build a church, they still felt a "strong attach-
ment to their mother Church."[17] Their repeated pleas to Scotland for
Presbyterian ministers went unheeded but, by the mid-1820s, the Church
of Scotland was at least in a position to offer practical help when the
"Society (in connection with the Established Church of Scotland) for
Promoting the Religious Interests of Scottish Settlers in British North
America" was founded.[18] Having been established by Glaswegians in
1825, it understandably came to be known by its condensed name – "the
Glasgow Colonial Society." However the Society had to tread very care-
fully in Nova Scotia, where the indigenous and long-established
Presbyterian Church felt alarmed by what it saw as the intrusive activ-
ities of this new missionary group.[19]

Unfortunately, when they emigrated, Scots transferred the existing
internal divisions within the Presbyterian Church to Nova Scotia, which
led to much friction and dissension.[20] The Glasgow Colonial Society was
thus confronted by warring factions in Nova Scotia but, in Cape Breton,
where Presbyterianism was much slower to develop, there were few ten-
sions. While the Society received an unwelcoming response from mainland
Nova Scotia, Cape Breton was desperate to have missionaries. The plight
of its people was graphically described by Reverend John McLennan of
Belfast, Prince Edward Island, and Reverend Donald A. Fraser of East
River, Pictou, two ministers who had been sent, in 1827, by the Scotch
Presbytery of Halifax to tour the island. Their reports, detailing the poverty
of the people and lack of churches and ministers, stirred the Glasgow Colonial Society into action, but after an unsuccessful attempt to establish a
resident minister the Society lost interest.[21] However, the two ministers
had also caught the attention of Mrs. Isabella Gordon MacKay, an Edinburgh lady who was so moved by their reports that she dedicated her life
to raising funds for the Presbyterian Church in Cape Breton.

She founded the "Edinburgh Ladies Association," a group that under-
took to furnish Cape Breton with settled clergymen, churches and schools.
A thin "slightly built" women "with round-ruddy cheeks," Isabella had
enormous drive and a strong sense of duty. Her parents were Highlanders, and this might explain why she felt such sympathy for Cape

Breton Scots, while her husband's wealth and connections gave her the means to realize her philanthropic aims.[22] John Mackay, a minister, was educated at Edinburgh University where he became acquainted with Professor Dugald Stewart, a leading proponent of the so-called Scottish Enlightenment.[23] Perhaps the new thinking, which argued that the problems of the poor needed immediate and radical solutions, had struck a chord with her husband who in turn may have influenced Isabella. Lord Selkirk had grasped the new concepts of social justice and liberty, and offered emigration as a practical remedy for the poor and dispossessed.[24] Isabella would provide poor people, who had already emigrated, with the means to practise their religion and teach their children, believing that by nurturing the soul and mind, their lives would be greatly improved.

She was no empty-headed lady bountiful. She had the lobbyist's political and communication skills and a passionate belief in the importance of her mission. Through its fundraising activities and close collaboration with the Glasgow Colonial Society, the Edinburgh Ladies Association established Presbyterian congregations throughout the whole of Cape Breton. Isabella brought schools, books and churches to the people because she believed that by doing so she would be assisting in the "salvation" of their souls. We, in our modern world, care little for such thinking, but at this time many people were deeply religious and were desperate to have the sort of help that Isabella offered.

Her scheme worked on the principle that once missionaries arrived in Cape Breton and toured the island, they would soon attract parishes willing to employ them as their ministers. She knew that some communities had already built churches, but had failed to find resident clergymen. At Middle River, two hundred acres, intended as glebe land for a clergyman, had been secured and a church had been constructed "in anxious expectation that one day they should obtain a pastor from their beloved Kirk and country."[25] The Lake Ainslie settlers had "transmitted a bond to Scotland for a minister," while the inhabitants of Boularderie Island had already bound "themselves to pay £75 for one half of a Gaelic minister's service. The adjacent settlements are ready to contribute a like sum so that in this instance, likewise, no pecuniary aid will be required." The

Presbytery of Nova Scotia had also appointed ministers and catechists to Cape Breton. The Reverend William Millar worked as a resident minister at Mabou, even though he was "totally unacquainted with Gaelic," while John McCauley was "a travelling catechist about a place called St. Denys."[26] Thus it was case of building on known centres of Presbyterianism and helping them develop congregational structures.

Isabella MacKay used her husband's contacts to get herself heard in the higher echelons of government, but to no avail. Undaunted by this rejection, she extended her campaigning efforts and began collecting funds in earnest through bazaars and by seeking donations.[27] Selling needlework produced by acquaintances in Paisley and Edinburgh, Isabella ran her first bazaar in 1834 at Largs, near Glasgow, which yielded £75. In no time at all the Association was raising enough funds to send out their first missionaries and teachers. Over the next ten years no part of the Maritimes was "more carefully cultivated or more abundantly watered with the ministrations of the Gospel" than Cape Breton.[28] A once-neglected island acquired a great many thriving congregations and schools.[29] After her husband's death, Isabella sold her estate in order to donate even more funds to the Cape Breton mission. Her whole life had centred on the work of the Association. She corresponded directly with each of her ministers and teachers and always responded to their specific requests for financial help. When Reverend Murdoch Stewart visited her in 1842, Isabella was boarding "with a Christian lady – the widow of a Presbyterian Minister...occupying two, or at most three rooms, without a servant of her own, in order that she might be able to give more liberally for the cause of Christ at home and abroad."[30]

Isabella never went to Cape Breton, and it is doubtful that many settlers even knew of her existence. Her religious fervour seems somewhat eccentric in today's world but in her day religion was a dominant force in society. The Presbyterian Church never sought to extend its appeal to other religious denominations but only to preserve its influence within Scottish communities. Because Presbyterianism saw such a narrow role for itself, the extension of its scope and activities greatly reinforced Scottish values and customs. Highland traditions like the annual communal celebration of Communion were carried intact to Cape Breton, bringing thousands of people together to reaffirm their faith.[31] In furthering this and other aspects of Presbyterianism in Cape Breton, Isabella MacKay and her Association gave struggling pioneer communities a vital religious and cultural life-line. Isabella achieved so much; yet her immense contribution went largely unrecognized.

The Reverend Alexander Farquharson, the son of a prosperous Perthshire farmer, was the first of the Association's ministers to become installed, taking up the position of "Gaelic preacher" at Middle River in 1834. His appointment marked the end of a considerable wait by the congregation. Kenneth MacLeod, who was one of the earliest settlers, having arrived in 1814, secured "two hundred acres as glebe for a clergyman of our church," long before the prospect of a Church of Scotland minister was even in their sights.[32] So when Reverend Farquharson reached Middle River with his Bibles and Gaelic books there was already a church in place. He would serve this congregation for over twenty-four years.[33] One of his first duties, which was to tour the island and report on religious deficiencies, enabled him to witness the ongoing influx from Scotland:

> "Bridgeport Mines is ten miles from Sydney, where there are upwards of twenty families of Scotch Presbyterians maintaining a good character amongst Irish and Scotch Roman Catholics. Some are Highlanders from Tyree, Mull etc., and others miners from near Glasgow. There is amongst them a respectable schoolmaster. [At] River Mabou…from twenty to thirty families of Highlanders have lately settled on two branches at the head of this river. A pious man reads to them on the Sabbath."[34]

He met emigrants from Lewis at Washabuck, on the west side of Bras d'Or Lake, and settlers from Rhum at Margaree on the Western Shore. As a result, recent arrivals were scattered throughout the Island, having joined those settlements which best suited their community ties and land requirements.

At a conservative estimate, around 8,000 emigrants came to Cape Breton between 1833 and 1842.[35] Nearly all were Hebridean settlers. Four ships sailed from Stornoway to Sydney in 1831–32, and five ships left from Tobermory in 1832–33, taking a minimum of just over 1,400 emigrants (see Appendix II).[36] Deteriorating economic conditions, following the sharp decline in the kelp industry, from the mid-1820s, and the clearances of people from their holdings to make way for sheep farms, left countless numbers in a perilous and poverty-stricken state. By the early 1830s, when much of Scotland was gripped in an economic depression, large numbers of Scots were emigrating to Upper Canada. However, the Hebridean Islands bucked this trend. As the economic crisis in the Western Isles continued to worsen throughout the 1830s and 1840s, a sizeable proportion of people emigrated to Cape Breton, even though their prospects would have been far better in Upper Canada, which was, by then, getting the majority of all emigrant Scots. Placing a high value on preserving their lifestyles, Hebridean emigrants relinquished their economic prospects for the sake of living within communities that shared their culture and values.

With two successive failures in potatoes and grain crops in 1836 and 1837, people in the Western Isles were being pushed to the very edge of starvation. Poor and vulnerable to disease, many hundreds of them opted for Cape Breton. When the *Clansman* of Glasgow arrived at Sydney in 1836 "with a great number of Scotch emigrants...several of whom...are under the disease of smallpox," emergency measures had to be put in place to contain the spread of the disease. Having failed to observe the quarantine regulations, the captain had allowed his passengers to disembark "at the mouth of the Harbour.... A military force was immediately applied for, and obtained, which accompanied by magistrate, prevented any more persons being landed." It was soon discovered that "the greater number of" the passengers "were entirely destitute of provisions," some having been without food for more than twenty-four hours. They were given aid and said they intended to settle "about two miles or more below the town of Sydney," a place judged, by the customs officials, to be "one of the best" in the vicinity.[37]

The arrival of one hundred and four Sutherland emigrants at St. Anns in November of that same year was followed by an immediate request to the Nova Scotia government for help. Acting as their spokesman, Reverend Norman McLeod wrote a petition emphasizing the difficulties which people in St. Anns were having "at this time of noted scarcity."[38] A severe frost, four months earlier, had devastated potato and grain crops in many backland areas. Obviously, the emigrants had come at a particularly inopportune time. But for Norman they might have gone to Zorra, in western Upper Canada, which was, by then, the favoured destination of most Sutherlanders.[39] However, these were Assynt people, whose ties with St. Anns and Norman MacLeod ran very deep.

The forces of economic depression, particularly the perilous state of the fishing industry in northwest Sutherland, had no doubt been a factor in their decision to emigrate. St. Anns, founded by Assynt people some fifteen years earlier, had obvious advantages. However, judging from Norman MacLeod's comments that he and the other petitioners "had no hand in encouraging these emigrants into this country but have used strong arguments from experience to dissuade them," they were not exactly being welcomed with open arms. Nevertheless they came. Seventy-five people sailed on the *Albion* of Scarborough and the remainder probably travelled on the *Mariner* of Sunderland.[40]

Meanwhile, Reverend John Stewart, the second missionary to be sent out by the Edinburgh Association, was now ensconced at St. George's Channel, having taken up his appointment in 1835. A classical scholar, who spoke only a little Gaelic, he was full of complaints about his many ordeals, but was highly effective. He quickly established a coordinated system of education in his own parish, helped other communities to build churches and led campaigns, in his own area, to secure government funds for better roads and bridges.[41] The next to arrive was Reverend James Frazer, a Sabbath schoolteacher who had worked among the fishing population in Lochinver, in Sutherland. Taking charge of the Boularderie congregation in 1836, he completed his circuit of the island the following year, describing in vivid detail the instances of destitution which he witnessed. The Skye people he encountered at Whycocomagh could not have been in a more pitiful state:

> "In one house was an old man bed-ridden for two years with but one tattered rug or covering to protect him from the cold and the snow drifting in between the logs. His son-in-law, a poor creature who lived with him, occupied much of his time in preparing firewood to keep up a blazing fire…. There are children in abundance who, covered with rags, stretched all night alongside the fire on the floor from having no bed clothes to cover them and a person starts up every other hour to throw a log on the fire."[42]

While such poignant accounts might have assisted Isabella MacKay in her fundraising efforts, they were far from representative of life on the Island. Reverend Stewart was unlikely to have found similar examples of extreme poverty at his base in St. George's Channel, a place with many long-settled people of reasonable affluence. His touring thrust him into those remote and still undeveloped areas where new and recent arrivals struggled with the basics of life. Having arrived in a wretched

McDonald House c. 1830 at Iona Highland Village. It was moved from Stewartdale (Skye River) near Whycocomagh and re-assembled at this site. *Photograph by Geoff Campey.*

state, they settled in backland areas where they could barely support themselves. Reverend Frazer had appeared on the scene just after crop failures had been experienced. Being on the worst land, such failures would have hit them the hardest.

Judging from reports of destitution in the Western Isles, it would seem that the Islands of Tyree and Coll were "worse off than Mull...but it is in Skye and the Long Island [Outer Hebrides] that the greatest distress prevails."[43] When it came time to take the decision to emigrate, North Uist people certainly opted, most emphatically, to go to Cape Breton. Officials at Sydney were kept busy in 1841 dealing with the 1,500 emigrants who arrived that year from Lochmaddy in North Uist.[44] Most were completely destitute, having to rely on friends to get to their final destinations. Seen in a wider context these were emigrants from Lord MacDonald's estate who had been leaving North Uist in large numbers since 1839.[45] Around six hundred people had reached Prince Edward Island by 1841 and now several hundred more were relocating themselves to Cape Breton.[46] They almost certainly received some help with their transport costs from Lord MacDonald and the two Highland Relief Committees which were based in Glasgow and Edinburgh.[47] Fortunately when they got to Cape Breton there had been a good potato harvest, so there was no danger of food shortages and few required government assistance.

In 1840, people from Croick, in Ross-shire, had apparently "been urged to go to Cape Breton, where the people are so happy to have them, as to have promised to make provision for their reception."[48] Dr. Norman McLeod, the energetic Glaswegian clergyman who campaigned so forcefully through his *Gaelic Magazine* in support of Highland emigration to British America, had taken up their cause:

"The whole parish of Croick, in the north, are ready to go – to a man; and their clergyman has resigned his living, stipend, glebe and manse and will set off as soon as the necessary arrangements are entered into to provide a place for their reception and location. Thus the pastor and his whole flock will secure a home where they will not be exposed to a removal in the summary manner in which they have been warned to leave their present possessions.... Out of 350 ready to start, not more than twenty have sufficient means to ensure their own passage. Our [Glasgow] Destitution Committee voted them £250 last Tuesday to aid them in their outfit."[49]

It seems that these Croick people left before they were pushed. In just five years time, the people in neighbouring Glen Calvie would experience wholesale evictions to make way for sheep. Their sad plight was taken up initially by the *Scotsman* but, when their story found coverage in the *Times*, they gained national prominence. However, in spite of this publicity, the evictions proceeded. Some of the evicted families, having nowhere to go, camped beside Croick Church where they scratched a record of their stay on the glass in the church windows. Their eventual fate is unknown.[50]

In 1842, as more poor Scots continued to arrive at Sydney, the Justices of Sydney decided that the time had come to "erect a building...for the relief of newly arrived emigrants."[51] When ships reached Sydney Harbour, the passengers were "often exposed for days and nights on wharfs and beaches until their friends arrived from the interior to carry them away."[52] Something more humane was needed but the money was not forthcoming. Perhaps the government had anticipated that large-scale emigration to Cape Breton was coming to an abrupt end.[53] One of the last of the emigrant ships to leave Scotland was the *Catherine* which set out from Tobermory in 1843.

It could not have been a worse crossing. Problems occurred soon after she left. "After having been ten days at sea, the ship, through stress of weather, sprung a leak and was compelled to put back to Ireland to refit where she was detained ten or twelve days."[54] The three hundred passengers then transferred to the *John and Robert* and after "a very tedious passage they at length, in the Fall of 1843, arrived in the Gut of Canso [at Ship Harbour], most of them in a very destitute condition" Given that they had first set sail in May it really had been a lengthy voyage. The emigrants petitioned the Assembly for help and received £50 to buy seed potatoes in order to begin "their occupation of the wilderness lands." They "dispersed themselves here and there amongst their friends" and settled in Inverness County.[55]

Calvin Presbyterian Church, Loch Lomond, built in 1910. *Photograph by Geoff Campey.*

Most of the new arrivals to Cape Breton in the 1840s had originated from the Outer Hebrides, particularly from North Uist, but also from South Uist, Harris, Berneray and Pabbay, the latter two being islands to the south of Harris. Emigrants from Pabbay opened up new settlements at Cape North while Roman Catholics from South Uist went principally to the Sydney area, especially Sydney Mines, Mira, Gabarus Lake and East Bay.[56] Presbyterians from Harris and Berneray joined long-established communities at St. Anns, North River, Loch Lomond, Grand River and Framboise. Having acquired forty-three "Scottish Highlander" families by 1827, Grand River and Loch Lomond already had well-established Scottish communities by this time.[57] Many years later, in 1840, the *Cape Breton Advocate* would remind its readers of the area's Hebridean origins and describe the "large and neat-looking church" in what was then a "beautiful and thriving settlement."[58]

As more emigrant Scots arrived, the Edinburgh Ladies Association continued to extend its missionary program throughout Cape Breton. Having brought three Presbyterian ministers to Middle River, St. George's Channel and Boularderie by 1836, their fundraising and recruitment efforts intensified over the next decade. By the early 1850s they had established further congregations at Margaree, Malagawatch, St. Anns, the North West Arm of Bras d'Or, Loch Lomond and at South Sydney, Mira and Catalone.[59] Isabella MacKay's aim of providing Cape Breton with full-time ministers, lay catechists and teachers, presiding over Sabbath and Day schools and itinerant libraries, had finally become a reality. Reverend Hugh McLeod was the last of Isabella's missionaries, taking up his appointment at Mira Ferry in 1850. There he ministered to five hundred families who constituted nearly half the population of Cape Breton County.[60]

Disaster struck parts of Cape Breton between 1845 and 1849 when potato blight (or rot) devastated its crops.[61] As ever, it was the newly arrived, with the worst land, who suffered most. While the government's food aid in the form of flour, meal and seed potatoes ensured that few starved, the devastation suffered by backland farmers was considerable. Many of them, having arrived as destitute Scottish crofters, found themselves once more in dire poverty. Some had to sell their livestock and mortgage their land, falling deeply into debt. But farms on the better lands were relatively unscathed by the disease and many actually benefited from rising grain prices. And although conditions were grim, the suffering was relatively minor compared with the devastation being experienced in western Europe. The same disease, which appeared at roughly the same time, had a particularly lethal impact in the west Highlands and Islands, as well as in Ireland. Having climatic conditions and terrain which greatly encouraged the spread of the deadly spores, these areas suffered a great famine, on a scale not seen for hundreds of years. For almost a decade the potato crops failed, leaving thousands of people vulnerable to malnutrition and severe destitution.[62]

The blight had its most disastrous impact on the poorer crofting districts where dependence on the potato was greatest. These areas had the least resistance and fewest alternative resources. A huge exodus followed as deteriorating circumstanced caused around 11,000 people to emigrate to British North America in the decade from 1846 to 1856. While some people left unassisted, most were given financial help by landlords and various philanthropic societies. The main impact was felt in the Outer Hebridean Islands of Lewis, Barra, Benbecula and South Uist which together lost around 5,000 people, and in the Inner Hebridean Islands of Tyree and Mull, which lost around 2,300 people.[63] Surprisingly, these people did not go to Cape Breton, where they had many long-established communities, but went instead to Upper Canada. Anticipating their arrival, the Lieutenant Governor of Nova Scotia had intervened. Cape Breton could simply not cope with any more poor emigrants.

In 1847, at the height of the Cape Breton famine, Sir John Harvey wrote to Earl Grey, the Colonial Secretary, explaining that "this province is in no respect prepared for the reception of poor people...suffering as it is under the scarcity produced by the failure in the potato and grain crops in the last two seasons...those resorting to it, in the expectation of ameliorating their conditions, would be grievously disappointed."[64] The intervention had an immediate impact. Through press announcements and instructions sent to customs officials and emigration agents in Scotland, the Nova Scotia government headed off a further influx of pauper emigrants. While large numbers of destitute Scots arrived at Pictou in the following year, they avoided Cape Breton.[65]

That same year the *Presbyterian Witness* expressed its disapproval of what it saw as "the general prejudice against the emigration to Cape Breton. It is our decided opinion, founded upon pretty extensive observation, that Cape Breton is, generally speaking, superior in agricultural resources to any portion of the Lower Provinces," now known as Atlantic Canada. The newspaper was probably worried over the loss of Presbyterians, who would otherwise have come from the Hebridean Islands at this time, but nevertheless it was making a genuine point. Much of Cape Breton had good agricultural potential. While a great deal of poverty was to be found, most settlers were making a reasonable living from the land. The large numbers of petitions being sent to the Provincial Secretary asking for financial help in building mills, kilns and roads reveal a positively motivated population striving to improve their lot. These were the actions of people who had a stake in their future. Even in height of the famine, the losses being experienced in the backlands of Lake Ainslie were of substantial numbers of cattle and sheep. While there is no suggestion of great affluence, those claiming losses were not necessarily operating at the lowest levels of subsistence. People were usually willing to repay any help they got and were not simply looking for handouts. And when it came to raising funds, during the famine years, for the establishment of the Free Church College of Nova Scotia, it was the Cape Breton Presbytery which came forward more generously than any other part of the province.[66]

It is known from official papers that Cape Breton had great difficulties in dealing with destitute newcomers and in grappling with the effects of the potato famine, but this source should not be allowed to cloud the overall impression of its rural society. Some, but not necessarily most, people were being plunged into the depths of despair and extreme poverty. Reverend Norman McLeod had been quick to criticize what he saw as the excessive misrepresentation of conditions on the island by the Edinburgh Ladies Association's missionaries.[67] As far as he was concerned, they magnified the true situation in order to justify their own labours and the need for more missionaries. Equally, when the potato famine took hold, there are dangers in exaggerating its impact beyond the scraggy backlands where people struggled with the worst conditions imaginable on the island. They may not have significantly bettered their standard of living but they, at least, had their independence. Instead of living in an oppressive feudal society, which took their money and labours and gave them nothing but unremitting toil and subjugation in return, they now had some hope of a better future.

Moreover, these pioneer Scots were not without their entrepreneurs. Norman McLeod and his group of settlers had been building small fishing boats from the time they arrived at St. Anns. Graduating to bigger ocean-going ships, John Munro completed the 440-ton *Chieftain* by 1845, while John McLeod built the 247-ton *Norman* a year later. Then

John Munro completed the 725-ton *Flora* in 1848, one of the largest sailing vessels ever built in Cape Breton. With his fleet of ships, John Munro sent local timber to Scotland and in return received a range of food and manufactured goods which he could sell in his store.[68] Yet even with these obvious signs of prosperity and a vibrant local economy, all was not well in St. Anns.

Typically, Norman McLeod saw the blight as the Almighty's punishment for the misdeeds of his people. It was the "unthriftness and offensive indolence" of those who "can well feed and flutter, dress and dandle and carelessly chafe away with toddy and tobacco" which had caused "the Giver of all Good" to send "this disease of the potato."[69] While McLeod later escaped to New Zealand with his band of loyal followers, sixteen family heads from St. Anns took a more considered view.[70] They petitioned the government to pay for their relocation to Upper Canada, explaining that:

> "some of your petitioners are younger branches of families that emigrated to this Island about twenty years ago and who could not get land fit for supporting them after becoming of years and others of your petitioners have only emigrated from the Highlands in later years when all the good lots were also occupied thus keeping your petitioners in a constant state of dependence…. That the chief part of your petitioners have large families and owing to the failure of the crops of years past, found it difficult to get means of sustenance."[71]

Government funding was almost certainly not forthcoming. In any case these people were not on the brink of starvation. They simply wanted better land. Captain Donald McNeil, who lived at Mira River, would gladly have sold his 500-acre farm if he could get sufficient money from it "to bring us up to [Upper] Canada and purchase a small farm." He too, was seeking economic self-improvement. His youngest brother was a partner "in a mercantile house in Sydney," while his sister was married to a doctor who was employed by the General Mining Association at the Sydney coal mines.[72] They hardly qualify as a destitute family.

Thus, while the blight may have triggered off a desire to leave Cape Breton, those who reacted in this way were not necessarily facing imminent destitution. Another factor in the growing exodus from Cape Breton was the great difficulty being experienced in acquiring land. "The sole concern" of the many Highland families who moved during the 1840s to the Codroy Valley in southwest Newfoundland had been "to own a piece of land." Having settled in the Broad Cove and Margaree areas, along the Western Shore, they lived there but owned no land:

> "Although it was due to hardships they met with in Cape Breton that the Scots left and migrated to Newfoundland, it was not hard work which deterred them.... The most important thing was that they could at last own land."[73]

A study of the Cape Breton influx from the Highlands and Islands of Scotland inevitably focuses attention on the famine years and the hardships of the poorest settlers. However, the really intriguing aspect of this huge migration of people was not so much their poverty as the intensity of their loyalty to Cape Breton. Even when they there was uncertainty over whether they could acquire land, that most basic of all emigrant needs, they still came. They had resisted the prospects of the far better conditions that Upper Canada could offer for some twenty years. In the height of the potato famine the provincial authorities actually had to take steps to stop them from coming to Cape Breton. A desire to preserve their way of life outweighed any financial advantage they hoped to gain from emigrating. One suspects that, without the intervention of the Lieutenant Governor, the many thousands of Hebridean people who emigrated, during the decade from 1846 to 1856, would have continued to go to Cape Breton.

9
SHIPS AND ATLANTIC CROSSINGS

The plan you mention of getting a cargo of men and lassies and
bring back timbers might do well – the thing to consider is could
you get a cargo anywhere in the Highlands – McDonald and
elders at Skye used to be agents in this way and may assist you.[1]

JAMES MACALPIN, A TIMBER MERCHANT from Corpach, near Fort
William, had followed this plan once before. In 1817, his ship, the
Ardgour of Fort William, had sailed off to Quebec with 108 emigrants and almost certainly returned with a timber cargo.[2] Now MacAlpin
was searching for emigrants to take out once again. Like many other
shipowners, he sought to profit from this two-way traffic in timber and
emigrants. It was essentially a very simple process. Timber was loaded
into the ship's hold one-way and emigrants were accommodated in the
same hold the other way. Temporary wooden planking was placed over
cross beams and carpenters were called in to build temporary berths
along the sides. This was how most emigrants crossed the Atlantic. They
travelled as steerage passengers, below deck, in what were usually cramped
and uncomfortable conditions. There were no portholes, nor any means
of ventilation beyond the hatches. And, in stormy seas, the hatches could
be kept battened down for days.

However, because conditions were this basic, it should not be concluded
that emigrants were deliberately made to suffer by the people who

provided the shipping services. By looking more closely at the *Ardgour*, it can be determined that it was a brand new 166-ton snow, having been built in Fort William in 1817. Not only that, the insurance company, Lloyd's of London, had given it a top "A1" rating for the quality of its construction.[3] It was, in fact, one of the many new vessels being built at the time to meet the needs of the explosive growth in the North American timber trade. These emigrants had actually sailed to Quebec in a top-quality vessel.

Yet emigrant sea crossings seem always to conjure up a lurid image of brutal captains, leaky ships and wretched conditions. Travelling by sea at this time did come with many perils and discomforts. The accommodation was cramped, the legal requirement for the floor-to-ceiling height (between-deck) being only five-and-a-half feet, disease could flare up at any time, and most people succumbed to long bouts of seasickness. And there was little or no regulation of the services. Legislation had been in place from 1803, stipulating minimum space and food requirements for passengers, but there was no practical way of enforcing these regulations and they were therefore frequently ignored.[4] Against this backdrop we would expect emigrants to be easy prey for unscrupulous ship owners but this was not so. To get repeat business shippers needed good personal recommendation from emigrants and to achieve this they had to maintain good standards.

While conditions below deck could be grim, it should be remembered that this was a time when most people were accustomed to poor living conditions. Overcrowding and rudimentary sanitary facilities were facts of life. Finding such hardships on a ship was nothing new. The real question is whether steps were taken to minimize the emigrants' discomfort and suffering. A shipowner could not control the weather but he could choose the ship and captain, thereby setting the standard of service for the voyage. He could also choose to limit the numbers he allowed on board to avoid overcrowding. Did most emigrants travel in well-constructed ships, with adequate accommodation space, under experienced and caring captains? This is the ultimate test.

The two hundred and thirteen ships, identified in this study as having carried emigrant Scots to Nova Scotia and Cape Breton, are to be scrutinized. Fortunately, details of the quality of construction of the vessels used, and their condition, can be obtained from the *Lloyd's Shipping Register*, a documentary source which dates back to the late eighteenth century.[5] As major insurers, Lloyd's of London needed reliable shipping intelligence, which it procured through the use of paid agents in the main ports in Britain and abroad. Vessels were inspected by Lloyd's surveyors and assigned a code according to the quality of their construction and maintenance.[6] These codes were then used by insurers and shipowners to determine levels of risk and freight rates. Shipowners actually complained that the codes were too stringent, particularly in the way that a ship's age and place of construction could affect its classification.[7] Today these classification codes can be used to determine the overall quality of emigrant ships in the late eighteenth and early nineteenth centuries.

Because of gaps and inconsistencies in shipping sources, the identification of shipping codes can never be an exact science.[8] Shipping codes have been located for one hundred and thirty-eight of the two hundred and thirteen ships known to have carried emigrants from Scotland to Nova Scotia and Cape Breton – making this a substantial sample of the ships used (see Appendix III). Sixty-nine of the one hundred and thirty-eight ships with known codes were recently built first-class ships ("A1" code). A further thirteen were ranked just below the top rating. They had no defects, but their age put them just beyond the reach of an "A1" designation.[9] Thus a total of eighty-two ships, representing sixty per cent of the ships with known codes, were of the highest quality. Most of the remaining ships had an "E," or second class ranking, signifying that they were seaworthy, although they had minor defects. Only four ships – the *Hector* (in 1773), the *Lovelly Nelly* (in 1774–75), the *Tweed* of Ullapool (in 1802) and the *Elizabeth and Ann* of North Shields (in 1806) – were assessed as having been unsuitable for ocean travel. Their crossings had been some of the earliest. No examples were found of unsuitable ships after 1806. The popular image of leaky and sub-standard vessels is simply not born out by the evidence.

The *Lloyd's Shipping Register* thus gives us unequivocal evidence that emigrants were not offered the worst ships as is generally believed. Most

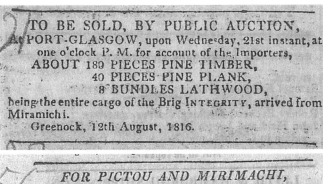

TO BE SOLD, BY PUBLIC AUCTION,
At PORT-GLASGOW, upon Wednesday, 21st instant, at
one o'clock P. M. for account of the Importers,
ABOUT 180 PIECES PINE TIMBER,
40 PIECES PINE PLANK,
8 BUNDLES LATHWOOD,
being the entire cargo of the Brig INTEGRITY, arrived from
Miramichi.
Greenock, 12th August, 1816.

FOR PICTOU AND MIRIMACHI,
The Brig INTEGRITY,
Captain EMMERSON,
burthen 163 tons, daily expected to arrive, and
will be dispatched in ten days. Shippers and
passengers may rely on there being no delay, as
the Vessel will sail with or without freight.
Apply to G. M'Gregor, Tontine Buildings, Glasgow; or
here, to
WILLIAM GALBRAITH.
Greenock, 24th July, 1816.

Advertisements in the *Glasgow Courier* (August 1816). *Top*, for the sale of
the *Integrity*'s Miramichi timber; *bottom*, the announcement of her return
voyage to Pictou and Miramichi. *Courtesy of The Trustees of the National
Library of Scotland.*

emigrants actually sailed in top-quality ships. Shipowners could have cut
their costs by offering inferior vessels but if they had done so, they would
have had no repeat business. Because emigrants were in such demand,
competition between shippers worked in the emigrants' favour. Even so,
ships were not selected with emigrants in mind. They were chosen solely
for their stowage capabilities and manoeuvrability in heavy seas. The needs
of passengers were quite secondary. They were just another cargo to be
taken on a westward journey. However, conditions for passengers improved
from the late 1820s, with the arrival of so-called "regular traders."[10]

Regular traders were more specialized vessels, being designed to handle
a wide range of cargoes and to accommodate around thirty passengers in
their cabins. They included vessels like the *Aberdeenshire* of Aberdeen and
Albion of Aberdeen, which sailed once or twice a year from Aberdeen to
Halifax, often arriving with small numbers of emigrants (see Appendix II).[11]

The *Acadian* of Glasgow and *Jean Hastie* of Grangemouth also crossed regularly to Halifax, leaving from Greenock, and occasionally taking small numbers of passengers. However, few emigrants could afford to pay for the extra space and privacy which cabins provided and between them, regular traders took only a tiny minority of the total number of emigrants who went to Nova Scotia or Cape Breton. Perhaps up to one or two thousand emigrant Scots went as cabin passengers to Halifax.[12] But many more thousands travelled as steerage passengers in the holds of timber ships. Unlike the regular traders, which crossed the Atlantic several times, most timber ships made a once-only appearance.[13] But, although the ships made fleeting appearances, the emigration agents who procured them were more permanent fixtures.

Agents were much vilified at the time for exploiting emigrants. Anti-emigration campaigners depicted them as opportunistic money-grubbers who performed no useful function, yet got large sums of money out of vulnerable and misguided emigrants. But the reality was quite different.[14] They were the vital lynch pin in the overall process. Because of the huge spare capacity on westward-bound routes, competition for emigrant fares was brisk. Acting as middlemen, the agents agreed on established terms and conditions with individual shipowners. Emigrants were sent

Halifax, Nova Scotia, c. 1840. Painting by John Stevenet Clow. *Courtesy of the National Archives of Canada, C-042271.*

a succession of ships, which had the appearance of a purpose-built shipping fleet, but, of course, they had no common owner and rarely did the same journey more than once. But the agent would have sought a consistent standard of shipping. Because his repeat business depended on a good "word of mouth" recommendation, he was under pressure to provide good ships and reliable captains.

The emigrants covered in this study left behind only snippets of information relating to their crossings. However, what is available is mainly positive. Some of the earliest feedback comes from the Hebridean emigrants who began sailing in large numbers to Pictou and Sydney, from 1816, once the Napoleonic Wars had ended. The 285 emigrants who sailed from Tobermory to Pictou in 1819, on the *Economy* of Aberdeen, praised Captain Frazier's "kind treatment" during a five-week passage, while the *Acadian Recorder* found them to have "landed in good health and spirits."[15] Captain Murray's "humane treatment" when in charge of the *Glentanner* of Aberdeen in 1820, and the "fine quality of the ship's' provisions" won commendations, as did Captain Watt who was at the helm of the *Emperor Alexander* of Aberdeen when she sailed from Tobermory to Sydney in 1823.[16] And, in charge of the *Hercules,* which took 122 passengers from Stornoway to Pictou in 1837, had been Duncan Walker, "a very clever, shrewd man with a good deal of experience."[17] Overseeing all of these crossings was Archibald McNiven, the man who took over Simon Fraser's role as the principal emigration agent for the northwest coast and the Hebridean Islands.

Looking back over the previous twenty years in 1841, McNiven announced that he had arranged ships for some 16,000 emigrants. Nearly 7,000 of the 12,000 or so emigrants he acted for, between 1820 and 1832, had gone to Cape Breton.[18] In 1826, he had organized a petition to Parliament on behalf of some 1,600 people in Mull, Benbecula, Barra and North Uist, who requested financial help to emigrate.[19] They failed to get public funds, but the great surge in the numbers who sailed to Sydney from Stornoway in 1828–29, when there were at least four crossings with around 1000 passengers, shows that they proceeded anyway, and on ships organized by McNiven.

The North East Highlands also experienced a steady exodus of people from 1815. Situated as it was midway between the Dornoch and Moray firths and having an excellent harbour, Cromarty became the principal collecting port for emigrants. Atlantic-bound ships from Aberdeen, Leith, Dundee and other eastern ports would call for them at Cromarty and, as the service developed, Thurso became a second collecting point (see Appendix II). However, serious problems occurred on one of the first sailings from Cromarty. The captain of the *Ann* of Banff, which sailed in 1819 with sixty passengers, actually faced criminal charges for the inadequate provisioning of his ship.[20] William Allan, a Leith ship broker, took charge of the service shortly after this and, when he did, emigrant crossings went far more smoothly and with little incident. When one of Allan's ships, the *Jane Kay* arrived at Pictou from Cromarty and Thurso in 1833 with 106 passengers, they were said to be "all in good health"[21]

But Allan's reputation took a severe knock in 1836 when the *Mariner* of Sunderland arrived at Quebec. Sixty-seven of the one hundred and forty-five passengers, who arrived from Thurso and Loch Eriboll, complained bitterly

The Emigration Stone at Cromarty, designed and carved by Richard Kindersley, 2002. The names of 39 ships which collected emigrants from Cromarty are carved around the edges. The inscription is from Hugh Miller's report in the *Inverness Courier* of the sailing of the *Cleopatra* in June 1831. *Courtesy of Richard Kindersley.*

that they thought that William Allan was going "to bring them out to Pictou."[22] This mix-up can be blamed on the changing focus of the timber trade which, by then, was firmly rooted in New Brunswick and the Saint Lawrence region. Most of the timber ships, which took passengers, were now Quebec-bound and, unless emigration agents stipulated that Pictou or Sydney stopoffs were required, their routes would not be altered. By the 1840s, when very few ships were advertised as calling at Pictou, agents were reduced to offering Quebec departures with "a safe and cheap conveyance" which would take emigrants back to Pictou only after they had landed at Quebec.[23]

With the great distress caused by the *Mariner*'s failure to berth first at Pictou being a possible factor, Allan's commanding position as an emigration agent for the Highlands came to an abrupt end. Taking over from him were Duncan MacLennan and John Sutherland, both of whom lived in the Highlands. MacLennan was an Inverness lawyer while Sutherland worked as the Wick agent for the British Fisheries Society, a body which promoted employment opportunities in fishing. Having lived for twenty years in Nova Scotia, Sutherland made great play of his personal knowledge of its opportunities.[24] What feedback exists about the partners is mainly favourable. The *Pictou Observer*'s welcome, in 1840, to the "140 passengers, chiefly from Sutherland-shire" who arrived at Pictou on the *Deveron* of Glasgow could not have been warmer. "They appear in excellent health and spirits and we hope will soon bury their regrets for their fatherland in prosperity and independence."[25] And the 191 emigrants who sailed to Pictou, two years later, on the *Superior* of Peterhead, under Captain Donald Manson, were particularly fulsome in their praise. The captain's "humane and gentlemanly conduct was such as will accrue for him a place in our remembrance while we live, in whatever corner of the globe providence may order our lot."[26]

However, the plight if the emigrants on board the *Lady Grey* of North Shields, when she arrived at Pictou in 1841, could not have been worse. Only seventy-five of her two hundred and forty passengers were due to disembark at Pictou, but because conditions were so bad it was decided to move everyone on shore, both sick and healthy, to allow the ship to be cleaned and fumigated before she went on to Quebec. Typhus had afflicted twenty-six passengers and there were six deaths. Two years later, the *Halifax Times* published an anonymous letter written by a Pictou gentleman, which recalled the "green hillocks in the grave yard at Carriboo Beaches" where the dead had been buried and the resultant consequences for Pictou. "The *Lady Grey* cost the Province upwards of five hundred pounds and Pictou one of its most estimable inhabitants – Dr. Martin, health officer at the port," who had caught the typhus.[27]

The *Times* correspondent made no mention of Captain William Grey's behaviour. As far as he was concerned, overcrowding was the sole issue. There is no doubt that her passenger to tonnage ratio was woefully over the limit. With the regulations stipulating five tons for every three passengers, she, as a 285-ton snow, should have had no more than 171 passengers, when in fact she carried 240 people. However, this is one of those very rare occasions where we actually have the emigrants' account of what happened. Strange as it may seem, their report makes no mention at all of overcrowding. They put the blame entirely on Captain Grey's inability to manage the vessel.

Soon after settling sail from Thurso, "a committee consisting of seven persons were chosen, who framed rules and regulations, for the better securing of cleanliness and good order on board, during the voyage, who agreed that all complaints should be laid before Captain Grey, who was requested to see such regulations put into force."[28] However, Captain Grey took no notice of them in spite of repeated complaints of "the inefficient state of the privies on deck" and general "want of cleanliness on board." Captain J.F. Simpson (a passenger, who was the Committee Chairman) was in no doubt that "the cause of sickness on board arose from the passengers having caught cold on deck in consequence of the decks being always wet and in a filthy condition…he conceived it to be the duty of the captain of the ship to see that the ship was kept in order."[29] Captain Grey insisted that his job was simply to get the vessel to Pictou and that he was not responsible for its cleanliness. But he should have been. Fortunately, his appalling behaviour was fully detailed in the *Mechanic and Farmer,* for the benefit of those who would follow:

> "Intending emigrants...will do well, previous to leaving their native homes, to enquire into the character and disposition of the masters of vessels, they intend sailing in, upon whom in a great measure, depends the lives of themselves and families, whilst under their charge."[30]

When the *George* of Dundee arrived at Pictou in August 1843, it looked as if MacLennan and Sutherland had another disastrous crossing on their hands. Arriving with 307 passengers, 95 of whom left at Pictou, the remainder sailing on to Quebec, the ship reeked of disease. Pictou health officials found conditions below deck "almost intolerable." Commenting on her arrival, our same anonymous *Times* correspondent was certain that unscrupulous agents were to blame for the "additional source of infection" which Pictou now had to contend with:

> "We have had occasion to observe a variety of circumstances in which the Emigration Act has been shamefully violated by those who call themselves agents.... The persons who are sent out in the capacity of surgeons are often no more than useless apothecaries apprentices, some of them addicted to drunkenness...the space between the platform and the lowest tiers of berths is seldom or ever what the Act requires...it is seldom that...the steerage passengers are furnished, as the law directs, with a copy of the Emigration Act, so they are left in ignorance of their rights...the water casks are old and have materials adhering to them which speedily taint the water and render it useless or worse...the proportion between the tonnage and the number of passengers is seldom observed. And in such cases nothing can be more convenient that touching at Cape Breton or Pictou when on their way to Quebec."[31]

However, this unsubstantiated diatribe can be contrasted with the comments made by the emigrants themselves. When the remaining passengers got to Quebec, they told Archibald Buchanan, the Quebec Immigration Agent, that because the *George* had called at three ports – Cromarty, Thurso and Loch Laxford, some passengers "were from 12 to 13 weeks on board and complained much of the detention they experienced owing to the vessel calling at so many ports, which they state they were not aware of when they engaged their passage." They were also detained some days owing to the sickness among the passengers and arrived here [Quebec] the 88th day from Dundee."[32] As a result, their provisions were hopelessly inadequate and they "arrived destitute of means." Thus there was a passing reference to illness, but what had really concerned them was the unexpectedly long journey time.

Looking more closely at the criticisms made by the *Times* correspondent, it is clear that these were baseless accusations. The *George's* Captain Frances Hanley, who would have overseen the passengers' medical needs, was apparently "well known for his kindness and attention to passengers."[33] Having a tonnage of 676 tons and carrying 307 passengers, she was well within her passenger to tonnage limit. Having some eight feet between decks and being one hundred and twenty fix feet long, this newly built ship was the epitome of spaciousness. Her headroom was far more generous than the legal limit, which was only five feet six inches. Being slightly ahead of her time, she offered accommodation in a second cabin which gave emigrants access to an intermediate standard, between cabin class and steerage.[34] Yes, the drinking water was foul-tasting because it was always stored for the duration of any journey in crude wooden casks. Emigrants had to accept this and they did what they could to counter the water's offensive taste by adding vinegar.

What about the "shameful" behaviour of "those who call themselves agents"? The agents were, of course, MacLennan and Sutherland. Sutherland usually managed the Pictou departures, and his reputation could not have been higher. The *Lady Emily* passengers, who sailed with him in the previous year, praised his "strict and unremitting attention to our health and comfort during a voyage protracted by calms and contrary winds. Particularly do we appreciate the kindness of Captain Stove, who at the sacrifice of his personal comforts, supplied some of us with the means of subsistence out of his own stores for a period of 20 days, and if he should continue in future to bring out passengers for Mr. Sutherland, we shall have great pleasure in recommending such of our friends as may be disposed to follow us to this, the land of our adoption, to take passage with Captain Stove." And they went on:

"In returning our warmest thanks to Mr. Sutherland for his uniform kindness and attention to our wants and requirements, we cannot help stating that from what we have seen of this country since we entered the port of Canso, we are convinced that the advantages held out by Mr. Sutherland to the poor and oppressed peasantry of Scotland may be realised by any sober and industrious person; and we trust that Mr. Sutherland may be successful in inducing thousands of our fellow countrymen to follow us."[35]

Back in Scotland, when news filtered through of the *Lady Emily's* safe arrival, the *John O'Groat Journal,* added its eulogies as well:

"The northern counties of Scotland are peculiarly indebted to Mr. Sutherland for laying on his vessels in this part of the country – for before he established himself, those desirous of emigrating had to bear the expense of removal to Greenock, which equalled if not exceeded the whole sum now charged for the passage to America. Nearly 2,000 emigrants have been sent out by him within two years in vessels of the first class. So far as we know Mr. Sutherland has left behind him a character for uprightness and integrity. His conduct to the poorer classes of emigrants has been very praiseworthy – he very frequently granted free passages to many members of a family where the head of it could not command sufficient means to carry them all out."[36]

Thus, the anonymous letter-writer, although totally uninformed of the facts, had hit out at the standard of shipping being offered to emigrants.

175

While allying himself with the plight of poor emigrants, his real motivation may have been closer to home. Pictou's inhabitants were growing weary of receiving the large numbers of desperately poor Scots, who were becoming a major burden on public finances. By decrying the overall process in this way, he may have hoped to add to the growing pressure being exerted on the British government to limit numbers on emigrant ships. However, in so doing, he was not necessarily furthering the interests of emigrant Scots. The evidence that does exist from them suggests that the shipper's low price, high volume policy suited them. They put a far higher premium on low fares than on having their creature comforts.

While the emigration agents played an essential role in coordinating services in the Highlands and Islands, they were only fixers. At sea everything depended on the captain's navigational skills and his attitude to his passengers. When emigrants relayed information about their crossings, highest priority was always given to the captain. A captain like Alexander Leslie, who was in charge of the *Albion* of Aberdeen during her many crossings between Aberdeen and Halifax from 1829 to 1853, soon built up a high reputation. The "unremitted assiduity with which Captain Leslie attended to our comfort during a tedious, stormy passage," on the *Albion*'s Spring crossing in 1836, earned him this accolade from his passengers:

"While we do not presume that we can add to the character which Captain Leslie has long since earned, and fully established on both sides of the Atlantic, we deem it a debt of gratitude due to him thus publicly to express our approbation of his conduct and we would strongly recommend to emigrants and others crossing the Atlantic to do so by the *Albion*, as from experience we can assure them that under the command of Captain Leslie the greatest care will be paid to their comfort and safety."[37]

Strong gales were a fairly common occurrence, but there were also occasions when the earliest ships to go out in the Spring could become ensnared in large icefields. Here again passenger survival depended on

Aberdeen Harbour from the Dock Gates, looking towards the city. Photograph by George Washington Wilson c. 1877. *Copyright of George Washington Wilson Collection, Aberdeen University.*

the captain's skill and cool head. When the *Thetis* "got caught in ice and was carried on the rocks in the vicinity of Arichat" as she approached the Strait of Canso in April, 1829, it had been possible to rescue all of the passengers.[38] The *Isabella* of Glasgow had a similar encounter with ice in 1842. Having first taken control of a disorderly crew, including an inebriated cook, "who struck one of the boys," her captain, Alexander Thomas, had to guide the *Isabella* through "a large field of ice" which was encountered near St. Paul's Island, off Cape Breton.[39] When she became "uncommandable, being jammed in the ice" a small boat with four passengers was sent ashore "to get information as there was houses to be seen from the ship," but they were uninhabited. "Three men belonging to a schooner that was beset in the ice off Cape North came on board and gave such dangerous information of the place which made the passengers make every preparation for going on shore." The following morning he and his crew put the passengers on boats and rowed them the three-quarter-mile distance to Aspy Bay.[40] Captain Thomas and his crew had saved their lives. And by grabbing his log book, as he abandoned ship, the captain saved the one piece of evidence which would prove that he had acted responsibly in all the circumstances.[41]

Next in importance to a good captain, was a reasonable standard of accommodation. From the late 1820s there had been a gradual move towards larger and roomier ships, although emigrants had to wait until 1842 before the legal limit of the floor to ceiling space, between decks, was raised to six feet. Before then the only stipulation was that "ships are not allowed to carry passengers to the Colonies unless they be of the height of five and a half feet between decks."[42] Again there are only odd snippets of data for the ships covered in this study. But what is available shows that many ships provided a space, between decks, well in excess of the legal limit. Even as early as 1817 the *Prompt* could offer six feet between decks, the *Tamarlane*, sailing in 1826, had seven feet, the *Romulus* offered 8 feet in 1831, the *Zephr* had upwards of seven feet in 1833, while the *Hercules* offered six feet three inches in 1837.[43] And the fact that the *Corsair* of Greenock was said to have "a high and roomy space between decks" may explain why she was used on four occasions, between 1827 and 1838, to carry substantial numbers of emigrants. While most timber ships were used only once, the *Corsair* carried 80 emigrants to Halifax on one crossing, 218 emigrants to Pictou and Quebec on a second crossing and 450 emigrants to Canso and Sydney on two further crossings.[44] However, in addition to vertical space, the question of overcrowding must also be considered. Here, the territory is more contentious and uncertain.

An overriding priority for emigrants was to have low fares.[45] Shippers wanted high volume and, to achieve this, many would lower their fares. Three hundred and forty people had been packed into the hold of the 240 ton *Northern Friends* of Clyde when she sailed, from Moidart to Sydney, in 1801. No doubt the emigrants had negotiated cheap fares but in doing so, they endured very overcrowded conditions. The *Northern Friends* was some three times over her legal limit when judged against the terms of the 1803 Passenger Act, which required two tons per person. While the 1803 legislation did reduce overcrowding for a period, its space requirements were relaxed in 1817, to one and one half tons per person, as a result of pressure from shipowners and agents. This was hailed in some quarters, as a great step forward because it enabled shipowners to reduce their fares:

"We are anxious to state what we believe is not generally known, that the Bill which has recently had the Royal assent gives great facilities to persons who are desirous of proceeding as settlers to ... North America, in as much as by reducing the tonnage to be allowed to each individual during the passage it enables the masters of vessels...to take passengers at a much lower rate than has been hitherto demanded."[46]

However, one effect of lowering the space limits was to produce odd examples of severe overcrowding, which were reminiscent of the pre-1803 days. The 141 ton *Morningfield* of Aberdeen, which sailed, in 1819, from Tobermory to Pictou with 264 emigrants, was actually three times over her legal limit. Regulations were tightened up in 1823 but were repealed once again, in response to continuing commercial pressures and, by 1828, the passenger-to-tonnage ratio was three passengers for every four tons. While the limits appear to have been widely followed, there were odd transgressions. That same year the 139 ton, *Two Sisters* of Pictou, sailed to Sydney with 160 passengers, fifty-six more than her legal limit allowed. When they arrived, the passengers were said to be "very much in want of provisions, having been on allowance all the voyage, owing as the master states, to deceptions which were practised with regard to the number of passengers and the stock of provisions put on board."[47] George McKenzie, who captained the *Two Sisters,* had clearly not been expecting these numbers, nor had her owner, James Carmichael, who was McKenzie's brother-in-law. The clear implication is that the emigrants themselves were responsible for the excess numbers and had consented knowingly to their overcrowded conditions. Thus, it was not the avarice of shipowners which caused these people to be crammed together, but their desire to have low fares and sail on this particular ship. One particularly strong reason for their choice of this ship was her captain.

George McKenzie was no ordinary captain. "As a commander he was daring, clear-headed, calm even under the most difficult circumstances, prompt in deciding upon his plans and energetic in having them executed." Captaining the *Two Sisters* once again in 1829, when she carried thirty emigrants:

> "in her he went up to Glasgow, and she was then noticed as the largest vessel that, up to that date, had gone so far up the Clyde. On her return, it was noticed in the Pictou paper, as something good, that she had made the round trip in twelve weeks. He then settled down in business in New Glasgow where he first built a schooner of 100 tons.... From this, he advanced to building vessels of 600 tons and then to others of 800, which were thought wonders for a time, but not content with this he soon was building still larger."[48]

McKenzie had been both captain and owner of the *Lulan* of Pictou, which took 167 South Uist emigrants from Glasgow to Pictou in 1848.[49] Built in James Carmichael's shipyard, in New Glasgow, she owed her name to a legendary figure in Mi'kmaw mythology. At the launching "one of the elder members...probably the Chief" was an honoured guest. When asked what he thought of the christening of the *Lulan*, he replied that he would "build big canoe, and call him Old Carmichael."[50] It is fitting that the *Lulan* should mark the end of this study. Her crossing from Glasgow to Pictou in 1852, with twenty-three passengers, was the last in this series. That same year the *Tongataboo* of New Glasgow, built at Fox Harbour, had also taken passengers on that same route. George McKenzie was part owner of her as well. So the era of emigrant sailing ships ended with Nova Scotia-built ships which were owned by Nova Scotia businessmen.

The eighty-year period under discussion began with the arrival of the *Hector*. A full-bottomed ship of uncertain age, she arrived in a decrepit state, while the brand new, streamlined, *Lulan,* the last to arrive, was in top, "A1," condition. While the *Lulan* could achieve far greater sailing speeds, there had actually been little advance in the overall technology. Shipping still depended on catching the wind in sails and passengers continued to be accommodated by placing temporary boards on beams which were hammered into a ship's hull. But with the arrival in the 1850s of specialist steamships, sea transport entered the modern era. Being no longer dependent on the vagaries of the weather and wind direction, and designed with passenger needs in mind, they could offer custom-built accommodation and work to predetermined schedules.

This study has followed the progress of some 30,000 of the 40,000 emigrants known to have arrived at Nova Scotia and Cape Breton during the period from 1773 to 1852. Most arrived safely and in a healthy state. The notable exceptions were the 138 passengers who had sailed on the *Rambler* of Leith in 1807, and lost their lives in a shipwreck. There were also some others who died during their crossings, or just after, as a result of contracting typhus, cholera, smallpox and other diseases. However, putting these deaths into context, they represent a tiny proportion of the total people involved. For throughout this period, irrefutable evidence exists demonstrating that ships of consistently high quality were used. There were plenty of exemplary captains and reliable agents who remained in charge of passenger services over long periods. A picture of a continuous nightmare of suffering on filthy, leaky and ill-managed ships can be conjured up, but it is totally unrepresentative. Contrary to popular depiction, emigrant Scots were well served by the men of the transatlantic passenger trade. Lurid descriptions of "slave trade" conditions and rotting ship hulls may titillate readers, but they bear little relation to the facts.[51]

∞ 10 ∞
THE SCOTTISH LEGACY

The arrival of the ship Hector was the first, as well as the most important event in the history of Highland emigration or indeed of any emigration to the Lower Provinces of British North America.[1]

THESE WORDS WERE SPOKEN BY Alexander MacKenzie of Inverness, during his evening lecture to the Buckie Literary Institution on the 8th of December, 1883. Buckie, then a prosperous fishing village on the Moray Firth in northeast Scotland, was the unlikely venue for this historic talk which covered, amongst other subjects, the sailing of the *Hector* from Loch Broom to Pictou in 1773. Some one hundred and ten years later, this event was being described in Buckie and recorded for posterity. Mackenzie would later extract this section of his lecture and have it published in the *Celtic Magazine*. He was, after all, its editor. A prolific author to boot, he saw his *History of the Highland Clearances*, a major anthology of his earlier writings, also appeared in print in that same year. Seeking ammunition in the *Hector* account for his own strongly held views on the wickedness of the clearances, he found demonic lairds where none existed. He described the "cruel tigers in human form" who had driven their tenantry in their thousands "out of their native land, not caring one iota whether they sank in the Atlantic." He must have had people on the very edge of their seats! Of course the *Hector* passengers had not been driven out. Mackenzie provided no evidence of this that evening, nor has anyone else since then. However, irrespective of this one lapse into rhetoric, he left behind an invaluable record of the 1773 crossing and, without it, the second chapter of this book could not have been written.

Mackenzie's lecture was not based on any written documentation. Because most of the *Hector* passengers had been unable to read or write in their mother tongue – which was Gaelic – no written records were available. No passenger list had been produced at the time of sailing in 1773, and it would take fifty years before one of the passengers would get around to writing one. However, verbal recollections survived by being passed through families. These were memories told and retold which Mackenzie recounted on that winter's evening. It is not known why he chose this time and place to deliver his lecture or from whom he had acquired his information, but in disclosing this material he elevated the spoken word to the written word. His article, "First Highland emigration to Nova Scotia: Arrival of the *Hector*," published in the Inverness-based *Celtic Magazine* in 1883, gives an account of what the settlers themselves said they experienced during their voyage and upon their arrival in Pictou.[2]

It was a minor miracle that any recollections survived at all. Within two or three generations, many of the descendants of the original settlers were probably seeking the better economic prospects which western Canada and the United States had to offer. Those who remained in the Maritimes were more likely to be found in industrial centres like New Glasgow and Sydney, which were expanding to meet the labour needs of their collieries, steel works and other industries.[3] As industrialization grew and agricultural opportunities declined, people moved off the land. Pasture and arable land became neglected and natural forest growth returned. Today, as one drives through parts of Nova Scotia and Cape Breton some telltale signs of deserted farms remain visible. The ruined remains of odd barns and houses and dark patches of new spruce forest mark the spots where emigrant Scots had once cultivated their land.

After the *Hector*'s arrival in 1773, Scots continued to stream into eastern Nova Scotia and Cape Breton for some eighty years. They colonized most of Cape Breton, predominated in Pictou, Antigonish and Guysborough counties, and made a sizeable impact on Colchester and

Cumberland counties. Like Pictou, Arisaig in Antigonish County was one of their earlier conquests. A plaque at the Arisaig pier records the site of its first agricultural community, which was founded by Catholic Highlanders in 1791. Their first log church was built a year later. While standing by the shore looking out to sea, it is easy to picture logs being loaded onto ships for export, and to get a sense of the importance placed on religion. Father MacEachern's visits were to such places. During his stay in 1798 "he was kept busy with marriages, baptisms, and in the administration of the other sacraments."[4] In addition to his annual visit to Arisaig, he frequently crossed the Northumberland Strait, from his base in Prince Edward Island, "in a boat on sick-calls."

Christmas Island, in Cape Breton, also had its beginnings by the water's edge. Here a cairn commemorates "the first Catholic Church on the Bras d'Or Lakes," which was built in 1814. Bishop Plessis came to visit in the following year, but his inability to speak Gaelic brought the settlers little benefit, although he did find a priest who could speak their language soon after.[5] However, the most evocative of any of the early pioneer sites is to be found at Indian Point in west Mabou.

Small stones lie in neat, long rows in the Indian Point pioneer cemetery, which overlooks the sea. The settlers, who mainly originated from Lochaber in west Inverness-shire, first began arriving there in the early 1800s.[6] No doubt they had been attracted by the extensive, naturally occurring fertile meadows, which are still visible along nearby rivers and streams. Looking at the fine harbour it is again easy to visualize ships being loaded with cut timber. Father MacDonald came to visit the area in the early years "and distributed Holy Communion under a tree."[7] These two themes – the timber trade and religion – are the ones that keep recurring. They were the bedrock and cement, which gave emigrant Scots their economic foothold and links with their distinctive culture and spiritual beliefs.

Settlements, such as these, developed a distinctive Scottish identity through their associations with particular regions of Scotland. Because most of the influx to mainland Nova Scotia and Cape Breton had been from the Highlands and Islands, where people emigrated in large groups,

The Mother of Sorrows Pioneer Shrine, Mabou. The church, built in the
late 1920s, had originally been situated at Indian Point. It was moved to its
present location in 1967 and dedicated to "the brave pioneers of Mabou."
Photograph by Geoff Campey.

distinctive settlement patterns soon emerged. Some settlers had originated from Lowland areas like Dumfries-shire, Aberdeenshire, Fife
and the Lothians, but they had come in small groups and were quickly
assimilated into a number of different communities. On the other hand,
when Highlanders emigrated, they transplanted whole communities.

Each new settlement that these Highlanders founded could trace its
roots back to a particular County or Island in Scotland. Pictou's intake
of Scots reflected the particular origins of the *Hector* arrivals, who had
strong associations with east Inverness-shire. Earltown in Colchester,
and St. Anns, Cape Breton, drew most of their initial settlers from
Sutherland. Having founded the Middle River settlement in Cape Breton,
Wester Ross emigrants continued to be drawn to this one community.
Similarly, Harris and North Uist settlers adopted Loch Lomond and
Leitches Creek as their own, while many Barra people congregated
around Iona and Christmas Island.

Early farms and houses were temporary features on the landscape, but the culture of the settlers who built them lives on. People in some of the more remote areas of Cape Breton still speak Gaelic and those who do will often pronounce their words according to the particular dialect of their ancestors. Thus they might have a Barra or North Uist accent.[8] Highlanders had an oral tradition and when memories faded much was lost, but some songs and poetry did survive. John MacLean's famous poem, "A' Choille Ghruamach" ("The Gloomy Forest") which gave early impressions of pioneer life, had an enormous impact. His heart-rending poem, written in 1819, just after he had arrived in Nova Scotia, conveyed the helplessness he felt when confronted by massive forests. It became one of the most celebrated pieces of literature ever written by a New World immigrant.[9] However, MacLean quickly adjusted to the forests. His decision to emigrate had not been a mistake after all. Through his later poems, also written in Gaelic, we see a more cheerful man who had begun to appreciate the great advantages which the New World had to offer. They are in fact more typical of other Gaelic accounts which stress the greater freedoms and better livelihoods which could be realized through emigration.[10]

Barn with a Gaelic name at Mount Auburn, east of Red Islands, Cape Breton. "Beinn Phadruig" is Gaelic for "Patrick's Mountain." *Photograph by Geoff Campey.*

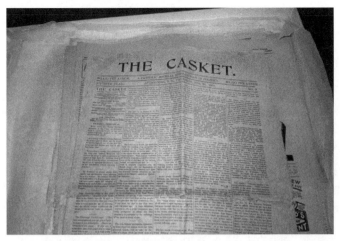

The Casket newspaper, Antigonish, 28 Feb. 1901 – " a Catholic Journal, non-partisan in politics." *Photograph by Geoff Campey.*

Highlanders came with traditions and customs which were centuries old. Their poems and songs were committed to memory and passed from person to person, although in time many were forgotten. The Reverend James MacGregor, Pictou's first Presbyterian minister, noted how "a good many of the older people from the Highlands could not read, but it is said that many of them could give a wonderfully correct account of the sermon and had much Scripture in their memories."[11] Newly arrived Highlanders complained when ministers read out their sermons. They respected the eloquence of the spoken word more highly than what was written down. "The people think that every sermon read is a borrowed one, and consequently they will not entertain for any length of time a high opinion of such as use their papers."[12] Although the Gaelic language struggled to survive, its usage in Antigonish was sufficiently widespread to give it coverage eventually in a local newspaper. When John Boyd of Antigonish first published *The Casket* in 1852, half of this newspaper was written in Gaelic. The sections devoted to songs, stories and editorials were in Gaelic, while the other half, a news section, was written in English. Despite this promising start, the Gaelic content was gradually reduced and, by 1857, it had all but disappeared.[13]

187

Sixty-five years later, John MacDougall wrote with sadness of Gaelic's steady decline:

"We realize that we have neglected our forebears; that we have not venerated their memory as we should; that we have made no attempt to preserve that which they regarded sacred, their mother-tongue.... We are sorry. We feel convinced of negligence and we wish to preserve what things they would wish us to have preserved."[14]

However, given the many ethnic influences at work it was inevitable that the Gaelic language would become weakened. Even some of their more fun-loving traditions like their fiddling had to withstand the jibes of stern clergymen who believed all musical merriment to be the work of the devil.[15] In more recent times, pipebands and tartans have given Scottish culture new life throughout the province. Some but not all of these more recent developments are rooted in early Highland traditions.[16] The Highland Society of Nova Scotia, founded in the late 1830s, did much to promote public displays of Highland symbolism and gave direction to this new movement which sought to preserve what it could of the province's Scottish heritage.[17] On all public occasions the Society's officers and members were to wear "scarves of the Highland tartan." They would seek "to improve the moral condition and, by extending the blessings of education" they would hope "to elevate the character of Scotchmen and their descendants. The distinction between Highlander and Lowlander is forgotten in a generous emulation to do good."[18] In extending "the blessings of education," the Society was building on the much-acclaimed work of men like Reverend Thomas McCulloch, who had been the force behind the establishment of the Pictou Academy in 1816. Becoming an excellent seat of learning, it was one of the most respected institutions of its time within the province. In fact, Pictou could boast of having sixty schools in place by 1826 and four years earlier it had established its first subscription library.[19]

The Antigonish Branch of the Nova Scotia Highland Society, which was formed later, concentrated more on outward expressions of Highland culture. It wished to preserve "the aesthetic in Scottish life and counter the impression that there was no artistry in the songs and poems and music of the Scottish Highlands."[20] Two years after its founding in 1861, the first Highland Games were held, after which time they became an annual event. A proliferation of clan associations and clan gatherings has followed throughout the province, bringing new life to early Scottish traditions.

The Antigonish Highland Society Memorial dedicated to "the Highland Pioneers who left the Isles and Highlands of Auld Scotland to settle in this part of New Scotland nearly two centuries ago." *Photograph by Geoff Campey.*

Thus, Scottish culture has been able to adapt to and reflect modern tastes. Although Gaelic has long been in decline, Scottish traditions persist. With the transformation from rural to industrial communities, fiddles and bagpipes remained in use but, by the 1920s, they were accompanied by pianos and brass bands.[21] This ability to assimilate new influences enabled Scottish culture to maintain its popularity, and appear modern and relevant to each new generation. However, it is deeply ironic that the traditions of people who were once regarded as barbaric and untutored should in later years become great positive symbols of Scottish culture.

When Highlanders first arrived in Nova Scotia, their illiteracy and bagpipes made them objects of ridicule. They were thought to be lazy and lacking in ambition. Commentators frequently bemoaned their "poor farming habits and apathy."[22] Yet, when it came to pioneering, Highlanders were second to none. Moreover they were certainly not lacking in intelligence or ambition. There are countless examples of humble crofters whose sons went on to be distinguished judges and successful merchants. Malcolm McNeil from Barra and Ellen Meagher, who were married in 1851 at Mabou, produced eleven children, of whom one became a bishop, two were lawyers (one of whom became a judge) one was a merchant, two were farmers, and one daughter became a nun.[23] People at the time wondered why "the people from Lake Ainslie [Cape Breton] do so well as doctors and lawyers and ministers." The answer according to "an old Cape Bretoner" was that "they were not afraid of anything or anybody.... They worked hard and accomplished whatever they set their mind to."[24]

While Highlanders may have been content with modest strides in their material living standards, they reached for the sky when it came to their achievements in business, the professions and public service. Their strong feeling of self-worth and clear sense of identity, no doubt, helped them to succeed. These attributes may also help to explain why Scottish culture became so deeply rooted. It was certainly not connected with their numbers. By 1941 only 27 per cent of Nova Scotia's population was of Scottish ancestry.[25] In numeric terms Scottishness has declined, but in cultural terms it has gone from strength to strength. Even Acadian music must bow to Scottish superiority in Cape Breton. The many French names appearing in *The Cape Breton Fiddler,* the definitive work on Cape Breton fiddling, attest to the widespread appeal of Highland music across modern-day ethnic boundaries.[26]

When the *Hector* settlers first approached Pictou Harbour in 1773, some of the younger men were "donned in their national dress" and in celebration of their arrival "the piper blew up his pipes with might and main."[27] Highland dress was banned in Scotland and so being able to wear the kilt was their first real demonstration of freedom. In going to Pictou they had defied public opinion in Scotland which was hotly opposed to emigration. They would continue to defy regulations and authority. They grabbed the best lands, even though initially they had no legal entitlements to them, and quickly established themselves as successful settlers and entrepreneurs. Their pride in their national traditions was an important part of their success. They believed in themselves and what they could achieve. This was a triumph of the common people. They had no well-heeled proprietors to help them. They overcame huge obstacles and seized their opportunities. As they "communicated with their friends" and family back in Scotland and told them of the opportunities to be had "the stream [of emigrants] continued to deepen and widen."[28] Before long Scots dominated the eastern half of the province and they would firmly stamp their culture on Atlantic Canada.

APPENDIX I

EXTANT PASSENGER LISTS FOR SHIP CROSSINGS
FROM SCOTLAND TO NOVA SCOTIA AND CAPE BRETON

The fifteen passenger lists recorded below are the only lists known to have survived. Primary sources are recorded but, where possible, transcripts have been taken from secondary sources: Bumsted, *People's Clearance*, 243–61; MacLaren, *Pictou Book*, 31–4, 105, 108–18; MacDougall, *The History of Inverness County Cape Breton*, 126–31.

The lists vary in the amount of information given. Emigrant locations in Scotland are more likely to be found in the earlier lists. Ages were often recorded since fares were normally based on a sliding scale according to age.

1. The *Hector*, John Spier (Master) sailed 8th July 1773 from Loch Broom to Pictou
No passenger list was compiled at the time of the *Hector*'s departure. The list which follows was compiled by William (Squire) MacKay, a passenger on the *Hector*, some fifty years later. It names 179 people who boarded ship at Loch Broom and a further ten people who had got on the ship at Glasgow. The list was reprinted in MacLaren, George, *The Pictou Book: Stories of our Past* (New Glasgow, N.S., 1954), 31–4. The original list is held by Nova Scotia Archives and Records Management.

The divisions in the list suggest the probable price differences in fares. Passengers over 8 years old would have paid the full fare, children aged between 2 to 8 years would have paid half fares, while infants under 2 probably travelled free of charge. In the section listing infants under the age of 2, the mother's or father's name is listed first and then the child's.

APPENDIX I

Passengers from Loch Broom – Full passengers above eight years

Alex Cameron
Donald Cameron
Sarah Campbell
Archibald Chisholm
Colin Douglas
Alex. Falconer
Mary Forbes
Hugh Fraser
Thomas Fraser
Ann Fraser
Hugh Fraser
William Fraser
Mrs. Fraser
Kenneth Fraser
Janet Fraser
Alex Fraser
Donald Graham
Christopher Grant
Donald Grant
John Grant
James Grant
Alex Grant
Robert Innis
Robert Lyon
Margaret Lyon
Donald McDonald
James McDonald
John McDonald
Alex McDonald
Mary McDonald
William McDonald
James McDonald
John McGregor
Colin McKay
Roderick McKay
Donald McKay

Donald McKay
William McKay
Margaret McKay
Christopher McKay
Catherine McKay
Margaret McKay
John McKay
Mary McKay
William McKay
Donald McKay
William McKay (piper)
Magdalene McKenzie
John McKenzie
Colin McKenzie
Isabel McKenzie
William McKenzie
Angus McKenzie
Alex McKenzie
Donald McKenzie
Elspa McKenzie
William McKenzie
Alex McKenzie
Kenneth McKritchie
Margaret McKritchie
Catherine McLean
Alex. McLean
Mary McLean
Margaret McLean
John McLennan
William McLennan
James McLeod
Elspeth McLeod
Janet McLeod
Hugh McLeod
David McLeod
Mary McLeod

Finlay McLeod
Marion McLeod
William McLeod
Alex McLeod
Charles Matheson
William Mathewson
Mary Mathewson
Janet Munroe
Donald Munroe
John Munroe
James Murray
Margaret Murray
Adam Murray
Abigail Murray
Christopher Murray
Walter Murray
Ann Patterson
Rebecca Patterson
Janet Ross
Alex Ross
Donald Ross
Alex Ross
William Ross
Alex Ross
Marion Ross
William Ross
Ann Smith
Lily Sutherland
John Sutherland
Mary Sutherland
Betty Sutherland
John Sutherland
David Urquhart
Christian Urquhart

Passengers from two to eight years old

Alex Cameron
Mary Cameron

Janet McDonald
Mary McDonald

George McLeod
Katherine McLeod

194

APPENDIX I

Passengers from two to eight years old

Margaret Douglas
Alex Fraser
Catherine Fraser
Jean Fraser
Isabel Fraser
Isabel Fraser
Mary Fraser
Simon Fraser
Margaret Grant
Mary Grant
Andrew McDonald
Catherine McDonald
Elizabeth McDonald

Alex McKay
George McKay
James McKay
John McKay
Roderick McKay
William McKay
Adam McKenzie
Jane McKenzie
Katherine McKenzie
Kenneth McKenzie
Kenneth McKenzie
James McKritchie
Angus McLeod

Marion McLeod
Ann Matheson
Christopher Murray
George Murray
Alex Ross
Catherine Ross
Christina Ross
Donald Ross
Mary Ross
Walter Ross

Children under two years of age

Janet Cameron
Janate Cameron
Colin Douglas
Hugh Fraser
James Grant
Robert Innes
Alex McDonald
William McDonald
Alex McDonald
Colin McKay
John McKay
Colin McKay
Roderick McKay
William McKay
Donald McKenzie
Colin McKenzie
Donald McKenzie
Finlay McLeod
Alex McLeod
Finlay McLeod
Andrew Mains
William Mathewson
George Morrison
Walter Murray
Alex. Ross
John Sutherland

child of John
child of Hugh
child of Alex
child of Donald
child of Jane
child of Duncan
child of Hugh
child of Ann
child of James
child of Colin
child of Ann
child of Alex
child of Ann
child of Flora
child of Elizabeth
child of Colin
child of William
child of Jannet
child of Donald
child of William
child of Andrew
child of John
child of Hector
child of Elizabeth
child of Catherine
child of William

APPENDIX I

Full passengers from the Clyde

James Campbell
Jane Forbes
Charles Fraser
Jane Gibson

Andrew Hain
George McConnel
George Morrison
and child

John Patterson
John Stewart

2. The *Dove* of Aberdeen, Crane (Master) sailed in June, 1801 from Fort William to Pictou
[NAS RH2/4/87 ff. 73–75. Corrected spellings of place names are given in square brackets.]

Names of Passengers	The Age of those under 16 years without trades further than Labouring & Industry	Occupation	Place of residence: Parish, Country, and Shire
Archibald MacKay		Farmer	Kilmorack
James Fraser		Labourer	Kilmorack
Barbara McKay		Spinster[1]	Kilmorack
Isobel McKay		Spinster	Kilmorack
Ann Thomson		Spinster	Kilmorack
Elizabeth MacKenzie		Spinster	Kilmorack
Janet MacKenzie		Spinster	Kilmorack
Marg't Fraser		Spinster	Kilmorack
Ann MacKay	12	Spinster	Kilmorack
Flory MacKay	7		Kilmorack
Al. Cameron		Tenant	Kilmorack
Janet Cameron		Spinster	Kilmorack
Al'r Cameron		Labourer	Kilmorack
John Cameron	14		Kilmorack
Isobel Cameron	12		Kilmorack
Ann Cameron	4		Kilmorack
Hugh Cameron		Farmer	Kilmorack
Margaret Cameron		Spinster	Kilmorack
Marg't Cameron	4		Kilmorack
William MacLean		Farmer	Kilmorack
Mar MacLean		Spinster	Kilmorack
Donald MacLean		Labourer	Kilmorack

[1] Spinster denotes an adult female—both married and unmarried.

Names of Passengers	The Age of those under 16 years without trades further than Labouring & Industry	Occupation	Place of residence: Parish, Country, and Shire
Marg MacLean		Spinster	Kilmorack
Kath MacLean		Spinster	Kilmorack
Isobel Cameron		Spinster	Kilmorack
John MacLean	10		Kilmorack
Wm MacLean	8		Kilmorack
Don'd Cameron		Tenant	Kilmarnock
Kath'r Cameron		Spinster	Kilmarnock
Margaret Cameron		Spinster	Kilmarnock
Cath Cameron		Spinster	Kilmarnock
James Cameron	13		Kilmarnock
Hugh Cameron	11		Kilmarnock
Isobel Cameron	7		Kilmarnock
Alexander Fraser		Farmer	Kilmarnock
Margaret Fraser		Spinster	Kilmarnock
Mary Fraser	14		Kilmarnock
Margaret Fraser	9		Kilmarnock
Janet Fraser	7		Kilmarnock
Alex'r Fraser	5		Kilmarnock
Robert Fraser	3		Kilmarnock
Donald MacLeod		Tenant	Kilmarnock
Ann MacLeod		Spinster	Kilmarnock
Ann MacLeod	10		Kilmarnock
Alex'r MacLeod	8		Kilmarnock
Andrew MacLeod	5		Kilmarnock
Dav'd MacLeod	3		Kilmarnock
James Cameron		Labourer	Killarkty [Kiltarlity]
Janet Cameron		Spinster	Killarkty
James Cameron	6		Killarkty
Donald Cameron	2		Killarkty
Hugh Cameron		Farmer	Killarkty
Ann Cameron		Spinster	Killarkty
Mary Cameron	8		Killarkty
James Cameron	3		Killarkty
Alex'r MacLean		Labourer	Kilmarnock[1]

[1] Probably Kilmarnock, Ayrshire, although it may be a misspelling of Kilmorack.

197

Names of Passengers	The Age of those under 16 years without trades further than Labouring & Industry	Occupation	Place of residence: Parish, Country, and Shire
Kath MacLean		Spinster	Kilmarnock
John Bethune		Labourer	Kilmarnock
James Bethune		Labourer	Kilmarnock
Rod'k MacKenzie		Labourer	Kilmarnock
Kenneth MacLeod		Labourer	Kilmarnock
Donald Fraser		Labourer	Kilmarnock
John Jack		Labourer	Knockbain
Alex'r Ross		Labourer	Kincardine
Alex'r Chisholm		Labourer	Ercless
Alex'r Fraser		Labourer	Killarkty [Kiltarlity]
James MacDonald		Labourer	Kilmorack
William Chisholm		Labourer	Killarkty [Kiltarlity]
John Chisholm		Labourer	Kilmorack
William Chisholm		Labourer	Kilmorack
Donald MacDonald		Labourer	Kilmorack
Donald Fraser		Labourer	Killarkty [Kiltarlity]
John Forbes		Labourer	Killarkty
John MacDonald		Labourer	Killarkty
Kath Chisholm		Spinster	Kilmarnock
James Chisholm		Labourer	Kilmarnock
Rod'k Chisholm		Labourer	Kilmarnock
James Forbes		Labourer	Kilmarnock
Charles Forbes		Labourer	Kilmarnock
Ranald MacDonald		Farmer	Arisaig
Kath MacDonald		Spinster	Arisaig
Kath Gillis		Spinster	Arisaig
Alexander Gillis		Labourer	Arisaig
John MacDonald	6		Arisaig
Janet MacDonald	3		Arisaig
Donald MacLellan		Tenant	Moron [Morar]
Mary MacLellan		Spinster	Moron
Karin MacLellan	7		Moron
Marg't MacLellan	5		Moron
Patrick MacLellan	3		Moron
Alex'r MacLellan	2		Moron
Alex'r McLean		Farmer	Moidart

APPENDIX I

Names of Passengers	The Age of those under 16 years without trades further than Labouring & Industry	Occupation	Place of residence: Parish, Country, and Shire
Marion McLean		Spinster	Moidart
A Boy	3		Moidart
An Infant			Moidart
Lauchlan McDonald		Tenant	Moidart
Cath McDonell		Spinster	Moidart
A Girl & Infant	3		Moidart
John McDonald		Farmer	Moidart
Cath McDonald		Spinster	Moidart
A girl	1		Moidart
John McDonald		Labourer	Moidart
Marian McDonald		Spinster	Moidart
Alex'r McDonald	8		Moidart
An Infant	-		Moidart
Hugh McDonald		Tenant	Moidart
Ann McDonald		Spinster	Moidart
A Boy	4		Moidart
A Boy	2		Moidart
John McDonald		Farmer	Moidart
Cath McDonald		Spinster	Moidart
Peggy McDonald	14		Moidart
Cath McDonald	9		Moidart
Janet McDonald	5 1/2		Moidart
Mary McDonald	3yr		Moidart
Angus Beaton		Farmer	Bad enough [Badenoch]
Isobel Beaton		Spinster	Bad enough
Alex'r Beaton		Labourer	Bad enough
Angus Beaton		Labourer	Bad enough
Donald Beaton		Labourer	Bad enough
Marian Beaton		Spinster	Bad enough
Ann Beaton		Spinster	Bad enough
Ann Beaton		Spinster	Bad enough
Archibald Beaton	14		Bad enough
John Beaton	12		Bad enough
Finlay Beaton	9		Bad enough
Margaret Beaton	7		Bad enough

APPENDIX I

Names of Passengers	The Age of those under 16 years without trades further than Labouring & Industry	Occupation	Place of residence: Parish, Country, and Shire
Catherine Beaton	5		Bad enough
Archibald McFarlane		Farmer	Arisaig
Dougald McFarlane		Labourer	Arisaig
Peter McFarlane		Labourer	Arisaig
John McFarlane		Labourer	Arisaig
Peggy McFarlane	12		Arisaig
Angus McFarlane	7		Arisaig
Donald MacInnes		Tenant	Arisaig
Cath MacInnes		Tenant	Arisaig
Angus McInnes		Labourer	Arisaig
Duncan McInnes	5		Arisaig
Jean M Innes	7		Arisaig
John Mac Isaach		Labourer	Arisaig
his spouse		Spinster	Arisaig
Angus MacIsaach		Labourer	Arisaig
Catherine MacIsaach		Spinster	Arisaig
Duncan MacIsaach		Labourer	Arisaig
Mary MacIsaach		Spinster	Arisaig
John Boyd		Tenant	Arisaig
Cath Boyd		Spinster	Arisaig
Kate McPherson		Spinster	Arisaig
Anne Boyd		Spinster	Arisaig
Angus Boyd		Labourer	Arisaig
John Boyd	7		Arisaig
Hugh Boyd		Labourer	Arisaig
Mary Boyd		Spinster	Arisaig
Bell MacFarlance	12		Arisaig
Mary Boyd	4		Arisaig
Alex'r Boyd		Labourer	Arisaig
Mary Boyd		Spinster	Arisaig
Cath McDougald		Spinster	Arisaig
John McDonald		Tenant	Arisaig
Mary McDonald		Spinster	Arisaig
Peggy MacFarlane		Spinster	Arisaig
Donald McMillan		Farmer	Locharigag [Loch Arkaig]

APPENDIX I

Names of Passengers	The Age of those under 16 years without trades further than Labouring & Industry	Occupation	Place of residence: Parish, Country, and Shire
Marian McMillan		Spinster	Locharigag
Angus McMillan		Labourer	Locharigag
John McMillan		Labourer	Locharigag
Angus Gillies		Farmer	Locharigag
Ann Gillies		Spinster	Locharigag
Ann Gillies		Spinster	Locharigag
Janet Gillies		Spinster	Locharigag
Mary Gillies		Spinster	Locharigag
Donald Gillies		Labourer	Locharigag
John Gillies	12		Locharigag
Kenneth Chisholm		Labourer	Strathglass
Chisholm his spouse		Spinster	Strathglass
a Child			Strathglass
Donald Gillies		Farmer	Knoydart
Ann Gillies		Spinster	Knoydart
Alex'r Gillies	3		Knoydart
Hugh Gillies	2		Knoydart
Mary McDonald		Spinster	Lochaber
Mary Fraser		Spinster	Kilmorack
Fraser her daughter		Spinster	Kilmorack
Finlay Cameron		Labourer	Lochbroom
John McIntosh		Farmer	Glenelg
Ann McIntosh		Spinster	Glenelg
Mary McIntosh		Spinster	Glenelg
Finlay McLellan		Labourer	Glenelg
John McMillan		Farmer	Locharigag [Loch Arkaig]
John McMillan		Labourer	Locharigag
Jean McMillan		Spinster	Locharigag
Isobel McMillan		Spinster	Locharigag
Mary McMillan		Spinster	Locharigag
John McMillan		Labourer	Locharigag
Martha McMillan		Spinster	Locharigag
Marian McMillan		Spinster	Locharigag
John McMillan		Tenant	Locharigag
Alex'r McMillan	12		Locharigag

Names of Passengers	The Age of those under 16 years without trades further than Labouring & Industry	Occupation	Place of residence: Parish, Country, and Shire
Donald McMillan			Locharigag
Ewen Cameron		Farmer	Kinlochmorer
Donald Cameron		Labourer	Kinlochmorer
James Cameron		Labourer	Kinlochmorer
Rod Cameron		Labourer	Kinlochmorer
Eliza Cameron	14		Kinlochmorer
Mary Cameron	4		Kinlochmorer
Marg't Cameron	3		Kinlochmorer
Christian	1 1/2		Kinlochmorer
Angus Gillies		Labourer	Morar
Mary Gillies		Spinster	Morar
Alex Stewart		Tenant	Athol, Perth [Blair Atholl]
Mary Stewart		Spinster	Athol, Perth
Alex'r Urquhart		Tenant	Calder [Cawdor], Nairnshire
Patrick Tulloch		Tenant	Callader R'shire Callander, Perthshire?
Mrs. Mary Fraser		Spinster	Kirkhill
Jean Fraser & her daughter	8	Spinster	Kirkhill

In all 219. Including men women & Children and Infancy making the number of full passengers to be 176 calculating the age of those under sixteen being 447 years and thereafter dividing by 16 years making a full passenger.

Those above 16 years	149
Those below by the above calculation	27

176 to go on board the Ship *Dove* burdened 186 tons.

3. The *Sarah* of Liverpool, Smith (Master), sailed in June 1801 from Fort William to Pictou
[NAS RH2/4/87 ff. 66–71]

Names of Passengers	The Age of those under 16 years	Occupation	Places of Residence Shire Parish or Country
Arch'd Chisholm		Late Farmer	Kilmorack, Inv.
Cath Chisholm		Spinster[1]	Kilmorack
Isobel Chisholm		Spinster	Kilmorack
Ann Chisholm		Spinster	Kilmorack
Cath Chisholm	12		Kilmorack
John McIntosh		Late Farmer	Kilmorack
Janet McIntosh		Spinster	Kilmorack
Flora McIntosh	5		Kilmorack
John McIntosh	3		Kilmorack
An Infant			Kilmorack
Duncan Chisholm		Late Farmer	Kilmorack
Ann Chisholm		Spinster	Kilmorack
One Infant			Kilmorack
Thomas McDonald		Labourer	Kilmorack
Janet McDonald		Spinster	Kilmorack
Duncan Chisholm		Labourer	Kilmorack
Ann Chisholm		Spinster	Kilmorack
Donald McIntosh		Late Farmer	Kilmorack
Alexander McIntosh		Late Farmer	Kilmorack
Cath McIntosh		Spinster	Kilmorack
Janet McIntosh		Spinster	Kilmorack
Marg't McIntosh	14		Kilmorack
John Chisholm		Late Farmer	Kilmorack
Cath Chisholm		Spinster	Kilmorack
Don'd Chisholm		Labourer	Kilmorack
Colin Chisholm		Labourer	Kilmorack
Will'm Chisholm		Labourer	Kilmorack
Margaret Chisholm	12		Kilmorack
Donald McKenzie		Labourer	Kilmorack
Ann McKenzie		Spinster	Kilmorack
John McKenzie	4		Kilmorack
Donald McKenzie		Farmer	Kiltarlity, Inv.
Donald McDonald		Farmer	Kiltarlity

[1]Spinster denotes an adult female—both married and unmarried.

APPENDIX I

Names of Passengers	The Age of those under 16 years	Occupation	Places of Residence Shire Parish or Country
John McDonald		Labourer	Kiltarlity
Rod. McDonell		Labourer	Kiltarlity
Ann McDonald		Spinster	Kiltarlity
Cath McDonald		Spinster	Kiltarlity
Janet McDonald		Spinster	Kiltarlity
John McDonald	2		Kiltarlity
A Child			Kiltarlity
Duncan McDonald		Farmer	Kilmorack
Janet McDonald		Spinster	Kilmorack
Mary McRae		Spinster	Kilmorack
Murdoch McRae	7		Kilmorack
Ann McRae		Spinster	Kilmorack
Duncan McRae	5		Kilmorack
Margaret McRae	4		Kilmorack
Farquhar McRae	1 1/2		Kilmorack
William Grant		Labourer	Kilmorack
Janet McDonald		Spinster	Kilmorack
Christian McDonald		Spinster	Kilmorack
Alexander Chisholm		Farmer	Strathglass
Mary Chisholm		Spinster	Strathglass
Duncan Chisholm	14		Strathglass
Cath McDonald	7		Strathglass
Cath Chisholm	4		Strathglass
Patrick Chisholm	3		Strathglass
Janet Chisholm		Spinster	Kilmorack
Donald McPherson		Farmer	Strathglass
Mary McPherson		Spinster	Strathglass
Ann McPherson		Spinster	Strathglass
Hugh McPherson		Labourer	Strathglass
Ann Fraser		Spinster	Ereless
Marg't Fraser		Spinster	Ereless
John Chisholm		Labourer	Kiltarlity
Flora Chisholm		Spinster	Kiltarlity
John Chisholm		Farmer	Kilmorack
Rod'r Chisholm		Farmer	Kilmorack
Arch'd Chisholm		Farmer	Kilmorack
William McDonald		Late Farmer	Kiltarlity
Janet McDonald		Spinster	Kiltarlity
Mary McDonald	13		Kiltarlity

APPENDIX I

Names of Passengers	The Age of those under 16 years	Occupation	Places of Residence Shire Parish or Country
Ann McDonald	10		Kiltarlity
John McDonald	8		Kiltarlity
Cath McDonald	5		Kiltarlity
Henny McDonald	3		Kiltarlity
An Infant			Kiltarlity
John Fraser		Farmer	Kiltarlity
Christian Fraser		Spinster	Kiltarlity
William Fraser		Labourer	Kiltarlity
Bell Fraser		Spinster	Kiltarlity
Ann Fraser	3		Kiltarlity
Arch'd Chisholm		Labourer	Kiltarlity
Colin Chisholm		Labourer	Kiltarlity
Alex'r Chisholm		Farmer	Kilmorack
Helen Chisholm		Spinster	Kilmorack
Cath'n Chisholm		Spinster	Kilmorack
Marg't Chisholm	14		Kilmorack
Ann Chisholm	12		Kilmorack
Alex'r Chisholm	10		Kilmorack
Helen Chisholm	8		Kilmorack
Isobel Chisholm	6		Kilmorack
Colin Chisholm	2		Kilmorack
An Infant			Kilmorack
Duncan McDonald		Tenant	Kilmorack
Isobel McDonald		Spinster	Kilmorack
Hugh McDonald	3		Kilmorack
An Infant			Kilmorack
John Duff		Labourer	Kilmorack
Catherine Duff		Spinster	Kilmorack
An Infant			Kilmorack
Arch'd Chisholm		Tenant	Kilmorack
Ann Chisholm		Spinster	Kilmorack
An Infant			Kilmorack
Margaret Chisholm		Spinster	Kilmorack
Rory McDonald		Labourer	Kilmorack
Cath McDonald		Spinster	Kilmorack
William Chisholm		Farmer	Kilmorack
Mary Chisholm		Spinster	Kilmorack
Alex'r Chisholm		Labourer	Kilmorack
Donald Chisholm		Labourer	Kilmorack

Names of Passengers	The Age of those under 16 years	Occupation	Places of Residence Shire Parish or Country
Marg't Chisholm		Spinster	Kilmorack
Cath Chisholm	14		Kilmorack
Kenneth Chisholm	8		Kilmorack
William Chisholm	4		Kilmorack
Colin Chisholm	3		Kilmorack
An Infant			Kilmorack
Angus Grant		Farmer	Glenmoriston
Duncan Grant	11		Glenmoriston
Patrick Grant		Farmer	Glenmoriston
John McDonald		Farmer	Glenmoriston
Arch'd McArthur		Labourer	Kilmonivaig
Christian McArthur		Spinster	Kilmonivaig
An Infant			Kilmonivaig
Paul McDonald		Farmer	Urquhart
Ann McDonald		Spinster	Urquhart
John McDonald	10		Urquhart
Donald McDonald	8		Urquhart
Marg't McDonald	6		Urquhart
Alex'r McDonald	4		Urquhart
Alex'r McDonald		Labourer	Appin, Argyle
Ann McDonald		Spinster	Appin
Finlay McDonald		Farmer	Urquhart, Inv.
Ann McDonald		Spinster	Urquhart
John McDonald	13		Urquhart
Ann McDonald	10		Urquhart
Donald McDonald	6		Urquhart
Christian McDonald	4		Urquhart
Duncan McDonald	1 1/2		Urquhart
Finlay McIntosh		Farmer	Urquhart
Ann McIntosh		Spinster	Urquhart
Elizabeth McIntosh		Spinster	Urquhart
Isobel McIntosh		Spinster	Urquhart
James McIntosh	14		Urquhart
Christian McIntosh	8		Urquhart
William McIntosh	6		Urquhart
An Infant			Urquhart
Duncan McDonald		Farmer	Urquhart
Isobel McDonald		Spinster	Urquhart
Mary McDonald	5		Urquhart

APPENDIX I

Names of Passengers	The Age of those under 16 years	Occupation	Places of Residence Shire Parish or Country
John McDonald	2		Urquhart
John McDonald		Farmer	Urquhart
Eliz McDonald		Spinster	Urquhart
Duncan McDonald	6		Urquhart
Janet McDonald	3		Urquhart
Donald McDonald		Labourer	Urquhart
John Grant		Farmer	Urquhart
Margaret Grant		Spinster	Urquhart
Alex'r Grant		Labourer	Urquhart
Donald Grant		Labourer	Urquhart
Marg't Grant		Spinster	Urquhart
Eliz Grant		Spinster	Urquhart
Patrick Grant	6		Urquhart
Cath Grant	6		Urquhart
William Grant	4		Urquhart
Robert Grant	2		Urquhart
Simon Fraser		Labourer	Kilmorack
Ann Fraser		Spinster	Kilmorack
Alex'r McGregor		Farmer	Urquhart
Christian McGregor		Spinster	Urquhart
William McGregor	3		Urquhart
Rory McDonald		Tenant	Urquhart
Mary McDonald		Spinster	Urquhart
Cath McDonald		Spinster	Urquhart
Janer McDonald	5		Urquhart
Donald McIntosh		Farmer	Urquhart
Janet McIntosh		Spinster	Urquhart
Isobel McIntosh	3		Urquhart
Robert McIntosh		Farmer	Urquhart
Janet McIntosh		Spinster	Urquhart
Janet McIntosh	3		Urquhart
John McMillan		Labourer	Urquhart
William McDonald		Labourer	Urquhart
Alexander McDonald		Tenant	Kilmorack
Ann McDonald		Spinster	Kilmorack
Alex'r McDonald	8		Kilmorack
John McDonald	4		Kilmorack
Patrick McDonald		Labourer	Urquhart
John Fraser		Labourer	Kirkhill

APPENDIX I

Names of Passengers	The Age of those under 16 years	Occupation	Places of Residence Shire Parish or Country
Christian Fraser		Spinster	Kirkhill
Isobel Fraser	2		Kirkhill
Alexander Stuart		Tenant	Kiltearn, Ross.
May Stuart		Spinster	Kiltearn
Murdo Stuart	9		Kiltearn
Donald Stuart	4		Kiltearn
Ann Stuart	2		Kiltearn
An Infant			Kiltearn
John McLean		Labourer	Kiltearn
Ann McLean		Spinster	Kiltearn
Isobel McLean		Spinster	Kiltearn
Alexander Cameron		Farmer	Urquhart
Helen Cameron		Spinster	Urquhart
Alex'r Cameron		Labourer	Urquhart
Ann Cameron	13		Urquhart
Flory Cameron	7		Urquhart
Mary Cameron	3		Urquhart
Ewen McDonald		Labourer	Strathglass
John Chisholm		Farmer	Strathglass
Ann Chisholm		Spinster	Strathglass
John Chisholm	9		Strathglass
Alex'r Chisholm	7		Strathglass
Colin Chisholm	5		Strathglass
David Chisholm	2		Strathglass
Alexander Chisholm		Labourer	Strathglass
Margaret Chisholm		Spinster	Strathglass
Marg't Chisholm		Spinster	Strathglass
Angus McDonald		Farmer	Knoydart
Margaret McDonald		Spinster	Knoydart
Mary McDonald		Spinster	Knoydart
Allan McDonald		Labourer	Knoydart
Donald McDonald	10		Knoydart
Samuel McDonald	6		Knoydart
Peggy McDonald	4		Knoydart
Mary McDonald	2		Knoydart
Alexander McLean		Tenant	Urquhart
Margaret McLean		Spinster	Urquhart
Becky McLean	4		Urquhart
Ann McLean	1 1/2		Urquhart

APPENDIX I

Names of Passengers	The Age of those under 16 years	Occupation	Places of Residence Shire Parish or Country
Alexander Grant		Farmer	Urquhart
Hannah Grant		Spinster	Urquhart
Alex Grant	4		Urquhart
Isobel Grant	1 1/2		Urquhart
William McKenzie		Farmer	Urquhart
Flory McKenzie		Spinster	Urquhart
Isobel McKenzie	5		Urquhart
John McKenzie	2		Urquhart
Janet Grant		Spinster	Red Castle
John McMillan		Blacksmith	Strathglass
Cathrine McMillan		Spinster	Strathglass
Eliz McMillan	7		Strathglass
Will'm McMillan	5		Strathglass
John Robertson		Tenant	Rannach [Perth-
Janet Robertson		Spinster	Rannach shire]
Alex'r Robertson		Labourer	Rannach
Eliz. Robertson		Spinster	Rannach
Donald Robertson	13		Rannach
Janet Robertson	11		Rannach
Duncan Robertson	5		Rannach
James Robertson		Labourer	Rannach
Donald Smith		Tenant	Rannach
Smith, his wife		Spinster	Rannach
James Robertson		Farmer	Rannach
Christian Robertson		Spinster	Rannach
Eliz Robertson	6		Rannach
Janet Robertson	3		Rannach
Duncan Robertson	2		Rannach
Donald Robertson		Farmer	Rannach
Janet Robertson		Spinster	Rannach
Peggy Robertson	6		Rannach
Janet Robertson	4		Rannach
John Robertson	2		Rannach
Murdo McLennan		Farmer	Aird, Inv.
Janet McLennan		Spinster	Aird
Murdo McLennan	3		Aird
John McLennan		Labourer	Aird
Christian McLennan		Spinster	Aird
Kate McLennan	3		Aird

Names of Passengers	The Age of those under 16 years	Occupation	Places of Residence Shire Parish or Country
Angus McDonald		Labourer	Glengarry
Janet McDonald		Spinster	Glengarry
Rachael McDonald		Spinster	Glengarry
Janet McDonald	3		Glengarry
Kath McDonald			Glengarry
James Chisholm		Farmer	Urquhart
Martha Chisholm		Spinster	Urquhart
Isobel Chisholm	14		Urquhart
Mary Chisholm	12		Urquhart
James Chisholm	10		Urquhart
Cath Chisholm	7		Urquhart
John Chisholm	5		Urquhart
Ewan Chisholm	2		Urquhart
Donald Grant		Farmer	Urquhart
Janet Grant		Spinster	Urquhart
Alex Grant	9		Urquhart
Christian Grant	6		Urquhart
Isobel Grant	3		Urquhart
Duncan McDonald		Labourer	Urquhart
Janet McDonald		Spinster	Urquhart
Duncan Chisholm for Janet Chisholm		Spinster	Urquhart
Donald McGregor		Farmer	Kiltarlity
Isobel McGregor		Spinster	Kiltarlity
Mary McGregor	11		Kiltarlity
John McGregor	9		Kiltarlity
Jean McGregor	8		Kiltarlity
Alex'r McGregor	6		Kiltarlity
Andrew McGregor	4		Kiltarlity
Kate McGregor	2		Kiltarlity
Alexander Chisholm		Farmer	Strathglass
Mary Chisholm		Spinster	Strathglass
Betsey McRae		Spinster	Strathglass
William McKenzie		Labourer	Strathglass
Cath McKenzie		Spinster	Strathglass
Don'd McKenzie for Alex'r McGregor	8		Strathglass
John Chisholm	15		Strathglass
Hugh Bain	10		Strathglass

APPENDIX I

Names of Passengers	The Age of those under 16 years	Occupation	Places of Residence Shire Parish or Country
John Grant		Farmer	Strathglass
Cath Grant		Spinster	Strathglass
James Grant	10		Strathglass
John Grant	8		Strathglass
Alex'r Grant	6		Strathglass
Donald Grant	4		Strathglass
Farquhar McKenzie		Labourer	Strathglass
Cath Fraser		Spinster	Strathglass
Don'd McIntosh		Farmer	Glenelg
Mary McIntosh		Spinster	Glenelg
Surmy McIntosh	12		Glenelg
Anne McIntosh	8		Glenelg
Donald McIntosh	5		Glenelg
Mary McIntosh	2 1/2		Glenelg
Finlay McIntosh		Tenant	Glenelg
Anne McIntosh		Spinster	Glenelg
Anne McIntosh	4		Glenelg
Donald McIntosh	2		Glenelg
Arch'd McLellan		Farmer	Brincory of Morar
Isobel McLellan		Spinster	Brincory
Angus McLellan	2		Brincory
Mary McLellan	3		Brincory
Anne McDougald		Spinster	Knoydart
Ereck McDougald		Spinster	Knoydart
Janet McLean		Spinster	Beaulyside
William McLean		Labourer	Beaulyside
Alex'r Fraser		Tacksman	Kiltarlity
Medley Fraser		Spinster	Kiltarlity
Mary Fraser	12		Kiltarlity
Eliz Fraser	6		Kiltarlity
Marg't Fraser	3		Kiltarlity
William Chisholm		Taylor	Strathglass
Caith Chisholm		Spinster	Strathglass
Cath Chisholm	9		Strathglass
Anne Chisholm	4		Strathglass
Alex'r Chisholm	3		Strathglass
Rory Chisholm		Tenant	Strathglass
Mary Chisholm		Spinster	Strathglass
Mary Chisholm		Spinster	Strathglass

Names of Passengers	The Age of those under 16 years	Occupation	Places of Residence Shire Parish or Country
Christian Chisholm	12		Strathglass
Donald McDonald		Labourer	Alness, Ross
Hector Thomson		Tenant	Kilmorack
Janet Thomson		Spinster	Kilmorack
Simon Thomson	3		Kilmorack

In all 350 including Men, Women, Children & Infants making the Number of full Passengers to be 250. Calculating the age of those under sixteen at 830 1/2 years & thereafter dividing by 16 making a full passenger

Those above 16 years   199
Those below by above cal   51

         Total   250   To go on board Ship *Sarah* burdened 350 tons.

4. The *Commerce,* Robert Galt (Master), sailed 10th August, 1803 from Port Glasgow to Pictou
[NLS MS 1053 ff.104–9]
{All were from Perthshire but their parish or place of origin is not given.}

Name	Ages	Cause of Emigration	Occupation
James McLawson	60	Farm taken from him.	Farmer
Isabella McLawson	58		Wife
John McLawson	21		Child
James McLawson	18		Child
Eliza McLawson	11		Child
James Stewart	37	Farm taken from him.	Farmer
Janet Stewart	37		Wife
Donald Stewart	11		Child
Isabella Stewart	9		Child
Janet Stewart	7		Child
Charles Stewart	1 1/4		Child
Donald Gordon	40	Rent raised and could not live by it.	Farmer
Christian Gordon	31		Wife
Isabella Gordon	6		Child

Name	Ages	Cause of Emigration	Occupation
Henry Gordon	5		Child
James Gordon	3		Child
Donald Gordon	9 mos.		Child
Duncan McGregor	41	Farm taken from him.	Farmer
Margaret McGregor	30		Wife
Katherine McGregor	8		Child
Charles McGregor	6		Child
Hugh McGregor	4		Child
Jessie McGregor	1 1/2		Child
Alexander McGregor	60	Farm taken from him.	Farmer
Margaret McDonald	40		—
Donald McLauren	33	Farm taken from him.	Farmer
Eliza McLauren	32		Wife
James McLauren	6		Child
Janet McLauren	4		Child
John McLauren	2		Child
William McLauren	25	Rent raised and could not live by it.	Farmer
Janet McLauren	20		Wife
Donald McLauren	1		Child
Alex'r Stewart	20	Want of employment.	Labourer
Donald Kennedy	45	Rent raised and could not live by it.	Farmer
Margaret Kennedy	35		Wife
Janet Kennedy	10		Child
John Kennedy	8		Child
Robert Kennedy	6		Child
Donald Kennedy	3		Child
Duncan Robertson	42	Farm taken from him.	Farmer
Isabella Robertson	31		Wife
Alexander Robertson	6 1/4		Child
Eliza Robertson	4 1/4		Child
Margaret Robertson	1 1/4		Child
Isabella Robertson	3 mos.		Child

Name	Ages	Cause of Emigration	Occupation
John Reid	25	Farm taken from him.	Farmer
Eliza Reid	23		Wife
Alexander Reid	3 1/4		Child
Ann Reid	1 1/4		Child
John McFarlane	41	Rent raised and could not live by it.	Farmer
Ann McFarlane	39		Wife
Eliza McFarlane	10		Child
James McFarlane	8		Child
John McFarlane	6		Child
Ann McFarlane	4		Child
Margaret McFarlane	2		Child
Janet McFarlane	2 mos.		Child
Alexander McIntosh	42	Rent raised and could not live by it.	Farmer
Agnes McIntosh	34		Wife
John McIntosh	13		Child
Margaret McIntosh	11		Child
James McIntosh	9		Child
William McIntosh	3		Child
James Bullians	24		—
Charles McDonald	35		Farmer
Agnes McDonald	31		Wife
Eliza McDonald	9		Child
Alexander McDonald	2		Child
James McDonald	9 mos.		Child.

5. Memorial of the Emigrants who sailed on the *Prince William* from Cromarty/ Thurso to Pictou in 1815
[NSARM MG100 Vol226 #30, *The Pictou Advocate*, Nov. 20, 1931]

"TO HIS EXCELLENCY Sir John Coape Sherbrooke, Knight of the most Honourable Order of the Bath, Lieutenant Governor and Commander in Chief of His Majesty's Province of Nova Scotia and its Dependencies etc., etc.

The memorial of the Subscribers late emigrants in the Brigantine *Prince William* from the Shire of Sutherland near Britain most Humbly Sheweth –

That your Memorialists Nineteen heads of Families as numbered annexed to their names have lately arrived in this Port been obliged to look for an Assylum in this His Majesty's Province owing to the Land Holders of their Native Country having disspossed them by letting the Farms which they and their forefathers Occupied to Sheepholders.

Your Memorialists have served His Majesty on the Local Militia of Scotland and taken the Oath of Alleigiance they have been and ever will continue loyal Subjects – and they most Humbly pray your Excellency will be pleased to order them a Location of Lands in this District or in its Vicinity when vacant in proportion to the number in their families, and as in Duty bound shall ever pray –

Name	No in Family	No. of Acres
John MacKay	8	400
Robert McKay	4	300
John McKay	9	450
Hugh McKay	3	250
Donald McKay Sr.	6	300
Donald McKay Jr.	3	250
Robert McKenzie	11	500
Wm. McIntosh	12	500
Wm. McKay	5	300
John McKay	8	400
Alex. Munro	5	300
Kenneth Munro	6	300
John McKay	10	500
Wm. Ross	5	300
Wm. Neall	8	400
Widow McKay her husband dies of his wounds in Ireland	5	300
James McKay	3	250
Hugh McKay	6	300
William McKay	5	300

Endorsements

1. The Petition of John McKay and 18 others for land at Pictou, Received 4th Oct. 1815.
2. Personally appeared before me One of His Majesty's Justices of the Peace for the county of Halifax – The within named petitioners who being duely sworn depones that whatever they have stated in the same is truth – Sworn before me at Pictou this 30th September 1815.
   HUGH DENOON, J., P.
3. Recommended for the proportions pencilled opposite to the names of the Petitioners – "

6. The *Ossian*, Hill (Master), sailed 25th June 1821 from Cromarty to Pictou, [*Inverness Journal*, June 29, 1821]

"We have been favoured with the following list of the emigrants from Sutherlandshire who sailed from Cromarty, for Pictou, on Monday the 25th inst. per the *Ossian* of Leith, Captain Hill, with the particulars of the aid afforded to them from the fund raised by subscription in Bengal, and remitted by Messrs. MacKintosh & Co. 'for Relief of the Expatriated Highlanders of Sutherland.'"

Name	Aged	Family Adults Under 14	Cash £.	S.	D.	Hat chets	Pick axes	Spa des	Saws	Nails 1000	Eng / Gaelic Bibles		Tartan Yds	Barrels Pork
Jo. Sutherland, Miller	70	8	5	45	15	6	3	3	2	3	2	2	2	36	1/2
Dd. Suthd. M'Quarlish	50	4	5	5	15	6	2	2	1	2	1	1	2	20	1/2
Angus MacKay	40														
William Miller	36	4	1	10	0	0	2	2	2	2	2	1	2	24	1/2
Al. Suthd. M'Quarlish	50	3	5	20	9	6	1	1	1	1	1	1	1	15	1/4
Margt. Baillie, widow	55	8	1	39	7	6	4	4	2	2	2	2	2	36	1/2
Donald Sutherland	46	2	4	15	15	0	1	2	1	1	1	1	2	15	1/4
Robert McKay	70	7	1	30	0	0	1	2	1	1	2	1	2	18	1/2
William McDonald	55	5	5	31	0	0	2	3	2	1	1	2	2	24	1/2
George Baillie	46	4	5	26	15	6	2	2	2	1	1	2	2	25	1/2
Mgt. McDonald, widow	60	4	0	18	18	0	2	2	1	1	1	2	2	12	1/4
Ann Sutherland, widow	55	4	0	14	14	0	2	2	1	1	1	1	1	12	1/4
Don. & Chr. Ross	19&20	2	0	9	9	0	0	0	0	0	0	1	2	6	1/4
Hugh McLeod	50	6	0	28	7	0	2	2	1	1	1	1	1	15	1/2
Donald Douglas	30	1	0	0	0	0	1	1	0	0	0	1	1	3	0
Norman Douglas	18	1	0	0	0	0	1	1	0	0	0	1	0	3	0
Jean Sutherland	22	1	0	0	0	0	0	0	0	0	0	0	1	3	0
Margaret Murray	30	1	0	4	14	6	0	0	0	0	0	0	0	3	0
Donald McDonald	16	1	0	4	14	6	0	1	0	0	0	0	1	5	0
Jean Murray	25	1	0	4	14	6	0	0	0	0	0	0	1	3	0
Alex. Grant, and	34														
Alex. McLeod	32	5	4	29	18	6	3	3	2	2	2	1	2	30	1/2

The *Ossian* was chartered to carry the Sutherland emigrants at the very moderate rate of Four Guineas and a Half for adults, and One Guinea and a Half for passengers under fourteen years of age. Her stores, of all descriptions, were laid in at Leith, of the best quality, at the sight of the Freighter."

7. The *Emperor Alexander* of Aberdeen, Alexander Watt (Master) sailed from Tobermory to Sydney, Cape Breton, July 1823*
[*Inverness Journal*, Jan. 30, 1824]

"This is to certify that Mr John McEACHERN, the steward on board the *Emperor Alexander*, of Aberdeen, for Mr Archibald McNIVEN#, has done all manner of justice to us and all our fellow-passengers during out passage; and we further declare , that Captain ALEXANDER WATTS behaved to all his passengers with great humanity. SYDNEY, CAPE BRETON ISLAND, 16th Sept. 1823

Kintail

> DUNCAN MACRA
> GEORGE MACRA
> ALEX. MACRA
> DONALD MACCULLOCH
> JOHN MACLENNAN
> MALCOLM McCRIMMAN
> JOHN McEARLICH
> RODk. McLENNAN
> ALLAN MACDONALD

S. Uist

	his	
ALLAN	X	MACDONALD
	mark	
	his	
DONALD	X	MACDONALD
	mark	
	her	
CHRISTIAN	X	MACDONALD
	mark	
	his	
RONALD	X	MACINTYRE
	mark	

JOHN	his X mark	MACINTYRE
EFFY	her X mark	MACINTYRE
MARION	her X mark	MORISON
JOHN	his X mark	O'HEULY
ALEX.	his X mark	MACINTYRE
ANGUS	his X mark	MACINTYRE
JOHN	his X mark	CURRIE
JOHN	his X mark	STEEL
NIEL	his X mark	BEATON
RANALD	his X mark	O'HEULY
ANGUS	his X mark	O'HEULY
ALEXANDER	his X mark	STEEL
JOHN	his X mark	SMITH

APPENDIX I

Benbecula

	his	
DUNCAN	X	MACINTYRE
	mark	
	his	
ANGUS	X	MACINTYRE
	mark	

Badenoch

ARCHIBALD MACDONALD

Arisaig

JOHN MACDONALD

Barra

	his	
MALCOLM	X	MACDOUGALL
	mark	

N. Uist

MALCOLM MACDONALD
ANGUS MACDONALD

* The *Emperor Alexander* of Aberdeen sailed on to Quebec where a further 49 emigrants disembarked (*QM* Oct 7, 1824)
# Archibald Mc Niven was the principal Emigration Agent in the Hebrides from 1820 to 1840.

8. The *St Lawrence* of Newcastle, Jonathan Cram (Master) sailed 12th July 1828 from Leith to Ship Harbour, Cape Breton
[Source: MacDougall, *History of Inverness County*, 126–31.]

No.	Name	Age	Former Residence	Port of Landing
1	Hugh McLean	49	Rhum	Gut of Canso
2	Marion McLean	45	"	"
3	Flory McLean	19	"	"
4	John McLean	13	"	"
5	Angus McLean	10	"	"
6	Mary McLean	6	"	"

No.	Name	Age	Former Residence	Port of Landing
7	Catherine McLean	4	Rhum	Gut of Canso
8	Hector McLean	3	"	"
9	Allan McLean	Infant	"	"
10	Lauchlin McLean	45	"	"
11	Mary McLean	45	"	"
12	Marion McLean	24	"	"
13	Hugh McLean Jr	27	"	"
14	Catherine McLean	60	"	"
15	Donald McLean	48	"	"
16	Mary McLean	40	"	"
17	Hector McLean	60	"	"
18	Effie McLean	60	"	"
19	Angus Campbell	19	"	"
20	Neil McQuarrie	55	"	"
21	Marion McQuarrie	50	"	"
22	Simon Dalgleish	62	"	"
23	Penny Dalgleish	23	"	"
24	Donald McKay	27	"	"
25	Neil McKay	30	"	"
26	Charles McKay	24	"	"
27	Catherine McKay	60	"	"
28	Jean McKay	22	"	"
29	Catherine McKay	13	"	"
30	John McKay	19	"	"
31	Peter McKay	35	"	"
32	Flory McKay	32	"	"
33	Lauchlin McKay	5	"	"
34	Donald McKay	3	"	"
35	Angus McKay	2	"	"
36	John McKay	Infant	"	"
37	Jonathan McKinnon	30	"	"
38	Archy McKinnon	28	"	"
39	Ann McKinnon	60	"	"
40	Mary McKinnon	26	"	"
41	Ann McKinnon	5	"	"
42	John McKinnon	3	"	"
43	Flory McKinnon	Infant	"	"
44	Alexander McKinnon	28	"	"
45	Margaret McKinnon	60	"	"
46	Marion McKinnon	28	"	"
47	Jessie McKinnon	26	"	"

APPENDIX I

No.	Name	Age	Former Residence	Port of Landing
48	John McKinnon	24	Rhum	Gut of Canso
49	Catherine McKinnon	16	"	"
50	Charles McLean	30	"	"
51	Flory McLean	62	"	"
52	John McQuarrie	65	"	"
53	Marion McQuarrie	60	"	"
54	Allan McQuarrie	30	"	"
55	Donald McQuarrie	28	"	"
56	Rachel McQuarrie	26	"	"
57	Margaret McQuarrie	24	"	"
58	Bell McQuarrie	20	"	"
59	Lauchlin McInnes	55	"	"
60	Mary McInnes	48	"	"
61	Penny McInnes	25	"	"
62	Allan McInnes	23	"	"
63	Hector McInnes	21	"	"
64	Mary McInnes	19	"	"
65	Donald McInnes	17	"	"
66	Marion McInnes	10	"	"
67	Flory McInnes	8	"	"
68	Jessie McInnes	6	"	"
69	Neil McLean	40	"	"
70	Mary McLean	30	"	"
71	Margaret McLean	10	"	"
72	John McLean	6	"	"
73	Alexander McLean	5	"	"
74	Ann McLean	3	"	"
75	Donald McLean	Infant	"	"
76	Rory McIsaac	85	"	"
77	Mary McIsaac	40	"	"
78	Peggy McLean	80	"	"
79	Donald McPhaden	54	"	"
80	Flory McPhaden	50	"	"
81	Hector McPhaden	19	"	"
82	Ann McPhaden	13	"	"
83	Donald McPhaden	10	"	"
84	John McPhaden	8	"	"
85	Angus McPhaden	6	"	"
86	Hector McLean	32	"	"
87	Catherine McLean	29	"	"
88	Mary McLean	Infant	"	"

No.	Name	Age	Former Residence	Port of Landing
89	Malcolm McKinnon	45	Rhum	Gut of Canso
90	Bell McKinnon	35	"	"
91	Catherine McKinnon	18	"	"
92	Christina McKinnon	15	"	"
93	John McKinnon	13	"	"
94	Marion McKinnon	10	"	"
95	Peggy McKinnon	6	"	"
96	Flory McKinnon	4	"	"
97	Bell McKinnon	2	"	"
98	Margaret McKinnon	60	"	"
99	Flory McKinnon	30	"	"
100	Catherine McKinnon	28	"	"
101	Lauchlin McKay	28	"	"
102	Mary McLean	50	"	"
103	Donald McKinnon	47	"	"
104	Margaret McKinnon	46	"	"
105	Jessie McKinnon	21	"	"
106	Lauchlin McKinnon	20	"	"
107	Donald McKinnon	16	"	"
108	John McKinnon	13	"	"
109	Catherine McKinnon	10	"	"
110	Angus McKinnon	6	"	"
111	Peter McKinnon	3	"	"
112	John McKinnon	48	"	"
113	Ann McKinnon	45	"	"
114	Bell McKinnon	20	"	"
115	Donald McKinnon	18	"	"
116	Mary McKinnon	15	"	"
117	Neil McKinnon	12	"	"
118	John McKinnon	6	"	"
119	Donald McKinnon	3	"	"
120	Hugh McLean	29	"	"
121	Marion McKinnon	28	"	"
122	Rachel McKinnon	Infant	"	"
123	Allan McLean	89	"	"
124	Ann McLean	62	"	"
125	Peggy McLean	40	"	"
126	Peggy McArthur	12	"	"
127	Hector McArthur	6	"	"
128	Donald McKay	54	"	"
129	Christine McKay	49	"	"

No.	Name	Age	Former Residence	Port of Landing
130	Mary McKay	20	Rhum	Gut of Canso
131	Flory McKay	18	"	"
132	John McKay	15	"	"
133	Donald McKay	10	"	"
134	Neil McKay	6	"	"
135	Jean Cameron	48	"	"
136	Peggy McKinnon	20	"	"
137	Loddy McKinnon	17	"	"
138	Catherine McKinnon	15	"	"
139	Mary McKinnon	13	"	"
140	Archy McKinnon	10	"	"
141	Lauchlin McKinnon	40	"	"
142	Marion McKinnon	35	"	"
143	Lauchlin McKinnon	12	"	"
144	Catherine McKinnon	10	"	"
145	Archy McKinnon	8	"	"
146	Donald McKinnon	6	"	"
147	Mary McKinnon	Infant	"	"
148	Donald McKay	65	"	"
149	Christina McMillan	60	"	"
150	Alexander McLean	26	"	"
151	Neil McLean	28	"	"
152	Catherine McLean	33	"	"
153	Archy McMillan	27	"	"
154	Jessie McMillan	28	"	"
155	Donald McMillan	2	"	"
156	Neil McMillan	Infant	"	"
157	Angus McMillan	38	"	"
158	Marion McMillan	40	"	"
159	Ann McMillan	28	"	"
160	Neil McMillan	24	"	"
161	Marion McMillan	17	"	"
162	Ann McKay	40	"	"
163	Duncan McKay	20	"	"
164	Mary McKay	25	"	"
165	Neil McKay	18	"	"
166	Donald McMillan	57	"	"
167	Marion McMillan	52	"	"
168	John McMillan	67	"	"
169	Catherine McMillan	26	"	"
170	Mary McMillan	24	"	"

No.	Name	Age	Former Residence	Port of Landing
171	Ann McMillan	23	Rhum	Gut of Canso
172	Neil Stewart	26	"	"
173	Marion Stewart	20	"	"
174	Flory McMillan	17	"	"
175	Neil McMillan	13	"	"
176	Donald McMillan	48	"	"
177	Catherine McKinnon	50	"	"
178	Marion McMillan	88	"	"
179	Flory McKinnon	18	"	"
180	Marion McKinnon	16	"	"
181	Ann McKinnon	12	"	"
182	Allan McKinnon	18	"	"
183	Neil MacKay	60	"	"
184	Mary McKay	57	"	"
185	Mary McKay	35	"	"
186	Donald McKay	23	"	"
187	Peggy McKay	30	"	"
188	Neil McKay	28	"	"
189	John McKay	26	"	"
190	Christina McKay	21	"	"
191	Jessie McKay	33	"	"
192	Ann McKay	Infant	"	"
193	Duncan McKinnon	63	"	"
194	Mary McKinnon	58	"	"
195	Alexander McKinnon	30	"	"
196	Ann McKinnon	25	"	"
197	Lauchlin McKinnon	24	"	"
198	Ann McKinnon	20	"	"
199	Catherine McKinnon	15	"	"
200	Donald McKinnon	19	"	"
201	Flory McKinnon	40	"	"
202	Margaret McKinnon	38	"	"
203	Allan McKay	12	"	"
204	Allan McLean	58	"	"
205	Christina McLean	42	"	"
206	John McLean	13	"	"
207	Malcolm McLean	11	"	"
208	Flory McLean	9	"	"

APPENDIX I

9. The 49 families from Skye who sailed on the *Malay* to Sydney in 1830
[NSARM RG1 Vol. 67 Doc. 19]

	Heads of Families	Women	Children
1	BEATON, Alexander	Mary	Anne, Ket, Donald, Isabel, John
2	BEATON, Samuel	Ket	Mary, Donald
3	McINNES, John	Flora	
4	BEATON, John	Margaret	Mary
5	GILLES, Murdo	Margaret	Christy, Angus, Malcolm, James, Donald, Susan
6	GILLES, Archibald	Ket	Murdo, Margaret, Angus
7	ROSS, John	Mary	
8	CAMPBELL, Murdo	Anne	
9	McDERMIT, Neil	Margaret	
10	GILLES, John	Flora	Sarah, Duncan, Mary, Archibald, Christy
11	McKENZIE, Malcolm	Christy	Rod., John, Flora
12	STEWART, Peter	Margaret	Allan
13	GILLES, John	Jannet	John
14	STEWART, John	Christy	Ket, Jennet
15	McKINNON, John	Flora	John, Christy, Alexander
16	BUCHANNON,	Jannet	Duncan, Malcolm, Alexander
17	ROSS, Donald	Ket	Ket, Margaret, Mary
18	McKINNON, Neil	Marion	Malcolm, Mary, Ket., Maragret
19	McINNES, Malcolm	Marion	Marion, Neil, Ket
20	McINNES, Angus	Margaret	Mary, Angus
21	BEATON, John, widower		Anne, John, Betsy, Isabel, Donald
22	BEATON, Malcolm	Mary	
23	BEATON, William	Mary	Donald, Neil, Jannet
24	GILLES, Angus	Flora	
25	McKENZIE, Donal	Anne	Peggy, Duncan, Alexander
26	CAMPBELL, Alexander	Ket	Anne, Ket, Duncan
27	CAMPBELL, Malcolm	Anne	
28	McLEAN, Norman	Peggy	John, Norman, Maragret
29	McPHERSON, Donald	Marion	Donald, John, Alexander, Mary, Margaret
30	STUART, Alexander	Mary	Donald, Agnes, Anne, Jannet, John
31	NICHOLSON, Alex.	Margaret	John, Donald

225

Heads of Families	Women	Children
32 CAMPBELL, Alexander	Christy	John
33 CAMERON, Donald	Anne	Anne, Charles, Mary
34 McINNES, Miles	Mary	Mary, Christy, John, Flora
35 ROSS, John	Mary	Mary, Angus, Christy, Bell, Murdo
36 —		
37 McKINNON, Donald	Christy	
38 FINLAYSON, Alex.	Christy	Angus, Christy, Anne
39 NICHOLSON, Duncan	Anne	
40 NICHOLSON, James	Margaret	Anne, John
41 ROSS, Alexander	Anne	Mary, John, Donald, Bain., Flora
42 McDONALD, Duncan	Christy	Flora, Donald
43 BEATON, Donald	Jannet	Malcolm
44 McNAB, John	Ket	Mary, Anne, Andrew, John, Marion
45 McLEOD, Donald	Mary	John, Anne, Maragret, Donald, Malcolm, Roderick, Samuel, Mary
46 McDONALD, Duncan	Anne	
47 McKENZIE, John	Ket	
48 NICHOLSON, Samuel	Ket	John, Norman, Alex., Mary, Norman
49 McDONALD, Donald	Bell	Duncan, also stepsons: Collin, Charles & Lach. CAMPBELL

Total: 49 Men, 48 Women, 123 Children in all 220 souls.

10. The *Lady Grey* of North Shields, William Grey (Master) sailed June 1841 from Cromarty and Thurso with 240 passengers to Pictou and Quebec [NAS RH 1/2/908]

List of passengers who protested about their ill-treatment during the voyage. All had disembarked at Pictou:

John F. Simpson	Wm. McDonald
James Allen	Donald Sutherland
John Ross	Hugh Ross
John Campbell	Angus McLean

Hector Holm Jr.
Donald Gordon
James Ross
Donald Ross
John McKay
Hugh Fraser
Duncan McDonald
John Bannerman (weaver)
Alex. McDonald
Rob't Ferguson
Donald McKenzie
Donald McLean
Hugh MacKay
Hugh Ross
John McLellan
Alex. Sutherland
Wm. McIntosh
John Campbell

Donald Bannerman
John Murray
Wm. Chisholm
Colin McDonald
James McPherson
Hugh Beaton
Robert Lillie
George McKay
John Sutherland
Wm. Bannerman
Wm. Gunn (tailor)
Hugh Murray
Alex. Taylor
Angus McLeod
Hector Holm Sr.
Wm. Ross
Alex. Campbell

11. The *Hope* of Glasgow, William Grange (Master) sailed 5th April 1848 from Glasgow to Pictou.
[NSARM Vol. 257 Doc. 99]

\# People who had travelled on the *Hope* but left Pictou to settle in the United States.

David McLean
Martha McLean
Robert McLean
Martha McLean

Joseph Robertson
Rosanna Robertson
Joseph Robertson
George Robertson
William Robertson
Mary Robertson
James Robertson
Jane Robertson
Isabella Robertson

James Robertson#
Jane Robertson#

Elizabeth Robertson#
William Robertson#

Pettigrew Robertson#
Margaret Robertson#
John Robertson#
Elizabeth Robertson#
Jane Robertson#

George Robertson
Anne Robertson
Margaret Robertson
Anne Robertson
Sarah Robertson
Charles Robertson

George Robertson#

John Greenhorn
Margaret Greenhorn
Anne Greenhorn
John Greenhorn

Robert Borland#
Elizabeth Borland#
John Borland#
Robert Borland#
Elizabeth Borland#
Joseph Borland#

John Borland#
Jane Borland#
Janet Borland#
John Borland#
Isabella Borland#

227

George Robertson#
Jane Robertson#
James Robertson#
Anne Robertson#
Charles Robertson#
John Robertson#

Edward Robertson
Margaret Robertson
Mary Robertson
Peter Robertson
Barbara Robertson
George Robertson

Walter Robertson#
Isabella Robertson#
Isabella Robertson#
Jane Falkin
Tabitha Falkin

Robert Cullin
Janet Cullin
Thomas Cullin
David Cullin
Anne Cullin
Jane Cullin
Margt. Cullin
Elizt. Cullin
Martha Cullin

Archibald Niven

James Stevenson#
Helen Stevenson
John Picken#
Margaret Picken
Francis Stevenson
James Stevenson
Janet Stevenson
Helen Stevenson

John Blue#

Mary Robertson#
Anne Robertson#
Mary Robertson#

William Robertson

John Robertson
Maria Robertson
James Robertson

Andrew Gilmour
Anne Gilmour
Jane Gilmour
Robert Gilmour
Anne Gilmour
Helen Gilmour
Robert Wilson

John Morison#
Jane Morison#
Elizabeth Morison#
Robert Morison#
John Morison#
Jane Morison#

William Baird#
Margaret Baird#
Margaret Baird#
Mary Baird#
Gavin Baird#
Jane Baird#
Robertson Baird#
Janet Baird#

Joseph Martin#
Jane Martin#
Joseph Martin#

James Houston
Jane Houston

John Bowman#
Mary Bowman#
John Bowman#
Mary Bowman

Samuel McDougall#
Ann McDougall#
John McDougall#
Murdoch McDougall#
Agnes McDougall#
Euphemia McDougall#

William Falkin
Elizabeth Falkin
Margaret Filkin
John Falkin
James Houston

William Storie

William McLeay

John Wood

Elizabeth Greenhorn

Agnes Weir
Mary Weir
Agnes Weir

John Clark

In Cabin
George Walker
Mrs. Walker
Janet Walker
Anne Walker
Andrew Walker
Robert Walker
George Walker
Mary Jane Walker

Totals: 70 adults, 67 children.

12. The *Ellen* of Liverpool, Dugald McLachlan (Master) sailed 22nd May 1848 from Loch Laxford to Pictou
[NSARM Vol. 257 Doc. 110]

Donald Kerr
Sarah Kerr
William Kerr
John Kerr
Ann Bethune
Meran Bethune
Barbara Bethune
John Bethune
Ann Bethune
Johan Bethune

Angus McKay
Elizt. McKay
Barbara McKay
William McKay
Georgina McKay
Margaret McKay

W. Meran McLeod

Ann McKay
Elizt. McKay
Margt. Adam

Murdo Morrison

Flora Kerr
Cathie Kerr

Hugh McIntosh
Elspet McKay
Georgina MacKay
Diana McKay

Roderick McKay
Barbara McKay

John McLeod
Ann McLeod
Isabella McLeod
Jean McLeod
Barbara McLeod

Donald McLeod
Margaret McLeod
Colin McLeod
Simon McLeod
Thos. McLeod
Janet McLeod

George McIntosh

Barbara McIntosh
Elizabeth McIntosh

John Bethune
Hecato McKenzie
Donald McKenzie
Angus McKenzie
Margt. McKenzie

Benjamin Gunn
Flora Gunn
Donald Gunn

Fingal Morrison

Hector Falconer
Mary Falconer
Flora Falconer
Catharine Falconer
Alexander Falconer
Hughina Falconer
Mary Falconer
James Falconer
Johan Falconer
Peter Falconer

Elizt. Morrison
Ann Morrison
Alex. Morrison
John Morrison
Donald Morrison

William McKay
Janet McKay
Catherine McKay
Neilina McKay
Roderick McKay
Murdo McKay

Donald McKay
Jean McKay
Maria McKay
Donald McLeod
Johan McLeod
Hugh McLeod
Lucy McLeod
Robertina McLeod
David McLeod
Betty McLeod

Donald McLeod
Mary McLeod
George McLeod
Mary McLeod

George McLeod
Nancy McLeod
Margt. McLeod

Neil McLeod
Catherine McLeod

James McKay
Bessy McKay

Janet McIntosh

Donald McKenzie
Ann McIntosh
Robina McIntosh
Donaldina McIntosh
Cina McIntosh
Roderick McIntosh
Hughina McIntosh

John McKay
Jess McKay
Georgine McKay

Hugh McKenzie
Betty McKenzie
William Gunn
Christy Gunn
Donald Gunn

McKenzie Gunn
Merran Gunn
John Gunn
Mary Gunn
Jane Gunn
Donald Gunn
Robert Gunn
Angus Gunn
William Gunn

Jane Lamond
Merran Lamond

John Matheson
Johan Matheson
William Matheson
John Matheson
Patrick Matheson
Kenneth Matheson

Kathel Kerr
Ann Kerr
John Kerr
George Kerr
Bell Kerr
William Kerr
Barbara Kerr

Mary McKenzie

Donald McLeod
Betty McLeod
Hugh McLeod
Christy McLeod
Ann McLeod
Elspet Matheson
Robert Matheson

Donald McKenzie
Mary McKenzie
Alex McKenzie
Donald McKenzie
Murdoch McKenzie
Henry McKenzie
John McKenzie
Mary McKenzie
Flora McKenzie

Ann Sutherland
Fairly McKay
Jean McKay

David McKay
(Cabin Passenger)
Dond. Morrison
Cathrine McKay
(wife)
Peter Morrison

Margaret Matheson having failed to appear after the ship was cleared, the following parties are now substituted in their stead vizt.

Mrs. Ann Sutherland 80   Fairly McKay 24   Ann McKay 18
Jean McKay 26

13. The *London* of Glasgow, John McDonald (Master) sailed 11th April 1848 from Glasgow to Pictou
[NSARM Vol. 257 Doc. 104]

Dond. Nicholson

James Reid

Dond. Kennedy
Jane Kennedy

Janet Pitbluda

Jas. McDonald
Janet McDonald

Daniel Robertson
Grace Robertson
James Robertson

Thos W. Kennedy
Elizabeth Kennedy

John Foley
Elizabeth Foley
John Pitbluda

James Pitbludie
Catherine Pitbludie
Ann K. Pitbludie
Alex. McDonald

John Butler
Mary Butler
Sally Butler
John Butler

Anne Pitbluda
Chas. B. Pitbluda
P. McD. Pitbluda
Anne Pitbluda
Catherine Pitbluda
John Pitbluda

Hugh Butler
James Butler
Jane Butler
Henry Butler
In Cabin
Mrs. Miller
Mrs Robertson of
      Nova Scotia
Mrs Elizabeth Chase

14. The *London* of Glasgow, John McDonald (Master) sailed 14th July 1848 from Glasgow to Pictou
[NSARM Vol. 257 Doc. 131]

John McDonald
Una McDonald
Catherine McDonald
June McDonald
Murdoch McDonald

John McInnes
Elizabeth Baird
Donald Ross
Janet Irvine

William Stevenson
Neil McLeod
Catherine McDonald
Robert Dick
Mary McIntosh
Ann McIntosh
Susan McIntosh
William Burgess
Catherine Wallace
Alex. Laurie

Malcolm McKenzie
Beth McKenzie
Marion McKenzie
Ewen McKenzie
(written on backo
  For P. E. Island
Neal McLeod
Murdoch McDonald
John McInnis

15. The *Lulan* of Pictou, George McKenzie (Master) sailed 17th August 1848 from Glasgow to Pictou.
[NSARM Vol. 257 Doc. 167]

George Cowie
John Ferguson
David Moses
Thomas Lower
William Burt
Jas. Neilson
Andrew Neilson
Wm. Grant

Geo. Prentice
Jane Prentice

Peter Samson
Janet Sampson
Peter Samson
Margaret Samson
Agnes Samson
Jane Samson
Robert Samson

Wm. Fleming
Elizabeth Fleming
Alexander Fleming
Jane Fleming
Hugh Fleming
Elizabeth Fleming

Hugh Maxwell

James Neilson
Marion Neilson
Mary Neilson
John Neilson
Catherine Neilson

Murdo McLeod
Catherine McLeod
Margaret McLeod

John Pollock
Colin McLuckie
Wm. McCalloch
John Fairlie
Robt. Sillars
John Gillies
Ann Gillies
Flora Gillies
Margaret Gillies
Christina Gillies
Catherine Gillies

Angus McPhee
Marion McPhee
Ronald McPhee
Angus McPhee
Christina McPhee

Hugh McLean
Jessie McLean
Marion McLean
Effie McLean
Catherine McLean
Donald McLean
Mary McLean

Archibald McAulay
Catherine McAulay

Anne McLellan
Penny McLellan

Archibald McLeod
Hector McLeod
Marion McLeod
Christine McLeod
Jessie McLeod
John McLeod

Effie McAulay
Donald McAulay

Rory McLellan
Flora McLellan
Hugh McLellan
Margaret McLellan
Mary McLellan
Donald McLellan
Catherine McLellan
Rory McLellan

Neil McPherson
Catherine McPherson
Donald McPherson
Samuel McPherson
Marion McPherson
Angus McPherson
Fergus McPherson

Duncan McIntyre
Mary McIntyre
Mary McIntyre
Catherine McIntyre
Anne McIntyre
Neil McIntyre
Effie McIntyre

Angus McDonald
Marion McDonald
Ann McDonald
Mary McDonald
Neil McDonald
Donald McDonald
Christina McDonald

John McIntyre

Mary McLeod

Malcom McDonald
Ann McDonald
Ronald McDonald
Donald McDonald
Christina McDonald
Mary McDonald
John McDonald

Donald McDonald
Malcom McLellan

Alex Gillies
Flora Gillies

John Morrison
Isabella Morrison
Ann Morrison
Angus Morrisonq

Finlay McInnes
Penny McInnes
Donald McInnes

Finlay McLellan
Mrs. R. Grant
Mr. J. A. Dawson

Ewing McLeod
Mary McLeod

Peter McIntyre
Gormal McIntyre
Donald McIntyre
Ann McIntyre
Angus McIntyre
John McIntyre
Peggy McIntyre

Ronald McDonald
Donald McDonald
Mary McDonald
Peggy McDonald

Allan Black
Margaret Black
Duncan Black
John Black

Donald McDonald
Catherine McDonald
Mary McDonald
Donald McDonald
Miss J. Dawson
Mr. Honeyman

Catherine McIntyre
Mary McIntyre
Effie McIntyre
Mary McIntyre
Christina McIntyre
Effie McIntyre
Donald McIntyre

Anne Morison
Anne Morison
Mary Morison
James Morison
Allan Morison

Mary Morison

Neil McCormaig
Mary McCormaig
Donald McCormaig

John Clarkson
Mrs Clarkson
   Cabin Passengers
James Carmichael
Jessy Carmichael
Mrs. Honeyman
Mr. Faickny

APPENDIX II

Emigrant Ship Crossings from Scotland to Nova Scotia and Cape Breton, 1773–1852

Year	Mth	Vessel	Master	Psgr. Nos.	Departure Port	Arrival Port
1773	06	*Hector*	Spiers, John	190	Loch Broom from Greenock	Pictou

Passenger List: MacLaren, *Pictou Book*, 31–4. Reconstructed passenger list (Appendix I). Patterson, *History, Pictou County*, 450–6; Adams & Somerville, *Cargoes of Despair and Hope*, 76; MacKay, *Scotland Farewell*, 89–105.
Most passengers originated from Wester Ross, Sutherland and East Inverness-shire. Ship arrived Sept. 15. The emigrants were recruited by John Ross, an agent for the Philadelphia Land Company which owned 200,000 acres of wilderness land in Pictou. The *Hector* was owned by John Pagan.

Year	Mth	Vessel	Master	Psgr. Nos.	Departure Port	Arrival Port
1774		*Lovelly Nelly*	Sheridan, William	67	Whitehaven	PEI

Passenger List: PRO T 47/12. The passenger list is undated but almost certainly refers to a 1774 crossing.
Passengers came from Kirkcudbrightshire and Dumfriesshire Many of the emigrants later moved on to Pictou. The group included 4 masons, 1 blacksmith, 2 wheelwrights, 2 farmers, 3 joiners, 9 labourers and 1 sailor. The Captain's name is given as William Sherwin in the *Lloyds Shipping Register*.

Year	Mth	Vessel	Master	Psgr. Nos.	Departure Port	Arrival Port
1774	04	*John and Jean*		59	Aberdeen	Halifax & Quebec

Adams & Somerville, *Cargoes of Despair and Hope*, 124, 217; NSARM MG7 Vol. 3A. "Brought a number of settlers and some indented servants." Arrived Halifax June 7, 1774.

Year	Mth	Vessel	Master	Psgr. Nos.	Departure Port	Arrival Port
1775	05	*Lovelly Nelly*	Sheridan, William	82	Dumfries	PEI

Passenger List: PRO T 47/12
Passengers came from Dumfriesshire, Kirkcudbrightshire & Peebleshire. The group included 2 joiners, 2 weavers, 12 labourers, 1 gardener, 1 chapman (pedlar), 1 blacksmith, 1 school master, 1 mariner, 1 clerk and 1 farmer. Some of the emigrants later moved to Pictou.

Year	Mth	Vessel	Master	Psgr. Nos.	Departure Port	Arrival Port
1783		*Sally*		n/k	Aberdeen	Halifax

Bumsted, *People's Clearance*, 72.
Arrived in August. 39 died on the crossing and others died soon after arriving.

Year	Mth	Vessel	Master	Psgr. Nos.	Departure Port	Arrival Port
1784		*Glasgow*		> 100	Greenock	Halifax

Lawson, *The Emigrant Scots*, 39; NSARM MG7 Vol. 3A.
Ship carried "indented passengers." The arrivals petitioned for land in Pictou.

Year	Mth	Vessel	Master	Psgr. Nos.	Departure Port	Arrival Port
1784		*John*	Allen, Robert	n/k	Aberdeen	Halifax, Shelbourne, N.S. & Philadelphia, U.S.A.

Patterson, *History, Pictou County*, 122–3, 465; *AJ* Feb. 23 & May 17, 1784; Patterson, *Memoir of John MacGregor*, 81; MacKay, *Scotland Farewell*, 167.
In 1784 "a few families of Highlanders...arrived at Halifax, removed to Pictou, and settled on the East River." They probably sailed on the *John*. She was to call at Cromarty to collect passengers. The brig was "to be fitted up entirely for the reception and accommodation of passengers" and would be "supplied with plenty of the best provisions."

Year	Mth	Vessel	Master	Psgr. Nos.	Departure Port	Arrival Port
1785		unnamed vessel		n/k	Glasgow	Halifax

NSARM MG7 Vol. 3A.

Year	Mth	Vessel	Master	Psgr. Nos.	Departure Port	Arrival Port

1791   *Dunkenfield*   650   West Highland Pictou
            and another vessel   port of Glasgow

MacLaren, *Pictou Book*, 118; MacDonald, "Early Highland Emigration to Nova Scotia and PEI," 44; MacKay, *Scotland Farewell*, 182–3.

Vessel also known as the *Dunkeld*. Simon Fraser was the emigration agent. Mainly Roman Catholics from the Western Isles. Dispersed to PEI, Antigonish and Cape Breton.

1801   *Alexander*   n/k   Fort William   Pictou

Johnston, *History of the Catholic Church in Eastern Nova Scotia*, 163.

Many Catholics from the West Highlands and Western Isles.

1801   *Good Intent*   Beverly,   n/k   Fort William   Pictou
            of Aberdeen   Robert

MacLaren, *Pictou Book*, 118; Johnston, *History of the Catholic Church in Eastern Nova Scotia*, 163.

Vessel incorrectly recorded as *Golden Text*. Passage of 3 months. Passengers mainly Roman Catholics from Glen Moriston.

1801   *Hope* of Lossie   100   Isle Martin   Pictou
                                         (Ullapool)

NLS MS9646; Telford, *Survey, Central Highlands*.

A total of 122 souls from the estate of Struy (Strathglass) on board. They were calculated as being equivalent to 100 adults (children and infants totalled separately and recomputed as adult equivalents). George Dunoon was the shipping agent.

1801   *Nora*   500   Fort William   Pictou

MacLaren, *Pictou Book*, 118; Johnston, *History of the Catholic Church in Eastern Nova Scotia*, 163.

NAS RH4/188/2.

Smallpox broke out on the passage and 65 children under 5 died. Most arrivals moved to PEI, Truro, Antigonish and Cape Breton

1801   06   *Dove*   Crane   219   Fort William   Pictou
            of Aberdeen

Passenger List: NAS RH2/4/87 (Appendix I).

NLS MS9646; Adams & Somerville, *Cargoes of Despair & Hope*, 193; *PP* 1802–03; Johnston, *History of the Catholic Church in Eastern Nova Scotia*, 163; Bumsted, *People's Clearance*, 91–2.

There were 153 adults and 66 children under 16 years. Most of them originated from Inverness-shire. Hugh Dunoon, the emigration agent, was on board. George Dunoon from Pictou also named as an agent.

Year	Mth	Vessel	Master	Psgr. Nos.	Departure Port	Arrival Port
1801	06	*Sarah* of Liverpool	Smith	350	Fort William	Pictou

Passenger List: NAS RH2/4/87 (Appendix I).
NLS MS9646; Adams & Somerville, *Cargoes of Despair & Hope*, 193; *PP* 1802–03; Johnston, *History of the Catholic Church in Eastern Nova Scotia*, 163; Bumsted, *People's Clearance*, 91–2.
Most passengers originated from Inverness-shire. Hugh and George Dunoon were agents. Ship arrived in August.

1802		*Tweed* of Ullapool		70	Isle Martin (Ullapool)	Pictou

NLS MS9646; Brown, *Strictures and Remarks on Earl of Selkirk's Observations*, Appendix, State of Emigrations, 1801, 1802 and 1803; *PP* 1802–03.
Settlers probably originated from Sutherland and Wester Ross. Agent was A. McMillan.

1802		two unnamed vessels		900	Lochboisdale	Pictou

NLS MS9646; Brown, *Strictures and Remarks on Earl of Selkirk's Observations*; *PP* 1802–03; Johnston, *History of the Catholic Church in Eastern Nova Scotia*, 197.
Emigration agent was J. Ure. Catholics from the Clanranald estate in South Uist and Barra who mainly settled in Antigonish and Cape Breton.

1802	05	*Northern Friends* of Clyde		340	Moidart from Greenock	Sydney

NLS MS9646; Brown, *Strictures and Remarks on Earl of Selkirk's Observations*; *PP* 1802–03; NAS RH4/188/2.
Emigration agent was Andrew McDonald. There were 340 souls, who were recalculated as 250 adult passengers (converting children and infants to adult equivalents). Mainly Catholics from Inverness-shire.

1802	07	*Aurora* of Greenock	MacLean Alan	128	Fort William from Greenock	Pictou

NLS MS9646; Brown, *Strictures and Remarks on Earl of Selkirk's Observations*; Telford, *Survey, Central Highlands*; Johnston, *History of the Catholic Church in Eastern Nova Scotia*, 197; Patterson, *History, Pictou County*, 232–3.
Simon Fraser was emigration agent. There were 82 passengers above 16 years and 46 below. Mostly Catholics from Inverness-shire who settled in Antigonish.

Year	Mth	Vessel	Master	Psgr. Nos.	Departure Port	Arrival Port
1803		*Alexander* & 2 other ships		600	Stornoway	Pictou

Brown, *Strictures and Remarks on Earl of Selkirk's Observations*; Telford, *Survey, Central Highlands*; NAS GD 46/17 Vol. 23.
Two vessels provided by R. Macever (who was probably Roderick MacIver of Stornoway) and the third by J. MacKenzie of Lochead.

Year	Mth	Vessel	Master	Psgr. Nos.	Departure Port	Arrival Port
1803		Four unnamed vessels		480	Moray Firth	Pictou

Brown, *Strictures and Remarks on Earl of Selkirk's Observations*.
Settlers from Strathglass. Four vessels each carrying 120 passengers. Agents were D. Forbes and a Mr. Clark. One of the ship crossings was organised by "a club of Strathglass people".

Year	Mth	Vessel	Master	Psgr. Nos.	Departure Port	Arrival Port
1803		Two unnamed vessels		n/k		Pictou

Brown, *Strictures and Remarks on Earl of Selkirk's Observations*.
Vessels arranged "by Major Simon Fraser who has made a trade of the business since 1790."

Year	Mth	Vessel	Master	Psgr. Nos.	Departure Port	Arrival Port
1803	06	*Favourite* of Kirkaldy	Ballantyne	500	Isle Martin (Ullapool)	Pictou

Brown, *Strictures and Remarks on Earl of Selkirk's Observations*; Telford, *Survey, Central Highlands*.
The *Favourite* sailed with another vessel. Both were owned by Major Melville of Ullapool. The agent was D. Roy from America. Most passengers probably originated from Sutherland and Wester Ross.

Year	Mth	Vessel	Master	Psgr. Nos.	Departure Port	Arrival Port
1803	08	*Commerce*	Galt, Robert	70	Port Glasgow	Pictou

Passenger List: NLS MSS 1053 (Appendix I).
Settlers from Perthshire. Most said they had emigrated because their farms "had been taken" from them, or their rents had been raised.

Year	Mth	Vessel	Master	Psgr. Nos.	Departure Port	Arrival Port
1804	06	*North Star*		n/k	Leith via Greenock	Pictou (for repair)

NAS CS.96/3355; *GA*, Apr. 6.
The *North Star* set out with passengers bound for Pictou but had to return to Leith for repairs.

Year	Mth	Vessel	Master	Psgr. Nos.	Departure Port	Arrival Port
1805		*Polly*		n/k	n/k	Canso, Cape Breton

MacDonald, "Early Highland Emigration to Nova Scotia and PEI," 44.

| 1805 | | *Sir Sydney Smith* | | n/k | Stornoway | Pictou |

MacLaren, *Pictou Book*, 119; MacKay, *Scotland Farewell*, 196.

| 1805 | 05 | *Nancy* | Church, W.S. | 32 | Tobermory | PEI |

PAPEI RG9; *GA* 12 March 1805; Harvey, *Journeys to the Island*, 76–77.
The *Greenock Advertiser* stated: "for freight or charter to Halifax, New Brunswick, Pictou or Newfoundland; The schooner Nancy…would engage to carry out a load of passengers. Alan Ker & Co." The passengers were landed at Three Rivers.

| 1806 | 07 | *Pallas* | | n/k | Greenock | PEI, Sydney, Pictou, Quebec |

GA 11 June; *QM* 24 Sept.
"If sufficient numbers of passengers offer, *Pallas* will be able to call at a port in the Highlands to take them on board and will land them at the Island of Saint John, Sydney, Pictou or any other convenient port in the Gulf of St. Lawrence as they many incline."

| 1806 | 08 | *Elizabeth and Ann* of North Shields | St Girese, Thomas | 107 | Thurso | PEI |

Passenger List: *PAPEI 2702*.
GA 13 August 1806; E.504/7/5. According to the *Greenock Advertiser*, the *Elizabeth and Ann* was destined for Pictou. Passengers from North East Highlands, some from Durness and Tongue.

| 1806 | 08 | *Hope* | Henry, Matthew | 47 | Port Glasgow | Halifax & Quebec |

QM Oct 30; *GA* Aug 20.
47 steerage passengers disembarked at Quebec. She was also to call at Halifax.

| 1807 | 09 | *Rambler* of Leith | Norris, J. | 130 | Stromness from Thurso | Pictou |

E.504/7/5; *IC* Oct. 9,1807, Feb. 8, 1808.
Wrecked on October 29th near Newfoundland. A total of 138 people perished. The *Rambler* had taken emigrants in the previous year to PEI. The passengers on this crossing originated from Sutherland (Farr, Lairg and Rogart parishes) and Caithness.

Year	Mth	Vessel	Master	Psgr. Nos.	Departure Port	Arrival Port
1810	08	*Favourite* of Grangemouth	McDonald, Alexander	31	Oban	Pictou

E.504/25/3.
Journey time of 12 weeks

1811	03	*Ploughman* of Aberdeen	Yule, Alexander	28	Aberdeen	Pictou

E.504/1/24.

1811	04	*Malvina* of Aberdeen	Smith, John	12	Aberdeen	Quebec

E.504/1/24.
No record in *Quebec Gazette* of passenger arrivals. They may have disembarked at Nova Scotia.

1811	04	*Mary* of Aberdeen	Morrison, James	30	Aberdeen	Halifax

E.504/1/24.

1811	05	*Anne* of North Shields	Tod, James	26	Stornoway	Pictou

E.504/33/3.
A surgeon travelled.

1811	07	*Centurion* of Aberdeen	Morrison, James	18	Aberdeen	Halifax

E.504/1/24.

1812	03	*Ploughman* of Aberdeen	Main, James	12	Aberdeen	Pictou

E.504/1/24

1812	04	*Mary* of Aberdeen	Morrison, James	20	Aberdeen	Halifax

E.504/1/24; *AJ* Jan. 29.

1812	05	*Cambria* of Aberdeen	Pirie, James	33	Aberdeen	Halifax & Quebec

E.504/1/24; *AJ* Jan. 29.

Year	Mth	Vessel	Master	Psgr. Nos.	Departure Port	Arrival Port
1813	03	*Cambria* of Aberdeen	Oswald, James	25	Aberdeen	Halifax

E.504/1/24

1813	03	*Ploughman* of Aberdeen	Main, James	7	Aberdeen	Halifax

E.504/1/24

1814	03	*Mary* of Aberdeen	Oswald, James	30	Aberdeen	Halifax

E.504/1/25

1814	07	*Perseverance* of Aberdeen	Moncur	n/k	Cromarty	Pictou

IJ May 27.
Agents were: Peter Ritchie, Aberdeen; Alex McKenzie, Cromarty; James Lyon, Inverness.

1814	08	*Cambria* of Aberdeen	Clayton, James	35	Aberdeen	Halifax

E.504/1/25

1814	08	*Halifax Packet* of Sunderland	Hogg, John	7	Aberdeen	Halifax

E 504/1/25.

1815		*Prince William*		95	Cromarty or Thurso	Pictou

Passenger List: NSARM MG100 Vol. 226 #30 (Appendix I).
Nineteen families from Sutherland who petitioned for land in West Pictou. Some of the petitioners had served in the Local Militia of Scotland, probably the Reay Fencibles.

1815	03	*Amethyst* of Aberdeen	Greig, H.	29	Aberdeen	Halifax

E.504/1/25.

1815	03	*Fame* of Aberdeen	Masson, George	4	Aberdeen	Halifax

E.504/1/25.

Year	Mth	Vessel	Master	Psgr. Nos.	Departure Port	Arrival Port
1815	03	*Mary* of Aberdeen	Oswald, James	35	Aberdeen	Halifax

E.504/1/25.

| 1815 | 04 | *Halifax Packet* of Sunderland | Hogg, John | 3 | Aberdeen | Halifax |

E 504/1/25.

| 1815 | 04 | *John* of Berwick | Forster, Joseph | n/k | Fort George (near Inverness) | Halifax |

IJ Apr. 7.
Agents were: John Stevenson, Fortrose; James Lyon, merchant, Inverness.

| 1815 | 04 | *Perseverance* of Aberdeen | | n/k | Cromarty | Halifax |

IJ Apr 7.
Agents were: George Logan from America at Dornoch and James Campbell, Star Inn, Inverness.

| 1815 | 04 | *Seven Sisters* of Aberdeen | Brown, A. | 19 | Aberdeen | Halifax |

E.504/1/25.

| 1815 | 07 | *Ruby* of Aberdeen | Love, Thomas | 2 | Aberdeen | Halifax |

E.504/1/25.

| 1815 | 08 | *Glentanner* of Aberdeen | Laird, James | 17 | Aberdeen | Halifax & Pictou |

E.504/1/25.

| 1815 | 08 | *Helen* | Moore, James | 4 | Aberdeen | Halifax |

E.504/1/25.

| 1816 | 03 | *Amethyst* of Aberdeen | Greig, H. | 36 | Aberdeen | Halifax |

E.504/1/26.

Year	Mth	Vessel	Master	Psgr. Nos.	Departure Port	Arrival Port
1816	03	*Louisa* of Aberdeen	Oswald, James	36	Aberdeen	Halifax, Pictou & Miramichi

E.504/1/26; *AJ* Feb. 14
55 packages passengers' wearing apparel and belongings

Year	Mth	Vessel	Master	Psgr. Nos.	Departure Port	Arrival Port
1816	03	*Ythan* of Aberdeen	Craigie, Alexander	17	Aberdeen	Halifax & Miramichi

E.504/1/26.

Year	Mth	Vessel	Master	Psgr. Nos.	Departure Port	Arrival Port
1816	04	*Aurora* (Est)		70	Leith	Halifax & Pictou

Martell, *Immigration Nova Scotia, 1815–38*, 40–1; E.504/22/72; NSARM RG1 Vol. 227, Doc.116.
Passengers of "a superior class to those of last year".

Year	Mth	Vessel	Master	Psgr. Nos.	Departure Port	Arrival Port
1816	04	*Phesdo* of Aberdeen	Pennan, Andrew	37	Aberdeen	Halifax & Saint John, N.B.

E.504/1/26; *AJ* Jan. 3; *New Brunswick Royal Gazette*, June 29.
90 packages passengers' wearing apparel and bedding.

Year	Mth	Vessel	Master	Psgr. Nos.	Departure Port	Arrival Port
1816	04	*Ploughman* of Aberdeen	Duncan, Alexander	7	Aberdeen	Halifax & Pictou

E.504/1/26; *IJ* Mar. 15.
20 packages passengers wearing apparel and bedding.

Year	Mth	Vessel	Master	Psgr. Nos.	Departure Port	Arrival Port
1816	04	*Surry* of London	Meys, Richard	23	Greenock	Halifax

E.504/15/112.

Year	Mth	Vessel	Master	Psgr. Nos.	Departure Port	Arrival Port
1816	04	*Tartar* of Perth	Kelly, W.	144	Tobermory from Dundee	Pictou

Partial passenger list: Punch, "Scots Settlers to Long Point, 1816," 88–9.
E.504/35/2.
42 of the passengers petitioned for land in Long Point, Cape Breton.

Year	Mth	Vessel	Master	Psgr. Nos.	Departure Port	Arrival Port
1816	04	*William* of Aberdeen	Laird, James	6	Aberdeen	Halifax

E.504/1/26; Martell, *Immigration Nova Scotia, 1815–38*, 40.
20 packages passengers' wearing apparel and belongings.

Year	Mth	Vessel	Master	Psgr. Nos.	Departure Port	Arrival Port
1816	05	*Cambria* of Aberdeen	Lawrence, Alexander	12	Aberdeen	Pictou & Miramichi

E.504/1/26.

25 packages passengers' wearing apparel and bedding.

Year	Mth	Vessel	Master	Psgr. Nos.	Departure Port	Arrival Port
1816	05	*Dorset* of Grangemouth	Scott, Andrew	83	Leith	Halifax

E.504/22/73.

Year	Mth	Vessel	Master	Psgr. Nos.	Departure Port	Arrival Port
1816	06	*Lovely Mary* of Dumfries	Hudson, John	29	Dumfries	Pictou

E.504/9/9; *DGC* June 3.

Year	Mth	Vessel	Master	Psgr. Nos.	Departure Port	Arrival Port
1816	06	*Sprightly* of Dundee	Philip, Alexander	20	Aberdeen	Halifax, Pictou & Miramichi

E.504/1/26; E.504/11/18; *DC* Jan 17, 1817

Year	Mth	Vessel	Master	Psgr. Nos.	Departure Port	Arrival Port
1816	06	*Vine* of Peterhead	Pirie, Alexr.	81	Cromarty & Thurso	Pictou

E.504/7/5; *IC* 28 June, *IJ* Apr 26.

A muster list is noted but does not survive. Engaged by Mr George Logan, a settler in Canada. A medical person in attendance.

Year	Mth	Vessel	Master	Psgr. Nos.	Departure Port	Arrival Port
1816	07	*Aimwell* of Aberdeen	Morrison, John	139	Thurso from Aberdeen	Halifax

E.504/1/26, 7/5; Martell, *Immigration Nova Scotia, 1815–38*, p.40.

Martell states "139 passengers mostly farmers and mechanics," arrived from Aberdeen on the *Aimwell* in Sept. The Scottish Customs records show that there were "74 passengers as particularly specified in a list signed by the captain" who left from Thurso. They had 65 chests, 18 boxes and 6 trusses of wearing apparel and passenger luggage. The Scottish Customs records also show that 27 people left from Aberdeen and they had 45 packages of wearing apparel and luggage.

Year	Mth	Vessel	Master	Psgr. Nos.	Departure Port	Arrival Port
1816	08	*Diadem* of St John	Wells, George	2	Greenock	Halifax

E.504/15/113.

Year	Mth	Vessel	Master	Psgr. Nos.	Departure Port	Arrival Port
1816	08	*Good Intent* of Aberdeen	Beverly, Robert	69	Fort William	Pictou

E.504/12/6; Martell, *Immigration. Nova Scotia, 1815–38*, 41;
69 men, women and children. The journey time was 2 to 3 months. The *Good Intent* arrived back in Aberdeen from Pictou in December with a timber cargo.

| 1816 | 08 | *Lord Gardner* | Brown, John | 12 | Greenock | Halifax & Pictou |

Martell, *Immigration. Nova Scotia, 1815–38*, 40; E.504/15/113.
Ship arrived in October after a crossing of 59 days.

| 1816 | 08 | *Nymph* | Hutchinson, J. | 55 | Fort William | Pictou |

E.504/12/6.
"55 men, women & children"; provisions listed.

| 1816 | 08 | *Protector* of New Brunswick | Simpson, Walter | 8 | Greenock | Saint John N.B. & Halifax |

E.504/15/113.

| 1816 | 08 | *Three Brothers* of Hull | Maddison | 306 | Stornoway from Leith | Pictou & Miramichi |

E.504/33/3; E.504/22/74.
148 passengers boarded ship at Stornoway and 158 at Leith.

| 1816 | 09 | *Louisa* of Aberdeen | Oswald, James | 13 | Aberdeen | Halifax |

E.504/1/26
25 packages passengers' wearing apparel and luggage.

| 1817 | 03 | *Aimwell* of Aberdeen | Morrison, John | 32 | Aberdeen | Halifax |

E.504/1/26; *AJ* May 8.
100 packages passengers' wearing apparel and belongings.

| 1817 | 03 | *Good Intent* of Aberdeen | Rodgers, Alexander | 30 | Aberdeen | Pictou |

E.504/1/26.
120 packages passengers' wearing apparel and belongings.

Year	Mth	Vessel	Master	Psgr. Nos.	Departure Port	Arrival Port
1817	03	*Louisa* of Aberdeen	Oswald, James	65	Aberdeen	Halifax

E.504/1/26.
90 packages passengers' wearing apparel and belongings.

1817	03	*Phesdo* of Aberdeen	Pennan, Andrew	8	Aberdeen	Halifax

E.504/1/26.
25 packages passengers' wearing apparel and bedding.

1817	03	*Skeene* of Leith	Mason, James	100	Leith	Halifax

E.504/22/76.

1817	03	*Margaret* of Peterhead	McIntosh, Andrew	72	Leith	Halifax

E.504/22/76.

1817	03(Est)	*Protector* of New Brunswick	Simpson	n/k	Greenock	Halifax & Saint John NB

Martell, *Immigration. Nova Scotia, 1815–38*, 43; *GA* Feb. 25.
A number of farmers and mechanics

1817	04	*Augusta* of Dumfries	Davidson, Wm.	115	Dumfries	Pictou & Miramichi

DGC Apr. 15.

1817	04	*Douglas* of Aberdeen	Morrison, John	7	Aberdeen	Halifax

Martell, *Immigration Nova Scotia, 1815–38*, 43; E.504/1/27.
Journey of 63 days.

1817	04	*Hunter* of Aberdeen	Logan, James	5	Aberdeen	Halifax

E.504/1/27.

1817	04	*Nancy* of South Shields	Allan, Richard	164	Leith	Halifax & Quebec

Martell, *Immigration. Nova Scotia, 1815–38*, 43; *QM* Aug. 1. E.504/22/77.
Arrived Halifax in July & Quebec in August; 130 passengers left at Halifax & 34 settlers at Quebec.

Year	Mth	Vessel	Master	Psgr. Nos.	Departure Port	Arrival Port
1817	06	*Prompt* of Bo'ness	Coverdale	193	Leith	Halifax & Quebec

Martell, *Immigration. Nova Scotia, 1815–38*, 43; *QM* July 8; *GA* Mar 21; *Kelso Mail,*
June 26. E.504/22/77.
William Allan agent – sub-agents at Hawick & Kelso; Greenock agent Robert Hunter.
133 settlers left at Quebec & 60 at Halifax.
Scottish Customs records, "only 56 passengers shipt" from Leith.

Year	Mth	Vessel	Master	Psgr. Nos.	Departure Port	Arrival Port
1817	05	*Agincourt* of Leith	Matheson	200	Leith	Halifax & Quebec

QM Aug 11; *SM* LXXIX, 477.
73 settlers left at Quebec

Year	Mth	Vessel	Master	Psgr. Nos.	Departure Port	Arrival Port
1817	05	*Amity* of Peterhead	Anderson, Alexander	126	Thurso	Halifax

E.504/7/5; Martell, *Immigration Nova Scotia, 1815–38*, 43.

Year	Mth	Vessel	Master	Psgr. Nos.	Departure Port	Arrival Port
1817	05	*Helen* of Kirkaldy	Wilson, A	93	Kirkaldy	Halifax

Martell, *Immigration Nova Scotia, 1815–38*, 43; *SM* LXXIX p 477.

Year	Mth	Vessel	Master	Psgr. Nos.	Departure Port	Arrival Port
1817	05	*Traveller* of Leith	Bishop, J.	40	Leith	Halifax

Martell, *Immigration Nova Scotia, 1815–38*, 43; E.504/22/77.
Foundered about May 23. Crew and passengers saved and landed at Charlottetown
PEI.
Scottish Customs records "only 29 passengers shipt" from Leith.

Year	Mth	Vessel	Master	Psgr. Nos.	Departure Port	Arrival Port
1817	06 (Est)	*Hope*	Normand, George	161	Greenock	Sydney

Harvey, "Scottish Immigration to Cape Breton," 315–6; Martell, *Immigration Nova
Scotia, 1815–38*, 44; NSARM RG1 Vol. 329 Doc. 109.
Emigrants from Barra who settled near the Narrows. Simon Fraser was the agent.

Year	Mth	Vessel	Master	Psgr. Nos.	Departure Port	Arrival Port
1817	06	*Minerva* of Aberdeen	Strachan, W.	26	Fort William	Halifax & Quebec

E.504/33/3.
26 men, women & children. The *Minerva* arrived back in Aberdeen from Quebec in
November with a timber cargo.

Year	Mth	Vessel	Master	Psgr. Nos.	Departure Port	Arrival Port
1817	06 (Est)	*William Tell*	Boan, John	221	Greenock	Canso, Cape Breton

Harvey, "Scottish Immigration to Cape Breton," 315–6; Martell, *Immigration Nova Scotia, 1815–38*, 44; NSARM RG1 Vol. 329 Doc. 109.
Barra people who settled near the Narrows, Cape Breton. Simon Fraser was the agent. Another vessel carrying 250 Barra passengers was expected.

Year	Mth	Vessel	Master	Psgr. Nos.	Departure Port	Arrival Port
1817	07	*Earl of Dalhousie* of Aberdeen	Levie, John	24	Aberdeen	Halifax

E.504/1/27.

Year	Mth	Vessel	Master	Psgr. Nos.	Departure Port	Arrival Port
1817	07	*General Goldie* of Dumfries	Smith, William	18	Dumfries	Pictou, Miramichi, Quebec.

QM Sept. 16, *DGC* June 24.
18 settlers left at Quebec.

Year	Mth	Vessel	Master	Psgr. Nos.	Departure Port	Arrival Port
1817	08	*Anacreon* of Newcastle	Wilson, W.	166	Tobermory	Pictou & Quebec

E.504/35/2.
No passengers noted at Quebec. The agent was A. MacLochlan.

Year	Mth	Vessel	Master	Psgr. Nos.	Departure Port	Arrival Port
1817	08	*Frances Ann* of Irvine	Stoke, J.	136	Fort William	Pictou

E.504/12/6; MacLaren, *Pictou Book*, 119.
136 men, women & children were on board. The Rev. Norman MacLeod came on this vessel. Provisions listed.

Year	Mth	Vessel	Master	Psgr. Nos.	Departure Port	Arrival Port
1817	08	*Louisa* of Aberdeen	Oswald, James	19	Aberdeen	Halifax

E.504/1/27.

Year	Mth	Vessel	Master	Psgr. Nos.	Departure Port	Arrival Port
1817	08 (Est)	*Prince Leopold*		30	Leith	Halifax

Martell, *Immigration Nova Scotia, 1815–38*, 44.

Year	Mth	Vessel	Master	Psgr. Nos.	Departure Port	Arrival Port
1817	08 (Est)	*Scotia*		120	Leith	Halifax

Martell, *Immigration Nova Scotia, 1815–38*, 44.

Year	Mth	Vessel	Master	Psgr. Nos.	Departure Port	Arrival Port
1818		*Perseverance* of Aberdeen		150	Lochinver	Pictou

MacLaren, *Pictou Book*, 119; Patterson, "More studies in Nova Scotia History (1941)," 91–5. The passengers wanted to settle near Norman MacLeod at Pictou but there was insufficient land. They later moved to St Anns, Cape Breton.

Year	Mth	Vessel	Master	Psgr. Nos.	Departure Port	Arrival Port
1818		*Rowena*		n/k		Pictou

MacLaren. *Pictou Book*, 119.

Year	Mth	Vessel	Master	Psgr. Nos.	Departure Port	Arrival Port
1818	03	*Aimwell* of Aberdeen		33	Aberdeen	Halifax

Martell, *Immigration Nova Scotia, 1815–38*, 45

Year	Mth	Vessel	Master	Psgr. Nos.	Departure Port	Arrival Port
1818	03 & 07	*Louisa* of Aberdeen		40	Aberdeen	Halifax

Martell, *Immigration Nova Scotia, 1815–38*, 45–6
25 left Aberdeen in March and 15 in July.

Year	Mth	Vessel	Master	Psgr. Nos.	Departure Port	Arrival Port
1818	04	*Augusta* of Dumfries	Whitehead, Robert	120	Dumfries	Pictou & Miramichi

E.504/9/9; *DWJ* Feb. 17 & Apr. 21.
66 chests wearing apparel; *Dumfries Weekly Journal* gives 56 passengers for Miramichi while the Customs Records show 120 passengers.

Year	Mth	Vessel	Master	Psgr. Nos.	Departure Port	Arrival Port
1818	04(Est)	*Skeene* of Leith		85	Leith	Halifax

Martell, *Immigration Nova Scotia, 1815–38*, 45; *Kelso Mail*, Feb. 6, 1817.
In 1817 *Skeene's* departure advertised in *Kelso Mail*.

Year	Mth	Vessel	Master	Psgr. Nos.	Departure Port	Arrival Port
1818	05	*Lovely Mary* of Dumfries	Hudson, John	53	Dumfries	Pictou

E.504/9/9. Provisions listed

Year	Mth	Vessel	Master	Psgr. Nos.	Departure Port	Arrival Port
1818	07	*Ann*		129	Cromarty from Leith	Halifax

IJ June 19. Martell, *Immigration Nova Scotia, 1815–38*, 46
Agent was James Campbell, Star Inn, Inverness.

Year	Mth	Vessel	Master	Psgr. Nos.	Departure Port	Arrival Port
1818	07 (Est)	*British Queen*		131	Leith	Halifax

Martell, *Immigration Nova Scotia, 1815–38*, 46.

Year	Mth	Vessel	Master	Psgr. Nos.	Departure Port	Arrival Port
1818	08	*Bassettere* of Greenock	McMorland, W.	113	Fort William	Pictou

E.504/12/6.
113 Men, women & children "per muster roll"; provisions listed. "All inhabitants of the Highlands of Scotland."

Year	Mth	Vessel	Master	Psgr. Nos.	Departure Port	Arrival Port
1819		*Victory*		n/k		Pictou

Martell, *Immigration Nova Scotia, 1815–38*, 49; MacDonald, "Early Highland Emigration to Nova Scotia and PEI," 45.
Passengers from Canna.

Year	Mth	Vessel	Master	Psgr. Nos.	Departure Port	Arrival Port
1819	03	*Louisa* of Aberdeen		n/k	Aberdeen	Halifax

Martell, *Immigration Nova Scotia, 1815–38*, 47

Year	Mth	Vessel	Master	Psgr. Nos.	Departure Port	Arrival Port
1819	03 (Est)	*Skeene* of Leith	Mason	150	Leith	Halifax & Quebec

Martell, *Immigration Nova Scotia, 1815–38*, 47; SM IV 1819, 465.
113 people left at Halifax. Passengers included entire families with small properties. 1 family from West Calder (with 10 children) - 6 of the sons took out nearly £1,000.

Year	Mth	Vessel	Master	Psgr. Nos.	Departure Port	Arrival Port
1819	04 (Est)	*Mary*	Munro	32	Leith	Halifax & Quebec

SM 1819 IV, 465.

Year	Mth	Vessel	Master	Psgr. Nos.	Departure Port	Arrival Port
1819	04 (Est)	*Percival*	Scott	85	Leith	Halifax & Quebec

SM IV 1819, 465; *PC* Feb. 25.
Agent was William Allen.

Year	Mth	Vessel	Master	Psgr. Nos.	Departure Port	Arrival Port
1819	05 (Est)	*Agincourt* of Leith	Matthews	200	Leith	Halifax & Quebec

Martell, *Immigration Nova Scotia, 1815–38*, 47; SM IV 1819, 465.
135 left at Halifax

Year	Mth	Vessel	Master	Psgr. Nos.	Departure Port	Arrival Port
1819	05 (Est)	*Leopold* of Leith	Wilson, John	150	Leith	Halifax & Quebec

Martell, *Immigration Nova Scotia, 1815–38*, 47; *PC* May 13.
127 people left at Halifax and 23 travelled on to Quebec.

Year	Mth	Vessel	Master	Psgr. Nos.	Departure Port	Arrival Port
1819	06	*Speculation*	Allen	150	Oban	Pictou & Quebec

Martell, *Immigration Nova Scotia, 1815–38*, 49; *IJ* June 4; MacDonald, "Early Highland Emigration to Nova Scotia and PEI," 45. *QM* Sept. 14.

Emigrants from Lochaber. Fares for crossing: age over 14 price seven guineas, age 3 to 14 price five guineas, age 2 to 8 price three guineas. Passengers to be landed at Montreal but a 5 % reduction in fare if landed at Pictou or Quebec. Twenty-three left at Pictou. *Quebec Mercury* records 87 arrivals. Total passengers stated as 150.

Year	Mth	Vessel	Master	Psgr. Nos.	Departure Port	Arrival Port
1819	07 (Est)	*Caledonia* of Alloa	Liddell	n/k	Alloa & Greenock	Halifax & Pictou

Martell, *Immigration Nova Scotia, 1815–38*, 47; E.504/2/13; *PC* May 13.
Agent was William Allan

Year	Mth	Vessel	Master	Psgr. Nos.	Departure Port	Arrival Port
1819	07 (Est)	*Garland*		90	Leith	Halifax

Martell, *Immigration Nova Scotia, 1815–38*, 48

Year	Mth	Vessel	Master	Psgr. Nos.	Departure Port	Arrival Port
1819	07	*Louisa* of Aberdeen	Oswald, James	120	Tobermory	Pictou

E.504/35/2; Martell, *Immigration Nova Scotia, 1815–38*, 49

Year	Mth	Vessel	Master	Psgr. Nos.	Departure Port	Arrival Port
1819	07 (Est)	*Minerva*	Williamson	47	Leith	Halifax & Quebec

Martell, *Immigration Nova Scotia, 1815–38*, 48; *PC* June 10. John Skene, Leith, agent.

Year	Mth	Vessel	Master	Psgr. Nos.	Departure Port	Arrival Port
1819	07	*Morningfield* of Aberdeen	Laing	264	Tobermory	Pictou & Charlottetown

E.504/35/2; *PEI Gazette*, Sept. 3. 64 people arrived at Pictou and 200 at Charlottetown.

Year	Mth	Vessel	Master	Psgr. Nos.	Departure Port	Arrival Port
1819	08	*Economy* of Aberdeen	Frazer, James	285	Tobermory	Pictou

E.504/35/2; Martell, *Immigration Nova Scotia, 1815–38*, 49
The *Acadian Reporter* published a commendation to the Captain from the passengers "for the kind treatment they received from him for a passage which consisted of 5 weeks." It also reported that the passengers "were landed in good health and spirits" and that 4 children "were born upon the passage."

Year	Mth	Vessel	Master	Psgr. Nos.	Departure Port	Arrival Port
1819	09	*Ann* of Banff		60	Cromarty	Pictou

Martell, *Immigration Nova Scotia, 1815–38*, 49; NAS GD 263/63/2/54.
The master was charged with having inadequate provisions for the passengers; court case held in Stromness; schooner owned by Captain.

Year	Mth	Vessel	Master	Psgr. Nos.	Departure Port	Arrival Port
1820		*Dunlop*		n/k	Tobermory	Pictou

MacLaren, *Pictou Book*, 119.

| 1820 | 05 | *Speculation* | Douglas | 120 | Greenock | Halifax, Saint John & Quebec |

QM June 30; PRO CO 384/6. 120 settlers arrived at Quebec; Colonial Office correspondence indicates vessel was due to disembark passengers at Halifax & Saint John N.B.

| 1820 | 05(Est) | *Manchester* | | 26 | Leith | Halifax |

Martell, *Immigration Nova Scotia, 1815–38*, 50

| 1820 | 07 | *Glentanner* of Aberdeen | Murray, George | 141 | Tobermory | Cape Breton & Quebec |

E.504/35/2; *QM* Aug 25; *IJ* Nov 23
123 arrivals at Cape Breton and 18 at Quebec. The *Inverness Journal* printed a commendation to Captain Murray for his humane treatment and to the owners for the good quality of the provisions from 4 people who had made the crossing, one of whom was John Macra a surgeon from Plockton.

| 1820 | 08 (Est) | *Recovery* | | 14 | Greenock | Halifax |

Martell, *Immigration Nova Scotia, 1815–38*, 50.

| 1821 | | *Harmony* | | 350 | | Sydney |

Martell, *Immigration Nova Scotia, 1815–38*, 52. MacMillan, Hill of Boisdale, 35.
350 settlers from Barra and Uist. Most settled at Boisdale.

| 1821 | | *Tamerlane* | | n/k | | Halifax |

MacDonald, "Early Highland Emigration to Nova Scotia and PEI," 45

| 1821 | 03 | *Louisa* of Aberdeen | | 9 | Aberdeen | Halifax |

Martell, *Immigration Nova Scotia*, 52

| 1821 | 04 | *Thompson's Packet* of Dumfries | | 80 | Dumfries | PEI, Pictou, Miramichi, Richibucto |

Martell, *Immigration Nova Scotia, 1815–38*, 52; *DGC* Jan.30 & Apr. 10.
Eighty passengers are known to have left at Pictou.

Year	Mth	Vessel	Master	Psgr. Nos.	Departure Port	Arrival Port
1821	06	*Prompt* of Bo'ness	Jack, W.	n/k	Fort William & Tobermory	Nova Scotia & Quebec

IJ June 22; *QM* Oct. 30.
52 settlers left at Quebec. Numbers who may have left at a port in Nova Scotia are not known.

1821	06	*Ossian* of Leith	Hill	108	Cromarty	Pictou

Passenger List: *IJ* June 29 (Appendix I).
Twenty-two families in all. Fares were: 4 1/2 guineas per adult and 1 1/2 guineas for passengers under 14 years of age. Agent: William Allan of Leith.

1822		*Commerce*		n/k	Tobermory	Port Hastings Cape Breton

MacDonald, "Early Highland Emigration to Nova Scotia and PEI," 45.
Settlers from Muck who went to Plaster Cove, Cape Breton (now Port Hastings).

1822	04(Est)	*Union*	Scott	14	Greenock	Pictou

Martell, *Immigration Nova Scotia, 1815–38*, 53; *AR*, June 15.

1822	05	*Thompson's Packet* of Dumfries	Lookup, T.	133	Dumfries	Pictou & Quebec

Martell, *Immigration Nova Scotia, 1815–38*, 53; *QM* Oct. 30.
40 emigrants went on to Quebec.

1822	06	*Harmony* of Aberdeen	Murray, George	125	Cromarty	Pictou

E.504/17/9; *IJ* July 12.
Tenants from the Duke of Sutherland's estate. Together the *Harmony* and *Ruby* took 250 passengers. Spades, saw and nails given free by the association at Edinburgh "for persons emigrating from Sutherland to North America."

1822	06	*Ruby* of Aberdeen	Bodie, J.	125	Cromarty	Pictou

See comments for *Harmony* of Aberdeen.

1823	06	*Atlantic* of Stornoway	MacLeod, R.	n/k	Lochalsh	Pictou & Cape Breton

IJ May 2.
Vessel to call for passengers at Plockton, Lochalsh and Ardintoul Bay in Wester Ross.

Year	Mth	Vessel	Master	Psgr. Nos.	Departure Port	Arrival Port
1823	07	*Emperor Alexander* of Aberdeen	Watt,	160	Tobermory	Sydney & Quebec

Passenger List: *IJ* Jan 30, 1824 (Appendix I).
QM Oct. 7, 1823
Many of the passengers originated from South Uist. In the following year, the *Inverness Journal* printed a list of 30 heads of families giving parish origins. The humanity of the Captain was praised and John McEachern was named as the "steward on board." The Agent was Archibald McNiven. The *Quebec Mercury* recorded the arrival of 49 settlers at Quebec.

Year	Mth	Vessel	Master	Psgr. Nos.	Departure Port	Arrival Port
1824	07	*Dunlop*	Mandell	227	Greenock	Sydney & Quebec

Martell, *Immigration Nova Scotia, 1815–38*, 54; *QM* Aug. 31.
96 settlers left at Sydney & 131 at Quebec

Year	Mth	Vessel	Master	Psgr. Nos.	Departure Port	Arrival Port
1826		*Northumber-land*	Stevenson	c. 100	Greenock	St Andrews

MacDonald, "Early Highland Emigration to Nova Scotia and PEI," 45; MacDougall, *History of Inverness County*, 501–4.
Thirty-one families travelled on the *Northumberland* from the Hebrides. Many moved on to Inverness County, Cape Breton.

Year	Mth	Vessel	Master	Psgr. Nos.	Departure Port	Arrival Port
1826	03 (Est)	*Mercator*	Thomson	5	Greenock	Halifax

E.504/15/155.

Year	Mth	Vessel	Master	Psgr. Nos.	Departure Port	Arrival Port
1826	04(Est)	*Thetis*	Coverdale	n/k	Greenock	Pictou

E.504/15/155; *GA* Mar. 20 1827.
Vessel carried 16 chests, 7 trunks, 5 boxes & 10 bundles passengers luggage.

Year	Mth	Vessel	Master	Psgr. Nos.	Departure Port	Arrival Port
1826	06	*Tamerlane*	McKellop	>55	Greenock	Quebec & Sydney

E.504/15/156; MacDonald, "Early Highland Emigration to Nova Scotia and PEI," 45; *QM* Aug. 5.
55 settlers arrived at Quebec. Vessel landed at Sydney with passengers from North Morar. She left Greenock with 56 chests, 64 barrels, 6 half-barrels, 33 bags & 2 boxes passenger luggage.

Year	Mth	Vessel	Master	Psgr. Nos.	Departure Port	Arrival Port
1826	07	*Highland Lad*	Vickerman	>16	Tobermory	N. Scotia & Quebec

QM Sept 23; Martell, *Immigration Nova Scotia, 1815–38*, 57.
16 settlers left at Quebec.

Year	Mth	Vessel	Master	Psgr. Nos.	Departure Port	Arrival Port
1826	08	*Cadmus*	Snowdon	n/k	Tobermory	Canso, Cape Breton & Quebec

QM Oct. 3
Passengers landed at Gut of Canso.

Year	Mth	Vessel	Master	Psgr. Nos.	Departure Port	Arrival Port
1826	08	*Mercator* (Est)		n/k	Greenock	Halifax

E.540/15/157.
Vessel carried 11 trunks, 2 portmanteaux, 13 boxes, 1 barrel, 2 bundles 1 parcel passenger luggage.

Year	Mth	Vessel	Master	Psgr. Nos.	Departure Port	Arrival Port
1826	09	*Thetis* (Est)	Coverdale	n/k	Greenock	Pictou

E.504/15/157.
Vessel carried 6 chests, 2 bundles passenger luggage.

Year	Mth	Vessel	Master	Psgr. Nos.	Departure Port	Arrival Port
1826	10	*Douglas* (Est)	Athol	n/k	Greenock	Halifax

E.504/15/157.
Vessel carried certain passengers luggage

Year	Mth	Vessel	Master	Psgr. Nos.	Departure Port	Arrival Port
1827		*Aurora*		n/k		Port Hastings N.S.

MacDonald, "Early Highland Emigration to Nova Scotia and PEI," 45.
Passengers from Edinburgh.

Year	Mth	Vessel	Master	Psgr. Nos.	Departure Port	Arrival Port
1827	03	*Aberdeenshire* of Aberdeen	Oswald, James	23	Aberdeen	Halifax

Martell, *Immigration Nova Scotia, 1815–38*, 58

Year	Mth	Vessel	Master	Psgr. Nos.	Departure Port	Arrival Port
1827	03	*Mars* of Alloa	Mitchell	n/k	Alloa	Quebec

E.504/2/14.
"Baggage belonging to the passengers containing only wearing apparel, bedding and small items of provisions." Some passengers are likely to have disembarked at Halifax or Pictou.

Year	Mth	Vessel	Master	Psgr. Nos.	Departure Port	Arrival Port
1827	04	*Mercator* (Est)		18	Greenock	Halifax

Martell, *Immigration Nova Scotia, 1815–38*, 58

Year	Mth	Vessel	Master	Psgr. Nos.	Departure Port	Arrival Port
1827 (Est)	06	*Harmony* of Whitehaven	Young	236	Stornoway from Leith	Halifax & Quebec

Martell, *Immigration Nova Scotia, 1815–38*, 59; QM Sept. 1
Harmony arrived in Halifax in August. 200 passengers left at Halifax & 36 settlers left at Quebec. Thirteen people died during the crossing.

1827	07	*Active*	Walker, A.	200	Tobermory	Cape Breton & Quebec

E.504/35/2; QM Sept. 21.
40 settlers left at Quebec.

1827	08	*Columbus*	Fleck, A.	228	Tobermory	Cape Breton

E.504/35/2; MacMillan, *Hill of Boisdale*, 24.
Some of the emigrants settled at Leitches Creek.

1827	08	*George Stevens*	Potts, J.	193	Tobermory	Cape Breton

E.504/35/2; MacMillan, *Hill of Boisdale*, 24.
Settlers from North and South Uist, Benbecula and Barra. Some of the emigrants settled at Leitches Creek.

1827	08	*Isabella* of Dundee	Donaldson, James	24	Dundee & Tobermory	Cape Breton

E504/35/2; NAS CE 70 11/2.

1827	08	*Stephen Wright* of Newcastle	Gibson, N.	170	Tobermory	Sydney

E.504/35/2; MacMillan, *Hill of Boisdale*, 24.
More than a third of the passengers got smallpox. There were three deaths during the passage, 10 while in port and 2 after landing. Some of the emigrants settled at Leitches Creek.

1827 (Est)	08	*Corsair* of Greenock		80	Greenock	Halifax

Martell, *Immigration Nova Scotia, 1815–38*, 58

1828		*Commerce*		n/k	Stornoway	Sydney

MacMillan, *Hill of Boisdale*, 24.
Emigrants from Carinish, North Uist. Most settled at Loch Lomond, Cape Breton. A few went to Leitches Creek.

Year	Mth	Vessel	Master	Psgr. Nos.	Departure Port	Arrival Port

1828 *Mary* 135 Stornoway Sydney

Martell, *Immigration Nova Scotia, 1815–38*, 61; MacMillan, *Hill of Boisdale*, 23–4.

1828 04 *Caroline* of Rea, James 36 Inverness and PEI, Pictou,
Liverpool Fort William Miramichi

Martell, *Immigration Nova Scotia, 1815–38*, 62; *IJ* Feb 29; E.504/5/1.
According to the *Inverness Journal*, the *Caroline* was due to call at Pictou, PEI and the Miramichi in New Brunswick. Thirty-six passengers are known to have arrived at Pictou. The *Caroline* sailed from Inverness to Fort William through the Caledonian Canal. Passenger fares were £3.10.s. (with passengers providing their own food).

1828 04 *Thetis* 30 Greenock Pictou
(Est)

Martell, *Immigration Nova Scotia, 1815–38*, 62; *GA* Mar. 20, 1827.

1828 05 *Ann* 209 Stornoway Sydney
(Est)

Martell, *Immigration Nova Scotia, 1815–38*, 61

1828 05 *Mercator* 12 Greenock Halifax
(Est)

Martell, *Immigration Nova Scotia, 1815–38*, 61

1828 05 *Universe* 464 Stornoway Sydney,
of Aberdeen

Martell, *Immigration Nova Scotia, 1815–38*, 61; MacMillan, *Hill of Boisdale*, 23–4.
Two other vessels followed the *Universe* and were expected to follow to Bras d'Or Lake.

1828 07 *St. Lawrence* Cram, 208 Leith Ship Harbour,
of Newcastle Jonathan Cape Breton

Passenger List: MacDougall, *History of Inverness County*, 126–31 (Appendix I).
Martell, *Immigration Nova Scotia, 1815–38*, 62
Passengers from Rhum. Vessel landed at Ship Harbour in the Gut of Canso.

1828 07 *Two Sisters* McKenzie, 160 Greenock Sydney
(Est) of Pictou George

Martell, *Immigration Nova Scotia, 1815–38*, 61. Forty passengers got smallpox. No deaths.

1828 08 *Aberdeenshire* Oswald, 8 Aberdeen Halifax
of Aberdeen James

Martell, *Immigration Nova Scotia, 1815–38*, 61

Year	Mth	Vessel	Master	Psgr. Nos.	Departure Port	Arrival Port
1828	08 (Est)	*Isabella* of Glasgow		n/k	Greenock	Halifax

Martell, *Immigration Nova Scotia, 1815–38*, 61
"Several in the steerage."

Year	Mth	Vessel	Master	Psgr. Nos.	Departure Port	Arrival Port
1829		*Louisa* of Aberdeen		170	Stornoway	Sydney

Martell, *Immigration Nova Scotia, 1815–38*, 63.
Seventy of the 170 passengers went on to Prince Edward Island. Passengers were described as very poor. None suffered from disease on arrival.

Year	Mth	Vessel	Master	Psgr. Nos.	Departure Port	Arrival Port
1829		*Two Sisters* of Pictou		30	Clyde	Pictou

MacLaren, *Pictou Book*, 120

Year	Mth	Vessel	Master	Psgr. Nos.	Departure Port	Arrival Port
1829	03	*Albion* of Aberdeen	Leslie, Alexander	18	Aberdeen	Halifax

NAS GD316/15; Martell, *Immigration Nova Scotia, 1815–38*, 62
Receipt for £35 for 5 people who travelled as cabin passengers.

Year	Mth	Vessel	Master	Psgr. Nos.	Departure Port	Arrival Port
1829	04	*Mary Kennedy*		300 (approx.)	Skye	PEI

MacQueen, *Skye Pioneers and the Island*, 72, 93–99; *PEI Gazette*, June 2, 1829.
Passengers originated mainly from Uig in Skye. The *PEI Gazette* reported that 84 immigrants from Skye (who were heads of households) had arrived on a ship, which had also called at Cape Breton. Given the heads of households arrived with their families, passenger numbers on board the *Mary Kennedy* can be estimated at around 300.

Year	Mth	Vessel	Master	Psgr. Nos.	Departure Port	Arrival Port
1829	04 (Est)	*Thetis*			Greenock	Arichat, Cape Breton

Martell, *Immigration Nova Scotia, 1815–38*, 64; MacDonald, "Early Highland Emigration to Nova Scotia and PEI", 45
The schooner *Mermaid* picked up all of the *Thetis'* passengers after she was wrecked off Cape Breton (no lives lost).

Year	Mth	Vessel	Master	Psgr. Nos.	Departure Port	Arrival Port
1829	05 (Est)	*Hero*		157	Greenock	Pictou

Colonial Patriot, May 20. "To the mining company."

Year	Mth	Vessel	Master	Psgr. Nos.	Departure Port	Arrival Port
1829	06 (Est)	*Nero*			Greenock	Pictou

Martell, *Immigration Nova Scotia, 1815–38*, 64

Year	Mth	Vessel	Master	Psgr. Nos.	Departure Port	Arrival Port
1829	06	*Vestal*		301	Tobermory	PEI

Jones and Fraser, *Those Elusive Immigrants (Part 1)*, 41.
Mainly emigrants from Skye. Seventy people moved on to Cape Breton.

Year	Mth	Vessel	Master	Psgr. Nos.	Departure Port	Arrival Port
1829	07	*Aberdeenshire* of Aberdeen	Oswald, James	27	Aberdeen	Halifax

Martell, *Immigration Nova Scotia, 1815–38*, 62

Year	Mth	Vessel	Master	Psgr. Nos.	Departure Port	Arrival Port
1830	07 (Est)	*Corsair* of Greenock		206	Greenock	PEI

Warburton, *History of Prince Edward Island*, 381; *IJ* 6 Aug; Martell, *Immigration Nova Scotia, 1815–38*, 66.
Rev. John MacDonald led this group of Roman Catholics, who included some people from Ireland. Most settled in PEI but 38 people disembarked at Canso, Cape Breton. They later recorded their gratitude to the Captain and the Chief Mate "for their unremitting attention to us."

Year	Mth	Vessel	Master	Psgr. Nos.	Departure Port	Arrival Port
1830		*Dunlop*	Brown, John		Greenock	n/k

MacDonald, "Early Highland Emigration to Nova Scotia and PEI," 45. "settlers for Nova Scotia"

Year	Mth	Vessel	Master	Psgr. Nos.	Departure Port	Arrival Port
1830	03	*Albion* of Aberdeen	Leslie, Alexander	7	Aberdeen	Halifax

Martell, *Immigration Nova Scotia, 1815–38*, 64.

Year	Mth	Vessel	Master	Psgr. Nos.	Departure Port	Arrival Port
1830	04	*Aberdeenshire* of Aberdeen	Oswald, James	6	Aberdeen	Halifax, Pictou & Mir.

Martell, *Immigration Nova Scotia, 1815–38*, 64; *IJ* Feb. 12; *Elgin Courier* Feb. 5.
Ship crossing advertised in Inverness and Elgin newspapers.

Year	Mth	Vessel	Master	Psgr. Nos.	Departure Port	Arrival Port
1830	07 (Est)	*Malay*	Coverdale	270	Tobermory	Sydney & Quebec

Passenger List: NSARM RG1 Vol. 67 Doc.19 (Appendix I).
Martell, *Immigration Nova Scotia, 1815–38*, 65–6; *IJ* Aug 6; *QM* Sept. 11.
Vessel also referred to as the *Mallory*. Passengers consisted of 49 families from Skye who disembarked at Sydney and 50 more settlers who went to Quebec. Each family was granted 100 acres land in Cape Breton. Later given $100 relief by Halifax Council. The group eventually founded Skye Glen to the south of Lake Ainslie.

Year	Mth	Vessel	Master	Psgr. Nos.	Departure Port	Arrival Port
1831	03	*Albion* of Aberdeen	Leslie, Alexander	17	Aberdeen	Halifax

Martell, *Immigration Nova Scotia, 1815–38*, 68.

1831	03 (Est)	*Romulus* of Greenock			Greenock	Halifax

Martell, *Immigration Nova Scotia, 1815–38*, 68.
Vessel went ashore in the Bay of Islands 70 miles east of Halifax. Passengers and crew were saved.

1831	05 (Est)	*Six Sisters*		140	Stornoway	Wallace N.S. & Cape Breton

Martell, *Immigration Nova Scotia, 1815–38*, 69,70.
120 passengers landed at Cape Breton and 20 at Wallace.

1831	06	*Corsair* of Greenock	Scott	218	Cromarty from Leith	Pictou & Quebec

Martell, *Immigration Nova Scotia, 1815–38*, 70; *IJ* May 27, *QM* Aug. 30.
Fifty-seven left at Quebec. The 161 who landed in Pictou were in good health. The agent was William Allan of Leith.

1831	06	*Rover*	Briggs, Allan	116	Cromarty, Thurso from Leith	Pictou

Martell, *Immigration Nova Scotia, 1815–38*, 70; *IJ* May 27.
Agent: William Allan of Leith,

1831	07	*Aberdeenshire* of Aberdeen	Oswald, James	20	Aberdeen	Halifax

Martell, *Immigration Nova Scotia, 1815–38*, 68.

1831	07	*Industry*	Carr	57	Cromarty	Pictou & Quebec

Martell, *Immigration Nova Scotia, 1815–38*, 70; *IJ* June 24, *QM* Sept. 29.
Agent: William Allan of Leith.

1831	07	*Lord Brougham*	Watt, James	n/k	Cromarty	Pictou & Quebec

Martell, *Immigration Nova Scotia, 1815–38*, 70; *IJ* June 24.
Vessel collected passengers at Invergordon, near Cromarty.

Year	Mth	Vessel	Master	Psgr. Nos.	Departure Port	Arrival Port
1831 (Est)	08	*Breeze*		267		Sydney

Martell, *Immigration Nova Scotia, 1815–38*, 69.

1831 (Est)	08	*Cumberland*		392		Sydney

Martell, *Immigration Nova Scotia, 1815–38*, 69.

1832		*Charlotte Kerr*		98	Glasgow & Tobermory	Pictou

MacLaren, *Pictou Book*, 121.

1832	03 & 08	*Aberdeenshire* of Aberdeen	Oswald, James	79		Halifax

Martell, *Immigration Nova Scotia, 1815–38*, 71. 40 left in March and 39 in August.

1832	03	*Albion* of Aberdeen	Leslie, Alexander	31	Aberdeen	Halifax

Martell, *Immigration Nova Scotia, 1815–38*, 71.

1832	03	*Clyde*		14	Greenock	Halifax

Martell, *Immigration Nova Scotia, 1815–38*, 71.

1832 (Est)	03	*Isabella* of Glasgow		10	Greenock	Halifax

Martell, *Immigration Nova Scotia, 1815–38*, 71.

1832	04	*Phoenix*		150	Greenock	PEI

Jones and Fraser, *Those Elusive Immigrants (Part 2)*, 35.
Twelve families (30 to 40 people) left at Three Rivers, PEI Another 30 to 40 families landed at Pictou. All were reported to be in good health.

1832	05	*Sylvanus* of North Shields	Lawson	237	Cromarty	Pictou & Quebec

Martell, *Immigration Nova Scotia, 1815–38*, 73; *IJ* April 20; *QM* July 26.
Agent: William Allan of Leith. 41 settlers left at Quebec and 196 left at Pictou.

1832	06	*Blagdon*	Thomson	132	Cromarty	Pictou & Quebec

Martell, *Immigration Nova Scotia, 1815–38*, 73; *IJ* May 18; *QM* Aug 20.
132 settlers left at Quebec. Agent: William Allan of Leith.

Year	Mth	Vessel	Master	Psgr. Nos.	Departure Port	Arrival Port
1832	06	*Canada*	Hunter	241	Cromarty	Pictou & Quebec

Martell, *Immigration Nova Scotia, 1815–38*, 73; *QM* Aug. 22.
Landed 130 passengers at Pictou and 111 passengers at Quebec; Agent: Duncan MacLennan of Inverness.

Year	Mth	Vessel	Master	Psgr. Nos.	Departure Port	Arrival Port
1832	06 (Est)	*Mary Ann*	Robertson, D.	121	Stornoway	Sydney

Martell, *Immigration Nova Scotia, 1815–38*, 72.

Year	Mth	Vessel	Master	Psgr. Nos.	Departure Port	Arrival Port
1832	06 (Est)	*Six Sisters*	McIver, D.	102	Stornoway	Sydney

Martell, *Immigration Nova Scotia, 1815–38*, 72.

Year	Mth	Vessel	Master	Psgr. Nos.	Departure Port	Arrival Port
1832	07 (Est)	*Albion* of Glasgow	McMaster	240	Loch Indaal (Islay) & Tobermory	Sydney & Quebec

Martell, *Immigration Nova Scotia, 1815–38*, 72; *QM* Sept. 16.
181 settlers arrived at Quebec. Fifty-nine people landed at Sydney.

Year	Mth	Vessel	Master	Psgr. Nos.	Departure Port	Arrival Port
1832	07(Est)	*Earl of Fife*	McRitchie, D.	20	Stornoway	Sydney

Martell, *Immigration Nova Scotia, 1815–38*, 72.

Year	Mth	Vessel	Master	Psgr. Nos.	Departure Port	Arrival Port
1832	08 (Est)	*Eldon*	McAlpine, J.	121	Tobermory	Sydney

Martell, *Immigration Nova Scotia, 1815–38*, 72.

Year	Mth	Vessel	Master	Psgr. Nos.	Departure Port	Arrival Port
1832	08 (Est)	*Jessie*	Bolton, W.	313	Tobermory	Sydney

Martell, *Immigration Nova Scotia, 1815–38*, 72.

Year	Mth	Vessel	Master	Psgr. Nos.	Departure Port	Arrival Port
1832	08 (Est)	*Northumber-land*	Mitchell, W.	355	Tobermory	Sydney

Martell, *Immigration Nova Scotia, 1815–38*, 72; Brehaut, "Early Immigration (from UK) to PEI, 1767–1818." Settlers from South Uist.

Year	Mth	Vessel	Master	Psgr. Nos.	Departure Port	Arrival Port
1832	09	*Acadian* of Glasgow		9	Greenock	Halifax

Martell, *Immigration Nova Scotia, 1815–38*, 71.

Year	Mth	Vessel	Master	Psgr. Nos.	Departure Port	Arrival Port
1833		*Charles Hockin*		50	Glasgow	Pictou

MacLaren, *Pictou Book*, 121.

Year	Mth	Vessel	Master	Psgr. Nos.	Departure Port	Arrival Port
1833	03 & 08	*Aberdeenshire* of Aberdeen	Oswald, James	34	Aberdeen	Halifax

Martell, *Immigration Nova Scotia, 1815–38*, 74–5.
13 left in March and 21 in August.

Year	Mth	Vessel	Master	Psgr. Nos.	Departure Port	Arrival Port
1833	03 & 08	*Albion* of Aberdeen	Leslie, Alexander	57	Aberdeen	Halifax

Martell, *Immigration Nova Scotia, 1815–38*, 74–5.
26 left in March and 31 in August.

Year	Mth	Vessel	Master	Psgr. Nos.	Departure Port	Arrival Port
1833	03	*Jean Hastie* of Grangemouth		6	Greenock	Halifax

Martell, *Immigration Nova Scotia, 1815–38*, 74.

Year	Mth	Vessel	Master	Psgr. Nos.	Departure Port	Arrival Port
1833	03	*John*		3	Greenock	Halifax

Martell, *Immigration Nova Scotia, 1815–38*, 74.

Year	Mth	Vessel	Master	Psgr. Nos.	Departure Port	Arrival Port
1833	03 (Est)	*Acadian* of Glasgow		8	Greenock	Halifax

Martell, *Immigration Nova Scotia, 1815–38*, 74.

Year	Mth	Vessel	Master	Psgr. Nos.	Departure Port	Arrival Port
1833	04	*Highlander* of Aberdeen		41	Leith	Halifax

Martell, *Immigration Nova Scotia, 1815–38*, 74.

Year	Mth	Vessel	Master	Psgr. Nos.	Departure Port	Arrival Port
1833	05 (Est)	*Charlotte Kerr*	Anderson	50	Glasgow	Pictou

Martell, *Immigration Nova Scotia, 1815–38*, 76. Two passengers from Islay.

Year	Mth	Vessel	Master	Psgr. Nos.	Departure Port	Arrival Port
1833	05	*Poland*	Ridley, John	n/k	Cromarty	Pictou & Quebec

IJ Apr. 26
Due to call at Cromarty in early May to pick up passengers. Agent: Duncan MacLennan.

Year	Mth	Vessel	Master	Psgr. Nos.	Departure Port	Arrival Port
1833	06	*Economist* of Newport	Slocomb	89	Cromarty from Leith	Pictou & Quebec

Martell, *Immigration Nova Scotia, 1815–38*, 76; *IJ* May 17; *QM* Aug. 25.
Vessel registered at Newport on Tay near Dundee. Agents: William Allan of Leith.
47 settlers left at Quebec & 42 at Pictou.

Year	Mth	Vessel	Master	Psgr. Nos.	Departure Port	Arrival Port
1833	06	*Jane Kay*	Toft, Daniel	170	Cromarty & Thurso	Pictou & Quebec

Martell, *Immigration Nova Scotia, 1815–38*, 75; *IJ* May 17; *QM* Aug. 12.
Agent: Duncan MacLennan, Inverness. 106 for Pictou; 66 settlers left at Quebec; all reported to be in good health at Pictou.

1833	06	*Jean Hastie* of Grangemouth		8	Greenock	Halifax

Martell, *Immigration Nova Scotia, 1815–38*, 75.

1833	06	*Zephyr*	Tucker	150	Cromarty	Pictou & Quebec

Martell, *Immigration Nova Scotia, 1815–38*, 76; *IJ* May 31; *QM* Aug. 21.
"William Allan (shipping agent) is now at Cromarty superintending the fitting up; upwards of 7 ft. between decks, second cabin to be fitted up if passengers wish it. The *Staffa* steam boat will leave the Sea Loch at Clachnaharry with passengers for the *Zephyr*, returning home the same day." 99 settlers left at Quebec and 51 at Pictou.

1833	07 (Est)	*Amity* of Glasgow		258	Tobermory	Ship Harbour, Cape Breton

Martell, *Immigration Nova Scotia, 1815–38*, 77; NSARM RG1 Vol. 282, Doc. 77.
Vessel landed at Ship Harbour in the Gut of Canso on August 21st. A number of these passengers later moved on to PEI.

1833	07	*Robert & Margaret*	Ash	66	Cromarty	Pictou & Quebec

Martell, *Immigration Nova Scotia, 1815–38*, 76; *IJ* May 14, June 21.
"A most desirable conveyance being upwards of 6 feet between decks;" Agent: Duncan Maclennan of Inverness "'who accompanies the passengers; also a surgeon".

1833	08	*Adrian*	Forster	>106	Tobermory	Sydney & Quebec

QM Oct. 5.
106 settlers left at Quebec, unknown numbers left at Sydney.

1833	09	*Acadian* of Glasgow		11	Greenock	Halifax

Martell, *Immigration Nova Scotia, 1815–38*, 75.

1834	03 & 08	*Aberdeenshire* of Aberdeen	Oswald, James	35	Aberdeen	Halifax

Martell, *Immigration Nova Scotia, 1815–38*, 78.
24 left Aberdeen in March and 11 in August.

APPENDIX II

Year	Mth	Vessel	Master	Psgr. Nos.	Departure Port	Arrival Port
1834	04	*Acadian* of Glasgow		14	Greenock	Halifax

Martell, *Immigration Nova Scotia, 1815–38*, 78.

1834	04	*Jean Hastie* of Grangemouth		13	Greenock	Halifax

Martell, *Immigration Nova Scotia, 1815–38*, 78.

1834	06	*Chieftain* of Kirkaldy	Spark	119	Cromarty	Pictou

Martell, *Immigration Nova Scotia, 1815–38*, 79.

1834	06	*William Henry*		102	Cromarty	Pictou

Martell, *Immigration Nova Scotia, 1815–38*, 79.

1834	07	*Albion* of Aberdeen	Leslie, Alexander	31	Aberdeen	Halifax

Martell, *Immigration Nova Scotia, 1815–38*, 78.

1834	07 (Est)	*George Barclay*		47	Greenock	Pictou

Martell, *Immigration Nova Scotia, 1815–38*, 79.

1834	07 (Est)	*Mercator*		5	Greenock	Pictou

Martell, *Immigration Nova Scotia, 1815–38*, 79.

1834	09	*Jean Hastie* of Grangemouth		7	Greenock	Halifax

Martell, *Immigration Nova Scotia, 1815–38*, 78.

1835	03	*Albion* of Aberdeen	Leslie, Alexander	25	Aberdeen	Halifax

Martell, *Immigration Nova Scotia, 1815–38*, 80; *AJ* Jan. 21.

1835	03 & 08	*Aberdeenshire* of Aberdeen	Oswald, James	14	Aberdeen	Halifax

Martell, *Immigration Nova Scotia, 1815–38*, 80. 7 left in March and 7 in August.

Year	Mth	Vessel	Master	Psgr. Nos.	Departure Port	Arrival Port
1835	08	*Acadian* of Glasgow		6	Greenock	Halifax

Martell, *Immigration Nova Scotia, 1815–38*, 80.

Year	Mth	Vessel	Master	Psgr. Nos.	Departure Port	Arrival Port
1835	08	*Paragon*	Goodchild	100	Cromarty	Pictou & Quebec

MacLaren, *The Pictou Book* p.121; *QM* Oct. 27.
QM states 46 arrived at Quebec. Some settlers left at Pictou.

Year	Mth	Vessel	Master	Psgr. Nos.	Departure Port	Arrival Port
1836	04	*Albion* of Aberdeen	Leslie, Alexander	49	Aberdeen	Halifax

Martell, *Immigration Nova Scotia, 1815–38*, 82; *AH* July 23; *AJ* June 29.
The Albion returned in July with timber from Miramichi which was due to be sold by public auction "on the Links adjoining the Works of the Aberdeen Rope and Sail Company."

Year	Mth	Vessel	Master	Psgr. Nos.	Departure Port	Arrival Port
1836	05 & 08	*Ann Grant* (Est)		22	Greenock	Pictou

Martell, *Immigration Nova Scotia, 1815–38*, 84.

Year	Mth	Vessel	Master	Psgr. Nos.	Departure Port	Arrival Port
1836	06	*Albion* of Scarborough	Hicks, Michael	75	Cromarty & Loch Eriboll from Leith	St. Anns, Cape Breton & Quebec

Martell, *Immigration Nova Scotia, 1815–38*, 84; *IJ* June 10, July 1; *QM* Sept. 16, NSARM RG1 Vol. 313 Doc. 82
Agent: William Allan of Leith. "Who is now at Tongue. Vessel will lay by for eight days at Loch Eribol to embark passengers." Customs officer at Sydney reported 75 passengers landed on 6 Dec. 1836. Heads of households are listed in a petition requesting financial assistance for 104 Highlanders who "lately arrived" at St. Anns, Cape Breton.

Year	Mth	Vessel	Master	Psgr. Nos.	Departure Port	Arrival Port
1836	07	*Mariner* of Sunderland	Collins	145	Thurso & Loch Eriboll	Quebec

PP w/e 10 Sept.; *QM* Sept 6; *IJ* July 1; *JJ* July 1.
Agent: William Allan of Leith. One hundred and forty-five steerage passengers disembarked at Quebec but 67 had intended to leave at Pictou. They had been misled by the agent who had told them that *Mariner* would stop at Pictou. They sought "legal redress" but were unsuccessful. Many were said to be waiting in Quebec for an opportunity to get to Pictou.

Year	Mth	Vessel	Master	Psgr. Nos.	Departure Port	Arrival Port
1836	08	*Albion* of Aberdeen	Leslie, Alexander	42	Aberdeen	Halifax

Martell, *Immigration Nova Scotia, 1815–38*, 82; *AH* Aug. 6.

Year	Mth	Vessel	Master	Psgr. Nos.	Departure Port	Arrival Port
1836	08 (Est)	*Clansman* of Glasgow	Scott	206		Sydney & Quebec

Martell, *Immigration Nova Scotia, 1815–38*, 83; *QM* Oct. 11; NSARM RG1 Vol. 150, Doc. 130.
Many passengers arrived with smallpox. Two hundred left at Sydney and six people went on to Quebec.

1837	03 & 08	*Albion* of Aberdeen	Leslie, Alexander	41	Aberdeen	Halifax

Martell, *Immigration Nova Scotia, 1815–38*, 85.
15 left in March and 26 in August.

1837	04 (Est)	*Henry and William*		43	Stornoway	Sydney

Martell, *Immigration Nova Scotia, 1815–38*, 87.

1837	04 (Est)	*Isabella* of Glasgow		190	Greenock	Pictou

Martell, *Immigration Nova Scotia, 1815–38*, 86.

1837	06	*Hercules* of Aberdeen	Walker, Duncan	112	Stornoway	Pictou & Quebec

Martell, *Immigration Nova Scotia, 1815–38*, 86; *QM* July 27.
42 passengers arrived at Quebec & 70 at Pictou.

1837	07 (Est)	*Eclipse*		100	Tobermory	Sydney

Martell, *Immigration Nova Scotia, 1815–38*, 87.

1837	07 (Est)	*Isabella* of Glasgow		124	Greenock	Sydney & Pictou

Martell, *Immigration Nova Scotia, 1815–38*, 87.
120 for Sydney & 24 for Pictou.

1837	07 (Est)	*Thistle*		65	Stornoway	Sydney

Martell, *Immigration Nova Scotia, 1815–38*, 87.

Year	Mth	Vessel	Master	Psgr. Nos.	Departure Port	Arrival Port
1838	07	*Corsair* of Greenock	Ritchie	250	Tobermory	Sydney & Quebec

Martell, *Immigration Nova Scotia, 1815–38*, 90; *QM* Sept 18; Brehaut, "Early Immigration (from UK) to PEI, 1767–1878."
155 left at Sydney. The *Quebec Mercury* reported that in all 250 passengers had landed; Brehaut states passengers from South Uist who came, on an unknown vessel that year, went to Grand Mira, Cape Breton.

Year	Mth	Vessel	Master	Psgr. Nos.	Departure Port	Arrival Port
1838 (Est)	07	*Isabella* of Glasgow		37	Greenock	Pictou

MacLaren, *Pictou Book*, 121; Martell, *Immigration Nova Scotia, 1815–38*, 90.
37 adults.

Year	Mth	Vessel	Master	Psgr. Nos.	Departure Port	Arrival Port
1838	08	*Albion* of Aberdeen	Leslie, Alexander	21	Aberdeen	Halifax

Martell, *Immigration Nova Scotia, 1815–38*, 88.

Year	Mth	Vessel	Master	Psgr. Nos.	Departure Port	Arrival Port
1839		*Isabella* of Glasgow		118	Greenock	Pictou

MacLaren, *Pictou Book*, 121.
"118 miners."

Year	Mth	Vessel	Master	Psgr. Nos.	Departure Port	Arrival Port
1839	05 & 08	*Albion* of Aberdeen	Leslie, Alexander	59	Aberdeen	Halifax

Morse, "Immigration to Nova Scotia, 1839–51," 104.
29 left in April and 30 in August.

Year	Mth	Vessel	Master	Psgr. Nos.	Departure Port	Arrival Port
1839 (Est)	09	*Acadian* of Glasgow	Auld, T.	33	Greenock	Halifax

Morse, "Immigration to Nova Scotia, 1839–51," 104.
12 passengers bound for Halifax and 21 for Charlottetown.

Year	Mth	Vessel	Master	Psgr. Nos.	Departure Port	Arrival Port
1840	04 & 08	*Albion* of Aberdeen	Leslie, Alexander	31	Aberdeen	Halifax

Morse, "Immigration to Nova Scotia, 1839–51," 104–5.
22 left in April and 9 in August (4 cabin and 5 steerage).

Year	Mth	Vessel	Master	Psgr. Nos.	Departure Port	Arrival Port
1840 (Est)	04	*Isabella* of Glasgow		37	Greenock	Pictou

MacLaren, *Pictou Book*, 122.

Year	Mth	Vessel	Master	Psgr. Nos.	Departure Port	Arrival Port
1840	04	*Osprey* of Leith	Kirk	150	Cromarty & Thurso	Pictou & Quebec

IC Aug. 5; *JJ* Apr. 10; *Moray, Nairn and Banff Courant*, Apr. 3.
One of three vessels (*British King, Quebec Packet*) chartered by Sutherland & MacLennan. A total of 403 people sailed on the three vessels of whom 248 were from Caithness. 60 landed at Pictou and the rest went on to Quebec.

Year	Mth	Vessel	Master	Psgr. Nos.	Departure Port	Arrival Port
1840	05 (Est)	*Deveron* of Glasgow	Maclean	140	Lochinver from Greenock	Pictou

MacLaren, *Pictou Book*, 122; *IC* Aug.; Morse, "Immigration, Nova Scotia, 1839–51," 105.
A passage of 27 days

Year	Mth	Vessel	Master	Psgr. Nos.	Departure Port	Arrival Port
1840	07	*British King* of Dundee	Brown, A.	157	Cromarty	Pictou & Quebec

PP w/e Aug. 22; *IC* Aug. 5; *JJ* May 29.
All who landed at Quebec were in good health and had brought capital of £7000 – £8000. 20 of the 157 passengers left the ship at Pictou and 10 left at PEI Also see comments for the *Osprey* of Leith (1840).

Year	Mth	Vessel	Master	Psgr. Nos.	Departure Port	Arrival Port
1840	07 (Est)	*Cruickston Castle* of Greenock	McKinley, D.	195	Stornoway	Sydney

Morse, "Immigration to Nova Scotia, 1839–51," 106.

Year	Mth	Vessel	Master	Psgr. Nos.	Departure Port	Arrival Port
1840	07 (Est)	*Isabella* of Glasgow		n/k	Greenock	Pictou

MacLaren, *Pictou Book*, 122.

Year	Mth	Vessel	Master	Psgr. Nos.	Departure Port	Arrival Port
1840	08	*Nith* of Liverpool	Shaw	550	Uig and Tobermory	PEI & Sydney

Jones and Fraser, *Those Elusive Immigrants (Part 3)*, 34; *IC* Aug. 12; *Cape Breton Advocate*, Sept. 15.
Some 400 passengers boarded at Uig in Skye and 150 at Tobermory in Mull. Passengers mainly from Skye (especially Snizort and northern parishes). Ninety-seven passengers disembarked at Sydney, while 315 left at Charlottetown. Agent was A. McNiven.

Year	Mth	Vessel	Master	Psgr. Nos.	Departure Port	Arrival Port
1840	08	*Rother*	Hall	150	Uig and Tobermory	PEI & Cape Breton

IC Aug. 12; Morse, "Immigration, Nova Scotia, 1839–51," 106.
See comments for *Nith*.

Year	Mth	Vessel	Master	Psgr. Nos.	Departure Port	Arrival Port
1840	09	*Acadian* of Glasgow	Auld	4	Greenock	Halifax

Morse, "Immigration, Nova Scotia, 1839–51," 105.

Year	Mth	Vessel	Master	Psgr. Nos.	Departure Port	Arrival Port
1841	04	*Pacific* of Aberdeen	Morrison, John	193	Thurso	Pictou & Quebec

PP 1842(301)XXXI; *JJ* Feb. 5.
Most passengers were former tenants of the Duke of Sutherland, twenty-two of whom left at Pictou. Advertisement states that "George McKay merchant in Reay will be every Friday at McKay's Hotel to enrol names." Agent: Alexander Cooper, shipowner, Aberdeen.

Year	Mth	Vessel	Master	Psgr. Nos.	Departure Port	Arrival Port
1841	06	*Lady Grey* of North Shields	Grey, William	240	Cromarty & Thurso	Pictou & Quebec

Passenger List: Maclaren, *The Pictou Book*, 104–5 (Appendix I).
PP w/e Aug. 28; *PP* 1842(301)XXXI; NAS RH 1/2/908; *IJ* June 25.
Seventy-five passengers destined for Pictou and the rest for Quebec but 135 stayed in Pictou. Typhus broke out causing six deaths on crossing. A partial passenger list records people protesting at the captain's ill-treatment. Principal Agents: MacLennan & Sutherland.

Year	Mth	Vessel	Master	Psgr. Nos.	Departure Port	Arrival Port
1841	07	*Mariner* of Sunderland	Henning, C.	35	Glasgow	Halifax

Morse, "Immigration, Nova Scotia, 1839–51," 107.

Year	Mth	Vessel	Master	Psgr. Nos.	Departure Port	Arrival Port
1841	07	*Unicorn* (Est)		105	Thurso	Pictou

Morse, "Immigration, Nova Scotia, 1839–51," 108.

Year	Mth	Vessel	Master	Psgr. Nos.	Departure Port	Arrival Port
1841	08	*Albion* of Aberdeen	Leslie, Alexander	28	Aberdeen	Halifax

Morse, "Immigration, Nova Scotia, 1839–51," 107.
28 steerage.

Year	Mth	Vessel	Master	Psgr. Nos.	Departure Port	Arrival Port
1841	08	*Banffshire* of Dundee		450	Lochmaddy	Cape Breton

Morse, "Immigration, Nova Scotia, 1839–51," 109.
1 of 3 vessels taking 1300 emigrants from N. Uist to Cape Breton, "of the poorest class."

| 1841 | 08 | *Cleostratus* | | 22 | Clyde | Pictou |

Morse, "Immigration, Nova Scotia, 1839–51," 108. 5 cases of small pox on board ship.

| 1841 | 08 | *George* of Dundee | | 400 | Lochmaddy | Cape Breton |

Morse, "Immigration, Nova Scotia, 1839–51," 109.
1 of 3 vessels taking 1300 emigrants from N Uist to Cape Breton, "of the poorest class."

| 1841 | 08 | *Tay* of Glasgow | | 450 | Lochmaddy | Cape Breton |

Morse, "Immigration, Nova Scotia, 1839–51," 109.
1 of 3 vessels taking 1300 emigrants from N. Uist to Cape Breton, "of the poorest class."

| 1841 | 09 | *Universe* of Aberdeen | | 124 | Thurso | Pictou & Quebec |

PP w/e Oct 9; MacLaren, *Pictou Book*, 122.
Most were former tenants of the Duke of Sutherland. 105 passengers left the vessel at Pictou; the remainder disembarked at Quebec to join relatives in vicinity of Kingston & Toronto. Agent: William Allan, shipowner, Aberdeen.

| 1842 | 04 | *Isabella* of Glasgow | Thomas, Alex. | 54 | Glasgow | Pictou |

MacLaren, *Pictou Book*, 122; Morse, "Immigration, Nova Scotia, 1839–51," 110; Flewwelling, "Immigration and Emigration Nova Scotia," 84; SRA Glasgow Shipping, TCN-21(2); NAS CS 96/1592.
Vessel stuck in ice off Cape North, Cape Breton; Captain, crew & passengers abandoned ship; treated badly on arrival by people in surrounding area. Passengers arrived at Pictou in good health and were warmly welcomed.

| 1842 | 04 | *Eagle* (Est) | | n/k | Glasgow | Pictou & Halifax |

MacLaren, *Pictou Book*, 122; Flewwelling "Immigration and Emigration Nova Scotia," 83; SRA Glasgow Shipping, TCN-21(3)
A group landed at Halifax and "behaved in a highly orderly, discreet and virtuous manner."

Year	Mth	Vessel	Master	Psgr. Nos.	Departure Port	Arrival Port
1842	05	*Superior* of Peterhead	Manson, Donald	191	Cromarty & Thurso	Pictou & Quebec

PP 1843 (109) XXXIV; *IJ* Mar. 18, 25, July 29; *Pictou Observer*, June 21, 1842.
Fifty-two left at Pictou; 139 left at Quebec. Captain Manson, a native of Cromarty was experienced and "known to possess that manner of urbanity that will secure to him the good will and respect of all the passengers." Agents: MacLennan & Sutherland.

Year	Mth	Vessel	Master	Psgr. Nos.	Departure Port	Arrival Port
1842	06 (Est)	*Cleostratus*	Levens	64	Glasgow	Pictou & Sydney

MacLaren, *Pictou Book*, 122; SRA Glasgow Shipping, TCN-21(2); *AH* Apr. 30; *Glasgow Herald*, Apr. 18. Sixty four passengers arrived at Pictou in August.

Year	Mth	Vessel	Master	Psgr. Nos.	Departure Port	Arrival Port
1842	06	*Lady Emily* of Sunderland	Stove	150	Cromarty, Thurso & Loch Laxford	Pictou & Quebec

MacLaren *Pictou Book*, 122; *IJ* June 10, Sept. 30; *Pictou Observer*, Sept. 6, 1842; *PP* w/e Oct. 1.
Eighty-six left at Pictou and 64 at Quebec. Passengers who disembarked at Pictou expressed their "heartfelt thanks" to Captain Stove for "his kindness" and they also expressed their "warmest thanks to Mr Sutherland for his uniform kindness and attention to our wants and requirements." Agents: MacLennan & Sutherland.

Year	Mth	Vessel	Master	Psgr. Nos.	Departure Port	Arrival Port
1842	06 (Est)	*St Andrew* of New Brunswick	Leith, J.	>133	Lochmaddy	Cape Breton & Quebec

PP w/e Aug 6; *IJ* Aug. 19.
The number of passengers who may have disembarked at Cape Breton is not know. Arrivals at Quebec were very poor and some could not pay for their passage.

Year	Mth	Vessel	Master	Psgr. Nos.	Departure Port	Arrival Port
1842	07 (Est)	*Hercules* of Liverpool	Postill, F	>59	Lochmaddy	Cape Breton & Quebec

PP w/e Sept 17; *IJ* Aug. 19;
Passengers who arrived at Quebec were very poor and some could not pay for their passage. The number of people who disembarked at Cape Breton is not known.

Year	Mth	Vessel	Master	Psgr. Nos.	Departure Port	Arrival Port
1842	08	*Acadian* of Glasgow	Auld, T.	16	Greenock	Halifax

Morse, "Immigration, Nova Scotia, 1839–51," 110; SRA Glasgow Shipping, TCN-21(2).
16 steerage passengers

Year	Mth	Vessel	Master	Psgr. Nos.	Departure Port	Arrival Port
1843	06	*George* of Dundee	Hanley, Francis	307	Cromarty, Thurso & Loch Laxford from Dundee	Pictou & Quebec

PP 1844(181)xxxv; *PP* w/e Sept. 16; *DC* Apr. 28; NSARM RG1 Vol. 255 Doc. 57.
Ninety-five left at Pictou; long delays caused by many port calls; disease broke out before arrival in Pictou and emigrants taken to temporary accommodation on beaches. Poster for crossing states "vessel has her cabins on deck, the whole space between decks nearly 8 ft in height and 126 ft in length. Is fitted expressly for intermediate and steerage passengers." Agents: MacLennan and Sutherland.

Year	Mth	Vessel	Master	Psgr. Nos.	Departure Port	Arrival Port
1843	07	*Catherine*	McKechney	275	Tobermory	Ship Harbour, Cape Breton, Quebec

*PP*1844(181)xxxv; *PP* w/e Oct. 14.
After 5 weeks at sea put into Belfast in distress. Passengers transhipped on *John & Robert*. 200 landed at Cape Breton & 22 at Quebec, all destitute.

Year	Mth	Vessel	Master	Psgr. Nos.	Departure Port	Arrival Port
1843	07	*Charles Hamerton* of Liverpool		405	Tobermory	Cape Breton & Quebec

*PP*1844(181)xxxv; *IC* Jul 13 & Aug 2.
Probably called at Cape Breton. The number of people who disembarked there is not known. 408 people disembarked at Quebec. The *Inverness Courier* recorded the departure of 16 families, chiefly Roman Catholic, from Eigg. It also reported the departure in July of 215 passengers from Gairloch and Torridon together with a few from Skye.

Year	Mth	Vessel	Master	Psgr. Nos.	Departure Port	Arrival Port
1844	04	*Albion* of Aberdeen	Leslie Alexander	13	Aberdeen	Halifax

AH Apr. 27, Jul. 20.
Vessel returned to Aberdeen from Miramichi in July.

Year	Mth	Vessel	Master	Psgr. Nos.	Departure Port	Arrival Port
1844	04	*Pacific* of Aberdeen	Morrison, John	n/k	Cromarty & Thurso	Quebec

IJ April 5.
Agents: MacLennan and Sutherland. Some passengers may have landed at Pictou.

Year	Mth	Vessel	Master	Psgr. Nos.	Departure Port	Arrival Port
1844	06	*Harriet*	Chambers, W.	n/k	Cromarty & Thurso	Quebec

IJ June 21.
Advert states that because of "unprecedented scarcity of suitable vessels for passengers" the owners will not allow the *Harriet* to call at Pictou – if a suitable place cannot be found to land passengers in Nova Scotia a "safe & cheap conveyance will be procured for them in Quebec." Agents: MacLennan & Sutherland.

Year	Mth	Vessel	Master	Psgr. Nos.	Departure Port	Arrival Port
1844	08	*Albion* of Aberdeen	Leslie, Alexander	13	Aberdeen	Halifax

AH Aug. 17.
30 packages of passengers luggage.

Year	Mth	Vessel	Master	Psgr. Nos.	Departure Port	Arrival Port
1845	04	*Albion* of Aberdeen	Leslie, Alexander	13	Aberdeen	Halifax

AH March 29.

Year	Mth	Vessel	Master	Psgr. Nos.	Departure Port	Arrival Port
1845	07	*Joseph Harrison*	Hutchison, John	n/k	Cromarty & Thurso	Quebec

IC June 18, 25.
New ship, great height between decks. Agents: MacLennan and Sutherland. Advert states steamers go regularly between Quebec and Pictou - fare only 8d.

Year	Mth	Vessel	Master	Psgr. Nos.	Departure Port	Arrival Port
1845	08	*Sovereign of Kirkwall*			Lochmaddy & Stromness (Orkney)	Sydney Pictou & Quebec

IC May 28 & Jul 16 advert.
Agent: D. MacLennan.

Year	Mth	Vessel	Master	Psgr. Nos.	Departure Port	Arrival Port
1847		*Serius*		117	Thurso	Pictou

MacLaren, *Pictou Book*, 122.
Duke of Sutherland's tenants.

Year	Mth	Vessel	Master	Psgr. Nos.	Departure Port	Arrival Port
1847	04	*London* of Glasgow	MacDonald, John	50	Greenock	Pictou

MacLaren, *Pictou Book*, 122.
Smallpox aboard

Year	Mth	Vessel	Master	Psgr. Nos.	Departure Port	Arrival Port
1848	04	*Hope* of Glasgow	Grange, William	137	Glasgow	Pictou

Passenger List: MacLaren, *Pictou Book*, 111–13 (Appendix I).
NSARM RG1 Vol. 257 Doc. 99; Morse, "Immigration, Nova Scotia, 1839–51," 97.
70 adults & 67 children, mainly colliers for Albion mines. The mining company obtained a refund for the head tax they had paid for those families (66 people) who went to the United States later.

Year	Mth	Vessel	Master	Psgr. Nos.	Departure Port	Arrival Port
1848	04 & 07	*London* of Glasgow	McDonald, John	62	Glasgow	Pictou

Passenger List: MacLaren, *Pictou Book*, 113–14 (Appendix I).
NSARM RG1 Vol. 257 Docs 104, 131; Morse, "Immigration, Nova Scotia, 1839–51," 97.
Three of the July passengers went to PEI. 36 travelled in May and 26 in July; April group included 7 labourers, 1 farmer, 1 weaver & 1 carpenter; July group included 5 labourers 2 farmers & 1 seaman

Year	Mth	Vessel	Master	Psgr. Nos.	Departure Port	Arrival Port
1848	05	*Ellen* of Liverpool	McLachlan, Dugald	154	Loch Laxford	Pictou

Passenger List: MacLaren, *The Pictou Book*, 108–10 (Appendix I).
Flewwelling, "Immigration and Emigration Nova Scotia," 94–95; NSARM RG1 Vol. 257 Doc. 110; Morse, "Immigration, Nova Scotia, 1839–51," 98.
The passenger list was compiled at Pictou on the vessel's arrival. A Pictou customs official commented that the Captain of the *Ellen* "acted indeed unto one and all of them, the passengers, more like the head of a family than a Shipmaster. No praise that they can bestow on him can be too great." The vessel had been chartered by the Duke of Sutherland. A head tax was levied on all passengers. A dispute broke out because the families who went to PEI had to pay twice.

Year	Mth	Vessel	Master	Psgr. Nos.	Departure Port	Arrival Port
1848	08	*Lulan* of Pictou	McKenzie, George	167	Glasgow	Pictou

Passenger List: MacLaren, *Pictou Book*, 114–18 (Appendix I).
NSARM RG1 Vol. 257 Doc. 167; Flewwelling, "Immigration and Emigration Nova Scotia," 95–96; MacDonald, *Mabou Pioneers*, 46; Morse, "Immigration, Nova Scotia, 1839–51," 98–99.
The South Uist emigrants were assisted by their landlord, Col. John Gordon. Unknown to the emigrants, they were initially put on vessel bound for Boston in the United States. The deception was discovered in enough time for the emigrants to abandon their vessel but they were forced to wait a long time in the Clyde for a vessel to Nova Scotia.

Year	Mth	Vessel	Master	Psgr. Nos.	Departure Port	Arrival Port

They arrived suffering from disease and in extreme poverty. By November, 24 emigrants had died of disease. The vessels which took the emigrants on to PEI and Cape Breton were hired at public expense. The Nova Scotia authorities had to pay £470 head tax for them. In all there were 9 cabin and 158 steerage passengers who included 30 men with families who intended to work in the Albion Coal Mines near Pictou. Seventy-two of the emigrants eventually moved to PEI.

Year	Mth	Vessel	Master	Psgr. Nos.	Departure Port	Arrival Port
1849	05	*Sarah Botsford* of Glasgow	MacDonald	50	Glasgow	Pictou

MacLaren, *Pictou Book*, 123.

Year	Mth	Vessel	Master	Psgr. Nos.	Departure Port	Arrival Port
1849	07	*Joseph Hutchison*	Stirling, Samuel		Glasgow	Cape Breton

SRA Glasgow Shipping, TCN 21/7.

Year	Mth	Vessel	Master	Psgr. Nos.	Departure Port	Arrival Port
1850	04 & 08	*Albion* of Aberdeen	Leslie, Alexander	21	Aberdeen	Halifax

AH Apr. 6, Aug. 17.
13 left in April and 8 in August.

Year	Mth	Vessel	Master	Psgr. Nos.	Departure Port	Arrival Port
1850	06	*George* of Dundee	Hanley, Francis	82	Cromarty, Thurso & Loch Laxford	Pictou & Quebec

IC May 16; *PP* 1851(348)XL
Passengers were to take *Maid of Morven* steamship from Invergordon, Burghead & Little Ferry to Cromarty free of charge. The *George* was due to call at Pictou but the number of passengers who may have landed at Pictou is not known. Eleven families arrived at Quebec from Oban. MacLennan & Sutherland were the agents.

Year	Mth	Vessel	Master	Psgr. Nos.	Departure Port	Arrival Port
1851	04	*Sarah Botsford* of Glasgow	Cameron	18	Glasgow	Pictou

SRA Clyde Bill of Entry, T/CN 26/5

Year	Mth	Vessel	Master	Psgr. Nos.	Departure Port	Arrival Port
1851	05	*Islay*		68	Stornoway & Glasgow	Quebec

Devine, *Highland Famine*, 219.
Sir James Matheson's tenants from Lewis. Some passengers may have landed at Sydney.

Year	Mth	Vessel	Master	Psgr. Nos.	Departure Port	Arrival Port
1851	05	*Marquis of Stafford*		500	Stornoway	Quebec

Devine, *Highland Famine*, 219; *IC* June 12.

Sir James Matheson's tenants from Lewis. Matheson apparently granted crofters arrears of rent amounting to about £1600 and purchased their stock at valuation. He also paid his tenants' passages. Some passengers may have landed at Sydney.

Year	Mth	Vessel	Master	Psgr. Nos.	Departure Port	Arrival Port
1852	04	*Lulan* of Pictou	McAlly	19	Glasgow	Boston & Pictou

SRA Clyde Bill of Entry, T/CN 26/7

Year	Mth	Vessel	Master	Psgr. Nos.	Departure Port	Arrival Port
1852	04	*Tongataboo* of New Glasgow	Peterson	26	Glasgow	Pictou

SRA Clyde Bill of Entry, T/CN 26/7

Year	Mth	Vessel	Master	Psgr. Nos.	Departure Port	Arrival Port
1852	08	*Lulan* of Pictou	Peterson	23	Glasgow	Pictou

SRA Clyde Bill of Entry, T/CN 26/7.

APPENDIX III

EXPLANATORY NOTES

Passenger Data

Passenger totals are provided for each vessel. Details of individual crossings together with documentary sources are to be found in Appendix II.

Passenger figures have been obtained from a wide variety of documentary sources. Some passenger figures are approximations and some are ambiguous. Uncertainties arise as to whether passenger numbers include all adults (not just heads of households) and children and infants. In some cases ships are reported to have carried passengers, but actual numbers are not given.

Vessel Details

Information on the tonnage, vessel type, year built, place built and the Lloyd's Code have been taken from the *Lloyd's Shipping Register*. Vessel dimensions, where available, have been taken from the shipping registers for Aberdeen (ACA CE 87/11), Dundee (DCA CE 70/11), Leith (NAS CE 57/11), Glasgow (SRA CE 59/11) and Pictou (NSARM RG 12A1 vols. 294–297).

Tonnage

This was a standard measure used to determine customs dues and navigation fees. Because it was a calculated figure, tonnage did not necessarily convey actual carrying capacity. Before 1836, the formula used to calculate tonnage was based only on breadth and length but after 1836 it incorporated the vessel's depth as well.

Vessel Type

The word "ship" can signify a particular vessel type as well as having a generic usage in denoting all types of sea-going vessels. Sailing ship rigs were many and varied. A major distinction was the alignment of the sails. There were the square-rigged vessels in which the sails were rigged across the vessel and the fore-and-aft rigs which followed the fore-and-aft-line of the vessel. The square rig was normally used on ocean-going vessels:

Brig (bg): a two masted vessel with square rigging on both masts.

Snow (sw): rigged as a brig, with square sails on both masts but with a small triangular sail mast stepped immediately towards the stern of the main mast.

Barque (bk): three-masted vessel, square rigged on the fore and main masts and fore-and-aft rigged on the third aftermost mast.

Ship (s): three-masted vessel, square-rigged on all three masts.

Schooner (sr): fore-and-aft sails on two or more masts. Some had small square topsails on the foremast. They were largely used in the coasting trade and for fishing, their advantage being the smaller crew than that required by square-rigged vessels of a comparable size.

Sloop (sp): single masted vessel, fore-and-aft rigged. Used in fishing and coastal trade.

Lloyd's Shipping Codes

These were assigned to vessels after periodic surveys according to their quality of construction, condition and age:

A – first class condition, kept in the highest state of repair and efficiency and within a prescribed age limit at the time of sailing.

AE – "second description of the first class," fit for safe conveyance, no defects but may be over a prescribed age limit.

E – second class vessels which, although unfit for carrying dry cargoes, were suitable for long distance sea voyages.

I – third class vessels only suitable for short voyages (i.e. not out of Europe).

The letters were followed by the number 1 or 2 which signified the condition of the vessel's equipment (anchors, cables and stores). Where satisfactory, the number 1 was used, and where not, 2 was used.

Failure to locate vessels in the *Register* does not in itself signify its exclusion from the Lloyd's classification system. To select the relevant vessel from the *Register* it is usually necessary to know the tonnage and captain's name, information which is often elusive and problematic because of gaps in the available shipping and customs records.

Multiple Crossings

The symbol # signifies a vessel which carried emigrants on more than one occasion (as shown in Appendix II).

Vessel		Tons	Capt.	Year(s) Sailed	Depart	Arrive	Psgr Nos	Year built	Place built	Lloyd's Code
#*Aberdeen-shire* of Aberdeen [Dimensions: 89′ x 25′ 2″ x 17′]	bg	240	Oswald, James	1827 −35	Aber-deen	Halifax	246	1825	Aber-deen	A1
#*Acadian* of Glasgow#	bk	385	n/k	1832 −42	Green-ock	Halifax	101	1832	Green-ock	A1
Active	n/k	n/k	Stirling, J.	1807	Fort William	Pictou	36	n/k	n/k	n/k
Active [Single deck with beams.]	s	351	Walker, A.	1827	Tober-mory	Cape Breton & Quebec	200	1826	N. Scotia	A1
Adrian [Two decks]	s	374	Forster	1833	Tober-mory	Sydney & Quebec	106	1819	Newcastle	E1
#*Agincourt* of Leith [Single deck with beams.]	s	347	Matheson	1817 −19	Leith	Halifax & Quebec	400	1804	North Shields	E1
#*Aimwell* of Aberdeen [Dimensions: 85′ x 25′ 10″ x 16′ 9′]	sw	232	Morrison, John	1816 −18	Thurso	Halifax & Aberdeen	204	1816	Aberdeen	A1
#*Albion* of Aberdeen [Single deck with beams. Dimensions: 94′ 2″ x 25′ 6″ x 17′ 2″]	bg	266	Leslie, Alexander	1829 −50	Aber-deen	Halifax	522	1826	Aberdeen	A1

Vessel		Tons	Capt.	Year(s) Sailed	Depart	Arrive	Psgr Nos	Year built	Place built	Lloyd's Code
Albion of Glasgow	bg	190	McMaster	1832	Loch Indaal (Islay) & Tobermory	Sydney & Quebec	240	1826	Campbel- town	E1
Albion of Scarborough	sw	287	Hicks, Michael	1836	Cromarty Loch Eribol, Lochinver & Tobermory	St. Anns & Quebec	103	1836	Sunderland	A1
Alexander & 2 other ships	n/k	n/k	n/k	1803	Storno- way	Pictou	600	n/k	n/k	n/k
#*Amethyst* of Aberdeen	sw	132	Greig, H.	1815 –16	Aber- deen	Halifax	65	1812	Aberdeen	A1
Amity of Glasgow	n/k	n/k	n/k	1833	Tober- mory	Ship Harbour	258	n/k	n/k	n/k
Amity of Peterhead	bg	197	Anderson, Alexander	1817	Thurso	Halifax	126	1817	Peterhead	A1
Anacreon of Newcastle [Single deck with beams.]	s	443	Wilson, W	1817	Tober- mory	Pictou & Quebec	166	1799	Sunderland	E1
Ann	n/k	n/k	n/k	1818	Cromarty from Leith	Halifax	129	n/k	n/k	n/k
Ann	bg	n/k	n/k	1828	Storn- oway	Sydney	209	n/k	n/k	n/k
#*Ann Grant*	s	378	n/k	1836 (twice)	Green- ock	Pictou	22	1806	Whitby	E1
Ann of Banff [Single deck]	sr	90	n/k	1819	Cromarty	Pictou	60	1817	Banff	A1

Vessel		Tons	Capt.	Year(s) Sailed	Depart	Arrive	Psgr Nos	Year built	Place built	Lloyd's Code
Anne of North Shields [Single deck with beams]	s	284	Tod, James	1811	Storn-oway	Pictou	26	1785	Bristol	EI
Atlantic of Stornoway [Single deck with beams.]	bg	131	MacLeod, R.	1823	Lochalsh	Pictou & Cape Breton	n/k	1823	Norway	AI
#*Augusta* of Dumfries [Two decks]	s	370	Davidson	1817 –18	Dumfries	Pictou & Miramichi	235	1796	Whitby	EI
Aurora [Two decks]	s	330	n/k	1816	Leith	Halifax & Pictou	70	1781	Whitby	EI
Aurora	n/k	n/k	n/k	1827		Port Hastings	n/k	n/k	n/k	n/k
Aurora of Greenock [Single deck with beams]	s	191	Mclean, Alan	1802	Fort William from Greenock	Pictou	128	n/k	Prize	EI
Banffshire of Dundee	s	471	n/k	1841	Loch-maddy	Cape Breton	450	1837	Pictou	AI
Bassettere of Greenock [Single deck with beams]	bg	123	McMorland, William	1818	Fort William	Pictou	113	n/k	America - Prize	EI
Blagdon	bg	289	Thomson	1832	Cromarty	Pictou & Quebec	132	1825	Shields	AI
Breeze	n/k	n/k	n/k	1831	n/k	Sydney	267	n/k	n/k	n/k
British King of Dundee	bg	239	Brown, A.	1840	Cromarty	Pictou & Quebec	157	1825	Sunder-land	AEI

Vessel		Tons	Capt.	Year(s) Sailed	Depart	Arrive	Psgr Nos	Year built	Place built	Lloyd's Code
British Queen [Two decks]	s	292	n/k	1818	Leith	Halifax	131	1785	Whitby	E1
Cadmus	n/k	n/k	Snowdon	1826	Tober-mory	Nova Scotia & Quebec	n/k	n/k	n/k	n/k
Caledonia of Alloa [Almost rebuilt 1819; Single deck with beams]	bg	291	Liddell	1819	Alloa & Greenock	Halifax & Pictou	n/k	Priza	America	E1
#Cambria of Aberdeen	bg	120	Pirie, James	1812 –16	Aber-deen	Halifax & Quebec	105	1808	Aberdeen	A1
Canada	s	269	Hunter	1832	Cromarty	Pictou & Quebec	241	1811	Montreal	E1
Caroline of Liverpool	n/k	140	Rea, James	1828	Inverness & Fort William	PEI, Pictou, & Miramichi	36	n/k	n/k	n/k
Catherine	s	448	McKechney	1843	Tober-mory	Ship Harbour & Quebec	275	n/k	n/k	n/k
Centurion of Aberdeen	bg	130	Morrison, James	1811	Aber-deen	Halifax	18	n/k	n/k	n/k
Charles Hamerton of Liverpool	n/k	640	n/k	1843	Tober-mory	Cape Breton	405	n/k	n/k	n/k
Charles Hockin	n/k	n/k	n/k	1833	Glasgow	Pictou	50	n/k	n/k	n/k
Charlotte Kerr Single deck with beams.]	bg	129	n/k	1832 –33	Glasgow	Pictou & Tobermory	148	1830	Nova Scotia	A1

283

Vessel		Tons	Capt.	Year(s) Sailed	Depart	Arrive	Psgr Nos	Year built	Place built	Lloyd's Code
Chieftain of Kirkaldy	bk	333	Scott, Andrew	1834	Cromarty	Pictou	119	1832	Leith	A1
[Three masts. Dimensions: 100′ 6″ x 27′ 9″ x 19′ 6″]										
Clansman of Glasgow	bk	348	Scott	1836	n/k	Sydney & Quebec	206	1823	New Brunswick	E1
#*Cleostratus*	bk	476	n/k	1841 –42	Clyde	Pictou	86	n/k	n/k	n/k
Clyde	n/k	n/k	n/k	1832	Green-ock	Halifax	14	n/k	n/k	n/k
Columbus	bg	322	Fleck, A	1827	Tober-mory	Cape Breton	228	1825	Pictou	A1
[Single deck with beams]										
Commerce	s	200	Galt, Robert	1803	Port Glasgow	Pictou	70	1772	River	E1
[Had two decks]										
#*Corsair* of Greenock	bg	273	n/k	1827 –38	Green-ock	Halifax, Pictou, C.B. & Quebec	691	1823	New Brunswick	E1
[Single deck with beams. Advertisement stated "high and roomy between decks" (*IJ* 27 May, 1831)]										
Cruickston Castle of Greenock	bk	382	n/k	1840	Storn-oway	Sydney	195	1822	New Brunswick	AE1
Cumberland	s	n/k	n/k	1831	n/k	Sydney	392	n/k	n/k	n/k
Deveron of Glasgow	bg	333	Maclean	1840	Loch-inver from Greenock	Pictou	140	1824	Nova Scotia	AE1
Diadem of St John	s	319	Wells, George	1816	Green-ock	Halifax	2	1805	New Brunswick	A1
[Single deck with beams]										

ssel		Tons	Capt.	Year(s) Sailed	Depart	Arrive	Psgr Nos	Year built	Place built	Lloyd's Code
rset Grangemouth ngle deck with beams]	s	194	Scott, Andrew	1816	Leith	Halifax	83	1802	Poole	E1
uglas	n/k	n/k	Athol	1826	Green-ock	Halifax	n/k	n/k	n/k	n/k
uglas Aberdeen imensions: 69′ 10″ x 21′ 9″ x 12′ 8″]	bg	135	Morrison, John	1817	Aber-deen	Halifax	7	1816	Aberdeen	A1
ve Aberdeen	n/k	186	Crane	1801	Fort William	Pictou	219	n/k	n/k	n/k
nkenfield d one other vessel [Three decks]	s	400	n/k	1791	n/k	Pictou	650	1783	n/k	A1
nlop wo decks]	bg	331	Mandell	1824	Green-ock	Sydney	227	1805	Montreal	E1
gle	bk	330	n/k	1842	Glasgow	Pictou & Halifax	n/k	1842	Quebec	A1
rl of alhousie Aberdeen	bg	183	Levie, John	1817	Aber-deen	Halifax	24	1817	Aberdeen	A1
rl of Fife ingle deck]	sp	42	n/k	1832	Storn-oway	Sydney	20	1820	Scotland	E1
lipse	n/k	n/k	n/k	1837	Tober-mory	Sydney	100	n/k	n/k	n/k
onomist Newport	bk	324	Stokeham	1833	Cromarty from Leith	Pictou & Quebec	89	1829	PEI	A1
onomy Aberdeen	n/k	n/k	Fraser, James	1819	Tober-mory	Pictou	285	n/k	n/k	n/k

Vessel		Tons	Capt.	Year(s) Sailed	Depart	Arrive	Psgr Nos	Year built	Place built	Lloyd's Code
Eldon	s	402	n/k	1832	Tober-mory	Sydney	121	1828	Quebec	A1
Elizabeth and Ann of North Shields [Single deck with beams. Had four guns.]	s	293	St Girese, Thomas	1806	Thurso from Port Glasgow	PEI & Pictou	107	1782	Whitby	I1
Ellen of Liverpool	bk	397	McLachlan, Dugald	1848	Loch Laxford	Pictou	154	1834	New Brunswick	AE1
Emperor Alexander of Aberdeen [Dimensions: 83′ 11″ x 25′ 8″ x 15′ 11″]	sw	236	Watts, Alexander	1823	Cromarty, Tober-mory (from Aberdeen)	Sydney & Quebec	160	1814	Sunderland	A1
Fame of Aberdeen	bg	141	Masson, George	1815	Aber-deen	Halifax	4	1810	Stockton	A1
Favourite of Grangemouth [Single deck with beams; had previously been *Favourite* of Kirkaldy – see below]	bg	165	McDonald, Alexander	1810	Oban	Pictou	31	1797	Kirkaldy	E1
Favourite of Kirkaldy & one other vessel [Single deck with beams]	bg	165	Ballantyne	1803	Isle Martin	Pictou	500	1797	Kirkaldy	A1
Frances Ann of Irvine [Single deck with beams]	bg	170	Stoke, J.	1817	Fort William	Pictou	136	1804	Prize	E1
Garland [Single deck with beams]	bg	180	n/k	1819	Leith	Halifax	90	1819	Sunderland	A1
General Goldie of Dumfries	sp	61	Smith	1817	Dumfries	Pictou, Miramichi, Quebec & Montreal	18	1812	Whitehaven	A1
George Barclay	bg	241	n/k	1834	Green-ock	Pictou	47	1834	Pictou	A1

APPENDIX III

Vessel		Tons	Capt.	Year(s) Sailed	Depart	Arrive	Psgr Nos	Year built	Place built	Lloyd's Code
#*George* of Dundee [Dimensions: 125′ 3″ x 27′ 4″ x 21′]	s	676	Hanley, Francis	1841 –50	Loch-maddy	C. B. Pictou, Quebec & Montreal	789	1839	Pictou	n/k
Glasgow	n/k	n/k	n/k	1784	Green-ock	Halifax	> 100	n/k	n/k	n/k
#*Glentanner* of Aberdeen [Dimensions: 77′ 10″ x 22′ 2″ x 13′ 6″]	bg	160	Laird, James	1815 & 1820	Aber-deen & Tobermory	Halifax, Pictou & Cape Breton	158	1811	Aberdeen	A1
#*Good Intent* of Aberdeen	n/k	n/k	Beverly, Robert	1801 & 1816	Fort William	Pictou, Halifax	99	n/k	n/k	n/k
#*Halifax Packet* of Sunderland	sw	185	Hogg, John	1814 –15	Aber-deen	Halifax	10	1814	Sunderland	A1
Harmony	n/k	n/k	n/k	1821	n/k	Sydney	350	n/k	n/k	n/k
Harmony of Aberdeen	sw	161	Murray, George	1822	Cromarty	Pictou	125	1801	Aberdeen	E1
Harmony of Whitehaven	bg	244	Young	1827	Storn-oway from Leith	Halifax & Quebec	236	1812	Whitehaven	A1
Harriet	n/k	n/k	Chambers, W.	1844	Cromarty & Thurso	Quebec	n/k	n/k	n/k	n/k
Hector	s	200	Spiers, John	1773	Loch Broom from Greenock	Pictou	190	n/k	Dutch Prize	I2

[Dimensions: 83′ x 24′ x 10′. Owned by J. Pagan & Co. A prize, Dutch-built and already old when acquired.]

Vessel		Tons	Capt.	Year(s) Sailed	Depart	Arrive	Psgr Nos	Year built	Place built	Lloyd's Code
Helen	bg	185	Moore, James	1815	Aber-deen	Halifax	4	1804	n/k	n/k
Helen of Kirkaldy [Single deck with beams]	sw	178	Wilson, A	1817	Kirk-aldy	Halifax	93	1814	Kirkaldy	A1

Vessel		Tons	Capt.	Year(s) Sailed	Depart	Arrive	Psgr Nos	Year built	Place built	Lloyd's Code
Henry and William	n/k	n/k	n/k	1837	Storn-oway	Sydney	43	n/k	n/k	n/k
Hercules of Aberdeen	bk	250	Walker	1837	Storn-oway	Pictou & Quebec	112	1781	Stockton	E1
[Dimensions: 88′ 6″ x 26′ 2″ x 6′ 3″ between decks, a former whaling ship.]										
Hercules of Liverpool	s	757	Postill, F.	1842	Loch-maddy	Cape Breton & Quebec	59	1836	Richibucto	AE1
Hero	bg	321	n/k	1829	Green-ock	Pictou	157	1823	New Brunswick	E1
Highland Lad	s	343	Vickerman	1826	Tober-mory	Nova Scotia & Quebec	16	1816	Quebec	E1
Highlander of Aberdeen	bg	174	n/k	1833	Leith	Halifax	41	1817	Aberdeen	E1
[Dimensions: 79′ 1″ x 22′ 11″ x 14′ 11″]										
Hope	bg	180	Henry, Matthew	1806	Port Glasgow	Halifax & Quebec	47	1803	Nova Scotia	A1
Hope	n/k	n/k	Normand, George	1817	Green-ock	Sydney	161	n/k	n/k	n/k
Hope of Glasgow	bk	513	Grange, William	1848	Glasgow	Pictou	137	1839	New Brunswick	AE1
Hope of Lossie	sp	74	Allan, J.	1801	Isle Martin	Pictou	100	1796	Banff	A1
[Single deck]										
Hunter of Aberdeeen	n/k	105	Logan, James	1817	Aber-deen	Halifax	5	n/k	n/k	n/k
Industry	bk	291	n/k	1831	Cromarty	Pictou & Quebec	n/k	n/k	Prize - 1808	n/k
[One and half decks. Three masts. Dimensions: 93′ 8″ x 27′ 6″ x 16′.]										

Vessel		Tons	Capt.	Year(s) Sailed	Depart	Arrive	Psgr Nos	Year built	Place built	Lloyd's Code
Isabella of Dundee	bg	304	Donaldson, James	1827	Dundee & Tobermory	Nova Scotia	24	1825	Dundee	EI
#*Isabella* of Glasgow [Single deck with beams.]	bk	376	n/k	1828 –42	Green- ock	Halifax, Sydney & Pictou	570	1828	New Brunswick	AEI
Islay	n/k	n/k	n/k	1851	Storn- oway & Glasgow	Quebec?	68	n/k	n/k	n/k
Jane Kay	sw	235	Toft, Daniel	1833	Cromarty & Thurso	Pictou & Quebec	170	1831	Sunderland	AI
#*Jean Hastie* of Grangemouth	s	280	n/k	1833 –34	Green- ock	Halifax	34	1826	New Brunswick	EI
Jessie	n/k	n/k	n/k	1832	Tober- mory	Sydney	313	n/k	n/k	n/k
John	bg	120	Allen, Robert	1784	Aber- deen	Halifax, Shelburne & Philadelphia	n/k	1772	America	EI
John	n/k	n/k	n/k	1833	Green- ock	Halifax	3	n/k	n/k	n/k
John and Jean	n/k	n/k	n/k	1774	Aber- deen	Halifax & Quebec	59	n/k	n/k	n/k
John of Berwick	n/k	n/k	Forster, Joseph	1815	Fort George	Halifax	n/k	n/k	n/k	n/k
Joseph Harrison	n/k	380	Hutchison, John	1845	Cromarty & Thurso	Quebec	n/k	n/k	n/k	n/k
Joseph Hutchison	n/k	n/k	Stirling, Samuel	1849	Glasgow	Cape Breton	n/k	n/k	n/k	n/k

Vessel		Tons	Capt.	Year(s) Sailed	Depart	Arrive	Psgr Nos	Year built	Place built	Lloyd's Code
Lady Emily of Sunderland	sw	285	Smith, James	1842	Cromarty, Thurso & Loch Laxford	Pictou & Quebec	150	1840	Sunderland	A1
Lady Grey of North Shields	sw	285	Grey, William	1841	Cromarty & Thurso	Pictou & Quebec	240	1841	Sunderland	A1
Leopold of Leith [Single deck with beams]	bg	184	Wilson, John	1819	Leith	Halifax & Quebec	89	1817	Leith	A1
#*London* of Glasgow	bk	239	MacDonald, John	1847 –48	Green- ock	Pictou	112	1833	Sunderland	A1
Lord Brougham	n/k	n/k	Watt, James	1831	Inver- gordon	Pictou & Quebec	n/k	n/k	n/k	n/k
Lord Gardner [Single deck with beams]	s	307	Brown, John	1816	Green- ock	Halifax & Pictou	12	1805	Quebec	E1
#*Louisa* of Aberdeen [Dimensions: 85′ 3″ x 24′ 2″ x 15′ 9″]	sw	213	Oswald, James	1816 –29	Aber- deen	Halifax, Pictou	472 etc.	1816	Aberdeen Sydney & Miramichi	E1
#*Lovelly Nelly*	bg	150	Sheridan, William	1774 –75	White- haven & Dumfries	Charlotte- town	149	1731	British	I2
#*Lovely Mary* of Dumfries [Single deck]	sr	90	Hudson, John	1816 –18	Dum- fries	Pictou	82	n/k	Denmark	E1
#*Lulan* of Pictou	bk	473	McKenzie, George	1848 –52	Glasgow	Pictou	209	1848	New Glasgow	A1
Malay	bg	215	n/k	1830	Skye	Sydney	211	1818	Greenock	E1
Malvina of Aberdeen	sw	203	Smith, John	1811	Aber- deen	Quebec	12	1806	Aberdeen	A1

Vessel		Tons	Capt.	Year(s) Sailed	Depart	Arrive	Psgr Nos	Year built	Place built	Lloyd's Code
Manchester [Single deck with beams.]	bg	173	n/k	1820	Leith	Halifax	26	1801	Hull	E1
Margaret [Single deck with beams.]	bg	218	Oliphant	1821	Green-ock	Halifax, Saint John & Quebec	180	1820	Kirkaldy	A1
Margaret of Peterhead	sw	201	McIntosh, Andrew	1817	Leith	Halifax	72	1811	Peterhead	A1
#*Mariner* of Sunderland	n/k	255	Collins	1836 & 1841	Thurso & Loch Eriboll; Glasgow	Cape Breton & Quebec; Halifax	180	n/k	n/k	n/k
Marquis of Stafford	n/k	n/k	n/k	1851	Storno-way & Troon	Quebec	500	n/k	n/k	n/k
Mars of Alloa [Single deck with beams]	bg	305	Mitchell	1827	Alloa	Quebec & Montreal	n/k	Prize from America		E2
Mary	n/k	n/k	n/k	1828	Storn-oway	Sydney	135	n/k	n/k	n/k
Mary [Single deck with beams]	s	308	Munro	1819	Leith	Halifax & Quebec	32	1780	Hull	E1
Mary Ann	n/k	n/k	n/k	1832	Storn-oway	Sydney	121	n/k	n/k	n/k
Mary Kennedy	n/k	n/k	n/k	1829	Skye	Sydney & PEI	c400	n/k	n/k	n/k
Mary of Aberdeen	bg	139	Morrison, James	1811 –15	Aber-deen	Halifax	115	1810	Aberdeen	n/k

Vessel		Tons	Capt.	Year(s) Sailed	Depart	Arrive	Psgr Nos	Year built	Place built	Lloyd's Code
#*Mercator*	n/k	n/k	Thomson	1826 –34	Green- ock	Halifax	40	n/k	n/k	n/k
Minerva	bg	166	Williamson	1819	Leith	Halifax & Quebec	47	1819	Anstruther	A1
[Single deck with beams.]										
Minerva of Aberdeen	sw	202	Strachan, W.	1817	Fort William	Halifax & Quebec	26	1813	Aberdeen	A1
[Single deck with beams]										
Morningfield of Aberdeen	bg	141	Laing	1819	Tober- mory	Pictou & PEI	264	1816	Aberdeen	A1
Nancy	sp	n/k	Church, W.S.	1805	Tober- mory	PEI	196	n/k	n/k	n/k
Nancy of South Shields	s	330	Allan, Richard	1817	Leith	Halifax & Quebec	164	1772	Scarborough	E1
Nelly	n/k	n/k	Manson	1803	Thurso from Leith	Pictou	60	n/k	n/k	n/k
Nero	n/k	n/k	n/k	1829	Green- ock	Pictou	n/k	n/k	n/k	n/k
Nith of Liverpool	n/k	650	Shaw	1840	Uig & Tober- mory	PEI & Sydney	550	n/k	n/k	n/k
Nora	n/k	372	n/k	1801	Fort William	Pictou	500	n/k	n/k	n/k
North Star	n/k	n/k	n/k	1804	Leith via Greenock	Pictou	n/k	n/k	n/k	n/k
Northern Friends of Clyde	s	240	n/k	1802	Moidart from Clyde	Sydney	340	1795	Finland	E1
[A prize. Single deck with beams.]										

Vessel		Tons	Capt.	Year(s) Sailed	Depart	Arrive	Psgr Nos	Year built	Place built	Lloyd's Code
Northum -berland [Two decks]	bk	361	Stevenson	1832	Green- ock	St. And- rews	355	1828	N.Brunswick	E1
Nymph [Single deck]	bg	121	Hutchinson, J.	1816	Fort William	Pictou	55	1813	Whitby	A1
Osprey of Leith	s	382	Kirk	1840	Cromarty & Thurso	Pictou & Quebec	150	1819	Greenock	AE1
Ossian of Leith	bg	194	Hill	1821	Cromarty	Pictou	108	1813	Leith	A1
#*Pacific* of Aberdeen [Dimensions: 102′ x 26′ 2″ x 18′ 7″]	bk	386	Morrison, John	1841 –44	Thurso from Aberdeen	Pictou & Quebec	193	1826	Aberdeen	AE1
Pallas	s	632	n/k	1806	Green- ock	Quebec	n/k	1802	Prussia	A1
Paragon	n/k	n/k	Goodchild	1835	Cromarty	Pictou & Quebec	146	n/k	n/k	n/k
Percival [Single deck with beams.]	bg	269	Scott	1819	Leith	Halifax, Quebec & Montreal	85	1811	Sunderland	A1
#*Perseverence* of Aberdeen Dimensions: 65′ 4″ x 20′ 10″ x 11′ 6″.]	bg	116	Moncur	1814 –18	Cromarty	Pictou	150	n/k	Foreign	n/k
#*Phesdo* of Aberdeen Dimensions: 87′ x 26′ 1″ x 16′ 9″.]	bg	245	Pennan, Andrew	1816 –17	Aber- deen	Halifax & Saint John	45	1815	Aberdeen	A1
Phoenix	n/k	n/k	n/k	1832	Green- ock	PEI, Pictou, Chaleur Bay	132	n/k	n/k	n/k

Vessel		Tons	Capt.	Year(s) Sailed	Depart	Arrive	Psgr Nos	Year built	Place built	Lloyd's Code
#*Ploughman* of Aberdeen	sw	165	Yule, Alexander	1811 −16	Aberdeen	Pictou	54	1804	Berwick	A1
Poland	s	350	Ridley, John	1833	Cromarty	Pictou & Quebec	n/k	n/k	n/k	n/k
Polly	s	281	Darby, Thomas	1805	n/k	Canso	n/k	1762	Whitby Nova Scotia	E1
Prince Leopold	bg	n/k	n/k	1817	Leith	Halifax	30	n/k	n/k	n/k
Prince William	n/k	n/k	n/k	1815	Cromarty or Thurso	Pictou	95	n/k	n/k	n/k
#*Prompt* of Bo'ness	bg	198	Coverdale	1817 & 1821	Leith	Halifax & Quebec	193	n/k	n/k	n/k

[Single deck with beams. Advertisement stated she had 6′ between decks (*IJ*, June, 1821).]

#*Protector* of New Brunswick	s	353	Simpson, Walter	1816 −17	Greenock	St John & Halifax	8	1814	N.Brunswick	A1

[Single deck with beams]

Rambler of Leith	bg	296	Norris, J.	1807	Stromness from Thurso	Pictou	130	1800	Leith	A1

[Shipwrecked in 1807 with the loss of 138 people.]

Recovery	n/k	n/k	n/k	1820	Greenock	Halifax	14	n/k	n/k	n/k
Robert & Margaret	s	420	n/k	1833	Cromarty	Pictou & Quebec	66	n/k	n/k	n/k
Romulus of Greenock	bk	467	n/k	1831	Greenock	Halifax	n/k	1831	Miramichi	AE1

[8′ between decks. (Advertisement *IJ* 8 July, 1836.)]

Rover	bg	165	Briggs, Allan	1831	Cromarty & Wick	Pictou	116	1800	Wemyss	E1

APPENDIX III

Vessel	Tons		Capt.	Year(s) Sailed	Depart	Arrive	Psgr Nos	Year built	Place built	Lloyd's Code
Rowena	n/k	n/k	n/k	1818	n/k	Pictou	n/k	n/k	n/k	n/k
#*Ruby* of Aberdeen [Dimensions: 67′ 9″ x 21′ 5″ x 11′ 1″.]	sw	128	Love, Thomas	1815 & 1822	Cromarty	Pictou	127	1805	Aberdeen	A1
Sally	n/k	n/k	n/k	1783	Aberdeen	Halifax	n/k	n/k	n/k	n/k
#*Sarah Botsford* of Glasgow	bk	306	MacDonald	1849 −51	Glasgow	Pictou	68	1840	New Brunswick	A1
Sarah of Liverpool	n/k	372	Smith	1801	Fort William	Pictou	350	n/k	n/k	n/k
Scotia	bg	244	n/k	1817	Leith	Halifax	120	1816	Sunderland	A1
Serius	n/k	n/k	n/k	1847	Thurso	Pictou	117	n/k	n/k	n/k
Seven Sisters of Aberdeen	bg	170	Brown, A	1815	Aberdeen	Halifax	19	n/k	n/k	n/k
Sir Sydney Smith	n/k	n/k	n/k	1805	n/k	Pictou	n/k	n/k	n/k	n/k
#*Six Sisters* [Single deck with beams]	sr	123	n/k	1831 −32	Stornoway	Wallace & C Breton	242	1830	Scotland	A1
Skeene of Leith [Single deck with beams.]	bg	250	Mason, James	1817 −19	Leith	Halifax	235	1815	Leith	A2
Sovereign of Kirkwall	bk	476	n/k	1845	Lochmaddy & Stromness	Sydney, Pictou & Quebec	n/k	1814	Hull	AE1

Vessel		Tons	Capt.	Year(s) Sailed	Depart	Arrive	Psgr Nos	Year built	Place built	Lloyd's Code
#Speculation	s	205	Douglas	1819– 1820	Fort William from Greenock	Pictou & Quebec	270	n/k	America	E1
[Single deck with beams]										
Sprightly of Dundee	bg	190	Philip, Alexander	1816	Aber- deen	Halifax, Pictou & Miramichi	20	n/k	Prize	E2
[Dimensions: 82′ 6″ x 24′ x 15′ 3″.]										
St. Andrew of New Brunswick	s	553	Leith, J.	1842	Loch- maddy	Cape Breton & Quebec	133	1835	Nova Scotia	n/k
St. Lawrence of Newcastle	s	335	Cram, J.	1828	Leith	Ship Harbour	208	1825	Newcastle	A1
Stephen	n/k	n/k	Potts, J.	1827	Tober- mory	New Brunswick	193	n/k	n/k	n/k
Stephen Wright	sw	262	Gibson, N.	1827	Tober- mory	Sydney	160	1820	Newcastle	A1
Superior of Peterhead	bk	306	Manson	1842	Cromarty & Thurso	Pictou & Quebec	191	1813	Shields	AE1
Surry of London	bg	145	Meys, Richard	1816	Green- ock	Halifax	23	1800	Spain	E1
[Single deck with beams]										
Sylvanus of North Shields	sw	263	Lawson	1832	Cromarty	Pictou & Quebec	237	1826	Sunderland	A1
Tamerlane	s	390	McKellop	1826	Green- ock	Quebec & Sydney	55	1824	New Brunswick	A1
[Single deck with beams. Advertisement claimed it offered 7′ between decks (*IJ*, April, 1833).]										
Tartar of Perth	s	330	Kelly, W.	1816	Tober- mory from Dundee	Pictou	144	1798	Perth	E1
[Two decks]										

Vessel		Tons	Capt.	Year(s) Sailed	Depart	Arrive	Psgr Nos	Year built	Place built	Lloyd's Code
Tay of Glasgow	bk	470	n/k	1841	Loch-maddy	Cape Breton	450	1840	N.Bruns'k	AE1
#*Thetis*	bg	327	Coverdale	1826 –29	Green-ock	Pictou	30	1810	Whitby	E1

[Single deck with beams. *Thetis* was wrecked in 1829 crossing, but no lives were lost.]

Vessel		Tons	Capt.	Year(s) Sailed	Depart	Arrive	Psgr Nos	Year built	Place built	Lloyd's Code
Thistle	n/k	n/k	n/k	1837	Storn-oway	Sydney	65	n/k	n/k	n/k
#*Thompson's Packet* of Dumfries	bg	201	Lookup	1821 –22	Dum-fries	Pictou & Quebec	213	1817	n/k	A1
Three Brothers of Hull	s	357	Maddison	1816	Storn-oway from Leith	Pictou & Miramichi	306	1801	Sweden	E1

[Two decks]

Vessel		Tons	Capt.	Year(s) Sailed	Depart	Arrive	Psgr Nos	Year built	Place built	Lloyd's Code
Tongataboo of New Glasgow	bk	533	Peterson	1852	Glasgow	Pictou	26	1851	Fox Harbour	A1

[George McKenzie was a part owner (NAS CE 59/11/14).]

Vessel		Tons	Capt.	Year(s) Sailed	Depart	Arrive	Psgr Nos	Year built	Place built	Lloyd's Code
Traveller of Leith	sw	191	Bishop, J.	1817	Leith	Halifax	40	n/k	Mediterranean	E1

[Single deck with beams]

Vessel		Tons	Capt.	Year(s) Sailed	Depart	Arrive	Psgr Nos	Year built	Place built	Lloyd's Code
Tweed of Ullapool	sp	75	McKenzie	1802	Isle Martin	Pictou	70	1763	Hull	I1
#*Two Sisters*	bg	139	McKenzie, George	1828– 1829	Green-ock	Sydney	190	1827	Pictou	A

[Single deck with beams.]

Vessel		Tons	Capt.	Year(s) Sailed	Depart	Arrive	Psgr Nos	Year built	Place built	Lloyd's Code
Unicorn	bk	n/k	n/k	1841	Thurso	Pictou	105	n/k	n/k	n/k
Union	s	231	Scott	1822	Green-ock	Pictou	14	1807	America	E1
Universe of Aberdeen	bk	281	Scott	1828 & 1841	Storn-oway	Sydney	588	1826	Aberdeen	A1

Vessel	Tons		Capt.	Year(s) Sailed	Depart	Arrive	Psgr Nos	Year built	Place built	Lloyd's Code
Vestal	n/k	n/k	n/k	1829	Tobermory	Sydney & PEI	301	n/k	n/k	n/k
Victory	n/k	n/k	n/k	1819	n/k	Pictou	n/k	n/k	n/k	n/k
Vine of Peterhead	bg	183	Pirie, Alex	1816	Cromarty & Thurso	Pictou	81	1802	Peterhead	E1
William Henry	n/k	n/k	n/k	1834	Cromarty	Pictou	102	n/k	n/k	n/k
William of Aberdeen	bg	172	Laird, James	1816	Aberdeen	Halifax	6	1815	Aberdeen	A1
William Tell	n/k	n/k	n/k	1817	Greenock	Canso	221	n/k	n/k	n/k
Ythan of Aberdeen	s	264	Craigie, Alexander	1816	Aberdeen	Halifax & Miramichi	17	n/k	Newburgh	A1
Zephyr	n/k	650	Tucker	1833	Cromarty	Pictou & Quebec	150	n/k	n/k	n/k

APPENDIX IV

[NAS CS 96/154, 96–103: William Liddell & Company, timber merchants, Glasgow, Sederunt Books, 1829–34.] These are the settlers who owed money to Edward Mortimer at the time of his death in 1819. The debts were transferred to his partner William Liddell of Glasgow and when he died in 1829 the debts remained unpaid.

Names of Debtors	Balance due 1 July 1827	Balance due 31 Dec 1828	Interest included in last balance
Donald King	£19.18.11	£9.7.2	£1.13.10
F. Falconer	£74.11.3	£45.1.10	£21.0.7
John Taylor		£6.10.0	
Thomas Dickson	£89.6.6	£225.9.10	
Johmnstone Knight		£42.15.3	
Peter Grant	£68.17.3	£73.15.4	£19.17.3
Counting House Furniture	£9.0.0.	£9.0.0	
Mr. Davison	£2.5.0		
William Fraser	£11.3.6		£0.16.6
William McDonald	£4.8.9		£1.15.3
John MacDonald	£5.8.0		
Dr. Murray	£1.19.10		£1.6.4
Mr. Murray	£5.4.6		£0.12.6
Rev. D. Fraser		£5.0.0	
Mr. McKay	£7.9.9	£4.3.9	
Angus Grant	£4.4.7	£6.6.3	£2.1.8
Donald MacDonald	£2.3.6		£0.6.0

Names of Debtors	Balance due 1 July 1827	Balance due 31 Dec 1828	Interest included in last balance
Mr. Copeland		£5.5.0	
D. Ross & D. McCoul	£3.5.0		
Boats Built, 1 sent home 2 here	£68.0.0		
D. Grants & Son	£29.10.10	£37.6.10	£7.16.0
Wm. Hattie Jnr.	£23.16.7	£3.0.7	£3.2.7
John MacDonald	£56.4.8	£13.7.6	£11.2.9
John Cameron	£14.13.19	£10.11.9	£5.17.7
Hector McLean	£0.13.0	£0.13.0	
John Rankine	£8.2.11	£10.1.11	£11.1.0
Widow McLean	£9.10.0	£12.0.0	£2.10.0
Alexr. McLean	£9.12.7		
D. McLean	£15.8.4	£11.10.4	£4.17.0
K. MacDonald		£16.13.7	
D. MacDonald	£15.7.3		£2.15.9
John Love		£5.6.4	
D. Loudon	£99.13.4	£99.13.4	
Alexr. McQuarry	£104.18.3	£47.0.0	£6.5.2
Alexr. Cameron	£21.0.0	£21.0.0	
D. Minor		£6.0.2	
James MacDonald	£9.9.4	£8.8.6	£3.9.8
Geo. Foster	£19.17.0	£13.0.6	£2.9.3
Charles MacDonald	£45.0.0	£46.11.0	£11.11.0
Alexr. Reid	£21.3.9	£27.14.8	£6.10.11
Colin Fraser	£4.0.2	£7.4.6	£7.13.5
A. Anderson	£20.9.4	£19.7.9	£10.9.5
J. MacDonald	£160.0.0	£160.0.0	
D. MacKenzie	£12.13.6	£15.7.6	£2.14.0
Will'm Beattie		£35.0.0	
Peter Grant	£86.5.4	£69.9.5	£21.11.9
George Foote	£160.7.6	£160.7.6	
Angus MacDonald	£9.10.9	£9.10.9	
Charles & Angus McDonald	£120.0.0	£155.18.10	£35.18.10
H. Blackadder	£25.0.0	£5.5.5	£1.15.0
John Ross	£23.5.0	£23.5.0	
Rod McKenzie	£8.5.6	£8.5.6	
William Fraser	£42.15.0		£10.18.10
John Gillies	£4.6.9	£4.6.9	
James Dewar	£21.18.10		£9.1.2
William Foster	£98.10.0	£83.10.0	£2.19.0
Alexr. MacDonald Senr.	£3.19.6		£1.1.0
Alexr. MacDonald Junr.	£52.4.2	£31.5.3	£13.17.0

APPENDIX IV

Names of Debtors	Balance due 1 July 1827	Balance due 31 Dec 1828	Interest included in last balance
Thomas MacPherson	£43.13.6	£40.0.9	£3.12.0
Estate of Pagan	£249.0.0	£103.12.7	£54.12.7
Paul Foster Error of £4.11/£151.1/			
	£147.0.0	£142.11.10	£16.12.4
William Adamson		£6.13.4	
John Fraser	£7.4.0		
James McPherson	£72.14.9	£50.11.5	£5.6.0
George Gordon	£20.15.6	£9.16.11	£5.14.10
John More	£84.11.0		£17.1.6
Donald MacDonald	£211.17.4	£211.17.4	
John McMillan	£49.18.5	£35.15.5	£3.13.0
James Bryden	£129.0.0	£186.10.9	£41.5.9
James Fraser	£59.0.0	£78.3.4	£19.3.4
Peter MacDonald	£40.10.0	£20.0.2	£14.13.9
Robert Dunn	£29.8.0		£9.6.6
F. Carmichael	£21.0.3	£25.5.3	£4.5.0
D. MacDonald	£64.7.6	£64.7.6	
A. Blackie	£7.15.8	£7.15.8	
D. McDougall	£42.6.4	£12.6.4	
L. Johnston Pd in full			£2.11.5
John McGregor	£1.1.0	£5.8.0	
E. & I. Harris	£10.0.0		£2.2.0
D. Gordon	£34.6.9	£34.6.9	
I. McDonald	£21.15.1	£10.17.1	£1.13.6
J.G. McKenzie	£170.0.0	£58.17.1	£10.15.0
J. Robertson			
(155 Tons Timber this date)			
J. McQuarry	£5.3.10	£0.13.10	£1.5.0
D. McLeod	£26.4.1	£26.5.0	£10.0.11
J. Stiles	£16.10.0	£8.7.6	£4.10.0
J. Smith	£25.11.9	£25.11.9	
D. McKeen	£30.0.0	£38.14.0	£8.14.0
John Robson	£193.4.8	£73.4.8	
J. McKell	£8.10.4	£11.10.11	£2.0.7
John Logan	£1.1.0	£1.1.3	
William Johnston	£23.5.0	£23.5.0	
John McIver	£16.7.8	£20.5.8	£3.18.0
Gregor McGregor	£39.16.9	£30.15.9	£12.9.0
Thomas Dodds	£7.8.0	£7.8.0	
Allan MacDonald	£0.13.6	£0.13.6	
George Smith	£28.9.1		£2.8.2

Names of Debtors	Balance due 1 July 1827	Balance due 31 Dec 1828	Interest included in last balance
John McLeod	£14.19.6	£14.19.6	
H. Dunn	£11.5.10	£13.17.10	£2.12.0
D. Sutherland	£43.7.1	£48.5.1	£11.5.10
(now A. Fraser's debt)			
H. Connor	£10.19.6		£1.18.7
Robt Smith Jr.	£42.10.0	£53.19.6	£11.9.6
R. McLeod	£65.0.0	£82.9.0	£17.9.0
Will'm McPherson	£45.0.0	£45.0.0	
Will'm Hunter	£31.0.0	£42.1.3	£11.1.3
William McClelland	£46.13.4		£8.6.8
James Reid	£198.12.0	£198.12.0	
John Blanchard	£33.10.6	£2.10.6	
(sale of Tuppers Land cancelled)			
Allan Cameron	£49.5.1	£45.19.2	£3.18.10
E. Tupper		£51.11.11	
A. & H. Fraser	£38.0.0	£1.0.8	£6.4.1
D. Stiles	£30.10.3	£32.18.9	£2.8.6
J. Campbell	£27.0.10	£27.0.10	
Rod'k McKenzie	£10.0.0		£5.0.0
John McMillan	£84.15.9	£19.10.0	£0.5.0
John McQuarry	£140.0.0	£116.17.6	£8.13.3
John Fraser	£32.7.4	£32.7.4	
Gregor McGregor	£167.0.0	£167.0.0	
J. McMillan	£12.0.0	£1.0.0	
Hector McQuarry	£100.0.0	£82.3.0	£7.3.0
H. McQuarry Jr.	£182.13.8	£182.13.8	
McDougall's Lot	£166.0.0		
Gallows Lot	£130.0.0	£130.0.0	
Hadley & Moorings	£950.0.0	£950.0.0	
D. Logan	£150.0.0	£150.0.0	
James Sturgeon	£146.15.8	£146.15.8	
Saw Mill site	£420.15.1	£420.15.1	
John McGregor Snr.	£22.1.1		£5.5.6
John Dunn	£91.0.0	£91.0.0	
Robert McKay	£50.10.5	£50.10.5	
Marshalls Lot	£700.0.0	£700.0.0	
Blanchards Farm	£1400.0.0	£1400.0.0	
Alexr. Campbell	£30.7.6		
D. Ferguson	£58.15.9	£0.3.0	£10.12.0
Wm. Mortimer	£116.4.0		
G. Smith		£66.6.0	£7.2.6

Names of Debtors	Balance due 1 July 1827	Balance due 31 Dec 1828	Interest included in last balance
G. MacDonald	£120.0.0	£131.14.0	£11.14.0
Land at Middle River	£118.15.0		
John R. Kitchen	£110.0.0	£7.16.1	£12.1.8
Robert Murray	£87.0.0	£64.5.6	£1.5.6
I. Maxwell		£73.10.9	£7.15.0
E.R. Fairbanks	£186.19.5	£186.19.5	
J. & R. Powell	£163.6.3	£109.2.2	£15.13.2
Thos. Henderson	£60.0.0		
Alexr. MacDonald		£90.0.0	
John Finlayson	£159.17.8	£191.19.5	£13.12.4
R. Gordon		£4.5.0	
Jas. & R. Kitchen (Old Jail Lot)	£250.12.6		
Jas. Pollok	£2.0.0		£1.19.0
Jas. McIntyre	£15.0.0		
Dr. Mitchell	£2.0.0		£1.0.0
Estate of R. Patterson for Thos. Dickson	£110.0.0	£110.0.0	
James Connal			£4.0.0
A.P. Olding			£112.0.6
J. Gordon)Parts of Debts		£23.19.8	
D. I. Pinis)last divided		£19.15.0	
William Blair)		£7.4.3	
Jas. Robson		£67.17.0	
Paul McDonald	£3.10.4		£2.10.7
John McDonald	£22.3.0	£24.0.0	£1.17.0
Thomas Copeland			£6.15.6
Alexr. Chisholm & Son, Peter			£1.2.0
W. Nicolson			£2.6.6
Allan McLeod			£3.7.1
	£10554.2.7	£9913.11.8	£711.7.6

Errors and Omissions Excepted. Pictou, N.S. the 30th Jan'y 1829 (signed) John Jamieson

	£10554.2.7		
Add price of Jail Lot	£220.0.0		
Do Debts last divided	£162.19.5	£9913.11.8	
Do Do Do	£67.17.0	£711.7.6	Off Interest
	£11004.19.0	£9202.4.2	
	£9202.4.2		
	£1802.14.10		

NOTES

CHAPTER 1 – THE NEW WORLD BECKONS

1 *Edinburgh Advertiser*, Sept. 28, 1773.

2 The French established Nova Scotia's earliest colonial settlement in 1605 at Port Royal, on the north shore of the Annapolis Basin. But after it was burned by the English in 1613, the French lost interest in the colony.

3 People who purchased the land would acquire the grandiose title of "baronet of Nova Scotia." J.M. Bumsted, *The Peoples of Canada: A Pre-Confederation History*, Vol. 1 (Toronto, 1992) 55. In spite of the demise of the proposed colony Nova Scotia survived as a geographical entity. The explanation for the name's survival was due not to any continuing connection with Scotland but to the growing assimilation of Scotland into British imperial designs before the Parliamentary Union of 1707. This would cause the Nova Scotia name to recur continually over the ensuing century. John G. Reid, "The Conquest of Nova Scotia; Cartographic Imperialism and the Echoes of a Scottish Past" in Ned C. Landsman (ed.) *Nation and Province in the first British Empire: Scotland and the Americas, 1600–1800* (Lewisburg, PA: Bucknell University Press, 2001) 39–59.

4 Steve Murdoch, "Cape Breton, Canada's 'Highland Island'?" *Northern Scotland*, Vol. 18 (1998) 31–42. Sir James Stewart, the fourth Lord Ochiltree, bought the Baronetcy of Cape Breton in 1629. He had previously purchased the lordship of Ochiltree from his cousin in 1615 having failed to obtain the earldom of Arran from his father in spite of being the eldest son.

5 However, the Acadian population only reached some 1,500 by 1700. For a general introduction to the Acadians, see Henri-Dominique Parette, *Acadians*. (Tantallon, N.S.: Four East, 1991). For a general introduction to the Mi'kmaq, see Stephen A. Davis, *Micmac*. (Tantallon, N.S.: Four East, 1991).

6 The Acadian population was estimated to be around 13,000 by 1752. Phillip Buckner, and John G. Reid (eds.), *The Atlantic Region to Confederation, A History* (Toronto: University of Toronto Press, 1993) 144–7, 164–5, 198–9.

7 The government did not wish to lose its own people to the colonies and these people had the advantage of already being acclimatized to North America. Most of the New Englanders came from Rhode Island, Connecticut and southeastern Massachusetts.

8 This was one of the very rare occasions when the government actually spent public

money in a colonization venture. Over £600,000 was spent in establishing a non-French population in Nova Scotia. Bumsted, *Peoples of Canada*, 121–2, 140–4.

9 Following her defeat in the Seven Years War (1756–63), France surrendered all of her North American territories to the British.

10 W.S. MacNutt, *The Atlantic Provinces; the emergence of Colonial Society 1712–1857* (London, 1965) 62–3, 113.

11 In addition 1,000 Yorkshiremen, who were tenants of the Duke of Rutland, settled in Chignecto (Cumberland County) during the 1770s. By 1775 around 20,000 people lived in Nova Scotia. Peter L. McCreath and John G. Leefe, *A History of early Nova Scotia* (Tantallon, N.S., 1990) 265–6.

12 Thomas Douglas, Fifth Earl of Selkirk, *Observations on the Present State of the Highlands of Scotland, with a view of the causes and probable consequences of emigration*, 1805 in J.M. Bumsted (ed.) *The Collected Writings of Lord Selkirk*, Vol. I (1799–1809) (Winnipeg: The Manitoba Record Society, 1984) 163–4. Hereafter this source is referred to as *Selkirk's Observations*.

13 John S. Moir, *The Church in the British Era, from the British Conquest to Confederation* (Toronto: McGraw-Hill Ryerson, 1972) 135–37.

14 Patrick Cecil Telford White (ed.) *Lord Selkirk's Diary 1803–04; A journal of his travels through British North America and the Northeastern United States* (The Champlain Society, Toronto, 1958) 44. Hereafter this source is referred to as *Lord Selkirk's Diary*.

15 George Patterson, *Memoir of the Rev. James MacGregor* (Philadelphia, 1859) 319–20, 252–3.

16 R.C. MacDonald, *Sketches of Highlanders; with an Account of their Early Arrival in North America; Their advancement in agriculture and some of their distinguished military services in the war of 1812* (Saint John, N.B., 1843) Appendix A (letter by Dr. Gesner, author of a treatise on the Geology of Nova Scotia, written 19 Aug. 1842).

17 The known emigrant ship crossings from Scotland to Nova Scotia and Cape Breton are listed in Appendix II. Emigrant ship crossings to Prince Edward Island are listed in Lucille H. Campey, *"A Very Fine Class of Immigrants": Prince Edward Island's Scottish Pioneers, 1770–1850* (Toronto: Natural Heritage, 2001) Appendix II.

18 Bumsted estimates that some 15,000 Scots emigrated to British North America between 1770 and 1815. Bumsted, *The People's Clearance*, 228.

19 Having a population of 65,000 in 1806, Nova Scotia's population rose to 104,000 by 1825. Joseph Bouchette, *The British Dominions in North America: a Topographical and Statistical Description of the Provinces of Lower and Upper Canada, New Brunswick, Nova Scotia, the Islands of Newfoundland, Prince Edward Island and Cape Breton*, Vol. II (London, 1832) 235.

20 J.S. Martell, *Immigration to and Emigration from Nova Scotia 1815–38* (Halifax: PANS 1942) gives data extracted from customs records and local newspapers. He estimates that about 43,000 immigrants arrived at Nova Scotia and Cape Breton, of which 37,500 arrived directly from the British Isles. However, except for the 1,700 Black refugees (former slaves from the southern American states) who had

been shipped to Halifax in 1815, most of the remainder were probably British-born. The figures only record 22,000 Scots but an additional 2000 can be added since these were Sydney and Pictou arrivals who were almost certainly Scottish. For more information on Black immigration to Nova Scotia, see Bridglal Pachai, *Blacks*. (Tantallon, N.S.: Four East Publications, 1987.)

21 A total of 13,500 British immigrants arrived during this period, of which 2,300 were Irish and 3,000 were English. Susan Longley Morse, "Immigration to Nova Scotia 1839–51" (Dalhousie, Nova Scotia, unpublished M.A. 1946) 121.

22 Plaque at Sydney Harbour commemorating the 1802 arrivals.

23 Martell, Ibid, 8–10.

24 The remaining population was descended from the Acadian, Irish and Loyalist settlers who came to Cape Breton before 1800. Stephen J. Hornsby, *Nineteenth Century Cape Breton; An Historical Geography* (Toronto, 1992) 31.

25 Through their "squatting," successive waves of Scottish settlers encroached on Mi'kmaw lands and threatened their way of life. The situation became so desperate by 1841 that the Mi'kmaw King, Louis-Benjamin Paussmigh, wrote personally to Queen Victoria for help. In 1842, the provincial government passed an act to address these problems, and six reserves covering 12,205 acres were established. However, in later years Scottish settlers encroached on the new Mi'kmaw reserves. See Steve Murdoch, "Cape Breton: Canada's 'Highland Island'?"

26 PRO CO 217/152, Sydney Customs Returns, June 1, 1831.

27 Martell, Ibid, 91–5. D.C. Harvey, "Scottish Immigration to Cape Breton," *Dalhousie Review*, Vol. xxi (1941) 313–24.

28 Morse, Ibid, 104–21.

29 Ralph Davis, *The Industrial Revolution and British Overseas Trade*, (Leicester: Leicester University Press, 1979) 48–49. Between 1814 and 1843 Baltic timber was sometimes shipped to North America and then back to Britain, as the saving of duty more than compensated for the double freight.

30 Church of Scotland clergymen were sent through the auspices of the Glasgow Colonial Society, formed in 1826, to establish Presbyterian congregations in British America.

31 NAC M-1354 Extracts of a letter from Rev. James Frazer, Jan. 31, 1837.

32 Campey, "*A Very Fine Class of Immigrants*," 32–47.

33 *Selkirk's Observations*, 169–70.

34 There were some who received financial assistance, but they were relatively few in number and most of them went to Upper Canada.

35 Kelp, made from burnt seaweed, was exported and used in various chemical processes. The kelp industry declined in the 1820s due to cheap foreign imports of similar products.

36 John L. MacDougall, *History of Inverness County* (Truro: New Pub. Co. Ltd., 1922) 542.

37 Plaque below the Highlander statue, overlooking Pictou Harbour which was erected by the Saint Andrews Society of New Glasgow.

CHAPTER 2 – THE *Hector* ARRIVES IN 1773

1 *Colonial Patriot* (Pictou), Aug. 20, 1831.

2 "Log Church, Loch Broom," Presbytery of Pictou. The original log church, built in 1787, was situated at the head of the harbour and near the Loch. The replica church was erected in 1973.

3 The geographical origins of most of the emigrants were recorded in George Patterson, *History of the County of Pictou, Nova Scotia* (Montreal: Dawson Bros., 1877) 450–6.

4 Donald MacKay, *Scotland Farewell: The People of the Hector* (Toronto: Natural Heritage, 1996) 45–8.

5 Sir John Sinclair, *First Statistical Account of Scotland*, 21 vols. (Edinburgh, 1791–99) Vol. xviii 337, 378, 412. MacKay, *Scotland Farewell*, 55, 59, 85. Some of the emigrants who are recorded as coming from Sutherland may have actually originated from Reay in Caithness. Several families from this parish were reported to have emigrated to North America in 1773. *SA*, Vol. xviii, 153.

6 MacKay, *Scotland Farewell*, 214–5.

7 NAC MG31-B4, Henry R. Beer Collection, Genealogical Sketch. William MacKay's list was reprinted in George MacLaren, *The Pictou Book: Stories of our Past* (New Glasgow, N.S.: Hector Pub. Co., 1954) 31–4 (see Appendix I). The original list is held by the Public Archives of Nova Scotia.

8 William MacKenzie's list was reprinted by Patterson, *History, Pictou County*, 450–6. The original list vanished.

9 MacKay, *Scotland Farewell*, 97–98.

10 Alexander MacKenzie, "First Highland Emigration to Nova Scotia: Arrival of the Ship *Hector*," *The Celtic Magazine*, vol. viii, (1883) 141–4. No contemporary reports were kept of the *Hector* crossing. Alexander MacKenzie's account of events was delivered in 1883 in Buckie (Banffshire). It is based on the memories which were passed down through the families of the descendants of the original emigrants. Hugh MacLeod's wife, Catherine, died soon after the ship arrived at Pictou. MacKay, *Scotland Farewell*, 100–1.

11 MacKenzie, "First Highland Emigration," 141–2.

12 *Dictionary of Canadian Biography* (hereafter *DCB*) Vol. v, 553–7.

13 *Scots Magazine*, Vol. xxxiv (1772), 482–4.

14 MacKenzie, "First Highland Emigration," 142.

15 NAC MG31-B4, Genealogical Sketch. MacKay, *Scotland Farewell*, 140–8.

16 Most settled near Truro and Onslow. MacKay, *Scotland Farewell*, 112–4.

17 The Pictou Harbour lands were owned by Major John Fisher and Alexander McNutt. The Philadelphia Company's land grant fell well short of the 200,000 acres that they had been promised. After complaining to the government, they were able to acquire additional land between Tatamagouche and Pictou. MacKay, *Scotland Farewell*, 120–1.

18 For instance, from 1768 to 1770, some 1600 people had left the Western Isles for Cape Fear, North Carolina. D. Vane Meyer, *The Highland Scots of North Carolina*,

1732–76 (Chapel Hill: University of North Carolina Press, 1961), 84. In 1769 a further 500 people left the Highlands for North Carolina. *SM*, Vol. xxi, 602.

19 They sailed on the *Betsey* of Rhode Island from Philadelphia in May, 1767. Patterson, *Memoir of Rev. James MacGregor*, 74–5. MacKay, *Scotland Farewell*, 125–34.

20 To preserve its hold on its vast tract of land, the Philadelphia Company was required to attract a minimum number of settlers within an agreed period of time. However, the company's grant was escheated by 1809, following its failure to comply with the settlement terms of the grant.

21 John Pagan was in business with his brothers, Robert and William. In partnership with the Greenock firm of Robert Lee and Joseph Tucker, they purchased goods from the West Indies in return for masts and timber. *DCB*, Vol. v, 645–7.

22 The second group of twenty was to pay one shilling per acre and the third group of twenty one shillings and sixpence. Additional land would also be made available to other family members. The advertisement stated that twenty families had already settled at Pictou and there was a school catering for about 30 children. *SM*, Vol. xxxiv (1772), 482–4.

23 MacKay, *Scotland Farewell*, 79.

24 *EA*, Oct., 1772.

25 Some of the press comment had been favourable. A correspondent calling himself "a bystander" argued that emigration was an important safety valve for relieving poverty and distress (*Caledonian Mercury*, Nov. 12, 1772). However the correspondent writing under the name of "Veritas" who believed that emigration was harmful and should be stopped was more typical (*SM*, Dec. 31, 1772). John Witherspoon, *The Works of John Witherspoon, D.D.*, Vol iii, *Essays and Sermons* (Edinburgh, 1805) 293–303.

26 Witherspoon belonged to the evangelical arm of the Presbyterian Church. He believed that ordinary people should be able to influence the selection of ministers and how the Gospel should be preached. Arthur Herman, *The Scottish Enlightenment, The Scots Invention of the Modern World* (London: Fourth Estate, 2001), 204–11.

27 MacKay, *Scotland Farewell*, 76–9.

28 The Forfeited Estates were lands on Highland estates which the Crown had seized following the Jacobite uprising of 1745–46. Other repressive measures were introduced including the proscription of Highland dress.

29 Pagan and Witherspoon agreed to survey 40,000 acres and divide it into lots of between 200 to 1000 acres and to supply provisions for one year, to be sold at cost to the emigrants. MacKay, *Scotland Farewell*, 84–5.

30 MacKenzie, "First Highland Emigration," 142. John Ross stayed on at Pictou as an ordinary settler.

31 MacKenzie, "First Highland Emigration," 143.

32 This is consistent with newspaper reports at the time which claimed that some Highlanders were leaving for North America with considerable sums of money. For example, a ship was said to have left Fort William in 1773 with 425 emigrants, who together carried £6000 sterling. Meyer, *Highland Scots of North Carolina*, 55. Also, the *Scots Magazine* published a letter in 1772, claiming that the people who

had emigrated from the Western Isles in 1768 "have carried with them at least £10,000 in specie [coin money]."

33 John Patterson remained behind but Robert Innes went to live at Minudie in Cumberland County. NAC MG31-B4, Genealogical Sketch.

34 MacKay, *Scotland Farewell*, 148–9.

35 NAC MG31-B4, Genealogical Sketch.

36 The "Official List of the number of families in the District of Pictou as of November 8, 1775," produced by John Harris, is printed in MacKay, *Scotland Farewell*, 213.

37 They had sailed on the *Lovely Nelly* in 1774 and 1775 and together totalled 149 people. Campey, *"A Very Fine Class of Immigrants,"* 29, 68, 71, 72, 137.

38 MacKenzie, "First Highland Emigration," 143–4.

39 NAC MG31-B4, "Rough Draft of the Pictou Highlanders," 123.

40 Thomas Chandler Haliburton, *An Historical and Statistical Account of Nova Scotia*, (Halifax: J. Howe, 1829) Vol. i, 50–8. Anon, *A General Description of Nova Scotia* (Halifax: Clement H. Belcher, 1825), 88, 91.

41 MacKenzie, "First Highland Emigration," 143.

42 The location of the twelfth Inverness-shire man is not known. Patterson, *History, Pictou County*, 450–6. NAC MG31-B4, Genealogical Sketch.

43 Patterson, Ibid, 450–6. At the time Pictou was a district within Halifax County. Pictou only became a county in its own right from 1835.

44 The *Lloyd's Shipping Register* gave the *Hector* an "I2" rating. She was 200 tons burthen and measured 83' long by 24' wide by 10' deep. MacKay, *Scotland Farewell*, 89.

45 The government also discriminated against Catholics. But, ironically, Donald Cameron was the first of the Highlanders to get a government grant for his land at East River.

46 Until 1863 Antigonish was a district within Sydney County. It became Antigonish County from 1864.

47 *Colonial Patriot*, March 2, 1828.

48 *Lord Selkirk's Diary*, 46. Lord Selkirk had come to Prince Edward Island in 1803 with several hundred Highlanders and assisted them in founding what would eventually become the large and flourishing settlements at Belfast. Lucille H. Campey, *The Silver Chief: Lord Selkirk and the Scottish Pioneers of Belfast, Baldoon and Red River* (Toronto: Natural Heritage, 2003) 24–50.

49 *Novascotian*, Aug. 3, 1826.

50 *Lord Selkirk's Diary*, 43.

CHAPTER 3 – THE LOYALIST EMIGRANTS

1 Patterson, *Memoir of Rev. James MacGregor*, 77–8.

2 Ibid.

3 William R. Brock, *Scotus Americanus, A Survey of the Sources for links between Scotland and America in the Eighteenth Century* (Edinburgh: Edinburgh University Press, 1982), 129–30.

4 Patterson, *History, Pictou County*, 458. Teignmouth had been suggested originally as a town name, but the old Mi'kmaw name of Pictou was adopted instead.

5 Helen Cowan, *British Emigration to British North America: The First Hundred Years* (Toronto: University of Toronto Press, 1961) 7–12. Most of the remaining 5,000 Loyalists settled in Upper Canada. Land to the west of Montreal was granted to some 1,800 Loyalist families, forming the nucleus of the defensive line between Cornwall and Kingston and in the Niagara Peninsula.

6 Bumsted, *Peoples of Canada*, 166–78. Marion Gilroy, *Loyalists and Land Settlement in Nova Scotia* (Halifax: PANS Publication No. 4, 1937).

7 Inverness-shire Scots were relocated from New York to Glengarry, on the Upper Saint Lawrence at the outbreak of the American War. A year after the war ended, in 1785, they were joined by further Inverness-shire emigrants, many of whom were veterans of the Glengarry Fencibles. This set in train a settlement cycle which drew emigrants from Inverness-shire over many years.

8 Neil MacKinnon, *This Unfriendly Soil: The Loyalist Experience in Nova Scotia 1783–1791* (Montreal: McGill-Queen's University Press, 1986), 158–79.

9 These Loyalists of African descent were mainly fugitive slaves from Virginia and South Carolina. Key factors in the lack of success of Black Loyalists was the tendency for their settlements to be on marginal land as well as white discrimination and racism. In 1800 Halifax lost many Maroons, who were the descendents of Black slaves from the old Spanish regime in Jamaica, to Sierra Leone further weakening the Black community. See S. Davis and L. Niven, "Birchtown: The History and Material Culture of an Expatriate African American Community," in *Moving on: Black Loyalists in the Afro-Atlantic Word*, John W. Paulis, ed. (New York: Garland Publishing Inc., 1998), 59–83. For more information on Black Loyalists, see James W. St. G. Walker, *The Black Loyalists: the search for a promised land in Nova Scotia and Sierra Leone, 1738–1870.* (Toronto: University of Toronto Press, 1992.)

10 G. Wynn, "A Region of Scattered Settlements and Bounded Possibilities: North eastern America 1775–1800," *Canadian Geographer*, Vol. 31 (1987) 319–38; Buckner and Reid, *Atlantic Region to Confederation*, 184–209. Around ninety percent of the New Brunswick Loyalists were American-born, and most originated from New York and New Jersey.

11 Disbanded Scottish soldiers were also prominent as early pioneers in New Brunswick. Argyll Highlanders (74th) were resettled in and around St. Andrews, while former Royal Highland Regiment members (42nd), who initially went to the Bay of Fundy, eventually settled in the Miramichi region. Esther Clark Wright, *The Loyalists of New Brunswick* (Fredericton, N.B., 1955), 120, 196–200.

12 F.W.P. Bolger (ed.) *Canada's Smallest Province: A History of Prince Edward Island*, (Halifax: Nimbus, 1991), 60. By the end of 1784, only about five to six hundred Loyalists remained and they were concentrated in the Malpeque Bay area and along the shores of Orwell Bay.

13 Hornsby, *Nineteenth Century Cape Breton*, 19–20, 23, 48, 120–21.

14 MacKinnon, *This Unfriendly Soil*, 57–66. Passenger list data for 1774–75 indicates

that North Carolina mainly attracted Scots from Argyll, the Western Isles and the North West Highlands. Viola Root Cameron, *Emigrants from Scotland to America 1774–75*. Baltimore: Genealogical Publishing Co., 1965. See, for example, pages 41–3 which shows the *Ulysses* bound for North Carolina in 1774 with 91 passengers, all from Argyll.

15 Meyer, *Highland Scots of North Carolina*, 84, 86. *SM*, Vol. xxx, 446, Vol. xxxi, 501, 602.

16 Meyer, *Highland Scots of North Carolina*, 160–1; Ian Charles Cargill Graham, *Colonists from Scotland: Emigration to North America 1707–83* (New York: Cornell University Press, 1956), 84, 85, 154. Some Scottish Loyalists from the North Carolina Volunteers took up land in the Miramichi area of New Brunswick. Wright, *The Loyalists of New Brunswick*, 198.

17 We have little quantitative data on the numbers of Scots who stayed behind in the United States after the American Revolution, or on the numbers of Scots who came to Nova Scotia and New Brunswick during the major Loyalist influx of 1784.

18 Hazel C. Mathews, *The Mark of Honour* (Toronto: University of Toronto Press, 1965) 122.

19 MacKinnon, *This Unfriendly Soil*, 60, 61, 199.

20 Although the Royal Highland Emigrants Regiment was formed in 1775, it was only officially recognized by the government in 1778. The first battalion helped to defend Quebec, while the second battalion was stationed in Nova Scotia. Jacqueline Rinn, "Factors in Scottish Emigration: A study of Scottish participation in the indentured and transportation systems of the New World in the seventeenth and eighteenth centuries" (Aberdeen University, unpublished Ph.D. thesis, 1979), 387–95.

21 Michael Brander, *The Scottish Highlanders and their Regiments* (Haddington: The Gleneil Press, 1996), 166, 167, 205. See also D. Smith, "From Swords to Ploughshares: The Context for Scottish Soldier Settlement in Central Nova Scotia 1749–1775," (Unpublished MA thesis, Saint Mary's University, Nova Scotia, 2003).

22 Meyer, *Highland Scots of North Carolina*, 153.

23 Patterson, *Memoir of Rev. James MacGregor*, 81.

24 While the indentured servants served with the regiment, their wives and children were taken to Halifax to be cared for by the army.

25 Rinn, "Factors in Scottish Emigration," 394.

26 In addition to Nova Scotia land, some former members of the Royal Highland Emigrants Regiment were also allocated land grants at Chatham township in Argenteuil County, a county in Lower Canada to the north of Glengarry.

27 NAS GD 174/2154/15: Lieutenant Hector MacLean to Capt. Murdoch MacLean of the 84th Regiment, 1784. A hand-drawn map shows the areas along the Nine Mile and the Shubenacadie rivers which had been reserved for the 84th Regiment.

28 Captains were actually entitled to at least 3000 acres and field officers could claim 5000 acres. Rinn, Ibid, 395.

29 NAS GD 174/2177/7: Memorial of Murdoch MacLean.

30 Ibid.

31 MacKinnon, *This Unfriendly Soil*, 46–7. Gilroy, *Loyalists and Land Settlement*, 60–2.

32 NAC M-1352: Rev. John Sprott to Rev. Robert Burns, Nov. 20, 1826.

33 In addition to living in major Loyalist settlements like Shelburne and Digby, Scots were also to be found in small Loyalist communities. For example, some of the *Hector* settlers moved out of Pictou and joined forces with Loyalists at a place in Halifax County which became known as "Meagher's Grant." Robert A. Logan, "Highlanders From Skye in North Carolina and Nova Scotia," *Scottish Genealogist*, Vol. 12 (1966), 92–107.

34 MacKinnon, *This Unfriendly Soil*, 174–5.

35 NAC M-1352: Rev. Gavin Lang to Rev. Robert Burns, Dec. 24, 1829.

36 MacKinnon, *This Unfriendly Soil*, 46, 174–5. PRO CO 700 N.S. No. 60.

37 Later census data reveals that the many Scottish-born American refugees who settled in Digby generally did not stay. The likelihood is that many moved to the Scottish strongholds in eastern Nova Scotia or to Upper Canada. Some are known to have returned to Britain. Isaiah W. Wilson, *A Geography and History of the County of Digby, Nova Scotia* (Belleville: Mika Studio, 1972 [originally published by the author in 1893]), 152.

38 *New Brunswick Gazette*, May 26, 1802;

39 MacKinnon, *This Unfriendly Soil*, 89–117.

40 Wynn, "A Region of Scattered Settlements," 321–25.

41 Census data for 1871 reported in Andrew H. Clark, "Old World Origins and Religious Adherence in Nova Scotia," *Geographical Review*, Vol. l (1960), 317–44.

42 This land had been granted to Major John Fisher before 1773. It later reverted by escheat to the Crown, possibly because Major Fisher died without heirs. MacKay, *Scotland Farewell*, 165. Some of the ex-servicemen from the 82nd Regiment, who settled in Merigomish, were Roman Catholic. Patterson, *History, Pictou County*, 443.

43 MacLaren, *The Pictou Book*, 72–6.

44 PRO CO 700 NS54.

45 Patterson, *Memoir of Rev. James MacGregor*, 80.

46 Patterson, *History, Pictou County*, 458–62.

47 MacLaren, *The Pictou Book*, 51.

48 D.F. Campbell and R.A. MacLean, *Beyond the Atlantic Roar: A Study of the Nova Scotia Scots* (Toronto: McClelland & Stewart, 1974), 38.

49 Patterson, *History, Pictou County*, 462–64. Finlay Cameron and John Chisholm drowned shortly after their arrival. Patterson, *Memoir of Rev. James MacGregor*, 80.

50 Patterson, *Memoir of Rev. James MacGregor*, 81. They probably sailed on the *John*, which had sailed from Aberdeen to Halifax (Appendix II). The passengers included Alexander Fraser (alias MacAndrew) John Robertson, William "Oig" Fraser and Alexander MacKay, all from Kilmorack parish. Private communication, Mr. George H. MacDonald, Stornoway, Lewis, May, 1995.

51 Patterson, *History, Pictou County*, 463–4.

52 Wynn, "Northeastern America 1775–1800," 323–4; MacKinnon, *This Unfriendly Soil*, 30–1.

53 A number of units serving in Island of St. John had been merged with Colonel Timothy Hierlihy's group to form the Volunteers. Hierlihy had commanded British troops in New York during the American War of Independence.

54 MacKinnon, *This Unfriendly Soil*, 44.

55 Angus Anthony Johnston, *A History of the Catholic Church in Eastern Nova Scotia*, Vol. 1 (Antigonish: St. Francis Xavier University Press, 1960), 126.

56 The St. Augustine Loyalists found their way to Guysborough. Having been driven out of the Carolinas and Georgia to Florida, they were exiled a second time when Britain gave up Florida in 1783 with many seeking refuge in Nova Scotia. PRO CO 700 NS No. 50. MacKinnon, *This Unfriendly Soil*, 30, 42–3.

57 NAC M-1354: Rev. William MacKenzie to Rev. Robert Burns, April 4, 1837. The Fraser Highlanders fought at Quebec under General Wolfe.

58 MacKinnon, *This Unfriendly Soil*, 42.

59 MacKay, *Scotland Farewell*, 166–7.

60 Patterson, *History, Pictou County*, 458–9.

CHAPTER 4 – CREATING A NEW SCOTLAND

1 NLS MS 9646: "On Emigration from the Scottish Highlands and Islands" attributed to Edward S. Fraser of Inverness-shire (1801–04) f. 41.

2 Kelp is burnt seaweed used in the manufacture of soap and glass. The industry was highly profitable from the late eighteenth century, reaching its high point around 1810. Landlords sought to maximize their profits from kelp production by encouraging their tenantry to live on ever smaller plots of land. This eventually created conditions of extreme congestion and overpopulation in regions which generally had very low soil productivity. Bumsted, *People's Clearance*, 41–3, 84–8.

3 Bumsted, Ibid, 118.

4 Tacksmen were an elite class in the Scottish feudal system who acted as factors or farm managers under a laird. They usually sublet much of their own land to sub-tenants who did most of the work on the great Highland estates. With the introduction of improved farming methods in the 1770s, the tacksmen's role became increasingly obsolete and many reacted to the sweeping changes by promoting emigration within their local population and were highly influential in encouraging large numbers to emigrate.

5 Simon Fraser of Fort William appears as an emigrant contractor in Robert Brown, *Strictures and remarks on the Earl of Selkirk's observations on the present state of the Highlands* (Edinburgh, 1806) Appendix (State of Emigrations, 1801, 1802 and 1803). Brown was a factor on Clanranald's Uist estates.

6 PRO CO 217/63: John Parr to Henry Dundas, Sept. 27, 1791.

7 Ibid: John Parr to Evan Nepean, 1791.

8 The British government would have preferred to have English-speaking, Anglican colonizers. However, most of the British arrivals to Nova Scotia before 1803 were, in fact, Gaelic-speaking Catholic Highlanders.

9 MacKay, *Scotland Farewell*, 182–4. Adams and Somerville, *Cargoes of Despair and Hope*, 193, 236.

10 Father Alexander MacDonald, writing in 1802, quoted by Bumsted, *People's Clearance*, 75.

11 John Lorne Campell, *Canna, the story of a Hebridean Island* (New York: Oxford University Press) 222. At this time Parrsboro was actually in Kings County.

12 NSARM MG9 Vol. 170 Scrap-book #170. The Eigg group who went to Parrsboro included John and Donald MacKinnon and families, Neil MacLeod and family, three families of MacIsaacs, two or three families of MacEacherns and Donald MacLeod from Canna. Johnston, *History of the Catholic Church in Eastern Nova Scotia*, 139–40.

13 Clark, "Old World Origins, Nova Scotia," 317–44.

14 For ease of reference, settlements are placed within the county boundaries which came into use later in the nineteenth century.

15 Campey, *"A Very Fine Class of Immigrants,"* 22–5.

16 The first resident priest was Father James McDonald who was succeeded by Father Alexander MacDonald in around 1800. After Father Alexander's death in Halifax in 1816, his parishioners carried his remains "through the woods all the way to Arisaig." Patterson, *History, Pictou County*, 443.

17 MacNutt, *The Atlantic Provinces*, 117–18; Campbell and MacLean, *Beyond the Atlantic Roar*, 210–13; Moir, *The Church in the British Era*, 135–37.

18 Father Ronald MacGillivray, a later pastor of Arisaig, quoted in Johnston, *History of the Catholic Church in Eastern Nova Scotia*, 160 (also see 157, 161–65).

19 Johnston, Ibid, 161.

20 NLS MS 9646 f. 26.

21 Ibid, f. 19. Appendix; Johnston, *History of the Catholic Church...* 163; NAS RH2/4/87.

22 Rankin, *County of Antigonish*, 14. Johnston, Ibid, 163.

23 *DCB*, Vol. vii, 244–46. Dunoon eventually became a Judge of the Court of Common Pleas, a Justice of the Peace, a Deputy Registrar of Deeds and a Collector of Customs for the district of Pictou. Patterson, *History, Pictou County*, 160.

24 NAS GD 248 3410/10: Duncan Grant to Sir James Grant, March 2, 1801.

25 Passenger lists for the *Dove* and *Sarah* crossings are taken from NAS RH2/4/87 ff. 66–75. They appear in Appendix I.

26 NLS MS 9646 ff. 15, 19.

27 Bumsted, *People's Clearance*, 88–95; MacKay, *Scotland Farewell*, 188–91; Patterson, *History, Pictou County*, 226–27.

28 Patterson, Ibid, 227–31.

29 NAS RH 2/4/87, ff. 72–77.

30 Lucille H. Campey, *"Fast Sailing and Copper-Bottomed": Aberdeen Sailing Ships and the Emigrant Scots They Carried to Canada 1774–1855* (Toronto: Natural Heritage, 2002), 105–6.

31 The 1803 Passenger Act introduced ostensibly for humanitarian reasons, stipulated minimum space and food requirements for passengers in ocean-going vessels.

However, it was generally accepted throughout Scotland that the Act would provide a temporary deterrent to emigration and allow time for the Highland improvement schemes being recommended by Thomas Telford, the renowned British Civil Engineer, to be implemented.

32 NSARM RG1 Vol. 227 Doc. 116.

33 NLS MS 9646 f. 21.

34 NAS GD 174/1615: Hector MacLean to Murdoch MacLean of Lochbuy on Mull, Dec. 14, 1803.

35 Patterson, *History, Pictou, County*, 232. The group probably included people from both Barra and South Uist.

36 NSARM RG1 Vol. 396B ff. 80–3: Charles Morris, Surveyor General to Richard Morris, District Surveyor, March 22, 1802. The "new road" was the link between Manchester and Antigonish whose route had been specified but not yet built.

37 Rankin, *County of Antigonish*, 12–5.

38 John Lorne Campbell (ed.), *The Book of Barra* (London: G. Routledge & Sons, 1936), 167.

39 Hornsby, *Nineteenth Century Cape Breton*, 23, 48–49. David Syrett, *Shipping and the American War 1775–83, A Study of British Transport Organisation*, (London: Athlone Press, 1970), 127, 169. J.S. Martell, "Early Coal Mining in Nova Scotia" in Don MacGillivray and Brian Tenyson (eds.) *Cape Breton Historical Essays* (Sydney: College of Cape Breton Press, 1981), 41–7.

40 Many Prince Edward Island settlers had to accept tenancies at the time.

41 Cape Breton was separated from Nova Scotia in 1784 and was re-annexed to it in 1820. During this period, Cape Breton was made an adjunct colony of Nova Scotia, seriously weakening the island's ability to organize its own affairs. It had an appointed Council, but no elected House of Assembly and was unable to collect taxes.

42 Campbell and MacLean, *Beyond the Atlantic Roar*, 65–70.

43 Migration records are available from 1796. See NSARM MG1 Vol. 1848 Folder.

44 Barbara Kincaid, "Scottish Emigration to Cape Breton, 1758–1838" (Dalhousie, Nova Scotia, unpublished Ph.D. thesis 1964). The Appendix (pp. 133–95) lists the surnames of Scottish householders who acquired land permits, together with their location on the Island and date of arrival. Geographical data for Nova Scotia and Cape Breton is taken from *A Map of the Province of Nova Scotia Canada* (Halifax: Province of Nova Scotia and Formac Pub. Co., 1992).

45 Kincaid, "Scottish Emigration to Cape Breton," 123–4.

46 John MacLean (1747–1848) later captured the dispiriting effects of the forests in his widely read poem "A' Choille Ghruamach" (The Gloomy Forest) written c. 1821. A native of Tyree, who emigrated to Nova Scotia in 1819, he was one of the most renowned of the Highland bards ever to come to North America.

47 Richard Brown, *A History of the Island of Cape Breton* (London: Sampson Low, Son and Marston, 1869), 404, 421–5.

48 Port Hood had 800 Catholic families by 1812.

49 Johnston, *History of the Catholic Church...*, 217. Judique's first pastor was Rev. Alexander MacDonell who served from 1818 until his death in 1841. His tombstone can be seen in St. Andrew's cemetery. Some of the passengers who sailed on the *Nora* in 1801 went to Judique.

50 Hornsby, *Nineteenth Century Cape Breton*, 3–5. At the beginning of the nineteenth century French-speaking Acadians were concentrated at Cheticamp, on the northwest coast and in the southwest corner of the island, particularly at Isle Madame.

51 A.M. MacKenzie, *The History of Christmas Island* (Cape Breton, 1983), 1–5; Kincaid, "Scottish Emigration Cape Breton," Appendix, 133–95.

52 Haliburton, *Nova Scotia*, 203. The main entrance to the Lake (Big Bras d'Or) and smaller entrance (Little Bras d'Or) a short distance to the east converge in a single body of water which is funnelled at the Grand Narrows into the central reservoir of Bras d'Or Lake (see Figure 8).

53 John, Parker, *Cape Breton Ships and Men* (Toronto: George J. McLeod Ltd., 1967), 71–4.

54 The Christmas Island settlement had its first Catholic Church by 1814.

55 He was not the same Hector MacNeil who settled at the Grand Narrows in 1804.

56 NAS RH4/188/2, f. 534; NLS MS 9646 f. 23.

57 Lacking a House of Assembly, taxes could not be collected. Despard got around this problem by introducing a tax on the liquor consumed by Cape Bretoners. He convinced the colonial authorities that his tax was legal and used it for the common good.

58 Robert Morgan, *Early Cape Breton, From founding to famine, 1784–1851* (Nova Scotia: Breton Books, 2000), 79–86. MacDougall, *History of Inverness County*, 641.

59 Kincaid, "Scottish Emigration Cape Breton," Appendix, 133–95.

60 1802–03 arrivals to Pictou from: NLS MS 9646, Brown, *Strictures and Remarks*, 36–8,112, Appendix and NAS RH 4/188/1–2: Vol. iii, 441, 475–92, 525.

61 MacLaren, *Pictou Book*, 78–9. Mr. Biggar is probably James MacGregor, who arrived in Pictou from Scotland in 1786. Duncan Ross arrived in 1795.

62 Patterson, *History of Pictou County*, 222.

63 Patterson, Ibid, 236.

64 Eric Richards, *The Highland Clearances* (Edinburgh: Berlinn Ltd., 2002), 113.

65 Brown, *Strictures and Remarks*, Appendix. Each vessel carried 120 passengers.

66 Haliburton, *Nova Scotia*, Vol. ii, 50.

67 Richards, *The Highland Clearances*, 114.

68 NLS MS 9646 f. 21: Brown, *Strictures and Remarks*, Appendix; PP 1802–03; Thomas Telford, *A Survey and Report of the Coasts and Central Highlands of Scotland* (London, 1803), 15.

69 Richards, *the Highland Clearances*, 82.

70 Patterson, *History of Pictou County*, 236–7. Brown, *Strictures and Remarks*, PP 1802–1803; NAS GD 46/17 Vol. 23.

71 *Lord Selkirk's Diary*, 47.

72, Ibid, 47

73 Ibid. The intervale lands, which were to be found along rivers and streams, were natural meadows.

74 James MacGregor had encountered four more Dumfries-shire families during his visit to the Middle River. Patterson, *Memoir of James MacGregor*, 105.

75 His father, also Anthony, had originated from Buittle near Kirkcudbright. See the passenger list for the 1775 *Lovely Nelly* crossing in Campey, *"A Very Fine Class of Immigrants,"* 109–11.

76 *Lord Selkirk's Diary*, 49.

77 Ibid, 50.

78 Ibid.

79 Ibid, 51.

80 NLS MS 1053 ff. 104–9. The passenger list for the *Commerce* crossing appears in Appendix I.

81 Patterson, *History, Pictou County*, 283–4.

82 NLS MS.35.6.18: "State of emigration from the Highlands of Scotland, its extent, causes and proposed remedy, London, March 21, 1803" f. 10.

83 Mackay, *Scotland Farewell*, 44–59. The Wester Ross contingent who had sailed on the *Hector* also came from Forfeited Estates. The estates forfeited after the Jacobite uprising of 1745–6 were returned to their original owners in the 1780s.

84 They were joined by many emigrants from Reay in Caithness. *SM*, Vol. xxxiv (1772) 395, 483, 515; Meyer, *Highland Scots of North Carolina*, 37, 43–44, 55, 86; Cameron, *Emigrants from Scotland*, 6–24; Adams and Somerville, *Cargoes of Despair and Hope*, 104–05; Sinclair, *First Statistical Account of Scotland*, Vol. xviii, 153, 337, 378, 412.

85 S.R. MacNeil, *All Call Iona Home*, (Antigonish: Formac Pub. Co., 1979) section headed "MacNeil."

86 The 1803 Passenger Act stipulated the daily requirements of beef, bread, biscuit or oatmeal, molasses and water to be provided to each passenger and a space allocation of one person for every two tons burthen. As a result of these regulations, fares more than doubled.

Chapter 5 – The Attractions of the Timber Trade

1 Patterson, *History, Pictou County*, 251.

2 Ibid.

3 Although William Liddell's timber interests were mainly based on trade with Saint Petersburg in Russia, he also formed other companies. In all he had co-partnerships with John Liddell (Halifax), John Clark (Miramichi), Edward Mortimer (Pictou) and Alexander Murison (Halifax). Liddell had debts of more than £50,000 to two Saint Petersburg companies at the time of his death in 1829. Most of Liddell's export trade came from the Baltic, while Mortimer's shipments came from Pictou. Mortimer entered into partnerships with John Liddell (Halifax) and John Clark (Miramichi). NAS CS96/154: William Liddell and Company merchants, Sederunt Books (1829–34).

4 *DCB*, Vol. v, 611–12. Patterson, *History, Pictou County*, 250–68. Mortimer obtained a 21 year lease for the Pictou coal mines in 1818.

5 Edward Mortimer was also a Judge of the Court of Common Pleas, a Chief Magistrate of Pictou and a generous benefactor of the Pictou Academy.

6 Patterson, *Memoir of James MacGregor*, 319–20.

7 Patterson, *History, Pictou County*, 252–3.

8 NAS CS96/154, 96–103.

9 Patterson, *History, Pictou County*, 252–3.

10 His firm continued under George Smith of Pictou for about 3 years. Smith later entered into a number of partnerships which all failed. NAS CS96/154, 84–95, 110–5.

11 Graeme Wynne describes the central role of merchants and storekeepers in the early nineteenth century development of the New Brunswick timber trade in *Timber Colony: an Historical Geography of early Nineteenth Century New Brunswick* (Toronto: University of Toronto Press, 1981), 84–86, 110–111, 113–137.

12 This practice continued for some time. Even in the early 1900s local farmers accounted for a substantial proportion of the timber production in the St. Marys River area of Guysborough County. Mike Parker, *Woodchips and Beans, Life in the early lumber woods of Nova Scotia*, (Halifax: Nimbus Pub. Ltd., 1992), 139–40.

13 Parker, Ibid, 1.

14 Patterson, *History, Pictou County*, 245.

15 Wynne, *Timber Colony*, 33–43.

16 The punitive tariffs on Baltic timber remained in force until 1860. Eric Sager, with G.E. Panting, *Maritime Capital: The Shipping Industry in Atlantic Canada 1820–1914* (Montreal: McGill-Queen's University Press, 1990), 38–46; Gerald S. Graham, *Sea Power and British North America 1785–1820: A Study in British Colonial Policy* (Cambridge, Mass.: Harvard University Press, 1941) Appendix C.

17 A. Shortt and A.G. Doughty (eds.), *Canada and its Provinces. A History of the Canadian people and their institutions. by one hundred associates* (Toronto: Publishers Association of Canada, 1913–17) Vol. xiii. 254–5. Nova Scotia also exported timber to the West Indies from the mid-1780s. While the trade was substantial, its relative importance to Nova Scotia declined when Britain used British North America as its primary source of timber.

18 NAS RH 2/4: Accounts of the Exports and Imports of the Provinces of North America, 1800–27.

19 With its considerable coastal trading links, its dominance of shipping, having nearly double the tonnage of Leith's shipping by 1820, and its extensive woollen industry, the Aberdeen economy was less adversely affected by the depression following the Napoleonic War years.

20 *AR* July 26, 1817. By this time most of the arrivals would have originated from Scotland and Ireland.

21 Martell, *Immigration Nova Scotia, 1815–38*, 40–1. NAS E.504/22/72.

22 NSARM RG1 Vol. 227, Doc. 116.

23 For example, the *Kelso Mail* carried an advertisement on June 26, 1817 for the *Prompt*, which sailed from Leith to Halifax and Quebec. Sixty emigrants left at Halifax and 133 sailed on to Quebec.

24 Martell, *Immigration Nova Scotia, 1815–38*, 43. SM Vol. lxxix, 477. The crossing from Kirkaldy to Halifax with emigrants was unusual. Most Fife people would have sailed to North America from Leith.

25 Campey, *"Fast Sailing and Copper-Bottomed,"* 59–79

26 They settled at Pictou, the Miramichi region of New Brunswick and Prince Edward Island. Campey, *"A Very Fine Class of Immigrants,"* 66–79.

27 Patterson, *History, Pictou County*, 278; Campbell and MacLean, *Beyond the Atlantic Roar*, 46; E.504/9/9 shows that four ships arrived at Pictou or the Miramichi from Dumfries in the period from 1816 to 1818.

28 *Reports from the Select Committee appointed to inquire into the expediency of encouraging emigration from the United Kingdom*, 1827, A 2391–2419. Woollen cloth was manufactured in many parts of the Borders. Fife was an important centre of linen production while the cotton industry was concentrated around the Clyde.

29 Patterson, Ibid, 280.

30 Ibid.

31 Ibid.

32 Ibid, 284.

33 *IJ*, May 13, 1813. The 600 acre holding was in west Pictou.

34 Richards, *Highland Clearances*, 119–39.

35 *IC*, Oct. 9, 1807, Feb. 8, 1808.

36 For example, *IJ*, Nov. 5, 1813.

37 *IJ*, May 28, 1815.

38 NSARM MG 100 Vol. 226 #30: Memorial of emigrants who arrived on the brigantine *Prince William* from the shire of Sutherland and requested land in Pictou, 30 Sept. 1815 (appears in Appendix I). The Reay Fencibles were disbanded in 1802.

39 MacLaren, *The Pictou Book*, 100–1.

40 *IJ*, April 7, 1815. Emigrants were invited to "apply to George Logan from America" at Dornoch.

41 Marjorie Hawkins et al., *Gairloch, Pictou County, Nova Scotia* (Oxford, N.S., 1977), 86–7. Although Gairloch attracted many Sutherland emigrants, its first founders came from Gairloch in Wester Ross. Arriving in 1805, they included Philip McDonald, Alexander McKenzie and Donald McPherson, who named the place after their native parish. Patterson, *History, Pictou County*, 241.

42 Patterson, Ibid, 277–9. Israel Longwith, *History of Colchester County, Nova Scotia* (Truro: The Book Nook, 1989 [originally published in c. 1886]), 82–5.

43 George R. Sutherland, *The Rise and Decline of the Earltown Community, 1813–1970* (Colchester Historical Society and Colchester Historical Museum, 1980), 13, 98–136.

44 Donald McLeod, *History of the Destitution in Sutherlandshire* (1841), 6–7.

45 NSARM RG1 Vol. 227 Docs. 116, 118. The Sutherland petitioners of 1815 who arrived on the *Prince William* can be found in this list.

46 PRO CO 217/99: Dalhousie to Bathurst, Jan. 2, 1817.

47 Rankin, *County of Antigonish*, 12–15.

48 Seven hundred of the 3,000 communicants lived in Cape Breton. Johnston, *History of the Catholic Church in Eastern Nova Scotia*, 205–6.

49 The earliest settlers in Ohio included Angus McInnes, Sergeant John McInnes, Donald McInnes, Angus McGillivary and Duncan McLean.

50 Campbell and MacLean, *Beyond the Atlantic Roar*, 61–62; Rankin, *County of Antigonish*, 12–7.

51 Rankin, *County of Antigonish*, 16.

52 Patterson, *History, Pictou County*, 285.

53 NSARM MG1 Vol. 1848, Folder 3.

54 Land grant permit data in Kincaid, "Scottish Emigration to Cape Breton 1758–1838." The appendix shows that most of the early arrivals settled at the Western Shore.

55 Johnston, *History of the Catholic Church in Eastern Nova Scotia*, 239–53.

56 Ibid.

57 Robert Greenhalgh Albion, *Forests and Seapower, the Timber Problems of the Royal Navy 1652–1862* (Cambridge, Mass., Cambridge, Mass.: Harvard University Press, 1926), 422. Figures taken from *Parliamentary Papers*, 1820 (269) iii, 381. Cape Breton exported 151 loads of pine or fir timber in 1804. By 1812 exports amounted to some 11,113 loads.

58 Haliburton, *Nova Scotia*, 257.

59 Land grant data in Kincaid, Ibid.

60 NSARM RG1 Vol. 329 Doc. 109. Harvey, "Scottish Immigration to Cape Breton," 313–24.

61 A.J. MacMillan, *To the Hill of Boisdale – A short history and genealogical tracing of the pioneer families of Boisdale, Cape Breton and surrounding area* (Sydney: the author, 1986), 24–7.

62 Ibid.

63 The 1838 *Census Returns* show large concentrations of MacNeils in Cape Breton County.

64 Campbell, *The Book of Barra*, 159–61. Letter from Roderick McNeil in Liverpool to Rev. Angus McDonald in Barra, June 6, 1816.

65 Ibid, 159.

66 Cowan, *British Emigration*, 58; Harvey, "Scottish Immigration to Cape Breton," 315–16.

67 P.J. MacKenzie Campbell, *A Highland Community on Bras d'Or* (Cape Breton, 1978), 115–125.

68 Kincaid, "Scottish Emigration to Cape Breton 1758–1838", Appendix.

69 Campbell, *The Book of Barra*, 167. A.D. MacDonald, *Mabou Pioneers, A genealogical tracing of some pioneer families who settled in Mabou district* (Antigonish: Formac Publishing Co., 1957). Where records exist, they show that between 1810 and 1820 a total of 159 people moved from Prince Edward Island to Cape Breton. NSARM MG1 Vol. 1848, Folder 3.

70 Few emigrant ships are known to have arrived in Pictou between 1806 and 1811. The *Active* arrived from Fort William in 1806 with 36 passengers, some of whom may have originated from the Western Isles. The *Favourite* of Grangemouth brought 31 emigrants from Oban. Some of them may have originated from the Argyll Islands. The *Ann* of North Shields carried 26 passengers from Stornoway in 1811. E.504/12/6, E.504/25/3. E.504/33/3.

71 MacAulay would have gained 1000 acres of land for himself if successful. Rusty Bittermann, "Economic Stratification and Agrarian Settlement: Middle River in the early Nineteenth Century" in Kenneth Donovan (ed.) *The Island, New Perspectives on Cape Breton History* (Fredricton: Acadiensis, 1990), 71–95; Rusty Bittermann, Robert A. MacKinnon and Graeme Wynne "Of Equality and Interdependence in the Nova Scotian Countryside 1850–70," *Canadian Historical Review* Vol. lxxiv (1993), 5–12. John Nicholson, *et al.*, *Middle River, Past and Present history of a Cape Breton community 1806–1985* (Cape Breton: 1985), 245–47.

72 Kincaid, Ibid.

73 Campey, *The Silver Chief*, 24–50.

74 Bittermann, "Middle River in the early Nineteenth Century," 79–81.

75 *IJ*, July 12, 1823.

76 The *Tartar* carried 144 passengers to Pictou. E.504/35/2. Terrance M. Punch, "Scots Settlers to Long Point, 1816," *Nova Scotia Genealogist*, Vol. 2 (1984), 88–9. The collapse of the kelp industry from the mid-1820s had caused extreme hardship in the Hebrides and greatly stimulated emigration. Great numbers arrived without the means to pay for land, which was being offered for sale on the basis of its commercial value. Because land purchase was beyond their means they squatted.

77 "Missionary Journey of Rev. John McLennan and Rev. Donald Fraser, 1827" in Rev. R.F. Binnington, "The Glasgow Colonial Society and its work in the development of the Presbyterian Church in British North America 1825–40" (Toronto, unpublished Th. D. thesis, 1960), 105–16. Campbell and MacLean, *Beyond the Atlantic Roar*, 65–6.

78 Rev. Farquharson writing in 1827. Anon., *Sketch of Missionary Proceedings at Cape Breton from August 1833 to September 1836* (1833–36) Aberdeen University Library Special Collections, Thomson Collection, T326/13, 10.

CHAPTER 6 – CAPE BRETON'S GROWING POPULARITY

1 PRO CO 217/146, Sir James Kempt to Wilmot Horton, Sept. 14, 1826.

2 Settlers paid £3 to £5 initially for a 100 acre lot. It was subject to an annual quit-rent of 2 s. payable after two years, but, in practice, quit-rents were never collected. Hornsby, *Nineteenth Century Cape Breton*, 48–53.

3 Martell, *Immigration Nova Scotia, 1815–38*, 61, 63, 65.

4 PRO CO 217/152, 413: Customs Returns, Sydney, June 1, 1831.

5 Flora McPherson, *Watchman Against the World, The Remarkable Journey of Norman McLeod and his People from Scotland to Cape Breton Island and New Zealand* (Cape

Breton: Breton Books, 1993), 24–32. Gordon Donaldson, *The Scots Overseas* (London: Robert Hale, 1966), 71–4.

6 The Assynt clearances began in 1812, and continued in 1819–1820, Richards, *Highland Clearances*, 131, 164–5.

7 MacLaren in *The Pictou Book* gives 400 passengers, but E.504/12/6 (Scottish Customs) records 136 passengers for the *Frances Ann*.

8 George Patterson, *More Studies in Nova Scotian History* (Halifax: Imperial, 1941), 91–5.

9 Laurie Stanley, *The Well-Watered Garden: The Presbyterian Church in Cape Breton 1798–1860* (Sydney, C.B.: University College of Cape Breton Press, 1983), 159; McPherson, *Watchman Against the World*, 40–1.

10 NSARM RG1 Vol. 334 Doc. 34. The fifteen family heads were: John McLeod (6), Neil McKenzie (5), Alexander MacKenzie (5), Roderick MacLeod (7), Duncan MacLeod (5), Donald MacLeod (7) Murdock MacLeod (10) John MacLeod (7) John Kerr (3) Alexander MacLeod (2), Donald McDonald (4), Donald McLeod Jr. (2), Donald Campbell (5), Norman MacLeod (8), Donald MacLeod (2).

11 McPherson, *Watchman Against the World*, 45–64. Some of the 1821 group may have sailed on the *Ossian* of Leith, which left Cromarty with 108 passengers. They included 22 families who are shown in a passenger list printed in *IJ* June 29, 1821 (Appendix I). In 1822, the *Ruby* of Aberdeen and the *Harmony* of Aberdeen each brought 125 people from Cromarty to Pictou. E.504/17/9, *IJ* July 12, 1822.

12 Bill Lawson, *A Register of Emigrants from the Western Isles of Scotland 1750–1900*, 2 vols. (Harris, the author, 1992).

13 For more information, see Chapter 8.

14 Norman McLeod accepted only the law of the gospel and refused to join the local Church of Scotland presbytery in Cape Breton.

15 Stanley, *Well-Watered Garden*, 160–3.

16 Stanley, *Well-Watered Garden*, 26–7. McPherson, *Watchman Against the World*, 125–6
.

17 McPherson, *Watchman Against the World*, 127–62. The community settled on the Waipu River. Between 1851 and 1859 more than 700 people travelled in six ships to their new location in New Zealand.

18 NSARM RG1 Vol. 334 Doc. 48. Laurence Kavanagh to R.D. George, Jan. 10, 1821. These Scottish emigrants may have sailed to St. Peter's from Tobermory on the *Glentanner* of Aberdeen, which had a total of 141 passengers, 18 of whom went on to Quebec. E.504/35/2.

19 Martell, *Immigration Nova Scotia, 1815–38*, 26–9, 59–83.

20 NAS GD 139/463/1: Alexander Keith, Halifax to George Sinclair, Wick, Feb. 18, 1835.

21 "Missionary Journney" in Binnington, "The Glasgow Colonial Society," 112.

22 Campbell and MacLean, *Beyond the Atlantic Roar*, 72–3; Johnston, *History of the Catholic Church in Eastern Nova Scotia*, 300–1; Lawson, *Register of Emigrants*.

23 "Missionary Journey" in Binnington, 107.

24 Nicholson, et al., *Middle River*, 245–7.

25 "Missionary Journey" in Binnington, 112–3.

26 Lawson, *Register of Emigrants*.

27 MacDougall, *History of Inverness County*, 466–8. Today Whycocomagh is the location of a modern First Nation's Reserve.

28 NAC M-1352: Rev. John Munro to Rev. David Welsh, Feb. 6, 1829. MacDougall, *History of Inverness County*, 471–3.

29 Kincaid, "Scottish Emigration Cape Breton" Appendix. By 1852 Malagawatch had 60 to 70 Presbyterian families, River Denys had 65 to 70 Presbyterian families and St. George's Channel had two Presbyterian churches. Stanley, *Well-Watered Garden*, 200.

30 Martell, *Immigration Nova Scotia, 1815–38*, 52; Colin S. MacDonald, "Early Highland Emigration to Nova Scotia and Prince Edward Island from 1770 to 1853," *Nova Scotia Historical Society (Collections)*, Vol. xxiii (1936), 41–48. MacDougall, *History of Inverness County*, 511. A list of the 30 heads of families, giving parish origins, who travelled on the *Emperor Alexander* was printed in *IJ*, Jan. 30, 1824 (Appendix I).

31 Kelp production was primarily concentrated in the Islands of North and South Uist, Benbecula, Barra, Harris, Lewis, Skye and Mull, and in the Argyll coastal mainland areas of Ardnamurchan, Sunart and Morvern. Malcolm Gray, *The Highland Economy 1750–1850* (Edinburgh: Oliver & Boyd, 1957), 126–51.

32 Richards, *Highland Clearances*, 184–92.

33 *Reports from the Select Committee appointed to inquire into the expediency of encouraging emigration from the United Kingdom*, 1826 Abstract of Petitions.

34 NAS GD 201/4/97: Duncan Shaw to Alexander Hunter – application to government for assistance in sending the extra population of Benbecula to America.

35 R.J. Uniacke was also a North Sydney merchant. *Select Committee, Emigration, 1826*, A 331. His view that Nova Scotia could absorb many more emigrants was not universally shared in Nova Scotia. Many people were concerned about the high cost to the government of caring for destitute emigrants and were loathe to see their numbers rise.

36 One of the families originated from South Uist. Martell, *Immigration Nova Scotia, 1815–38*, 56–7; MacDougall, *History of Inverness County*, 503–4; E.504/15/156; MacDonald, "Early Highland Emigration to Nova Scotia and P.E.I. 1770–1853," 45; *QM* Oct. 3, 1826.

37 "Missionary Journey," Binnington, 110.

38 NSARM RG1 Vol. 335 Doc. 64: Charles McNab to Sir James Kempt, Sept. 28, 1826.

39 Ibid.

40 Taken together, Loch Lomond, Grand River, St. Esprit and Framboise had 220 to 250 Presbyterian families in 1852. Stanley, *Well-Watered Garden*, 200.

41 Bras d'Or is separated from the sea at St. Peter's by just half a mile. The canal was begun in 1854.

42 Johnston, *History of the Catholic Church, Eastern Nova Scotia*, 300–4.

43 NSARM RG1 Vol. 336, Doc. 22, May 2, 1828. Only 23 heads of households (or 124 people) given in the petition (size of family in parentheses): John Campbell (12), John McEachern (13), Donald McDonald (3), John Mcinnes (2), Donald Currie (8), Lachlan Currie (2), John McIsac (3), John McIsac (5), Neil McIsac (5), James Mclean (8), Donald Mcleod (9), Norman McKinnon (2), Hector McKinnon (7), John McKinnon (2), Donald McMillan (5), Anne Steel [widow] (2), Sarah McInyre [widow] (2), Duncan McIntyre (8), Lachlan Mclean (3), Malcolm McPhie (9), Angus Morrison (3), Angus Morrison (4), Alexander McDonald (7).

44 MacMillan, *Hill of Boisdale*, 24, 170.

45 NSARM RG1 Vol. 307 Doc. 126: John Whyte, surgeon, to R.D. George, Dec. 19, 1827.

46 A total of 2,413 people originating from the "western parts of Scotland" had sailed to Sydney in 1828. This compares with a total of 944 in 1827. Martell, *Immigration Nova Scotia, 1815–38*, 61.

47 Martell, Ibid. Long boats were used to ferry small groups of people to and from ships once they had anchored offshore.

48 NSARM RG1 Vol. 336, Doc. 48: John G. Marshall to R.D. George, Sept. 9, 1828.

49 Ibid.

50 NSARM RG1 Vol. 336, Doc. 56. A total of £33.10s. was "paid for the relief of the poor and destitute Scotch emigrants landed in Cape Breton" in 1828.

51 Many of the North Uist settlers originated from Carinish. The North Uist and Harris emigrants sailed from Stornoway on the *Mary, Ann, Commerce* and *Universe* of Aberdeen. MacMillan, *Hill of Boisdale*, 23–24; Martell, *Immigration Nova Scotia, 1815–38*, 61.

52 Stanley, *Well-Watered Garden*, 20–21. Because of a long-running legal wrangle over escheat proceedings, the land records for Mira are incomplete.

53 A2654.

54 *Report from the Commissioners appointed for inquiring into the Administration and Practical Operation of the Poor Laws in Scotland, 1844;* Answers to Questions 30 to 32 in the Appendices (424–5).

55 Kincaid, "Scottish Emigration Cape Breton" Appendix.

56 Evidence given by Rev. Norman MacLeod to the Select Committee on Emigration in 1841 (A826). Dr. Norman McLeod, was an energetic Glaswegian clergyman who campaigned forcefully, through his *Gaelic Magazine*, in support of Highland emigration to British North America.

57 A total of 500 people were reported to have been "sent away " from Rhum. *Select Committee on Emigration* in 1841 (A209–A216). Evidence of John Bowie; MacDougall, *History of Inverness County*, 126–31.

58 They originated mainly from Kilmuir, Snizort and Portree parishes. Campey, *"A Very Fine Class of Immigrants,"* 80–9.

59 PRO CO 384/23, 484: Letter in the name of Donald Murchison, representing a group from Burnastill (probably Bernisdale) in Skye (1830).

60 NSARM RG1 Vol. 336, Doc. 90: C.E. Leonard & T.H. Clarke, J.P.s to R.D. George, May 26, 1829.

61 The 49 families are listed in NSARM RG1 Vol. 67, Doc. 19: R.H. Hay to Lt. Gov. Maitland, June 14, 1830. Martell, *Immigration Nova Scotia, 1815–38*, 65–66. The group's leader, Alexander Beaton, received 300 acres while the other families each got 100 acres. Fifty emigrants disembarked from the *Malay* at Quebec. *QM* Sept. 11, 1830.

62 The 1827 directive was ignored initially and was only complied with from 1832. Hornsby, *Nineteenth Century Cape Breton*, 51–7.

63 Hornsby, Ibid, 95–110; Lawson, *Register of Emigrants* shows 45% of all South Uist emigrants who arrived between 1840 and 1848 settled in the Sydney area.

64 NAC, M-1352: Rev. K.I. MacKenzie to Rev. David Welsh, Nov. 19, 1829.

65 Along with Father William Fraser, Father Alexander MacDonell presided over churches at Broad Cove, Mabou, Port Hood, Judique, River Inhabitants, Grand Narrows and East Bay. Johnston, *History of the Catholic Church in Eastern Nova Scotia*, 457, 460.

CHAPTER 7 – NOVA SCOTIA'S LINGERING APPEAL

1 NLS MS2543: Letter from Helen Creighton, wife of David Creighton, a Pictou merchant, to her uncle and aunt in Dundee, 1837.

2 Patterson, *History, Pictou County*, 366–7. Arthur R.M. Lower, *Great Britain's Woodyard: British America and the timber trade 1763–1867* (Montreal: McGill-Queen's University Press, 1973) 67–75. Coal had been mined commercially in Pictou County since 1815.

3 "Pictou Described in Joseph Howe's 'Eastern Rambles' in 1830" in MacLaren, *The Pictou Book*, 153–7.

4 Augustus Frederick, Duke of York (1773–1843) promoted benevolent schemes and was noted for his library which amounted to over 50,000 volumes, including 1,000 editions of the Bible.

5 The jewellers established an office for the General Mining Association in Ludgate Hill, in the City of London, near their premises. The firm also speculated in mining stock in South America with disastrous results. Paul Storr, *The Last of the Goldsmiths*, (London: Batsford, 1954) 76–7.

6 Until the late 1860s about two-thirds of the coal produced in Pictou was exported to the United States. Buckner and Reid, *Atlantic Region to Confederation*, 263–83. The General Mining Association established the Albion Foundry at Albion Mines in 1828. The enterprise brought to Nova Scotia its first steam engine and first steam-powered sawmill, along with the capacity to build more steam engines. Barbara Robertson, *Sawpower: Making Lumber in the Sawmills of Nova Scotia* (Halifax: Nimbus Pub. Ltd., & the Nova Scotia Museum, 1986) 59, 147.

7 The great gaps in the customs and shipping records for Pictou and Halifax prevent us from making any meaningful statistical assessment of the scale of the influx,

but the likelihood is that several thousand Scots had emigrated to eastern Nova Scotia by the late 1830s. Martell, *Immigration Nova Scotia, 1815–38*, 91–5.

8 Haliburton, *Nova Scotia*, 56–8.

9 "Pictou Described in Joseph Howe's 'Eastern Rambles' in 1830" in MacLaren, *The Pictou Book*, 155.

10 Ibid, 153–7.

11 "Population of the Pictou District, Oct. 2, 1828" in MacLaren, Ibid, 220.

12 NAC M-1352: Rev. D.A. Fraser to Rev. Dr. Scott, June 29, 1826.

13 Free Church of Scotland, *Report Presented to the Colonial Committee of the Free Church of Scotland on Canada and Nova Scotia by Rev. Dr. Burns, Paisley, one of the Deputies of the Free Church to America* (1844) [T27/4] 26–9.

14 NAC-1353: Copy of Bond, July 18, 1832.

15 NSARM RG1 Vol. 252, Doc. 69: Petition of the Inhabitants of the Upper Settlements of the West River of Pictou, Feb. 16, 1836. The petitioners were: Hugh Sutherland, George Baillie, Johan Baillie, John Baillie, Donald Baillie, James McLean, Roderick McLeod, Donald Campbell, Alexander Campbell, Angus Murray, Alexander Murray, William Mackenzie, William McLean, John McKay, Angus McKay, William Graham, Alexander McKay, Robert Thomson, Andrew Thomson, William Campbell, Thomas Fraser, Alexander Mckay, John Sutherland, Hugh McDonald, Alexander Brorason, Robert Morason.

16 Haliburton, *Nova Scotia*, 99.

17 These generous terms remained in place until 1827, when a less favourable system of land sales, at public auction, was introduced. Martell, *Immigration Nova Scotia, 1815–38*, 19–21.

18 NSARM RG1 Vol. 229, Doc. 34: George Smith to R.D. George (Provincial Secretary), June 30, 1820. PP 1828(148) Vol. XXI: Letter from Peter Crerar, Deputy Land Surveyor to John Spry Morris, May 14, 1827 in the Appendix to Lieut. Col. Cockburn's Report (on the granted and ungranted lands in the district of Pictou).

19 For more information on the Lowland Clearances see, Peter Aitchison and Andrew Cassell, *The Lowland Clearances: Scotland's Silent Revolution, 1760–1830.* (East Linton, Scotland: Tuckwell Press, 2003).

20 Richards, *Highland Clearances*, 119–79.

21 NLS SP Dep 313/1128/29: Letter from William Young to Earl Gower, May 1813.

22 Coming up against fierce opposition, the Red River settlement had to withstand the wrecking tactics of powerful men in the fur trade. Selkirk and his colonists persevered and in the end created an agricultural settlement deep in Canada's North West, which would have far-reaching consequences for Canada's future development. Campey, *The Silver Chief*, 77–105.

23 *IC*, Oct. 9, 1807; Feb. 8, 1808.

24 NLS SP Dep 313/1468: Francis Suther to James Loch, Dec. 24, 1817.

25 Ibid.

26 NLS SP Dep 313/1468: Francis Suther to James Loch, Nov. 7, 1817, April 4, 1818.

27 NLS SP Dep 313/1468: Francis Suther to James Stuart, July 21, 1819.

28 NLS SP Dep 313/1468: Francis Suther to James Loch, April 4, 1818. Meikle Ferry was near the boundary between Sutherland and Easter Ross. There was violent resistance to clearances in 1820 at Culrain, in Easter Ross, where 600 people were removed from their holdings at Strath Oykel. However, there was little emigration from Easter Ross until the 1830s. It was primarily a farming area which offered far more employment alternatives to displaced people than were available in Sutherland.

29 NLS SP Dep 313/1468: Francis Suther to James Loch, July 24, 1819. *IJ*, June 18, 1819.

30 NLS SP Dep 313/1139: James Loch to Francis Suther, Sept. 23, 1819.

31 Ibid, Dec. 24, Dec. 28, 1819.

32 John Prebble, *The Highland Clearances* (London: Penguin, 1969) 117–29.

33 One hundred and eight people sailed on the *Ossian* of Leith, while the *Harmony* of Aberdeen and the *Ruby* of Aberdeen together took 250 emigrants E.504/17/9; *IJ* July 12, 1822. The *Ossian*'s passengers included 22 families and 72 adults. A passenger list appears in *IJ*, June 29, 1821 (see Appendix I).

34 The unknown sources in Bengal were probably people connected with the East India Company, suggesting that the emigrants' benefactors were in commerce and trade.

35 The Assynt people were followers of Rev. Norman MacLeod and went to St. Anns, Cape Breton.

36 Sutherland, *Community of Earltown*, 4–11.

37 NSARM RG1 Vol. 229, Doc. 34.

38 Land grant data taken from Sutherland, *Community of Earltown*, 100–36.

39 NSARM MG1 Vol. 1848, Folder 1; NAC M-1352: Tour of Eastern Nova Scotia and Cape Breton Nov. 1829, Rev. Kenneth MacKenzie to Rev. David Welsh, Nov. 19, 1829.

40 Haliburton, *Nova Scotia*, 49.

41 NAC M-1353: Rev. Hugh MacKenzie to Rev. John Geddes, Nov. 4, 1832.

42 Sutherland, *Community of Earltown*, 45–56.

43 Free Church of Scotland, *Report Presented to the Colonial Committee of the Free Church of Scotland on Canada and Nova Scotia by Rev. Dr. Burns, Paisley, one of the Deputies of the Free Church to America* (1844) [Thomson collection in Aberdeen University Library].

44 "Petition 5th Nov., 1836 to Major General Sir Colin Campbell, Lt. Governor of Nova Scotia," printed in Sutherland, *Community of Earltown*, 15.

45 Patterson, *History, Pictou County*, 277–8.

46 NAC M-1352: Rev. Dugald McKichan to Rev. David Welch, June 2, 1829; NAC M-1354: Rev. Donald Macintosh to Rev. Robert Burns, May 1834.

47 Six hundred people had sailed from Stornoway to Pictou on three ships in 1803, the majority of whom settled at Wallace. Patterson, *History, Pictou County*, 236–7.

48 Martell, *Immigration Nova Scotia, 1815–38*, 69–70. The twenty Lewis people sailed on the *Six Sisters*.

49 NAC M-1352: Tour of Eastern Nova Scotia and Cape Breton Nov. 1829, Rev. Kenneth MacKenzie to Rev David Welsh, Nov. 19, 1829.

50 NSARM MG1 Vol. 1848, Folder 1. The Folley Lake is the source of the Ramsheg River (now Wallace River) which flows into Wallace Bay. Haliburton, *Nova Scotia*, 66–7.

51 NAC M-1352: Andrew Donald to Rev. Robert Burns, Dec. 10, 1829.

52 NAC M-1353: Rev. Hugh MacKenzie to Rev. John Geddes, Nov. 4, 1832. Settlements at Fox Harbour and Wallace were separated by two stretches of water (see Figure 5).

53 Patterson, *History, Pictou County*, 283–4.

54 John MacLean's famous poem, "The Gloomy Forest," which painted a dismal picture of early pioneer life may have deterred emigration for a period, particularly from his native Tyree.

55 NAC M1354: Petition of the Elders and Congregation of Barney's River, May 1834; Free Church of Scotland, *Report* (1844) 29.

56 Haliburton, *Nova Scotia*, 82.

57 NAC M-1352: Donald MacKenzie to Rev. Robert Burns, Dec. 16, 1826.

58 NSARM MG100 Vol. 167 #6e: The Giant Lake was discovered in 1840 by Donald McDonald, an Inverness-shire man of immense size and strength. The lake takes its name from him. The family heads of the community were: Angus, Duncan, Ronald, Donald and Angus McIsaac, Angus McDonald and John McNeil.

59 Patterson, *History, Pictou County*, 285.

60 Rev. George Patterson, *Sketch of the Life and Labours of the Rev. John Campbell of St. Marys, Nova Scotia* (New Glasgow: S.M. McKenzie, 1889) 7; NAC M-1354: Rev. Alexander McGillivray to Rev. Robert Burns, Feb. 12, 1835.

61 NAC M-1353: Rev. Lewis Rose to Mrs. MacKay, April 3, 1833.

62 Martell, *Immigration Nova Scotia, 1815–38*, 23–9.

63 PRO CO 217/154, 877: A. MacNiven to Lord Goderich, April 5, 1832.

64 MacLaren, *The Pictou Book*, 120–1.

65 This was the second Duke, George Granvill, Earl Gower, who held the title from 1833 until his death in 1861.

66 The opening up Zorra, Oxford County, in Upper Canada attracted large numbers of Sutherland emigrants during the 1830s and 1840s. This accounts for the rising number of ship crossings from Cromarty and Thurso to Quebec at this time. Campey, *"Fast Sailing and Copper-Bottomed,"* 138–40.

67 *Report from Commissioners, Poor Laws*, 402–3.

68 NAS RH 1/2/908, *Mechanic and Farmer*, Pictou. N.S., July 28, 1841. A partial passenger list records those who protested at the captain's ill-treatment on the voyage (NAS RH1/2/908). See Appendix I.

69 Susan Longley (Morse) Flewwelling, "Immigration to and Emigration from Nova Scotia 1839–51," *Nova Scotia Historical Society (Collections)*, Vol. xxviii (1949) 84–85; NSARM RG1 Vol. 255, Doc. 57.

70 When the passengers went on shore on Aspy Bay, they were treated "most shame-

fully" by people in the surrounding district although they got a warm welcome when they arrived in Pictou. *AR*, May 28, 1842. The Log Book for the crossing survives; see NAS CS 96/1592.

71 *Pictou Observer*, Sept. 6, 1842. MacLaren, *The Pictou Book*, 122.

72 Flewwelling, "Immigration and Emigration Nova Scotia," 82–3; *IJ*, March 18, March 25, July 29, 1842.

73 NAC MG25 G334: McKenna and MacDonald Family Genealogies.

74 T.M. Devine, *The Great Highland Famine: Hunger, Emigration and the Scottish Highlands in the Nineteenth Century* (Edinburgh: John Donald, 1988) 22, 177, 206, 323–26, 332.

75 The passengers would have included people from Scourie, a district which lost one-sixth of its population as a result of emigration. Devine, Ibid, 324–32. Most Sutherland people, who emigrated during the late 1840s and early 1850s went to Upper Canada rather than Nova Scotia. Campey, *"Fast Sailing and Copper-Bottomed,"* 138–40.

76 In addition to the Duke of Sutherland, other Highland landlords assisted considerable numbers of their estate tenants to emigrate during the period of the Great Famine, from 1846 to 1856. They included: Sir James Matheson (who owned Lewis), Col. J. Gordon of Cluny (who owned South Uist and Barra) and the Duke of Argyll (who owned Mull and Tyree). Devine, *Great Highland Famine*, 206.

77 Morse, "Immigration to Nova Scotia, 1839–51," 97–8. A passenger list was compiled at Pictou. NSARM Vol. 257, Doc. 110. See Appendix I.

78 The money raised from the head tax was to be used in caring for people who arrived without means, but in some years it was inadequate. Because of the particularly high expenses incurred in 1847 it was doubled during the following year. Flewwelling, "Immigration and Emigration Nova Scotia," 80–1.

79 *Journal of Assembly*, 1850, App. No. 49, quoted in Flewwelling, Ibid, 97.

80 Passenger lists for the *Hope* crossing in 1848 and the two crossings in 1848 of the *London* of Glasgow from Glasgow to Pictou are to be found in MacLaren, *The Pictou Book*, 111–4 (reprinted in Appendix I).

81 *AR*, Aug. 26, 1848. Similar ordeals were experienced by many of Gordon's other former tenants who went to Quebec. Richards *Highland Clearances*, 213–24.

82 Morse, "Immigration to Nova Scotia, 1839–51," 98–9. See MacLaren, 116–8 for the *Lulan* passenger list, which is reprinted in Appendix I.

Chapter 8 – Poor But Defiant: Cape Breton's Pioneer Scots

1 NAS GD 46/11/9: Extracts of letters (1835) from Rev. John Stewart, missionary in Cape Breton.

2 *1841 Emigration Select Committee*, A190. In addition, emigrants had to pay a head tax of 5s upon arrival in Cape Breton.

3 Hornsby, *Nineteenth Century Cape Breton*, 48–54. The new system of land sales at public auctions was introduced in 1827 but did not take effect until 1832.

4 NAC M-1354: Rev. John Stewart to Rev. Robert Burns, Dec. 25, 1834.

5 *1841 Emigration Select Committee*, A2798–A2799. The Long Island consists of Barra, South Uist, Benbecula and North Uist, which are separate islands, and Lewis and Harris, which are geographically one island.

6 Ibid, A1887 (Evidence of Mr. A.K. Mackinnon, a farmer from Skye).

7 Ibid, A640, A654.

8 Hornsby, Ibid, 21.

9 NAC M-1354, Stewart to Burns, Dec. 25, 1834.

10 Glasgow Colonial Society, *Eighth Annual Reports of the Glasgow Colonial Society for promoting the religious interests of the Scottish settlers in British North America* (Glasgow: 1835) 27.

11 Stanley, *The Well-Watered Garden*, 29–31. See also land grant data in Kincaid, "Scottish Emigration Cape Breton," Appendix.

12 Although Cape Breton's coal mines had been known from an early period, their productivity had initially been very low. With the General Mining Association's involvement, coal mining forged ahead. By 1846 the company had spent some £300,000 in Pictou's and Cape Breton's coal mines. Hornsby, *Nineteenth Century Cape Breton*, 95–107.

13 Cape Breton also exported large quantities of gypsum, used as a fertilizer, from 1817. Morgan, *Early Cape Breton*, 98–9.

14 Hornsby, *Nineteenth Century Cape Breton*, 101–3.

15 Jesuit missionaries from France had brought the Catholic faith to Cape Breton from the early seventeenth century.

16 Johnston, *History of the Catholic Church in Eastern Nova Scotia*, Vol. II, chart following page 374.

17 NAC M-1354 Stewart to Burns, Dec. 25, 1834; Glasgow Colonial Society, *Eighth Annual Report* (1835) 27.

18 Anglicans had begun their missionary endeavours in remote corners of the world far earlier, setting up the Anglican Church Missionary Society in 1790.

19 John S. Moir, *Enduring Witness: A History of the Presbyterian Church in Canada* (Toronto: McGraw-Hill Ryerson, 1975) 78–85. For more information on the Glasgow Colonial Society, see Elizabeth Ann Kerr McDougall and John S. Moir, eds., *Selected Correspondence of the Glasgow Colonial Society, 1825–40* (Toronto: Champlain Society, 1994) Chapter X.]

20 These divisions date back to 1733 when Secessionists, opposed to political patronage, broke away from the established Church of Scotland. Further divisions followed in 1748 when Secessionists disagreed over a religious clause in some oaths which needed to be taken and divided into the Burghers and Anti-Burghers.

21 Their "Missionary Journey" has been published in Binnington, "The Glasgow Colonial Society," 105–16.

22 Isabella Gordon Mackay (1778–1850) extended her Highland connections when she married. Her husband John Mackay came from Lairg in Sutherland where his father and grandfather had been Presbyterian ministers. By 1823, Isabella and John lived at Stafford Street, Edinburgh. Stanley, *The Well-Watered Garden*, 64–7.

23 Central to the new "enlightened" thinking was the belief that reason and observation should be used to formulate practical solutions to social problems.

24 Campey, *The Silver Chief*, 7–11.

25 NAS GD 46/11/8: Appendix to Memorial, Glasgow Colonial Society (1834).

26 "Missionary Journey" in Binnington, 109; NAC M-1353: John McAuley to Rev. David Welsh, Sept. 12, 1832; M-1353: Rev. Kenneth MacKenzie to Rev. Robert Burns, May 6, 1831.

27 Stanley, *The Well-Watered Garden*, 88–95.

28 *Halifax Guardian*, Sept. 15, 1843, quoted in Stanley, Ibid, 130.

29 Stanley, Ibid, 121–22, 192–201.

30 Rev. Murdoch Stewart quoted in Stanley, Ibid, 67. Within a year of her death the Edinburgh Ladies Association had disbanded.

31 Stanley, Ibid, 139–41.

32 Anon., *Sketch of Missionary Proceedings at Cape Breton from August 1833 to September 1836 (1833–36)*, 9–10; Stanley, Ibid, 100–1; Nicholson et al, *Middle River, Past and Present*, 31.

33 Stanley, Ibid, 73–8, 129–30. Rev. Farquharson was to get an annual salary of £150, half in cash and the remainder in cattle, sheep, butter and grain. However, he received only a portion the salary due to him. He and his family were thus very poor but so also was the community which he served.

34 Glasgow Colonial Society, *Eighth Annual Report* (1835), 61–2.

35 Johnston, *History of the Catholic Church in Eastern Nova Scotia*, Vol. II, 116.

36 Martell, *Immigration Nova Scotia, 1815–38*, 69, 70, 72.

37 NSARM RG1 Vol. 252, Doc. 88: John G. Marshall to T.W. James (deputy Provincial Secretary), Sept. 14, 1836.

38 NSARM RG1 Vol 313, Doc. 82: Petition of Norman McLeod and others to Lieutenant Governor, Major General Sir Colin Campbell, Nov. 8, 1836. The petitioners were: N. McLeod, Minister; D. McLeod, J.P.; John Munro, merchant; John McLeod, merchant; I. Fraser; Peter Fraser; R. Ross; R. McKenzie; D. McKenzie; H. Stuart; John McLeod; Hec. Sutherland; Don. McGregor; Donald Munro; Angus Houson; James Fraser; Donald Fraser; Andrew McIntosh; Mal. McDonald; Rory Fraser.

39 Campey, *"Fast Sailing and Copper-Bottomed,"* 138–40.

40 Martell, *Immigration Nova Scotia, 1815–38*, 84; *IJ*, June 10, July 1, 1836; *QM*, Sept. 16, 1836. Most of the people who sailed on the *Albion* boarded ship at Loch Eriboll in northwest Sutherland. The *Mariner* passengers had all been taken to Quebec even though 67 passengers had intended to disembark at Pictou. Claiming that they had been misled by the agent, they sought legal redress but to no avail. Many were apparently waiting for a vessel to take them to Pictou. *PP*, Quebec Immigration Agent's weekly report, w/e Sept. 10, 1836.

41 Stanley, *The Well-Watered Garden*, 78–87, 124–5.

42 NAC M-1354: Extracts of a letter from Rev. James Frazer, Jan. 31, 1837.

43 1841 *Select Committee on Emigration*, Appendix 1, R. Graham to F. Maule, May 6, 1837.

44 Morse, "Immigration to Nova Scotia, 1839–51," 109–10; Flewwelling, "Immigration and Emigration Nova Scotia," 85–7.

45 Campey, *"A Very Fine Class of Immigrants,"* 80–9.

46 A carefully documented account of the funds given to each person reveals that between 1839 and 1841 some 1,621 individuals from Skye and 841 from North Uist received financial help to emigrate to Prince Edward Island. The total amount granted was £2,250 or roughly £1 per person, with Lord MacDonald's contribution being matched by funds received from the Edinburgh and Glasgow Highland Relief Fund Committees. NAS GD 221/4434/1.

47 The scheme, in operation at the time throughout the Highlands, worked on the basis that each Committee paid a contribution of around 10s. per head to each emigrant provided this sum was matched by the proprietor.

48 Thomas Rolph, *Emigration and Colonization; Embodying the Results of a Mission to Great Britain and Ireland during the years, 1839, 1840, 1841 and 1842* (London: J. Mortimer, 1894) 24.

49 Ibid, 23–4.

50 Richards, *Highland Clearances*, 15–22. Some of their messages can still be read today—"Glen Calvie people was in the churchyard here, May 24, 1845."

51 NSARM MG100 Vol. 167: Application from Sydney Justices to J. Whidden, Nov. 15, 1842.

52 Ibid.

53 However, large-scale immigration to the Nova Scotia mainland continued. Pictou continued to receive Scottish immigrants and particularly large numbers of Irish immigrants arrived at Halifax following the great Irish exodus of 1847.

54 NSARM RG1 Vol. 255 Doc. 107: Petition to the Legislature of Nova Scotia, 19 March, 1844.

55 Ibid. PP, Quebec Immigration Agent's weekly reports, w/e Oct. 14, 1843. Passengers on the *Catherine*, sailing in 1843, included (ages shown in parentheses): Alexander Morison (40), Flora Morison (32), Mary Morison (9), Peggy Morison (7), Donald Morison (5), Effy Morison (2), John Morison (1), Duncan McLeod (32), Ann McLeod (26), Duncan McLeod (9 mo.), Dugald McEachern (32), Mary McEachern (55, widowed), Hugh McEachern (31), Angus McEachern (28), John McEachern (26), Ronald McEachern (20), Rory McEachern (18), James McEachern (16), Peggy McEachern (22), Mary McEachern (13). Quotes are from NSARM RG1 Vol. 255, Doc 107; list of petitioners from NSARM RG18(13).

56 Lawson, *A Register of Emigrants*. Land records for Mira are incomplete but census data reveals that there were at least two hundred and thirty-eight heads of households, of Scottish descent, living there by 1838. Kincaid, "Scottish Emigration Cape Breton," Appendix, 127.

57 "Missionary Journey" in Binnington, 105.

58 *Cape Breton Advocate*, Dec. 2, 1840.

59 Most Cape Breton Presbyterians joined the Free Church in 1843, when it withdrew from the established Church over political differences. Isabella and her

Association ministers had long supported Free Church principles and were thus highly supportive of the move. Stanley, *The Well-Watered Garden*, 132–9.

60 Stanley, Ibid, 120–32, 197–201. Rev. John Stewart left his congregation at St. George's Channel by 1838 to take up what he saw as a more secure position at New Glasgow. He was replaced by Rev. Murdoch Stewart.

61 The blight was caused by a fungus (*phytophthora infestans*) which attacks the leaves and tubers of potatoes.

62 Devine, *Great Highland Famine*, 33–56. Conditions were potentially as bad as the late 1690s when exceptionally high mortality rates had been caused by four successive years of crop failures and a murrain among the cattle.

63 Ibid, 192–211. The Lewis emigrants had been assisted by Sir James Matheson, the Barra, Benbecula and South Uist emigrants by Colonel John Gordon of Cluny, and the Tyree and Mull emigrants by the Duke of Argyll.

64 J. Harvey to Earl Grey, April 1, 1847, quoted in Devine, *Great Highland Famine*, 208–9.

65 Morgan, *Early Cape Breton*, 136–52.

66 Stanley, *The Well-Watered Garden*, 24–8, 118; Morgan, *Early Cape Breton*, 143–5.

67 McPherson, *Watchman against the World*, 71–5.

68 Parker, *Cape Breton Ships*, 120–3.

69 NSARM RG5 Series P, Vol. 84, # 68 (1848) quoted in Morgan, *Early Cape Breton*, 143.

70 Norman McLeod, at the time nearly 70, was among the 130 passengers who sailed to Australia in 1851 on the 236-ton *Margaret*, a vessel which had been built in a St. Anns shipyard. Later joined by others, around 700 of his St. Anns people would settle at Waipu in northern New Zealand. McPherson, *Watchman Against the World*, 135–47.

71 NSARM RG5 Series GP Vol. 6 #24: Petition, Feb. 6, 1849, listing sixteen family heads, representing 103 people (family size in parentheses): Murdoch Kerr (10), Angus McLeod (5), Angus Campbell (6), John McKenzie (6), John Cameron (9), John McLeod (10), Alexander McLeod (5), Murdock McLeod (8), John McKenzie (9), Donald McLeod (4), Murdoch McLeod (5), John McLeod (4), Angus McDonald (7), Murdoch Beaton (5), John McLeod (7), Donald Kerr (4).

72 NAS GD 403/27: Captain Donald McNeil to his brother Captain William McNeil, Feb. 27, 1847, June 25, 1849.

73 Margaret Bennett, *The Last Stronghold: Scottish Gaelic Traditions of Newfoundland* (Edinburgh: Canongate, 1989) 34–41. Bennett, Margaret, "Musical Traditions of the Scots in Newfoundland," *The London Journal of Canadian Studies*, Vol. 9 (1993) 63–64.

Chapter 9 – Ships and Atlantic Crossings

1 *NAS* CS 96/162: Sequestration papers for the estate of James MacAlpin, Vol. 2, 15–6. Letter, George Dempster to James MacAlpin (c. 1823) Vol. 1, 20, 128, 130.

2 E504/12/6; *QM*, Sept. 9, 1817. The *Ardgour* was jointly owned by James MacAlpin and John Wilson. Because MacAlpin was also a shipbuilder, her timber cargo may have been destined for his shipyard, although there is no record of her return in the Fort William customs records.

3 *Lloyd's Shipping Register*. See Appendix III for a further explanation of the Lloyd's Shipping Codes. A snow is a two-masted vessel with square rigging on both masts, but with a small triangular sail mast stepped immediately towards the stern of the main mast.

4 Oliver Macdonagh, *The Passenger Acts*, 54–62.

5 The *Lloyd's Shipping Register* is available as a regular series from 1775 apart from the years 1785, 1788 and 1817.

6 Still in use today and run by a Classification Society with a worldwide network of offices and administrative staff, the *Lloyd's Register* continues to provide standard classifications of quality for shipbuilding and maintenance.

7 The number of years that a ship could hold the highest code varied according to where it was built. In time, rivalries developed between shipowners and under-writers, and this led to the publication of two Registers between 1800 and 1833 – the Shipowners Register (Red Book) and the Underwriters Register (Green Book). Their coverage was similar but not identical. By 1834, with bankruptcies facing both sides, the two Registers joined forces to become the *Lloyd's Register of British and Foreign Shipping*.

8 To locate a ship's code from the *Register*, it is usually necessary to have the vessel name, the tonnage and/or captain's name. Such data is not always available and is highly problematic to locate. Some vessels may not have been offered for inspec-tion, particularly in cases where a shipowner could rely on his personal contacts for business. The lack of a survey might arouse our suspicions but is not neces-sarily conclusive proof of a poor quality ship.

9 According to the ratings: A – first class condition, kept in the highest state of repair and efficiency and within a prescribed age limit at the time of sailing; AE – "the second description of the first class," fit, no defects but may be over a prescribed age limit; E – second class, although unfit for carrying dry cargoes, were suitable for long distance sea voyages; I – third class, only suitable for short voyages (i.e. not out of Europe). These letters were followed by the number 1 or 2 which sig-nified the condition of the vessel's equipment (anchors, cables and stores). Where satisfactory, the number 1 was used, and where not, 2 was used. George Blake, *Lloyd's Register of Shipping 1760–1960* (London: Lloyd's, 1960) 12–13, 26–27.

10 The physical characteristics of a vessel greatly affected sailing performance as well as passenger comfort and safety. For an analysis of the different types of Aberdeen-registered vessels which were used to take emigrants to North America, see Campey, *"Fast Sailing and Copper-Bottomed,"* 80–98.

11 The *Aberdeenshire* carried a total of 246 passengers between 1827 and 1835, while the *Albion* carried a total of 522 passengers between 1829 and 1850.

12 Some people used Halifax as a convenient route for getting to the United States.

It was, in fact, the cheapest route to the United States from Britain. Thus, a significant proportion of Halifax arrivals are unlikely to have remained in Nova Scotia. Philip Buckner "The transformation of the Maritimes: 1815–60," *The London Journal of Canadian Studies*, Vol. 9 (1993) 18–9.

13 Some two hundred and thirteen ships were involved in the three hundred and thirty-one crossings, identified in this study. While a regular trader like the *Albion* of Aberdeen (266 tons), made 25 crossings with emigrants, vessels like the *Osprey* of Leith (382 tons), the *Pacific* of Aberdeen (402 tons) and *St. Andrew* of New Brunswick (553 tons) carried emigrants to Nova Scotia or Cape Breton on only one occasion (see Appendix III).

14 Occasionally, some agents did deliberately mislead and exploit emigrants, but they were a minority. Such people did no repeat business.

15 *AR*, Oct. 16, 1819; E.504/35/2.

16 *IJ*, Nov. 23, 1820, *IJ*, Jan. 30, 1824; E.504/1/26; E.504/7/5; Martell, *Immigration, Nova Scotia, 1815–38*, 40; *QM*, Oct. 19, 1821; *QM*, Oct. 7, 1823.

17 "Account of a Voyage from Aberdeen to Quebec," by William Shand, in George A. MacKenzie, *From Aberdeen to Ottawa in 1845: The Diary of Alexander Muir* (Aberdeen: Aberdeen University Press, 1990) 113–6.

18 PRO CO 384/67, 235–36: Archibald McNiven, Emigration Agent, Tobermory, to Lord John Russell, Jan. 19, 1841; PRO CO 217/154 p.877: Archibald McNiven to Lord Goderich, April 5, 1832.

19 PRO CO 384/15, 503: Archibald McNiven to Lord Bathurst, April 3, 1827.

20 NAS GD 263/63/2/54.

21 Martell, *Immigration to Nova Scotia, 1815–38*, 76.

22 *PP*, Quebec Immigration Agent's weekly reports, w/e Sept. 10, 1836.

23 For example, the advertisement for the *Harriet*, which was due to sail to Quebec in the summer of 1844. IJ, June 21, 1844.

24 Campey, *"Fast Sailing and Copper-Bottomed,"* 63–5, 67–9.

25 *Pictou Observer*, June 23, 1840.

26 *Ibid*, June 21, 1842. The commendation was signed by James Sutherland, John Gunn, William Jack, Hugh Craigie and George Ross.

27 *Halifax Times*, Aug. 22, 1843.

28 NAS RH1/2/908: *Mechanic and Farmer*, July 28, 1841. The *Mechanic and Farmer* was "devoted to the advancement of agriculture and the useful arts in the Colonies of Nova Scotia, Cape Breton, Prince Edward Island and New Brunswick.. neutral in politics and religion."

29 *Ibid*.

30 *Ibid*.

31 *Halifax Times*, Aug. 22, 1843.

32 PP, Quebec Immigration Agent's Report, w/e September 16, 1843.

33 DCA: Poster giving notice of the sailing of the *George*, from Dundee, under Captain Francis Hanley, on 27th May. No date was given, but details given in the poster strongly suggest that it was produced in 1843.

34 Report from the Select Committee on the Passenger Acts 1851, XIX, A911, A5054–5065.

35 *Pictou Observer*, Sept. 6, 1842.

36 *JJ* article in *IJ* July 1, 1842. Between 1840 and 1845, MacLennan and Sutherland arranged transport for nearly 3,000 emigrants in 19 vessels. PRO CO 384/77 ff. 461–69: Memorial to the Colonial Office from John Sutherland, Wick, 1846. The partners supplied 3 vessels in 1840 (369), 6 in 1841 (1037), 3 in 1842 (566), 3 in 1843 (416), 2 in 1844 (188) and 2 in 1845 (142). The numbers in parentheses are passenger totals.

37 *AJ*, June 29, 1836. The letter was signed by John Dickie, James Morrison, Joseph Elmsly, J. N. MacLean, William Primrose, John Duncan and George Nicol, on behalf of 49 passengers.

38 On "the following Sabbath" prayers of thanksgiving were said by one hundred worshippers, both Protestant and Catholic, "in an unfinished, unconsecrated Episcopal Church" in Arichat. Johnston, *Catholic Church in Eastern Nova Scotia*, Vol. II, 10.

39 The *Isabella* had taken 118 miners from Greenock to Pictou in 1839. She made seven crossings in all, from 1837 to 1842, taking nearly 600 passengers. MacLaren, *Pictou Book*, 121–2. Martell, *Immigration to Nova Scotia, 1815–38*, 86–7

40 Although the emigrants received a hostile reception from local residents, they were given a "substantial Nova Scotia supper" at the Royal Oak when they got to Pictou. Flewwelling, "Immigration to and emigration from Nova Scotia, 1839–51," 84.

41 NAS CS 96/1592: Captain Thomas' Log Book, barque *Isabella* of Glasgow.

42 SRO GD 46/13/184: Information published by His Majesty's Commissioners for Emigration respecting the British Colonies in North America (London, Feb., 1832) 6–7.

43 ACA CE 87/11, Advertisements in: *IJ*, June 1821, May 27, 1831, April 1833, May 31, 1833.

44 The 38 "passengers and heads of families," who arrived at Canso on the *Corsair* of Greenock recorded their gratitude to the captain and chief mate "for their unremitting attention to us." *IJ*, May 27, 1831. Martell, *Immigration Nova Scotia, 1815–38*, 58, 66, 70, 90.

45 For example, Donald MacCrummer, an emigration agent based in Skye, told the Colonial Office, in 1816, that the "kilted heroes of Waterloo" could not afford his fares at £6 or £7, but if the tonnage restrictions were reduced from 2 tons per passenger to 1 ton per passenger, he could reduce his fares to what they can afford—£4 or £5. PRO CO 42/170, 362.

46 *Dumfries Weekly Journal*, April 15, 1817.

47 NSARM RG1 Vol. 336, Doc. 48: John G. Marshall to R.D. George, Sept. 9, 1828.

48 Patterson, *History of Pictou County*, 431–5. Captain George McKenzie (1798–1876) built the 632-ton *Sesostris* in 1840, which carried over 300 emigrants from Glasgow to Quebec in 1851. NSARM RG12 A1 Vol. 294: Pictou Shipping Registers; *QM*, July 12, 1851.

49 George E.G. MacLaren, *Ship Building on the North Shore of Nova Scotia* (Halifax: Dec. 1962).

50 James Cameron, *Pictou County's History* (Kentville, N.S.: Kentville Pub. Co. Ltd., 1972) 73.

51 For example, Guillet reports commentators who claim that emigrant ships had worse conditions than those used in the slave trade. Edwin C. Guillet, *The Great Migration: The Atlantic Crossing by Sailing Ships Since 1770* (Toronto: University of Toronto Press, 1963) 12–3, 67–8.

CHAPTER 10 – THE SCOTTISH LEGACY

1 Mackenzie, "First Highland Emigration," 141.

2 The first passenger list, produced in around 1820 by William MacKay, was published in MacLaren, *The Pictou Book*, 31–4.

3 Campbell and MacLean, *Beyond the Atlantic Roar*, 84–6, 285–7.

4 Johnston, *History of the Catholic Church in Eastern Nova Scotia*, 157.

5 *Ibid*, 160–5, 300–4.

6 See the genealogical tracings in MacDonald's *Mabou Pioneers*. A smaller number of settlers had come from the Hebridean Islands, especially Barra.

7 Johnston, *History of the Catholic Church in Eastern Nova Scotia*, 216–7.

8 Kenneth MacKinnon, "Cape Breton Gaeldom in Cross-Cultural Context: The Transmission of Ethnic Language and Culture," in *Occasional Papers Series No. 11* (Hatfield Polytechnic School of Business and Social Sciences, 1983) 34 pgs. In the sample of Scots studied, it was found that Gaelic speakers tended to be most prevalent amongst older people, particularly people aged 65 and over.

9 Maureen Williams, "John MacLean: His Importance as a Literary and Social Personality," A paper read before the Antigonish Heritage Society, Sept. 9, 1985 (8 pgs.).

10 Michael Kennedy, "Lochaber No More: A Critical Examination of Highland Emigration Mythology," in Marjory Harper and Michael E. Vance (eds.), *Myth, Migration and the Making of Memory: Scotia and Nova Scotia, c. 1700–1990* (Black Point, NS & Edinburgh: Fernwood Publishing & John Donald Publishers, 1999) 267–97.

11 Patterson, *Memoir of Rev. James MacGregor*, 183.

12 NAC M-1352: Rev. K.I. MacKenzie to Rev. David Welsh, Nov. 19, 1829.

13 Buckner, *Transformation of the Maritimes*, 24.

14 MacDougall, *History of Inverness County*, 502.

15 Charles William Dunn, *Highland Settler: A Portrait of the Scottish Gael in Nova Scotia* (Toronto: University of Toronto Press, 1953) 54–5.

16 In fact, this trend had its beginnings in nineteenth century Scotland. Seeking a distinctive national identity, Scotland adopted the cultural emblems of its poorest region, the Highlands and Islands. Tartans and other Highland symbols came into vogue and provided an enhanced Scottish identity for the entire country, which was later exported to the New World. T.M. Devine, *The Scottish Nation* (Penguin,

1999) 231–45. The bagpipes had major cultural significance for the first three or four generations of Gaelic settlers in Nova Scotia and Cape Breton. For details of piping traditions in Cape Breton, see John Gibson, *Old and New World Bagpiping* (Montreal: McGill-Queen's University Press, 2002) 193–298. Also see John G. Gibson, *Traditional Gaelic Bagpiping 1745–1945.* (Montreal: McGill-Queen's University Press, 1998).

17 It was an offshoot of the Highland Society in London, founded in 1778, which did a great deal to preserve and rehabilitate these earlier Highland traditions. Thanks largely to its efforts, the wearing of the kilt, which had been banned following the Jacobite uprising of 1745–46, became the accepted national dress of Scotland.

18 Anon., *Constitution and First. Annual Report of the Highland Society of Nova Scotia with a list of Members and Office Bearers for 1839* (Halifax: 1839) 13. Branches were later established at Pictou, Antigonish and Lochaber (Guysborough County).

19 Campbell and MacLean, *Beyond the Atlantic Roar*, 45, 53, 124–5. Rev. McCulloch, who was born in Renfrewshire, emigrated to Pictou in 1803. In 1838, he became the first Principal of Dalhousie College in Halifax.

20 MacDougall, *History of Inverness County*, 502.

21 David Frank, "Tradition and Culture in the Cape Breton Mining Community in the early Twentieth Century," in Kenneth Donovan (ed.), *Cape Breton at 200: Historical Essays in honour of the Island's Bicentennial, 1785–1985* (Sydney, NS: University College of Cape Breton Press) 203–18.

22 Campbell and MacLean, *Beyond the Atlantic Roar*, 64. Dunn, *Highland Settler*, 108–9.

23 NAC MG25 G334: McKenna and MacDonald genealogical tracings.

24 Dunn, *Highland Settler*, 113–4.

25 Cambell and MacLean, *Beyond the Atlantic Roar*, 111.

26 Murdoch, *Cape Breton*, 39–40. While Cape Breton fiddling descended from Scottish fiddling, styles of music and playing have evolved to become quite distinct from their Scottish roots. See Kevin O'Shea, "Cape Breton Fiddle Music as Popular Culture" (105–10) and David Mahalik, "Music as a Living Tradition" (101–4) in C. Corbin and Judith A. Rolls, eds., *The Centre of the World at the Edge of a Continent: Cultural Studies of Cape Breton Island* (Sydney: University College of Cape Breton Press, 1996.)

27 Mackenzie, "First Highland Emigration," 141–2.

28 *Ibid*, 142.

BIBLIOGRAPHY

Primary Sources (Manuscripts)

Aberdeen City Archives (ACA)
CE 87/11: Register of Ships, Aberdeen.
Dundee City Archives (DCA)
CE 70/11: Register of Ships, Dundee.
National Archives of Canada (NAC)
M-1352, M-1353, M-1354: Glasgow Colonial Society Correspondence, 1829–37 (microfilm reels)
MG25: Family Genealogies.
MG31-B4: Henry R. Beer Collection.
National Archives of Scotland (NAS)
CE 57/11: Register of Ships, Leith.
CS 96/154: William Liddell and Company merchants, Sederunt Books (1829–34).
CS 96/162: Sequestration papers for the estate of James MacAlpin, Vol. 2.
CS 96/1592: Log Book, Barque *Isabella* of Glasgow.
CS 96/3355: Log Book, Ship *North Star*.
E.504: Customs records, collectors quarterly accounts, 1776–1830
/1 Aberdeen, /2 Alloa, /5 Banff, /7 Thurso, /9 Dumfries, /11 Dundee, /12 Fort William, /15 Greenock, /17 Inverness, /22 Leith, /25 Oban, /33 Stornoway, /35 Tobermory.
GD 46: Seaforth Papers.
GD 46/13/184: Information published by His Majesty's Commissioners for Emigration respecting the British Colonies in North America (London, Feb., 1832).
GD 139: Sutherland of Forse Papers.
GD 174: MacLean of Lochbuy Papers.
GD 201: Clanranald Papers.
GD 221: Lord MacDonald Papers.
GD 248: SeaField Papers.
GD 263: Heddle Papers.
GD 316: Matthew of Gourdiehill Papers.
GD 403: MacKenzie Papers.
RH 1/2/908: *Mechanic and Farmer*, Pictou. N. S., 28 July, 1841.

RH 2/4: Accounts of the Exports and Imports of the Provinces of North America, 1800–1827.

RH2/4/87 ff. 66–75 Passenger Lists, *Sarah* of Liverpool and *Dove* of Aberdeen, 1801.

RH4/188/2: Prize Essays and Transactions of the Highland Society of Scotland, Vol. iii, 1802–03.

National Library of Scotland (NLS)

MS 1053 ff.104–9: Passenger List, *Commerce*, 1803.

MS 9646: "On Emigration from the Scottish Highlands and Islands attributed to Edward S. Fraser of Inverness-shire (1801–04)."

MS2543: Lithgow Papers.

SP Dep 313: Sutherland Collection.

Nova Scotia Archives and Records Management (NSARM)

MG1: Papers of Families and Individuals.

MG7: Log Books, Ships and Shipping.

MG9: Miscellaneous.

MG100: Miscellaneous.

RG1: Bound Volumes of Nova Scotia Records.

RG5: Records of the Legislative Assembly.

RG12 A1 Vols 294–97: Pictou Shipping Registers.

RG 18: Immigration and Ship Passenger Lists.

Public Archives of Prince Edward Island (PAPEI)

MSS 2702: Passenger Lists, *Elizabeth and Anne*, *Spencer* of Newcastle, *Humphreys* of London and *Isle of Skye* of Aberdeen, 1806.

MSS 2704/4: 'Early British Emigration to the Maritimes. List of vessels carrying Scottish emigrants to the Maritimes' compiled by Mary Brehaut (1960).

RG9 #9: Collector of Customs, 1790–1847.

Public Record Office (PRO)

CO42: Correspondence, Canada.

CO 217: Nova Scotia and Cape Breton Original Correspondence.

CO 384: Colonial Office Papers on emigration containing original correspondence concerning North American settlers.

CO 700: Colonial Office Maps and Plans..

T 47/12: Passenger lists, *Lovelly Nelly* 1774–75.

Strathclyde Regional Archives (SRA)

CE 59/11: Register of Ships, Glasgow.

T/CN 26: Clyde Bills of Entry.

TCN-21: Shipping Report Books, Glasgow.

Printed Primary Sources and Contemporary Publications

Anon, *A General Description of Nova Scotia*, (Halifax, Clement H. Belcher, 1825)

Anon., *Constitution and FirSt. Annual Report of the Highland Society of Nova Scotia with*

BIBLIOGRAPHY

a list of Members and Office Bearers for 1839 (Halifax, Nova Scotia, 1839)

Anon., *Sketch of Missionary Proceedings at Cape Breton from August 1833 to September 1836 (1833–36)* [Thomson Collection in Aberdeen University Library].

Bouchette, Joseph, *The British Dominions in North America: a Topographical and Statistical Description of the Provinces of Lower and Upper Canada, New Brunswick, Nova Scotia, the Islands of Newfoundland, Prince Edward Island and Cape Breton*, Vol. II (London: H. Colburn & R. Bentley, 1832).

Brown, Richard, *A History of the Island of Cape Breton* (London: Sampson Low, Son and Marston, 1869)

Brown, Robert, *Strictures and remarks on the Earl of Selkirk's observations on the present state of the Highlands* (Edinburgh: Abemethy & Walker, 1806).

Douglas, Thomas, Fifth Earl of Selkirk, *Observations on the Present State of the Highlands of Scotland, with a view of the causes and probable consequences of emigration*, 1805 in Bumsted, J. M. (ed.), *The Collected Writings of Lord Selkirk*, Vol. I (Winnipeg: The Manitoba Record Society, 1984).

Census of Cape Breton, 1838.

Free Church of Scotland, *Report Presented to the Colonial Committee of the Free Church of Scotland on Canada and Nova Scotia by Rev. Dr. Burns, Paisley, one of the Deputies of the Free Church to America* (1844) [Thomson Collection in Aberdeen University Library].

Glasgow Colonial Society, *Eighth Annual Reports of the Glasgow Colonial Society for promoting the religious interests of the Scottish settlers in British North America* (Glasgow: 1835).

Haliburton, Thomas Chandler, *An Historical and Statistical Account of Nova Scotia*, 2 Vols. (Halifax: J. Howe, 1829).

Longwith, Israel, *History of Colchester County, Nova Scotia* (Truro: The Book Nook, 1989 [originally published c. 1886]).

Lloyd's Shipping Register 1775–1855.

MacDonald, R.C., *Sketches of Highlanders; with an Account of their Early Arrival in North America; Their advancement in agriculture and some of their distinguished military services in the war of 1812* (Saint John, N.B.: Henry Chubb & Co., 1843).

MacKenzie, Alexander, "First Highland Emigration to Nova Scotia: Arrival of the Ship *Hector*," *The Celtic Magazine*, Vol. VIII (1883) 141–4.

McLeod, Donald, *History of the Destitution in Sutherlandshire* (1841) [King Collection in Aberdeen University Library].

Patterson, George, *History of the County of Pictou, Nova Scotia* (Montreal: Dawson Bros., 1877).

Patterson, Rev. George, *Sketch of the Life and Labours of the Rev. John Campbell of St. Marys, Nova Scotia* (New Glasgow: S. M. McKenzie, 1889).

Patterson, George, *Memoirs of the Rev. James MacGregor* (Philadelphia: Joseph M. Wilson, 1859).

Sinclair, Sir John, *First Statistical Account of Scotland*, 21 vols. (Edinburgh, 1791–99).

Telford, Thomas, *A Survey and Report of the Coasts and Central Highlands of Scotland* (London, 1803).

BIBLIOGRAPHY

White, Patrick Cecil Telford, (ed.) *Lord Selkirk's Diary 1803–04; A journal of his travels through British North America and the Northeastern United States* (Toronto: The Champlain Society, 1958).

Wilson, Isiaiah W., *A Geography and History of the County of Digby, Nova Scotia* (Belleville: Mika Studio, 1972 [originally published by the author in 1893])

Witherspoon, John, *The Works of John Witherspoon, D.D.*, Vol III, *Essays and Sermons* (Edinburgh: Ogle & Aikman, 1805)

PARLIAMENTARY PAPERS

Annual Reports of the Immigration Agent at Quebec (1831–55).

Colonial Land and Emigration Commissioners, Annual Reports (1841–55).

Emigration Returns for British North America 1830–40.

Report from the Commissioners appointed for inquiring into the Administration and Practical Operation of the Poor Laws in Scotland, 1844; Answers to Questions 30–32 in the Appendices.

Report from the Select Committee on the Passenger Acts 1851, XIX.

Reports from the Select Committee appointed to inquire into the expediency of encouraging emigration from the United Kingdom, 1826, IV; 1826–27, V.

Report from the Select Committee appointed to enquire into the condition of the Population of the Highlands and Islands of Scotland, and into the practicability of affording the People relief by means of Emigration, 1841, VI.

NEWSPAPERS

Aberdeen Herald
Aberdeen Journal
Acadian Recorder
Caledonian Mercury
Cape Breton Advocate
Colonial Patriot
Dumfries and Galloway Courier
Dumfries Weekly Journal
Dundee Courier
Edinburgh Advertiser
Greenock Advertiser
Halifax Guardian
Halifax Times

Inverness Courier
Inverness Journal
John O'Groat Journal
Kelso Mail
New Brunswick Royal Gazette
Novascotian
PEI Gazette
Perthshire Courier
Pictou Advocate
Pictou Observer
Quebec Gazette
Quebec Mercury
Scots Magazine

SECONDARY SOURCES

Adams, Ian and Somerville, Meredyth, *Cargoes of Despair and Hope: Scottish Emigration to North America 1603–1803* (Edinburgh: John Donald, 1993).

342

BIBLIOGRAPHY

Aitchison, Peter and Andrew Cassell, *The Lowland Clearances: Scotland's Silent Revolution*, *1760–1830* (East Linton, Scotland: Tuckwell Press, 2003).

Albion, Robert Greenhalgh, *Forests and Seapower: The Timber Problems of the Royal Navy 1652–1862* (Cambridge, Mass.: Harvard University Press, 1926).

Bennett, Margaret, *The Last Stronghold: Scottish Gaelic Traditions of Newfoundland*, (Edinburgh: Canongate, 1989).

Bennett, Margaret "Musical Traditions of the Scots in Newfoundland," *The London Journal of Canadian Studies*, vol. 9 (1993).

Binnington, Rev. R. F., "The Glasgow Colonial Society and its work in the development of the Presbyterian Church in British North America 1825–1840" (Toronto, unpublished Th. D. 1960).

Bittermann, Rusty "Economic Stratification and Agrarian Settlement: Middle River in the Early Nineteenth Century" in Kenneth Donovan (ed.) *The Island: New Perspectives on Cape Breton History* (Fredricton: Acadiensis, 1990), 71–95.

Bittermann, Rusty, Robert A. MacKinnon and Graeme Wynne "Of Equality and Interdependence in the Nova Scotian Countryside 1850–70," *Canadian Historical Review* vol. lxxiv (1993), 5–12.

Blake, George, *Lloyd's Register of Shipping 1760–1960* (London: Lloyd's, 1960).

Bolger. F.W.P. (ed.) *Canada's Smallest Province: A History of Prince Edward Island*, (Halifax: Nimbus, 1991).

Brander, Michael, *The Scottish Highlanders and Their Regiments* (Haddington: The Gleneil Press, 1996).

Brock, William R., *Scotus Americanus: A Survey of the Sources for Links Between Scotland and America in the Eighteenth Century* (Edinburgh: Edinburgh University Press, 1982)

Buckner, Phillip and John G. Reid (eds.), *The Atlantic Region to Confederation: A History* (Toronto: University of Toronto Press, 1993).

Buckner, Philip "The Transformation of the Maritimes: 1815–1860," *The London Journal of Canadian Studies*, vol. 9 (1993), 13–30.

Bumsted, J.M., *The Peoples of Canada: A Pre-Confederation History*, vol. 1 (Toronto: Oxford University Press, 1992).

Bumsted, J.M., *The People's Clearance: Highland Emigration to British North America 1770–1815*, (Edinburgh: Edinburgh University Press, 1982).

Bumsted, J.M., 'Scottish Emigration to the Maritimes: A new look at an old theme', *Acadiensis*, vol. 10 (1981) pp.65–85.

Campbell, D.F. and R.A. MacLean, *Beyond the Atlantic Roar: A Study of the Nova Scotia Scots* (Toronto: McClelland & Stewart, 1974).

Campbell, John Lorne (ed.), *The Book of Barra* (London: G. Routledge & Sons, 1936).

Campell, John Lorne, *Canna: The story of a Hebridean Island* (New York: Oxford University Press).

Campbell, J. MacKenzie, *A Highland Community on Bras d'Or* (Cape Breton, 1978).

Campey, Lucille H., *"A Very Fine Class of Immigrants": Prince Edward Island's Scottish Pioneers, 1770–1850* (Toronto: Natural Heritage, 2001).

Campey, Lucille H., *"Fast Sailing and Copper-Bottomed": Aberdeen Sailing Ships and the Emigrant Scots They Carried to Canada* (Toronto: Natural Heritage, 2002).

Campey, Lucille H., *The Silver Chief: Lord Selkirk and the Scottish Pioneers of Belfast, Baldoon and Red River* (Toronto: Natural Heritage, 2003).

Cameron, James, *Pictou County's History* (Kentville, N.S.: Kentville Pub. Co. Ltd., 1972).

Cameron, Viola Root, *Emigrants from Scotland to America 1774–1775* (Baltimore: Genealogical Publishing Co., 1965).

Clark, Andrew H., 'Old World Origins and Religious Adherence in Nova Scotia', *Geographical Review*, vol. l (1960).

Cowan, Helen, *British Emigration to British North America: The First Hundred Years* (Toronto: University of Toronto Press, 1961).

Davis, Ralph, *The Industrial Revolution and British Overseas Trade*, (Leicester: Leicester University Press, 1979).

Davis, S. and L. Niven, "Birchtown: The History and Material Culture of an Expatriate African American Community," in *Moving On: Black Loyalists in the Afro-Atlantic World*, John W. Paulis, ed. (New York: Garland Publishing Inc., 1998) 59–83.

Davis, Stephen A., *Micmac* (Tantallon, N.S.: Four East, 1991).

Devine, T.M., *The Great Highland Famine: Hunger, Emigration and the Scottish Highlands in the Nineteenth Century* (Edinburgh: John Donald, 1988).

Dictionary of Canadian Biography, Vols. V–XIII (Toronto, 1979–85).

Donaldson, Gordon, *The Scots Overseas* (London: Robert Hale, 1966).

Donovan (ed.), Kenneth, *Cape Breton at 200: Historical Essays in Honour of the Island's Bicentennial, 1785–1985* (Cape Breton: University College of Cape Breton Press).

Dunn, Charles William, *Highland Settler: A Portrait of the Scottish Gael in Nova Scotia* (Toronto: University of Toronto Press, 1953).

Flewwelling, Susan Longley (Morse), "Immigration to and Emigration from Nova Scotia 1839–51," *Nova Scotia Historical Society (Collections)*, vol. xxviii (1949), 84–85.

Frank, David, "Tradition and Culture in the Cape Breton Mining Community in the early Twentieth Century," in Kenneth Donovan (ed.), *Cape Breton at 200: Historical Essays in Honour of the Island's Bicentennial, 1785–1985* (Cape Breton: University College of Cape Breton Press), 203–18.

Gibson, John, *Old and New World Bagpiping* (Montreal: McGill-Queen's University Press, 2002).

Gibson, John G., *Traditional Gaelic Bagpiping 1745–1945* (Montreal: McGill-Queen's University Press, 1998).

Gilroy, Marion, *Loyalists and Land Settlement in Nova Scotia* (Halifax: PANS Publication No. 4, 1937).

Graham, Gerald S., *Sea Power and British North America 1785–1820: A Study in British Colonial Policy* (Cambridge, Mass.: Harvard University Press, 1941).

Graham, Ian Charles Cargill *Colonists from Scotland: Emigration to North America 1707–83* (New York: Cornell University Press, 1956).

Gray, Malcolm, *The Highland Economy 1750–1850* (Edinburgh: Oliver & Boyd, 1957).

BIBLIOGRAPHY

Guillet, Edwin C., *The Great Migration, The Atlantic crossing by sailing ships since 1770* (Toronto: University of Toronto Press, 1963).

Harper, Marjory and Michael E. Vance, (eds.) *Myth, Migration and the Making of Memory: Scotia and Nova Scotia, c. 1700–1990* (Black Point, NS & Edinburgh: Fernwood Publishing & John Donald Publishers, 1999).

Harvey, Daniel Cobb (ed.), *Journeys to the Island of Saint John or Prince Edward Island 1775–1832* (Toronto: Macmillan of Canada, 1955).

Harvey, D. C., "Scottish Immigration to Cape Breton," *Dalhousie Review*, vol. xxi (1941).

Hawkins, Marjorie et al., *Gairloch, Pictou County, Nova Scotia* (Oxford, N. S., 1977).

Herman, Arthur, *The Scottish Enlightenment: The Scots Invention of the Modern World* (London: Fourth Estate, 2001).

Hornsby, Stephen J., *Nineteenth Century Cape Breton: An Historical Geography* (Montreal: McGill-Queen's University Press, 1992).

Johnston, Angus Anthony, *A History of the Catholic Church in Eastern Nova Scotia*, (Antigonish: St. Francis Xavier University Press, 1960) 2 Vols.

Kennedy, Michael, "Lochaber no more: a Critical Examination of Highland Emigration Mythology," in Marjory Harper and Michael E. Vance, (eds.) *Myth, Migration and the Making of Memory* (Fernwood & John Donald, 1999), 267–97.

Kincaid, Barbara, 'Scottish Emigration to Cape Breton 1758–1838' (Dalhousie, Nova Scotia, unpublished Ph. D. 1964).

Lawson, Bill, *A Register of Emigrants from the Western Isles of Scotland 1750–1900*, 2 vols. (Harris, 1992).

Lawson, James, *The Emigrant Scots* (Aberdeen: Aberdeen & North East Scotland FHS, 1988).

Lower, Arthur M., *Great Britain's Woodyard: British America and the timber trade 1763–1867* (Montreal: McGill-Queen's University Press, 1973).

McCreath, Peter L. and John G. Leefe, *A History of early Nova Scotia* (Tantallon, N.S.: Four East Pub., 1990).

Macdonagh, Oliver, *A pattern of government growth 1800–1860, The Passenger Acts and their enforcement* (London: Macgibbon & Kee, 1961).

MacDonald, A. D., *Mabou Pioneers, A genealogical tracing of some pioneer families who settled in Mabou district* (Antigonish: Formac Publishing Co., 1957).

MacDonald, Colin S., 'Early Highland Emigration to Nova Scotia and Prince Edward Island from 1770 to 1853', *Nova Scotia Historical Society (Collections)*, vol. xxiii (1936), 41–48.

MacDonald, Colin S., 'West Highland Emigrants in Eastern Nova Scotia', *Nova Scotia Historical Society (Collections)*, vol. xxxii (1959) pp.1–30.

MacDonald, Norman, *Canada, Immigration and Settlement 1763–1841* (London: Longmans & Co., 1939).

MacDougall, John L., *History of Inverness County* (Truro: New Pub. Co. Ltd., 1922).

MacKay, Donald, *Scotland Farewell: The People of the Hector* (Toronto: Natural Heritage, 1996).

MacKenzie, A.M., *The History of Christmas Island* (Cape Breton: 1983).

345

MacKenzie, George A., *From Aberdeen to Ottawa in 1845: The Diary of Alexander Muir* (Aberdeen: Aberdeen University Press, 1990).

MacKinnon, Kenneth "Cape Breton Gaeldom in cross-cultural context: the transmission of ethnic language and culture," in *Occasional Papers Series No. 11*(Hatfield Polytechnic School of Business and Social Sciences, 1983) 34 pgs. MacKinnon, Neil, *This Unfriendly Soil: The Loyalist Experience in Nova Scotia 1783–1791* (Montreal: McGill-Queen's University Press, 1986).

MacLaren, George, *The Pictou Book: Stories of our Past* (New Glasgow, N. S.: Hector Pub. Co., 1954).

MacLaren, George E. G., *Ship Building on the North Shore of Nova Scotia* (Halifax: Dec., 1962).

MacMillan, A. J., *To the Hill of Boisdale: A short history and genealogical tracing of the pioneer families of Boisdale, Cape Breton and surrounding area* (Sydney: the author, 1986).

MacNeil, S.R., *All Call Iona Home* (Antigonish: Formac Pub. Co., 1979).

MacNutt, W.S., *The Atlantic Provinces; the emergence of Colonial Society 1712–1857* (London: Oxford University Press, 1965).

MacPhie, J. P., *Pictonians at Home and Abroad* (Boston: Pinkhan Press, 1914).

MacQueen, Malcolm, *Skye Pioneers and the Island* (Winnipeg: Stovel Co., 1929).

Mahalik, David, "Music as a Living Tradition" in C. Corbin and Judith A. Rolls (eds.), *The Centre of the World at the Edge of a Continent: Cultural Studies of Cape Breton Island* (Sydney: University College of Cape Breton Press, 1996) 101–4.

A Map of the Province of Nova Scotia Canada (Halifax: Province of Nova Scotia and Formac Pub. Co., 1992).

Martell, J.S., "Early Coal Mining in Nova Scotia" in MacGillivray, Don and Brian Tenyson (eds.) *Cape Breton Historical Essays* (Sydney: College of Cape Breton Press, 1981).

Martell, J.S., *Immigration to and Emigration from Nova Scotia 1815–1838* (Halifax: PANS 1942).

Mathews, Hazel C., *The Mark of Honour* (Toronto: University of Toronto Press, 1965).

McDougall, Elizabeth Ann Kerr and John S. Moir (eds.), *Selected Correspondence of the Glasgow Colonial Society, 1825–1840* (Toronto: The Champlain Society, 1994).

McPherson, Flora, *Watchman Against the World: The Remarkable Journey of Norman McLeod and his People from Scotland to Cape Breton island and New Zealand* (Cape Breton: Breton Books, 1993).

Meyer, D. Vane, *The Highland Scots of North Carolina, 1732–1776* (Chapel Hill: University of North Carolina Press, 1961).

Miller, Thomas, *Historical and Genealogical Record of the First Settlers of Colchester County* (Belleville: Mica Studio, 1972).

Moir, John S., *Enduring Witness: A History of the Presbyterian Church in Canada* (Toronto: Presbyterian Church in Canada, 1975).

Moir, John S., *The Church in the British Era: From the British Conquest to Confederation* (Toronto: McGraw-Hill Ryerson, 1972).

Morgan, Robert, *Early Cape Breton: From Founding to Famine 1784–1851* (Nova Scotia: Breton Books, 2000).

Morse, Susan Longley, "Immigration to Nova Scotia 1839–51" (Dalhousie, Nova Scotia, unpublished M.A. 1946).

Murdoch, Steve, "Cape Breton: Canada's 'Highland Island'?," *Northern Scotland*, Vol. 18 (1998).

Nicholson, John, et al., *Middle River: Past and Present History of a Cape Breton Community 1806–1985* (Cape Breton, 1985).

Orlo, J. and Fraser D., 'Those Elusive Immigrants, Parts 1 to 3', *Island Magazine*, No. 16 (1984), 36–44, No. 17 (1985), 32–7, No. 18 (1985), 29–35.

O'Shea, Kevin, "Cape Breton Fiddle Music as Popular Culture" in C. Corbin and Judith A. Rolls (eds.), *The Centre of the World at the Edge of a Continent: Cultural Studies of Cape Breton Island* (Sydney: University College of Cape Breton Press, 1996) 105–10.

Parette, Henri-Dominique, *Acadians* (Tantallon, N.S.: Four East, 1991).

Parker, John P., *Cape Breton Ships and Men* (Toronto: George J. McLeod Ltd, 1967).

Parker, Mike, *Woodchips and Beans: Life in the Early Lumber Woods of Nova Scotia*, (Halifax: Nimbus Pub. Ltd., 1992).

Patterson, George, *More Studies in Nova Scotian History* (Halifax: Imperial, 1941).

Penzer, N.M., *Paul Storr: The Last of the Goldsmiths* (London: Batsford, 1954).

Prebble, John, *The Highland Clearances* (London: Penguin, 1969).

Punch, Terrance M., "Scots Settlers to Long Point, 1816," *Nova Scotia Genealogist*, Vol. 2(1984).

Rankin, D. J., Rev., *A History of the County of Antigonish, Nova Scotia* (Belleville, Ont.: Mika Publishing, 1972 [original published 1929]).

Reid, John G. "The Conquest of Nova Scotia; Cartographic Imperialism and the Echoes of a Scottish Past" in Ned C. Landsman (ed.), *Nation and Province in the first British Empire: Scotland and the Americas, 1600–1800* (Lewisburg, PA: Bucknell University Press, 2001) 39–59.

Richards, Eric, *A History of the Highland Clearances: Emigration, Protest, Reasons* (London: Berlinn Ltd., 1985).

Rinn, Jacqueline, "Factors in Scottish Emigration: A study of Scottish participation in the indentured and transportation systems of the New World in the seventeenth and eighteenth centuries" (Aberdeen University, unpublished Ph. D. 1979).

Robertson, Barbara, *Sawpower: Making Lumber in the Sawmills of Nova Scotia*, (Halifax: Nimbus Pub. Ltd., & the Nova Scotia Museum, 1986).

Rolph, Thomas, *Emigration and Colonization; Embodying the Results of a Mission to Great Britain and Ireland during the years, 1839, 1840, 1841 and 1842* (London, 1894).

Sager, Eric with G. E. Panting, *Maritime Capital: The Shipping Industry in Atlantic Canada 1820–1914* (Montreal: McGill-Queen's University Press, 1990).

Sherwood, Roland H., *Pictou Pioneers* (Windsor N.S.: Lancelot Press, 1973).

Shortt, A. and Doughty, A. G. (Ed.), *Canada and its Provinces: A History of the Canadian people and their institutions. by one hundred associates* (Toronto: Publishers Association of Canada, 1913–17).

Smith, D., "From Swords to Ploughshares: The Context for Scottish Soldier Settlement in Central Nova Scotia 1749–1775" (Saint Mary's University, Nova Scotia, unpublished MA Thesis, 2003).

Stanley, Laurie, *The Well-Watered Garden: The Presbyterian Church in Cape Breton 1798–1860* (Sydney, C.B.: University College of Cape Breton Press, 1983).

Sutherland, George R., *The Rise and Decline of the Earltown Community, 1813–1970* (Colchester Historical Society and Colchester Historical Museum, 1980).

Syrett, David, *Shipping and the American War 1775–83: A Study of British Transport Organisation*, (London: Athlone Press, 1970).

Walker, James W. St. G., *The Black Loyalists: The Search for a Promised Land in Nova Scotia and Sierra Leone, 1738–1870* (Toronto: University of Toronto Press, 1992).

Warburton, A.B., *History of Prince Edward Island* (St. John, N.B., 1923).

Williams, Maureen "John MacLean: His Importance as a Literary and Social Personality," A paper read before the Antigonish Heritage Society, Sept. 9, 1985 (8 pgs.).

Wilson, Isaiah W., *A Geography and History of the County of Digby, Nova Scotia* (Belleville: Mika Studio, 1972 [originally published by the author in 1893])

Wright, Esther Clark, *The Loyalists of New Brunswick* (Fredericton, N.B., 1955).

Wynn, G., 'A Region of Scattered Settlements and Bounded Possibilities: North eastern America 1775–1800', *Canadian Geographer*, Vol. 31 (1987).

Wynne, Graeme, *Timber Colony: an Historical Geography of early Nineteenth Century New Brunswick* (Toronto: University of Toronto Press, 1981).

INDEX

Aberdeen Harbour, 178

Aberdeen (Scotland), 55, 63, 88, 89, 110, 112, 131, 167, 170, 176, 178, 235, 240–250, 252, 255, 257–261, 263, 268, 271, 273, 274, 276, 278, 280, 281, 283, 285–290, 293–296, 298, 312, 318

Aberdeen Herald, 342

Aberdeen Journal, 240, 243

Aberdeen Rope and Sail Company, 266

Aberdeenshire (Scotland), 185

Acadia, Arcadian(s), 5, 304, 306, 316

Acadian(s), 4, 6, 71, 73, 191, 304, 306

Acadian deportation, 5, 6

Acadian Recorder, 169, 251

Adelaide (Australia), 112

Ainslie, George Robert (Major-Gen.) (Lieut. Gov.), 103

Albion Mines (New Glasgow), 125, 126, 139, 142, 275, 276, 325

Alexander, William (Earl of Stirling), 4

Allen, William (Leith ship broker agent), 132, 170, 171, 247, 250, 253, 260, 261, 263, 264, 266, 271

Alloa (Clackmannan), 251, 255, 283, 291

Alma (Nova Scotia), 110

American War of Independence (1775–1783), 6, 33, 36, 40, 42, 50, 54, 61, 63, 80, 81, 310, 311, 313

Anderson, Andrew, 47, 49

Andersons Mountain (Nova Scotia), 47, 49, 76

Anglican Church Missionary Society, 330

Annapolis, County of (Nova Scotia), 42, 48, 237

Annapolis Valley (Nova Scotia), 42

Anti-Burghers, 330

Antigonish County (Nova Scotia), 13, 48, 50, 53, 58, 60, 63, 66, 67, 73, 98, 99, 127, 129, 137, 138, 183, 184, 237

Antogonish Harbour, 50, 99, 127

Antigonish Highland Society Monument, 189

Antigonish (Nova Scotia), 32, 49, 50, 59, 68, 129, 137, 187, 236, 315, 338

Antigonish River, 68

Applecross (Ross-shire), 104, 106, 114

Arbuckles, Charles, 46

Ardintoul Bay (Wester Ross), 253

Argyll, Duke of, 333

Argyll Highlanders (74th), 310

Argyll (Scotland), 39, 311, 321, 323

Arichat (Cape Breton), 177

Arisaig (Inverness-shire), 72, 107, 219

Arisaig (Nova Scotia), 7, 59, 61–63, 65, 81, 99, 101, 127, 129, 184, 314

Arran, Isle of, 39

Aspy Bay (Cape Breton), 178, 328

Assynt (Sutherland), 15, 19, 107, 110, 111, 131, 132, 141, 154, 322, 327

Atlantic Canada, 160

Australia, 112, 333

Baddeck (Cape Breton), 36, 39, 72, 114, 147
Bagpipes, 190, 338
Baillie, John, 47, 49
Baileys Brook (Nova Scotia), 47–49
Ballantyne, David, 46
Baltic Sea, 89
Baltic timber, 87, 88, 306, 317, 318
Banff (Scotland), 19
Barneys River (Nova Scotia), 54, 77, 80, 127, 130, 137
Barra, Isle of, 48, 49, 60, 67, 68, 73, 74, 81, 102, 104, 113, 115, 116, 119, 146, 160, 169, 185, 186, 190, 219, 237, 247, 248, 252, 256, 315, 323, 329, 330, 333, 337
Battle of Culloden (1745–1746), 34, 80
Bay of Bulls, 91
Bay of Fundy, 4, 35, 38, 310
Bay of Islands, 260
Beaton, Alexander, 325
Beaton, Catherine, 106
Beauly (Inverness-shire), 19, 50, 64, 80, 90, 141
Beaver Cove (Cape Breton), 119
Belfast (Prince Edward Island), 14, 104, 105, 149, 273, 309
Benacadie (Cape Breton), 103
Benbecula, Isle of, 116, 119, 160, 169, 218, 256, 323, 330, 333
Ben Bhragaidh (Scotland), 77
Bengal, 134, 216, 327
Berneray, Isle of, 118, 158
Beyond the Atlantic Roar: A Study of the Nova Scotia Scots, xiii
Big Brook (Nova Scotia), 52
Big Pond (Cape Breton), 146
Big River (Nova Scotia), 76
Black Loyalists, 38, 310
Black Refugees, 305, 306

Black River (Nova Scotia), 141
Black, William (Rev.), 42
Blair Atholl (Perthshire), 80
Blue Mountain (Nova Scotia), 90
Boggey, David, 47
Boisdale (Cape Breton), 113, 114, 119, 252
Borders, The (Scotland), 89, 319
Boston (Massachesetts), 26, 42, 142, 275, 277
Boularderie (Cape Breton), 74, 113, 114, 147, 150, 154, 159
Boyd, John, 187
Bradshaw (Bradley), John, 47
Bras d'Or Lake, 68, 73, 74, 81, 102, 103, 105, 107, 113, 114, 117–119, 121, 147, 148, 152, 159, 184, 257, 316, 323
Bridgeport (Cape Breton), 148
Bridgeport Mines, 148, 152
Britain, British, see Great Britain
British Army, 81
British Fisheries Society, 171
British Navy, 65, 86
British North America, 6, 8–10, 24, 30, 32, 35, 44, 82, 87, 116, 132, 156, 160, 175, 182, 305, 318
Broad Cove (Cape Breton), 14, 72, 118, 123, 148, 163, 325
Brown, George, 46, 49
Brown Point (Pictou), 26, 27
Brown, Robert (Factor, Clanranald estates), 313
Brownfield, John, 46
Buchanan, Archibald, 174
Buckie (Banffshire), 182, 307
Buckie Literary Institute, 182
Buittle (Kircudbright), 317

Caithness (Scotland), also see Thurso, 92, 113, 133, 239, 269, 307, 317
Caledonia (Nova Scotia), 99, 138

Caledonian Canal, 257

Caledonian Mercury, 58

Calvin Presbyterian Church (Loch Lomond), 158

Cameron, Alexander, 17, 18, 30

Cameron, Alexander, 51

Cameron, Alexander, 52

Cameron, Angus, 93

Cameron, Ann, 95

Cameron, Archibald, 47

Cameron, Donald, 29, 32

Cameron, Donald, 50, 51, 309

Cameron, Duncan, 51

Cameron, Finlay, 50, 51, 312

Cameron, James, 53

Cameron, John, 51

Cameron, John, 93

Cameron, John, 99

Cameron, Samuel, 50, 51

Cameron, William, 93

Campbell, Angus, 106

Campbell, Donald, 322

Campbell James (Provost) (emigration agent), 24, 242, 249

Campbell, John (Rev.), 138

Campin, William, 47

Canna, Isle of, 58, 78, 146, 250, 314

Canso, see Gut of Canso

Cape Breton Advocate, 158

Cape Breton Fiddler, The, 191

Cape Breton Island: xiii–xvi, 4, 7–15, 17, 32, 36, 38, 39, 45, 55, 60, 62, 63, 66–68, 71, 72, 74, 77, 81, 87, 90, 98–112, 114–124, 140, 142–145, 147–149, 151, 153, 155, 156–163, 165, 166, 173, 177, 181, 183–186, 190, 191, 193, 217, 219, 234, 236, 237, 239, 243, 248, 249, 252, 255–256, 258–260, 264, 266, 268, 270, 271, 273, 276, 280, 282, 284, 289, 291, 295–297, 315, 320, 323, 329, 330, 332, 338

   Acadians, 4–6

   Baronetcy of, 304

coal mines, mining, 7, 39, 68, 330

crop failures, 156, 160, 333

   potato famines, blight, 159–161, 333

Cape Breton Presbytery, 161, 322

Cape d'Or (Nova Scotia), 58

Cape Fear (North Carolina), 307

Cape George (Nova Scotia), 46, 127

Cape North (Cape Breton), 111, 121, 148, 158, 177, 271

Caribou Harbour (Nova Scotia), 76

Carinish, (North Uist), 256, 324

Carmichael, James (New Glasgow shipbuilder), 46, 179, 180

Casket, The (Antigonish newspaper), 187

Catalone (Cape Breton), 121, 159

Catholic, see Roman Catholic

Celtic Magazine, xvi, 182, 183

Census Returns (1871), 59, 148

Chaleur Bay, 293

Chance Harbour (Nova Scotia), 47

Chantry, Francis, 77

Charlottetown (Prince Edward Island), 10, 247, 251, 268, 269, 290

Chatham Township (Lower Canada), 311

Chedabucto Bay (Nova Scotia), 53, 54

Cheticamp (Cape Breton), 123, 316

Chignecto (Nova Scotia), 305

Chisholm, Donald, 52

Chisholm, Donald Jr., 53

Chisholm, John, 50, 51

Chisholm, John, 53

Chisholm, John Jr., 51, 312

Chisholm, Kenneth, 70

Chisholm, Margaret, 64

Chisholm, William, 76

Cholera (on ship crossings), 113, 181

Christmas Island (Cape Breton), 73, 74, 81, 102, 103, 119, 184, 185, 316

Church of Scotland, 14, 25, 110, 129, 137, 149, 152, 306, 330

Churchville (Nova Scotia), 50, 52

Clanranald estate, 57, 59–61, 63, 74, 237, 313

Clark, John (Miramichi), 317

Clark, Mr. (emigration agent), 238

Clark, Robert, 51

Clark, Robert, 53

Clow, John Stevenet, 168

Clyne (Sutherland), 92, 98, 131, 134

Coal mines, 122, 125, 126, 318

Cobequid Bay (Nova Scotia), 40, 49

Cobequid Hills (Nova Scotia), 130, 134

Codroy Valley (Newfoundland), 163

Coigach Peninsula (Wester Ross), 18

Colchester County (Nova Scotia), 13, 23, 60, 76, 90, 92, 98, 129, 134, 183, 185

Coles Brook (Nova Scotia), 46

Coll, Isle of, 106, 107, 114, 147, 156

Colly, John, 47

Colonial Patriot, 258

Colonsay, Isle of, 115

Cooper, Alexander (emigration agent), 270

Copeland, R.S., 46

Cornwall (Upper Canada), 310

Corpach (Scotland), 164

Country Harbour (Nova Scotia), 53

Craigie, Hugh, 335

Creich (Sutherland), 19, 91

Creighton, David, 325

Creighton, Helen, 125

Creighton, Helen (Mrs.), 125, 325

Croick (Ross-shire), 156, 157

Cromarty Bay, 139

Cromarty (Easter Ross), xiv, 89, 92, 139, 140, 170, 174, 214, 216, 226, 235, 241, 242, 244, 249, 251, 260–266, 269, 270, 272–274, 276, 281–290, 293–296, 298, 322, 328

Cullen, Gerrard, 47

Culrain (Easter Ross), 327

Cumberland County (Nova Scotia), 58, 60, 63, 78, 184, 305, 309

Currie, Donald, 324

Currie, Lachlan, 324

Dalhousie College (Halifax), 338

Dalhousie Settlement (Nova Scotia), 90

Daniell, William, 89

Dansey (Dempsey), James, 47

Declaration of American Independence, 25

Denoon, Hugh (J.P.), see Hugh Dunoon

Denys Basin (Cape Breton), 114

Derry (Ireland), 46

Despard, John (Gen.), 74, 316

Dickie John, 336

Digby (Nova Scotia), 40, 42–44, 312

Dingwall (Easter Ross), 26

Dorchester (Nova Scotia), 50

Dornoch Firth, 170

Dornoch (Sutherland), 91, 98, 131, 133, 134, 242, 319

Douglas, Colin, 29

Douglas Township, Hants County, 41

Dudgeon, Thomas, 132–134

Duke of Cumberland's Regiment, 53

Duke of Hamilton's Regiment (the 82nd), 45, 46, 48, 49, 55

Dumfries and Galloway Courier, 235, 244, 246

Dumfries (Scotland), 89, 90, 235, 244, 246, 248, 249, 252, 253, 282, 286, 290, 297, 319

Dumfries-shire (Scotland), 28, 79, 90, 185, 234, 235, 317

Dumfries Weekly Journal, 249, 336, 342

Dunbar, Alexander, 53

Dunbar, Robert, 53

Dunbar, William, 53

Dundee (Angus), 170, 174, 243, 256, 263, 273, 278, 289, 296, 325, 335

Dundee Courier, 342

Dunfermline (Fife), 19

Dunn, Robert, 46
Dunoon, David, 64
Dunoon, George, 236, 237
Dunoon, Hugh (emigration agent), 53, 64–66, 76, 89, 215, 236, 237, 314
Dunrobin Castle, 77
Durness (Sutherland), 19, 81, 239

Eager, William, 126
Earltown (Nova Scotia), 92, 98, 134–137, 185
East Bay (Cape Breton), 147, 158, 325
East Inverness-shire (Scotland), 19, 26, 38, 50, 80, 90, 185, 234
East River (Pictou), 29, 30, 38, 49, 50–52, 64, 66, 76–79, 85, 90, 125, 127–129, 149, 235, 309
Eastern Maritimes, 6, 8–10, 13, 45, 59, 61, 87, 89, 90
Edinburgh Advertiser, 3, 24, 58
Edinburgh Ladies Association, 14, 149–152, 154, 159, 331, 333
Edinburgh (Scotland), 14, 67, 110, 134, 149, 151, 156, 253, 255, 330
Edinburgh University, 150
Eddrachilles (Sutherland), 92, 141
Eigg, Isle of, 58, 60, 63, 146, 273, 314
Elgin Courier, 259
Emigration; xiv, xv, 3, 6, 11, 15–17, 25, 45, 57, 80, 81, 89, 92, 110, 115, 120, 122, 131, 132, 136, 139, 141, 143, 150, 153, 156, 160, 182, 308, 313, 324, 327, 329, 332
    agent(s), agency, 22, 57, 132, 168, 169, 171, 176, 179, 234, 236, 237, 238, 242, 247–249, 251, 253, 254, 260–264, 266, 269, 270, 272–274, 276, 335
    causes, 3, 6–8, 13, 15–17, 57, 80, 115, 127, 131, 139, 141, 308
    financial assistance, 6, 74, 103, 116, 121, 122, 140, 141, 143, 156, 160, 306,
323, 329, 332
    opposition to, xv, 3, 15, 25, 58, 92, 168, 308
    Select Committee, 1826–27, 116, 117, 121, 324
    Select Committee, 1841, 145
Emigration Act, 173
English settlers, 45
Europe, 31, 159
Eves, John, 47
Evictions, see Highland Clearances

Falconer, Alexander, 31
Falkirk, 46
Farquharson, Alexander (Rev.), 152, 331
Farr (Sutherland). 19, 78, 81, 91, 92, 131, 132, 140, 239
Fearn (Ross-shire), 132
Ferdinand, Hardy, 48
Ferret (Gerrard), Robert, 48
Fiddling (music), 190, 191, 338
Field, Robert, 84, 127
Fife, County of (Scotland), 89, 185, 319
Fish Pools, 52
Fisher, John (Major), 307, 312
Fisher's Grant (Nova Scotia), 46–39
Flemming (Fleeman), Thomas, 48
Florida (USA), 313
Folley Lake (Nova Scotia), 328
Foot, John, 47
Forbes, D. (emigration agent), 238
Forbes, John, 52, 53
Forfeited Estates, 26, 80, 308, 317
Fort Augustus (Inverness-shire), 24
Fort George (Inverness-shire), 242, 289
Fort Louisburg (Cape Breton), 81
Fort William (Inverness-shire), xiv, 24, 56, 57, 63, 65, 67, 81, 87, 110, 164, 165, 196, 203, 236, 237, 245, 247, 248, 250, 253, 257, 282, 283, 285, 286, 292, 293, 295, 296, 308, 313, 321, 334

Fortrose (Easter Ross), 242
Fowler, John, 47
Fox Harbour (Nova Scotia), 136, 180, 328
Framboise (Cape Breton), 119, 148, 158, 323
Fraser, Alexander, 29, 34
Fraser, Alexander (MacAndrew), 312
Fraser, Donald, 128
Fraser, Donald A. (Rev.), 149
Fraser, Edward of Reelig, 63
Fraser Highlanders (71st & 78th), 40, 53, 54, 313
Fraser, Hugh, 29
Fraser, Hugh (weaver), 29, 33
Fraser, James, 50, 51
Fraser, James, 51
Fraser, James W. (Rev.), 51
Fraser, John, 46, 47
Fraser, John, 50, 52
Fraser John (Capt.), 4, 49, 55
Fraser, John "Collector," 46
Fraser, Kenneth, 23, 31
Fraser, Simon (Major) (emigration agent), 46, 55–58, 63, 67, 76, 92, 103, 132, 169, 236–238, 247, 248, 313
Fraser, Thomas, 52, 53
Fraser, Thomas Jr., 52
Fraser, William, 52, 312
Fraser, William (Father), 325
Frasers Mountain, 46, 49, 76, 91, 129
Frasers Point (Nova Scotia), 46, 49, 57
Frazer, James (Rev.), 14, 154, 156
Frazer, John, 127
Free Church College, 161
Free Church (Presbyterian), 332, 333
Freedom, British, 47
French River (Nova Scotia), 46, 47, 76, 90, 128

Gabarus Lake (Cape Breton), 158
Gaelic College of Celtic Arts and
Crafts, St. Anns (Cape Breton), 15, 16, 111
Gaelic Language, 13, 14, 54, 75, 112, 129, 134, 136, 150–152, 154, 183, 184, 186–188, 190, 337, 338
Gaelic Magazine, 156, 324
Gairloch Mountain (Cape Breton), 114
Gairloch (Nova Scotia), 92, 110, 132, 134, 136, 319
Gairloch (Ross-shire), 113, 114, 273, 319
Galloway Colony (Nova Scotia), 79
General Mining Association, 122, 126, 148, 162, 325, 330
Georgia (USA), 38, 313
Gerrond, John, 75
Giant's Lake (Nova Scotia), 138, 328
Gibson of Tain Academy, 133
Gigha, Isle of, 39
Gillies, Deffey (James), 46
Gillies, Donald, 69
Gillies, Ewen, 69
Gillis (Prince Edward Island), 116
Glasgow Colonial Society, 54, 149, 150, 306
Glasgow Courier, 167
Glasgow Destitution Committee, 157
Glasgow Herald, 272
Glasgow (Scotland), 19, 20, 24, 25, 46, 78, 83, 112, 140, 142, 151, 152, 156, 180, 193, 227, 231, 232, 236, 261–263, 270, 271, 275–278, 283, 285, 288, 289, 291, 295, 297, 299, 336
Glen Bard (Nova Scotia), 137
Glen Calvie (Ross-shire), 157
Glenelg (Nova Scotia), 99
Glengarry Fencibles, 310
Glengarry (Upper Canada), 310, 311
Glen Moriston (Inverness-shire), 236
Glen Urquhart (Inverness-shire), 90
"Gloomy Forest, The," 186, 315, 328
Golspie (Sutherland), 77, 91, 98, 131, 133
Gordon, Alexander, 48

Gordon, John (Col.) of Cluny, 142, 143, 275, 329, 333

Gore (Nova Scotia), 41

Governor Wentworth's Regiment, 48

Grand Mira (Cape Breton), 268

Grand Narrows (Cape Breton), 73, 81, 82, 102, 103, 148, 316

Grand River (Cape Breton), 107, 119, 121, 148, 158, 323, 325

Grant, Duncan, 64

Grant, James, 23, 29

Grant, James (Sir), 64

Grant, Peter, 51

Grant, William, 70

Gray, Archibald, 24

Great Britain, xiv, 5, 6, 8, 29, 44, 68, 87, 98, 101, 102, 126, 166, 214, 306, 312, 313, 318, 335

Green Hill (Nova Scotia), 76, 99

Greenock Advertiser, 238, 239

Greenock (Scotland), 74, 103, 112, 118, 120, 131, 139, 168, 175, 234, 235, 237–239, 243–248, 251–255, 265, 267, 268, 270, 271, 274, 280–282, 296–298, 308, 336

Grey, Earl (Col. Sec.), 160

Gulf of Mexico, 111

Gulf of St. Lawrence, 68, 239

Gulf Shore (Nova Scotia), 136

Gunn, Alexander, 92

Gunn, John, 335

Gut of Canso, Strait of Canso (Cape Breton), 72, 109, 118, 157, 175, 177, 178, 239, 248, 255, 257, 259, 264, 294, 298, 336

Guysborough County (Nova Scotia), 13, 50, 53, 98, 99, 129, 130, 137, 183, 313, 318, 333

∞

Halifax County, 84, 309, 312

Halifax (Nova Scotia), 10, 22, 29, 42, 48, 68, 88, 89, 91, 113, 120, 131, 167, 168, 176, 178, 235, 239–256, 259–261, 263–268, 270, 273, 276, 280–285, 288–296, 298, 306, 310–312, 314, 317, 319, 325, 332, 334, 335, 338

Halifax Guardian, 331, 342

Halifax Times, 172–174

Hants, County of, (Nova Scotia), 23, 41, 42, 49

Hardwood Hill (Nova Scotia), 76

Harris, Isle of, 107, 111, 114, 118, 120, 121, 145, 146, 158, 185, 323, 324, 330

Harris, John (company agent), 27

Harris, John (Dr.), 24

Harvey, D.C., 12

Harvey, John (Sir), 160

Hawick (Roxburgh), 247

Head Tax, see Immigrant Arrivals

Heads of Households, 322, 324, 328, 333

Hebridean Islands (Hebridean) (Western Isles) xv, 10, 12, 56, 57, 63, 72, 81, 98, 108, 109, 114–116, 118, 143, 153, 156, 160, 163, 169, 219, 236, 254, 307, 308, 311, 321, 337

Hector Heritage Quay (Pictou), 4, 5

Hierlihy, Timothy (Col.), 50, 313

Highland Clearances, xvi, 76–78, 91, 131–133, 141, 153, 157, 322, 327

Highland Dress, 188, 191, 308, 337

Highland Famine (1846-1856), 17

Highland Games, 189

Highland Relief Fund Committees, 156, 332

Highland Society of Edinburgh, 66, 338

Highlander(s), xiv, xv, 6–9, 26, 27, 32–34, 39, 40, 46, 50, 52, 60–62, 72, 74, 75, 78–80, 87, 99, 104, 105, 111, 117, 127, 129, 136–138, 143, 148, 149, 152, 158, 184–186, 188, 190, 235, 308, 309, 313

Highlands and Islands (Scotland), xiii, 7, 9, 23, 56, 57, 63, 67, 90, 100, 110, 115, 120, 141, 146, 147, 159, 163, 176, 184, 236, 337

History of the Highland Clearances, 182
Hopewell (Nova Scotia), 31, 53
Howe, Joseph, 125
Hunter, Robert (emigration agent), 247

∞

Ile Royale (later Cape Breton Island), 6
Ile Saint Jean (later Prince Edward
    Island), 6
Immigrant Arrivals:
    head tax, 139, 141, 143, 275, 329
    quarantine arrangements, 65, 113,
    139, 140, 153
Indentured Servants, 41, 311
Indian Point (Cape Breton), 184
Ingonish (Cape Breton), 148
Innes, Robert, 27, 309
Intervale lands, 29, 79, 99, 138, 317
Inveraray (Argyll), 24
Invergordon (Easter Ross), 260, 276
Inverness (Cape Breton), see Broad
    Cove
Inverness County (Cape Breton), 71,
    118, 157, 254
Inverness Courier, 170, 273
Inverness Journal, 90, 92, 216, 242, 244,
    249, 251–254, 257
Inverness (Scotland), 24, 29, 46, 52, 53,
    63, 128, 171, 183, 241, 242, 257, 259,
    262, 264, 283
Inverness-shire (Scotland), 6, 10, 19, 26,
    29, 38, 50, 60, 64, 65, 67, 72, 76, 80,
    90, 118, 123, 138, 143, 146, 184, 234,
    236, 237, 310, 328
Iona (Cape Breton), 73, 81, 82, 103, 116,
    185
Iona Highland Village, 105, 155
Ireland, 46, 48, 157, 159, 318
Irish settlers, immigrants, 45, 50, 306,
    332
Islay, Isle of, 39, 262, 263, 281
Isle Madame (Cape Breton), 316

Isle Martin (Ullapool), 63, 76, 81, 87,
    110, 236–238, 286, 288, 297
Ives, George, 48
Ives, John, 48

∞

Jack, William, 335
Jacobite Uprising, 1745–46, 308, 317,
    338
Jamieson, John, 303
John O'Groat Journal, 175
Jordan River (Nova Scotia), 40
Judique (Cape Breton), 72, 73, 101, 123,
    148, 316, 325
Jurra, Isle of, 39
Justaucorps (Cape Breton), 123

∞

Keith (Scotland), 84
Kelp, kelp industry, 16, 56, 81, 108, 115,
    153, 306, 313, 321, 323
Kelso Mail, 89, 247, 249, 319
Kelso (Roxburghshir), 247
Kempt, James (Sir) (Lieut. Gov.), 117
Kennedy brothers, 58
Kennetcook (Nova Scotia), 41
Kennetcook River (Nova Scotia), 41, 42
Kerr, John, 322
Kerr, Murdoch, 333
Kildonan (Sutherland), 81, 92, 131
Killearnan (Ross-shire), 64
Kilmorack (Inverness-shire), 19, 64, 312
Kilmuir (Skye), 324
Kiltarlity (Invernesss-shire), 19, 29, 33,
    64, 141
Kincaid, Barbara, "Scottish Emigration
    to Cape Breton, 1758–1838"
Kindersley, Richard, 170
King's Carolina Rangers, 36, 53
King's Casual Revenue, 122
Kings County (Nova Scotia), 23, 29, 314

Kingston (Upper Canada), 271, 310

Kintail (Ross-shire), 105, 106, 114, 115, 217

Kirk, William, 48

Kirkaldy (Fife), 89, 247, 287, 319

Kirkcudbrightshire (Scotland), 28, 79, 234, 235, 317

Kirkhill (Inverness-shire), 19

Knoydart (Inverness-shire), 65

Knoydarat (Nova Scotia), 127, 130

∞

Labrador, 112

Lairg (Sutherland), 78, 91, 98, 131, 132, 134, 239, 330

Lake Ainslie (Cape Breton), 107, 113, 118, 122, 147, 150, 161, 190, 259

Land acquisition:
backlands, 105, 145, 147, 154, 156, 159, 161
petitions for, 68, 235, 241, 243
purchase of, 109, 122, 130, 144, 145, 321, 329
regulations, 68, 72, 102, 109, 122
squatting, 39, 71, 72, 100, 102, 109, 122, 145, 306, 321

Lang, Gavin (Rev.), 43

Landlords, xvi, 3, 16, 56, 313

Largs (Scotland), 151

Lee, Robert, 308

Leitches Creek (Cape Breton), 119, 121, 185, 256

Leith (port of Edinburgh), 55, 88, 89, 131, 132, 170, 217, 219, 238, 243–253, 257, 260, 261, 263, 266, 278, 280–283, 285–288, 290–297, 318, 319

Lewis Cove (Cape Breton), 119

Lewis, Isle of, 78, 136, 146, 152, 160, 276, 277, 323, 327, 329, 330, 333

Liddell, John (Halifax), 317

Liddell, William (Glasgow merchant), 83, 299, 317

Lingan (Cape Breton), 148

Lismore (Nova Scotia), 130

Little Harbour (Nova Scotia), 48, 49

Little River (Nova Scotia), 76

Liverpool, Queens County (Nova Scotia), 30

Lloyd's of London, 165, 166, 278, 279, 280

Lloyd's Shipping Codes, 166, 334

Lloyd's Shipping Register, xv, 31, 166, 234, 278, 280, 309, 334

Loch Broom (Nova Scotia), 17–19, 30, 307

Loch Broom (Wester Ross), 18, 19, 21, 26, 182, 193, 234, 287

Loch Eriboll (Sutherland), 170, 266, 281, 291, 331

Loch Indaal (Islay), 262, 281

Loch Laxford (Sutherland), 140, 174, 229, 272, 273, 275–277, 286, 290

Loch Lomond (Cape Breton), 107, 118, 121, 148, 158, 159, 185, 256, 323

Lochaber (Inverness-shire), 48, 72, 104, 107, 184, 251

Lochaber Lake, 137, 138

Lochaber (Nova Scotia), 99, 338

Lochalsh (Ross-shire), 104, 105, 114, 253, 282

Lochboisdale (South Uist), 67, 237

Lochinver (Sutherland), 111, 140, 154, 249, 281, 284

Lochmaddy (North Uist), 156, 271, 272, 274, 282, 287, 288, 295–297

Logan, George (emigration agent), 92, 242, 244, 319

Loggan, Thomas, 47

London (Ontario), 51

Londonderry (Nova Scotia), 23, 28, 31

Long, Archibald, 47

Long Island (Cape Breton), 72, 107, 243

Long Island (Scotland), 145, 156

Long Point (Cape Breton), 72, 107

Loth (Sutherland), 131, 133, 134

Lothians, The (Scotland), 185
Lovat, Lord (Clan Fraser), 80
Lowlands, The (Scotland), 57, 89, 98, 185
Lowlanders, 88, 131, 188
Low Point (Cape Breton), 72, 101
Loyal Nova Scotia Volunteers, 36, 50, 313
Loyalists (United Empire), 34, 40, 42–45, 50, 53, 54, 65, 68, 71, 72, 81, 114, 129, 306, 310–312
Lyon, James (emigration agent), 241, 242
Lyons Brook (Pictou), 27

Mabou (Cape Breton), 72, 103, 123, 151, 184, 185, 190, 325
MacAlpin, James, 164, 334
MacAulay, Angus (Rev.), 104, 321
MacCrummer, Donald (emigration agent), 336
MacDonald, Alexander (Father), 314
MacDonald, Donald, 29
MacDonald, Donald and Janet, 141
MacDonald, James (agent), 24
MacDonald, James (Father), 314
MacDonald, John of Glenaladale (Capt.), 61
MacDonald, John (Rev.), 259
MacDonald, Lord, 121, 156, 332
MacDonell, Alexander (Father), 123, 316, 325
Macdonnell, Elizabeth, 76
MacEachern, Angus Bernard (Father) (later Bishop of Charlottetown), 7, 58, 62, 63, 99, 123, 184
MacEachern, John, 217, 254
MacGregor, James (Rev.), 7, 32, 54, 62, 187, 317
MacIntosh, Donald, 134
MacIntosh, Donald (Rev.), 129

MacIver, Roderick (emigration agent), 238
MacKay, Alexander, 312
MacKay, Colin, 29
MacKay, Donald, 30
MacKay, Isabella Gordon (Mrs.), 14, 149, 152, 155, 159, 330, 332
MacKay, John, 150, 215, 330
MacKay, Roderick, 29
MacKay, William (later Squire), 19, 21, 29, 33, 78, 193, 337
MacKenzie, Alexander, xvi, 182, 183, 307, 322
MacKenzie, Angus, 23
MacKenzie, Colin, 28, 30
MacKenzie, J. (emigration agent), 238
MacKenzie, Kenneth (Rev.), 136
MacKenzie, Roderick, 104, 105
MacKenzie, William, 20, 28, 30, 53
MacLean, Alexander, 50, 52
MacLean, Hector, 67
MacLean, Hector (Lieut.), 52, 53
MacLean, John (Gaelic Bard), 137, 188, 315, 328
MacLean, Murdoch (Capt.), 42
MacLean, R.A., xiii
MacLennan, Duncan (emigration agent), 171, 173, 174, 262–264, 269, 270, 272, 274, 276
MacLeod, Alexander, 33
MacLeod, Donald, 98
MacLeod, Duncan, 322
MacLeod, Hugh, 21, 31, 32, 307
MacLeod, James, 31
MacLeod, Kenneth, 104, 152
MacLeod, Murdock, 322
MacLeod, Norman (Rev.) (Glaswegian), 156
MacLeod, Roderick, 322
MacLochlan, A. (emigration agent), 248
MacNeil of Canna, 121
MacNeil, Donald, 81
MacNeil, Evin, 81

MacNeil, Hector, 68, 69, 74, 103, 316
MacNeil, John (born Colonsay), 115
MacNeil, John (born Barra), 48, 49, 81, 116
MacNeil, Katherine, 116
MacNeil, Malcolm, 190
MacNeil Monument, 82
MacNeil, Roderick (landlord), 103
MacNiven, Archibald (emigration agent), 139, 169, 217, 219, 254, 269
MacPhie, J.P., 75
Macra (Macrae?), John, 252
Malagawatch (Cape Breton), 114, 147, 159, 323
Malignant Cove (Nova Scotia), 127
Malpeque Bay (Prince Edward Island), 310
Manchester (Nova Scotia), 68, 315
Map of Cabotia…, 44
Margaree (Cape Breton), 72, 101, 122, 123, 148, 152, 159, 163
Maritimes, Maritime region, 14, 35, 36, 82, 84, 86, 183
Maroons (originally from Jamaica), 310
Marsden, Joshua (Rev.), 43
Martin, ___ (Dr.), 172
Maryburgh (Inverness-shire), 24
Marydale (Nova Scotia), 23, 68, 99
Maryland (USA), 24
Matheson, James (Sir), 276, 277, 329
Matheson, William, 23, 31
McCarthy, Hugh, 48
McCauley, John, 151
McCulloch, Thomas (Rev.), 188, 338
McDonald, Alex, 46
McDonald, Alexander, 69
McDonald, Andrew (emigration agent), 237
McDonald, Angus, 48, 67
McDonald, Colin "Cole," 46
McDonald, Donald, 69
McDonald, Donald (of Bann), 48
McDonald, Donald (of Lochaber), 48

McDonald, Donald Jr., 69
McDonald, Duncan, 51
McDonald, James, 69
McDonald, James (Hon.), 51
McDonald, John, 69
McDonald, John, 51
McDonald, John (2nd), 51
McDonald, Hugh, 51
McDonald, Philip, 319
McDonald, Roderick, 69
McDougall, Ann, 106
McDougall, Donald, 48
McDougall, John, 48
McDougall, John, 53, 188
McEachern, Mary, 332
McEichron, Alexander, 69
McEichron, Ewen, 69
McEichron, John, 69
McEichron, Margaret, 69
McGee, B., 46
McGilivray, ___ (Mr.), 79
McGillivary, Angus, 320
McGillivray, Ronald (Father), 314
McGilvray, Angus, 69
McGilvray, Donald, 69
McGilvray, Duncan, 69
McGilvray, John, 69
McGregor, Alex'r, 69
McGregor, David, 78
McGregor, John, 78
McInnes, Angus, Donald and John, 320
McIntosh, Alexander, 53
McIsaac, Margaret, 70
McIvor, ___ (Mr.), 78
McKay, George (emigration agent), 270
McKay's Cove (Nova Scotia), 90
McKelock, Ewen, 70
McKenzie, Alexander, 319
McKenzie, Alexander (emigration agent), 241
McKenzie, ___ (Mrs. John), 51
McKenzie, Neil, 322
McKenzie, Thomas, 52

McKinnon, Alexander, 47
McKinnon, Charles, 48, 49
McKinnon, Donald, 69, 314
McKinnon, Hector, 69
McKinnon, John, 314
McKinnon Point (Cape Breton),115
McLean, Alexander (Inverness-shire), 30, 123
McLean, Allan (Rev.), 101
McLean, David, 52
McLean, Duncan, 320
McLean, Isabella, 123
McLean, Marian, 93
McLellan, Anthony, 79
McLellan, Anthony Sr., 317
McLellan, Donald, 118
McLellan, James, 52
McLellan, John, 30
McLellan, John, 53
McLellan, Neil, 93
McLellan, William, 30
McLellans Brook (Nova Scotia), 30, 31, 100
McLellans Mountain (Nova Scotia), 66, 77, 90, 129
McLennan, John (Rev.), 118, 123, 149
McLennan, Mary, 106
McLeod, Donald, 69, 314
McLeod, Ewen, 69
McLeod, Hugh (Rev.), 159
McLeod, John, 161, 322
McLeod, Neil, 69, 314
McLeod, Norman (Rev.) (from Assynt, Sutherland), 15, 16, 107, 110–112, 148, 154, 161, 162, 249, 322, 327, 333
McMillan, A. (emigration agent), 237
McMillan, Hugh, 99
McMillan, Malcolm, 99
McNab's Cove (Cape Breton), 118
McNeil, Donald, 48
McNeil, Donald (Capt.), 81, 162
McNeil, John, 46
McNeil, John, 47

McNeil, John Jr., 48, 49
McNeil, Matthew, 48, 49
McNeil, Murdock, 48, 49
McNeil, Roderick (carpenter), 113
McNeil, Rory, 69, 81
McNutt, Alexander, 23, 29, 307
McPhail, Donald, 115
McPherson, Donald, 319
McPherson, James, 48
McPherson, John, 48
McPherson, Mary, 118
McQueen, Angus, 48, 49
McRae, Alexander, 106
McRae, Donald, 106
McVarish, Catherine, 123
McVie, William, 47
Meadow Green (Nova Scotia), 68, 99
Meagher, Ellen, 190
Meagher's Grant, 312
Mechanic and Farmer, 173, 335
Meickle Ferry Inn (Sutherland), 133, 327
Melbourne (Australia), 112
Melville, Major, of Ullapool, 238
Merigomish (Nova Scotia), 31, 46, 47, 63, 64, 76, 77, 128, 130
   Harbour, 54, 77, 127, 130
Messrs. MacKintosh & Co., 216
Methodist(s), 42, 43, 49
Middle River (Cape Breton), 14, 104, 106, 114, 147, 150, 152, 159, 185
Middle River (Pictou), 18, 29, 31, 47, 75, 76, 78, 92, 110, 125, 127–129, 132, 134, 317
Middle River Cemetery, 106
Mi'kmaw First Nation (Mi'kmaq), 4, 180, 304, 306, 310
Mill Brook (Nova Scotia), 78, 92, 132, 134
Millar, William (Rev.), 151
Miller, Hugh, 170
Miller, Robert, 47
Minas Basin (Nova Scotia), 5, 41, 42, 58

Minudie (Nova Scotia), 309

Mira (Cape Breton), 158, 159, 324, 332

Mira River, 121, 162

Miramichi (New Brunswick), 167, 243–246, 248, 249, 252, 257, 259, 266, 273, 282, 283, 286, 296–298, 310, 311, 317, 319

Missionaries, see Glasgow Colonial Society

Mitchell, ___ (Rev. Mr.), 90

Moidart (Inverness-shire), 65, 74, 107, 237, 292

Montgomerie Highlanders (77th), 40

Montreal (Quebec), 251, 286, 287, 291, 310

Moorson, William, 138

Morar (Inverness-shire), 65, 118

Moray Firth, 76, 89, 170, 182

Moray, Nairn and Banff Courant, 269

Morayshire, 5

Morison, Alexander, 332

Morison, Flora, 332

Morris, Charles (Survey Gen.), 69

Morristown (Nova Scotia), 127

Mortimer, Edward (Sir) (timber merchant), 8, 83–85, 88, 299, 317, 318

Mortimer's Point (Nova Scotia), 126

Mother of Sorrows Pioneer Shrine, 185

Mount Auburn, 186

Mount Thom (Nova Scotia), 66, 129

Moydart (Nova Scotia), 127

Muck, Isle of, 107, 115, 147

Muirhead, Andrew, 48

Mull Cove (Cape Breton) (later Orangedale), 114, 115

Mull, Isle of, 67, 106, 107, 114–116, 146, 152, 156, 160, 169, 269, 329, 333

Munroe, Donald, 23, 29

Munro, Ernest, 111

Munro, James (Rev.), 40, 42

Munro, John (Cape Breton merchant and shipbuilder), 107, 112, 161, 162

Murchison, Donald, 122, 324

Murison, Alexander (Halifax), 317

Murray, James, 23, 31

Murray, John, 22

Murray, William, 93

Napoleonic Wars (1803–1815), 10, 15, 81, 88, 90, 100, 104, 109, 126, 169, 318

Narrows (Cape Breton), 248, 249

Native Peoples, 4, 5

New Annan (Nova Scotia), 90, 135, 136

New Brunswick, 31, 38, 118, 125, 171, 239, 257, 296, 311, 319

New Brunswick Royal Gazette, 243

New England "Planters," 5

New Englanders, 4, 13, 304

New Glasgow (Nova Scotia), 85, 129, 180, 183, 333

New Jersey (USA), 25, 31, 39, 310

New Lairg (Nova Scotia), 78, 92, 129, 132, 134, 136

New York (New York), 42, 310, 313

New York (USA), 39, 40

New Zealand, 15,110, 112, 162, 322

Newfoundland, 21, 40, 65, 68, 91, 163, 239

Nine Mile River (Nova Scotia), 41, 42, 311

Norman Conquest, 35

North America, 3, 6, 40, 42, 43, 57, 64, 87, 145, 165, 179, 304, 308, 315, 319

North Carolina (USA), 23, 38–40, 81, 307, 308, 311, 313

North Carolina Volunteers, 81, 311

North East Highlands, 170

North Morar (Inverness-shire), 118, 254

North River (Cape Breton), 111, 148, 158

North Uist, Isle of, 107, 116, 118–121, 145, 146, 156, 158, 169, 185, 186, 219, 252, 256, 271, 323, 324, 330, 332

Northumberland Strait, 7, 61, 101, 184
Norway Point (Pictou), 88
Nova Scotia: xiii-xvi, 4–6, 8–10, 13–15,
  17, 18, 23, 24, 29, 32, 33, 35, 36, 38–4,
  44, 45, 51, 55, 56, 60, 61, 63, 66, 67,
  69, 71, 77, 81, 84, 87, 89, 90, 98–100,
  104, 109, 110, 117, 124–127, 129, 131,
  134, 136, 138–141, 143, 149, 160, 161,
  165, 166, 168, 181, 186, 190, 193, 234,
  240, 253, 254, 274–276, 283, 288, 289,
  304, 305, 311–312, 318, 323, 325, 326,
  329, 332, 335, 338
  Acadian deportation, 5, 6
  Baronet of Nova Scotia, 34
  Highland Society, 32
  division (1784), 315
  reintegration of Cape Breton (1820),
    315
  shipbuilding, 180
Nova Scotia Highland Society, 188
Nova Scotia Volunteers, see Loyal
  Nova Scotia Volunteers
Novascotian, 125

Oak River Cemetery (West River), 128
Oban (Argyll), 240, 251, 276, 286, 321
Ochiltree, Lord, 4
Ohio Lake, 99
Ohio (Nova Scotia), 99
Ohio (USA), 111, 320
Oliphant, of Gask, 46
Onslow (Nova Scotia), 23, 307
Orangedale, see Mull Cove
Orwell Bay (Prince Edward Island),
  310
Oswald, George, 7
Outer Hebrides, 78, 107, 111, 114, 145,
  156, 158, 160
Over-crowding, on ships, 66, 120, 165,
  172, 179

Pabbay, Isle of, 158
Pagan, John, 19, 24–26, 31, 80, 234, 287,
  308
Pagan, Robert, 19, 308
Pagan, William, 308
Paisley (Scotland), 24, 25, 27, 151
Parr, John (Lieut. Gov.), 57, 58
Parrsboro (Nova Scotia), 58, 314
Passenger Act (1803), 66, 81, 165, 178,
  314, 315, 317
Passenger lists:
  Alexander of Aberdeen, 217–219
  Commerce, 212–214
  Dove of Aberdeen, 196–202
  Ellen of Liverpool, 229–230
  Hector, 193–196
  Hope of Glasgow, 227–229
  Lady Grey, 226, 227
  London of Glasgow, 231
  Lulan of Pictou, 232, 233
  Malay, 225, 226
  Ossian, 216, 217
  Prince William, 214, 215
  Sarah of Liverpool, 203–212
  St. Lawrence of Newcastle, 219–224
Patterson, Agnes, 70
Patterson, George, 75, 90
Patterson, John, 27, 309
Patterson, Robert, 24, 27
Patterson, Robert, 47
Paussmigh, Louis-Benjamin (Mi'kmaw
  King), 306
Peacock, James, 47
Peebleshire (Scotland), 235
Pennsylvania (USA), 24
Perthshire Courier, 342
Perthshire (Scotland), 36, 80, 138, 152,
  212, 238
Petition of N. McLeod and others, 331
Petitioners of West River (1836), 326

Philadelphia Grant, 21, 25, 32
Philadelphia Land Company, 21,
    23–26, 31, 32, 234, 307, 308
Philadelphia (Pennsylvania), 23, 34, 42,
    235, 285, 308
Pictorians at Home and Abroad, 75
Pictou:
    Academy, 84, 188, 318
    coal mines, 125, 139, 318, 325, 330
    County of, 23, 48, 54, 60, 61, 64, 65,
        72, 76, 77, 80, 85, 86, 90, 92,
        98–100, 102, 128, 129, 130, 141,
        183, 309, 318, 319, 325
    Harbour of, 6, 8, 17, 18, 21, 22, 26,
        27, 29, 30, 32, 45, 46, 49, 54, 56,
        76, 78, 79, 81, 82, 83, 92, 126, 127,
        140, 191, 307
    Town of, xiii, xiv, 3–8, 10, 16–19, 21,
        23–29, 31–35, 37, 38, 45–47, 50, 54,
        57, 58, 62, 63, 65–67, 75, 76, 78,
        83–85, 87, 88, 90–92, 101, 107, 110–
        112, 124, 125–132, 134, 140–143, 160,
        167, 169–173, 176, 178–180, 182–185,
        187, 191, 196, 203, 212, 214–216, 226,
        227, 229, 231, 232, 234–245, 248–
        254, 257–178, 287, 280–290, 292–
        298, 307, 308, 312, 317, 319, 321,
        322, 325, 327, 329–331, 336, 338
Pictou Advocate, 214
Pictou County (Nova Scotia), 13
Pictou Observer, 140, 141, 171
Piedmont (Nova Scotia), 80
Planters, also see New Englander
    Planters, 5
Plaster Cove, see Port Hastings
Plessis, Joseph-Octave (Bishop), 101,
    119, 18
Plockton (Wester Ross), 252, 253
Pomquet River (Nova Scotia), 99, 128
Poor Law Amendment Act, 1845, 16,
    139
Population:
    Cape Breton, 12

Nova Scotia, 10, 38, 305
Port Glasgow (Scotland), 80, 212, 238,
    284, 286, 288
Port Hastings (Cape Breton), 115, 121,
    253, 255, 282
Port Hawkesbury, see Ship Harbour
Port Hood (Cape Breton), 72, 101, 123,
    315, 325
Port Roseway, see Shelburne
Port Royal (French), 304
Portree (Skye), 24, 324
Potato blight, see Cape Breton
Potato famine, see Cape Breton
Presbyterian Church (Scotland), 32, 308
Presbyterian clergymen, 14, 42, 62, 75,
    108, 110, 118, 129, 135, 136, 138, 144,
    149, 151, 159, 187, 188, 330
Presbyterian congregation(s) Presby-
    terian(s), xv, 7, 32, 40, 46, 52, 60, 63,
    65, 67, 75, 98, 104, 105, 113, 114, 119,
    123, 127–129, 136–138, 146–152, 154,
    158–160, 306, 323, 332
Presbyterian missionaries, 14, 43, 54,
    154, 159
Presbyterian Witness, 160
Presbytery of Nova Scotia, 151
Prince Edward Island, 7, 9, 14, 28, 36,
    38, 58, 60, 61, 63, 71, 72, 79, 84, 100,
    104, 105, 115, 116, 121–123, 141, 142,
    149, 156, 184, 234, 235, 236, 239, 247,
    257–259, 261, 264, 269, 270, 275, 276,
    283, 286, 291–293, 298, 309, 315, 319,
    320, 332
Prince Edward Island Gazette, 258
Princeton College (New Jersey), 25, 31
Protestant(s), 32, 59, 104, 107, 113, 114,
    118, 335

Quarantine, see Immigration
Quebec, 140, 148, 164, 165, 170–174,
    178, 219, 226, 235, 239, 240, 246–248,

250, 251, 253–256, 259–264, 266–274, 280–298, 311, 313, 319, 322, 325, 328, 331, 335, 336
Quebec Gazette, 240
Quebec Mercury, 219, 247, 251, 253, 254, 268

Ramsheg (Nova Scotia), 136
Rannoch (Perthshire), 80, 99
Reay (Caithness), 92, 270, 307, 317
Reay Fencibles, 92, 241, 319
Red Islands (Cape Breton), 74, 103
Red River, Colony of, 131
Regiments see, Duke of Cumberland's, Duke of Hamilton's (82nd), Fraser Highlanders, King's Carolina, Loyal Nova Scotia Volunteers, North Carolina Volunteers, Royal Highland, Royal Highland Emigrants (84th)
Religion, 14, 42, 59, 129, 135–18, 147, 151, 152, 184
Rhum, Isle of, 121, 146, 152, 257, 324
Richibucto, (New Brunswick), 252
Ritchie, Peter (emigration agent), 241
River Clyde, The, 21, 38, 55, 82, 87, 142, 180, 196, 258, 271, 275, 284, 292, 319
River Denys (Cape Breton), 114, 115, 147, 151, 323
River Inhabitants (Cape Breton), 73, 101, 123, 325
River John (Nova Scotia), 76, 92, 128, 129, 136
River Maboo (Cape Breton), 152
River Toney (Nova Scotia), 76
Robertson, Alex. (Col.), 46, 49
Robertson, ___ (Col.), 47
Robertson (Robinson), Charles, 47
Robertson, James, 47
Robertson, John, 50, 52, 312
Robertson, William, 52, 53

Robertson's Island (Nova Scotia), 46, 49
Rogart (Sutherland), 91, 92, 98, 131, 132, 134, 135, 140, 239
Rogers Hill (Nova Scotia), 31, 48, 75, 76, 91, 129
Roman Catholic Church, clergymen, 61, 62, 72
Roman Catholic congregations, Roman Catholic(s), xv, 7, 32, 49, 50–52, 57, 59, 60, 63, 65, 66, 67, 72–74, 98, 99, 102, 104, 105, 107, 113, 114, 125, 127, 129, 138, 146–148, 152, 158, 184, 236, 237, 259, 273, 309, 313, 315, 316, 330, 335
Rose, Lewis (Rev.), 139
Ross, Alexander, 28, 30
Ross, Duncan (Rev.), 75
Ross, George, 335
Ross, Janet, see Janet Cameron
Ross, John (emigration agent), 23, 26, 31, 234
Ross-shire (Scotland), 18, 28, 30, 31, 75, 104, 114, 115, 132, 133, 156
Roxburgh (Scotland), 89
Roy, D. (emigration agent), 238
Royal Highland Emigrants Regiment (84th), 40–42, 45, 49, 50–54, 311
Royal Highland Regiment (42nd), 40, 310
Royal North Carolina Regiment, 36, 53
Rundell, Bridge and Rundell, 126
Rutland, Duke of, 305

St. Andrews Channel (Cape Breton), 114, 119, 147
St. Andrews (New Brunswick), 117, 254, 293, 310
St. Andrews (Nova Scotia), 68, 73, 129
St. Andrews, Parish of, 72, 73, 101
St. Andrew's Roman Catholic Cemetery, 101, 113, 123, 316

St. Andrews Society (Nova Scotia), 306

St. Anns Bay, 110

St. Anns, (Cape Breton), 15, 16, 107, 111, 112, 148, 154, 158, 159, 161, 162, 185, 249, 266, 281, 327, 333

St. Augustine Loyalists, 313

St. Columba Church, 52

St. Columba Roman Catholic Cemetery, 116

St. Esprit (Cape Breton), 119, 323

St. George's Channel (Cape Breton), 73, 114, 147, 154, 155, 159, 323, 333

St. John, Island of, later Prince Edward Island, 39, 40, 239, 313

St. John River, 35

Saint John (New Brunswick), 243, 245, 246, 252, 291, 293, 294

St. Lawrence region, 171, 310

St. Lawrence River, 125

St. Margaret of Scotland Church (Arisaig), 65

St. Margaret of Scotland Roman Catholic Cemetery (Broad Cove), 118

St. Margaret, Queen of Scotland, 62

St. Marys Bay (Nova Scotia), 43, 44, 48

St. Marys (Nova Scotia), 130, 138

St. Marys River (Nova Scotia), 99, 130, 138, 318

St. Mary's Roman Catholic church, 130, 146

St. Patrick's Channel (Cape Breton), 114

St. Paul's Island, off Cape Breton, 51, 177

St. Peter's Canal, 119, 323

St. Peters (Cape Breton), 73, 112, 322

Scotchfort (Prince Edward Island), 60

Scotch Presbytery of Halifax, 149

Scots Hill (Nova Scotia), 76

Scots in Canada, 22

Scots Magazine, 25, 308

Scotsman, 133, 157

Scott, John, 47

Scottish Culture, 188–191

Scottish Enlightenment, 150, 331

Scottish Lowlands, 7

Scourie, 329

Selkirk, Lord (Thomas Douglas, 5th Earl of), 6, 8, 14, 15, 33, 78–80, 104, 105, 131, 150, 309, 326

Seven Years War (1756–1763), 40, 305

Sharp, William, 48

Shaw, Baillie Alexander, 24

Shaw, Donald, 53

Shaw, Duncan, 116, 121, 145

Sheep farming (Scotland), 16, 56, 76, 78, 80, 91, 110, 115, 131, 132, 153, 157, 215

Shelburne, formerly Port Roseway (Nova Scotia), 35, 40, 42, 43, 235, 289, 312

Ship captains:

Allan, J., 288, 292

Allan, Robert, 235, 289

Allen, ___, 251

Anderson, Alexander, 247, 263, 281

Ashi, ___, 264

Athol, ___, 255, 285

Auld, T., 268, 270

Ballantyne, ___, 238, 286

Beverly, Robert, 236, 245, 287

Bishop, J., 247

Boan, John, 248

Bodie, J., 253

Bolton, W., 262

Briggs, Allan, 260, 294

Brown, A., 242, 269, 282, 295

Brown, John, 245, 259, 290

Cameron, ___, 276

Carr, ___, 260

Chambers, W., 274, 287

Church, W.S., 239, 292

Clayton, James, 241

Collins, ___, 266, 291

Coverdale, ___, 247, 254, 255, 259, 294, 297

Craigie, Alexander, 243, 298
Cram, Jonathan, 219, 296
Crane, ___, 196, 236, 285
Darby, Thomas, 294
Davidson, Wm., 246, 282
Donaldson, James, 256, 289
Douglas, ___, 252, 296
Duncan, Alexander, 243
Fleck, A., 256, 284
Forster, ___, 264
Forster, Joseph, 242, 289, 289
Fraser, James, 285
Frazer, James, 251
Frazier, ___, 169
Galt, Robert, 212, 238, 284
Gibson, N., 256, 296
Goodchild, ___, 266, 293
Grange, William, 227, 275, 288
Greig, H., 241, 242, 281
Grey, William, 172, 226, 270, 290
Hall, ___, 270
Hanley, Francis, 174, 273, 276, 287, 335
Henning, C., 270
Henry, Matthew, 239, 288
Hicks, Michael, 266, 281
Hill, ___, 216, 253, 293
Hogg, John, 241, 287
Hudson, John, 244, 249, 290
Hunter, ___, 262, 283
Hutchison, John, 245, 274, 289, 292
Jack, W., 253
Kelly, W., 243, 296
Kirk, ___, 269, 293
Laing, ___, 251, 292
Laird, James, 242, 243, 287, 298
Lawrence, Alexander, 244
Lawson, ___, 261, 296
Leith, J., 272, 296
Leslie, Alexander, 176, 258–261, 263,
    265–268, 270, 273, 274, 276, 280
Levens, ___, 272
Levie, John, 248, 285
Liddell, ___, 251, 283

Logan, James, 246, 288
Lookup, T., 253, 297
Love, Thomas, 242, 295
MacDonald, ___, 276, 295
MacDonald, John, 231, 274, 290
Maclean, ___, 269
MacLachlan, Dugald, 141, 229
MacLeod, R., 253, 282
Maddison, ___, 245, 297
Main, James, 240, 241
Mandell, ___, 254, 285
Manson, Donald, 141, 171, 272, 292,
    296
Mason, James, 246, 295
Masson, George, 241, 286
Matheson, ___, 247, 280
Matthews, ___, 250
McAlly, ___, 277
McAlpine, J., 262
McDonald, Alexander, 240, 286
McDonald, John, 275
McIntosh, Andrew, 246, 291
McIver, D., 262
McKechney, ___, 273, 283
McKellop, ___, 254, 296
McKenzie, 297
McKenzie, George, 232
McKenzie, George, 179, 180, 257,
    275, 290, 297
McKinley, D., 269
McLachlan, Dugald, 275, 286
Mclean, Alan, 237, 282, 284
McMaster, ___, 262, 281
McMorland, William, 250, 282
McRitchie, D., 250, 282
Meys, Richard, 243, 296
Mitchell, ___, 255, 291
Mitchell, W., 262
Moncur, ___, 241, 293
Moore, James, 242, 287
Morrison, James, 240, 283, 291, 336
Morrison, John, 244–246, 270, 273,
    280, 285, 293

Munro, ___, 250, 291
Murray, ___, 169
Murray, George, 25, 253, 287
Normand, George, 247, 288
Norris, J., 239, 294
Oliphant, ___, 291
Oswald, James, 241–243, 245–247, 251, 255, 257, 259–261, 263–265, 280, 290
Peterson, ___, 277, 297
Pennan, Andrew, 243, 246, 293
Philip, Alexander, 244, 296
Pirie, Alexander, 244, 298
Pirie, James, 240, 283
Postill, F., 272, 288
Potts, J., 256, 296
Rea, James, 256, 283
Ridley, John, 263, 294
Ritchie, Thomas, 268
Robertson, D., 262
Rodgers, Alexander, 245
St. Girese, Thomas, 239, 286
Scott, ___, 250, 253, 260, 267, 284, 285, 293, 297
Scott, Andrew, 244, 284
Shaw, ___, 269, 292
Sheridan, William, 234, 235, 290
Simpson, ___, 246
Simpson, Walter, 245, 294
Slocomb, ___, 263
Smith, ___, 203, 237, 286, 290, 295
Smith, James, 290
Smith, John, 240, 290
Smith, William, 248
Snowdon, ___, 255, 283
Spark, ___, 265
Spiers, John, 193, 234, 287
Stevenson, ___, 254
Stirling, J., 280
Stirling, Samuel, 276, 289
Stoke, James, 247, 286
Stokeham, ___, 285
Stove, ___, 175, 272
Strachan, W., 247, 292

Thomas, Alexander, 177, 178, 271
Thomson, ___, 254, 261, 282, 292
Tod, James, 240, 282
Toft, Daniel, 263, 289
Tucker, ___, 263, 298
Vickerman, ___, 254, 288
Walker, A., 256, 280
Walker, Duncan, 169, 267
Watt, Alexander, 217, 286
Watt, James, 169, 254, 260, 290
Wells, George, 244, 284
Whitehead, Robert, 249
Williamson, ___, 251, 292
Wilson, A., 247, 287
Wilson, John, 250, 290
Wilson, W., 247, 281
Young, ___, 256, 287
Young, John
Yule, Alexander, 240, 294
Ship crossings, 234–277, 280–298
Ship Harbour (Port Hawesbury) (Cape Breton), 109, 121, 157, 219, 257, 264, 281, 283, 296
Ship Passenger Acts, see Passenger regulations
Ships:
  Aberdeenshire of Aberdeen, 167, 217, 255, 257, 259–260, 261–265, 280, 334
  Acadian of Glasgow, 168, 262–265, 268, 270, 272, 280
  Active, 256, 280, 321
  Adrian, 264, 280
  Agincourt of Leith, 247, 250, 280
  Aimwell of Aberdeen, 244, 245, 249, 280
  Albion, 258
  Albion of Aberdeen, 167, 176, 259–261, 263, 265–268, 270, 273, 274, 276, 280, 334, 335
  Albion of Glasgow, 262, 281
  Albion of Scarborough, 154, 266, 281
  Alexander (& 2 other ships), 63, 78, 236, 238, 281

Amethyst of Aberdeen, 241, 242, 281
Amity of Glasgow, 264, 281
Amity of Peterhead, 247, 281
Anacreon of Newcastle, 248, 281
Ann, 249, 257, 281, 324
Ann Grant, 266, 281
Ann of Banff, 170, 251, 281
Anne of North Shields, 240, 282, 321
Ardgour of Fort William, 164, 165, 334
Ark, 111
Atlantic of Stornoway, 105, 253, 282
Augusta of Dumfries, 246, 249, 282
Aurora, 88, 243, 255, 282
Aurora of Greenock, 67, 237, 282
Banffshire of Dundee, 282
Bassettere of Greenock, 250, 282
Betsey of Rhode Island, 26, 308
Blagdon, 261, 282
Breeze, 261, 282
British King of Dundee, 269, 282
British Queen, 249, 283
Cadmus, 118, 255, 283
Caledonia of Alloa, 251, 283
Cambria of Aberdeen, 240, 241, 244, 283
Canada, 262, 283
Caroline of Liverpool, 257, 283
Catherine, 157, 283, 332
Centurion of Aberdeen, 240, 283
Charles Hamerton of Liverpool, 273, 283
Charles Hockin, 262, 283
Charlotte Kerr, 261, 263, 283
Chieftain, 161
Chieftain of Kirkaldy, 265, 284
Clansman of Glasgow, 153, 267, 284
Cleopatra, 170
Cleostratus, 271, 272, 284
Clyde, 261, 284
Columbus, 119, 256, 284
Commerce, 80, 212, 238, 253, 256, 284, 317, 324

Corsair of Greenock, 178, 256, 259, 260, 268, 284
Cruickston Castle of Greenock, 269, 284
Cumberland, 261, 284
Deveron of Glasgow, 171, 269, 284
Diadem of St. John, 244, 284
Dorset of Grangemouth, 244, 285
Douglas, 255, 285
Douglas of Aberdeen, 246, 285
Dove of Aberdeen, 63–66, 76, 196, 202, 236, 285, 314
Dunkenfield [Dunkeld], 57, 236, 285
Dunlop, 252, 253, 259, 285
Eagle, 271, 285
Earl of Dalhousie of Aberdeen, 248, 285
Earl of Fife, 262, 285
Eclipse, 267, 285
Economist of Newport, 263, 285
Economy of Aberdeen, 169, 251
Eldon, 262, 286
Elizabeth and Ann of North Shields, 166, 239
Ellen of Liverpool, 141, 229
Emperor Alexander of Aberdeen, 115, 169, 217, 219, 323
Fame of Aberdeen, 241
Favourite of Grangemouth, 240, 321
Favourite of Kirkaldy, 76, 78, 238
Flora, 162
Francis Ann of Irvine, 110, 248, 322
Garland, 251
General Goldie of Dumfries, 248
George of Dundee, 140, 173, 174, 335
George Stevens, 119
Glasgow, 235
Glentanner of Aberdeen, 169, 242, 252, 322
Golden Text of Aberdeen, 63
Good Intent of Aberdeen, 236, 245
Halifax Packet of Sunderland, 241, 242

Harmony, 252
Harmony of Aberdeen, 134, 322, 327
Harmony of Whitehaven, 120, 256, 287
Harriet, 274, 287
Hector, xiii, xvi, 3–6, 8–10, 16–19, 21–23, 26, 28, 31–33, 35, 38, 45, 50, 54, 65, 78, 80, 81, 127, 131, 143, 166, 180, 182, 183, 193, 234, 287, 307, 309, 312, 317
Helen, 242
Helen of Heroen, 281
Helen of Kirkaldy, 89, 247, 287
Henry and William, 288
Hercules of Aberdeen, 169, 178, 288
Hercules of Liverpool, 288
Hero, 139, 288
Highland Lad, 288
Highlander of Aberdeen, 263, 288
Hope (1), 103, 142, 239, 247, 288
Hope (2), 247, 288
Hope of Glasgow, 227, 275, 288
Hope of Lossie, 63, 64, 236, 288
Hunter of Aberdeen, 246, 288
Industry, 288
Integrity, 167
Isabella of Dundee, 289
Isabella of Glasgow, 139, 140, 177, 258, 261, 267, 269, 271, 289
Islay, 289
Jane Kay, 170, 264, 289
Jean Hastie of Grangemouth, 168, 289
Jessie, 262, 289
John, 235, 289, 312
John, 263, 289
John and Jean, 235, 289
John and Robert, 157, 273
John of Berwick, 242, 289
Joseph Harrison, 274, 289
Joseph Hutchison, 276, 289
Lady Emily of Sunderland, 140, 174, 175, 272, 290

Lady Grey of North Shields, 140, 171, 172, 226, 270, 290
Leopold of Leith, 250, 290
London of Glasgow, 231, 274, 275, 290, 329
Lord Brougham, 260, 290
Lord Gardner, 245, 290
Louisa of Aberdeen, 122, 243, 245, 246, 248–252, 258, 290
Lovelly Nelly, 166, 234, 235, 290, 309, 317
Lovely Mary of Dumfries, 244, 249, 290
Lulan of Pictou, 142, 143, 180, 232, 275, 277, 290
Maid of Maven (steamship), 276
Malay (*Mallory*), 122, 225, 259, 290, 325
Malvina of Aberdeen, 240, 290
Manchester, 250, 291
Margaret, 291, 333
Margaret of Peterhead, 246, 291
Mariner of Sunderland, 154, 170, 171, 266, 270, 291, 331
Marquis of Stafford, 291
Mars of Alloa, 255, 291
Mary (1), 250, 291
Mary (2), 257, 291
Mary Ann, 262, 291
Mary Kennedy, 258, 291
Mary of Aberdeen, 240–242, 291, 324
Mercator, 254, 255, 257, 265, 292
Minerva, 251, 292
Minerva of Aberdeen, 247, 292
Morningfield of Aberdeen, 179, 251, 292
Nancy, 238, 292
Nancy of South Shields, 239, 246, 292
Nelly, 292
Nero, 259, 292
Nith of Liverpool, 269, 270, 292
Nora, 63, 68, 236, 292, 316

Norman, 161
North Star, 238, 292
Northern Friends of Clyde, 11, 74, 178, 237, 292
Northumberland, 117, 254, 262, 293
Nymph, 245, 293
Osprey of Leith, 269, 293, 335
Ossian of Leith, 134, 216, 217, 253, 293, 322, 327
Pacific of Aberdeen, 270, 273, 293, 335
Pallas, 239, 293
Paragon, 266, 293
Percival, 250, 293
Perseverance of Aberdeen, 92, 111, 241, 242, 249, 293
Phesdo of Aberdeen, 243, 245, 293
Phoenix, 261, 293
Ploughman of Aberdeen, 240, 21, 243, 294
Poland, 263, 294
Polly, 239, 294
Prince Leopold, 248, 294
Prince William, 92, 214, 241, 294, 319
Prompt of Bo'ness, 178, 247, 253, 294, 319
Protector of New Brunswick, 245, 246, 294
Quebec Packet, 269
Rambler of Leith, 91, 181, 239, 294
Recovery, 252, 294
Robert & Margaret, 264, 294
Romulus of Greenock, 178, 259, 294
Rother, 270
Rover, 260, 294
Rowena, 249, 295
Ruby of Aberdeen, 134, 242, 253, 295, 322, 327
St. Andrew of New Brunswick, 272, 296, 335
St. Lawrence of Newcastle, 219, 257, 296
Sally, 235, 295

Sarah Botsford of Glasgow, 276, 295, 314
Sarah of Liverpool, 63–66, 76, 203, 212, 237, 295
Scotia, 248, 295
Serius, 141, 274, 295
Sesostris, 336
Seven Sisters of Aberdeen, 242, 295
Sir Sydney Smith, 239, 295
Six Sisters, 260, 262, 295, 327
Skeene of Leith, 246, 249, 250, 295
Sovereign of Kirkwall, 274, 295
Speculation, 251, 252, 296
Sprightly of Dundee, 244, 296
Staffa (steamboat), 264
Stephen, 296
Stephen Wright of Newcastle, 119, 120, 256, 296
Superior of Peterhead, 140, 171, 272, 296
Surry of London, 243, 296
Sylvanus of North Shields, 261, 296
Tamerlane, 118, 178, 252, 254, 296
Tartar of Perth, 107, 243, 296, 321
Tay of Glasgow, 271, 297
Thetis, 177, 254, 255, 257, 258, 297
Thistle, 267, 297
Thompson's Packet of Dumfries, 252, 253, 297
Three Brothers of Hull, 245, 245, 297
Tongataboo of New Glasgow, 180, 277, 297
Traveller of Leith, 247, 297
Transport, 48
Tweed of Ullapool, 78, 166, 237, 297
Two Sisters of Pictou, 120, 179, 180, 257, 280, 297
Ulysses, 311
Unicorn, 270, 297
Union, 253, 297
Universe of Aberdeen, 120, 257, 271, 297
Vestal, 259, 298

Victory, 250, 298
Vine of Peterhead, 244, 298
William Henry, 265, 298
William of Aberdeen, 243, 298
William Tell, 103, 248, 298
Ythan of Aberdeen, 243, 298
Zephyr, 178, 264, 298
Sherbrooke, John Coape (Sir) (Lieut. Gov.), 214
Shipwreck(s), 91, 132, 181, 239, 258, 271, 294
Shubenacadie (Nova Scotia), 32
Shubenacadie River, 41, 311
Shunacadie (Cape Breton), 103
Sim, Robert, 31
Simpson, David, 47
Simpson, J.F. (Capt.), 172
Sir Edward Mortimer Inn, 83, 88
Sissibou River (Nova Scotia), 43
Skeene, John (emigration agent), 251
Skinner, James, 67
Skye Glen (Cape Breton), 122, 259
Skye, Isle of, 48, 49, 121, 122, 139, 146, 155, 156, 164, 225, 258, 259, 273, 290, 291, 324, 332, 336
Skye River, 155
Small, John, 48
Smallpox (on ships crossings), 63, 65, 113, 120, 140, 143, 153, 181, 236, 256, 257, 269, 274
Smashems Head, 47
Smith, George, 83, 318
Smith, John, 69
Smith, Robert, 47
Snizort (Skye), 269, 324
South Carolina (USA), 38, 39, 57, 310, 313
South Carolina Royalists, 53
South River (Antigonish), 127
South Uist, Isle of, 60, 67, 73, 74, 78, 102, 107, 113–116, 119, 122, 142, 143, 146, 158, 160, 217, 237, 252, 254, 262, 268, 275, 315

Southern Shore (Cape Breton), 72
Springville (Nova Scotia), 50, 52
Sprott, John (Rev.), 42
Squatters, squatting, 39, 71, 100, 102, 109, 122, 306, 321
Stafford, Lord, see Duke of Sutherland
Star Inn (Inverness), 242, 249
Steele, John, 70
Steerage (on ships), 164, 173, 174, 258, 272
Stellarton (Nova Scotia), 50, 52
Stevenson, John (emigration agent), 242
Stewart, Alexander, 47
Stewart, Alexander, 99
Stewart, Dougald, 24
Stewart, James (Sir) (4th Lord Ochiltree), 304
Stewart, Dugald (Prof.), 150
Stewart, Duncan, 99
Stewart, John, 99
Stewart, John (Rev.), 144, 148, 154, 155, 333
Stewart, Murdoch (Rev.), 151, 331, 333
Stewartdale (Cape Breton), 155
Stillwater (Nova Scotia), 99
Stornoway (Lewis), xiv, 78, 153, 169, 238, 239, 240, 245, 256–258, 260, 262, 267, 276, 277, 281, 282, 284, 285, 287–289, 295, 297, 321, 324, 327
Strait of Canso, see Gut of Canso
Strathglass (Inverness-shire), 50, 51, 72, 76, 236, 238
Strathnaver (Sutherland), 131, 132
Strath Oykel (Easter Ross), 327
Stromness (Orkney), 91, 251, 274, 294, 295
Struan (in Rannoch), 80
Struan House, 46
Struthers, James, 47
Suther, Francis, 132, 133
Sutherland and Transatlantic Friendly Society, 133, 134
Sutherland, Angus, 134

Sutherland, Countess of, 91, 131

Sutherland, County of (Scotland), 10, 19, 26, 30, 31, 46, 77, 78, 81, 92, 98, 107, 110, 129, 131, 132, 134, 135, 138, 141, 147, 154, 171, 191, 214, 216, 217, 234, 237–239, 307, 319, 327, 329, 330

Sutherland, Duke of (First) (George Granville Leveson-Gower), 77, 91, 253, 270

Sutherland Duke of (Second) (George Granville, Earl Gower), 140–142, 274, 275, 328, 329

Sutherland estate, 91, 131–137, 139–141, 143, 154

Sutherland, James, 335

Sutherland, John, 23, 31

Sutherland, John (emigration agent), 171, 173–175, 269, 270, 272, 274, 276, 336

Sutherland River (Nova Scotia), 31

Sutherland, William (Rev.), 135

Sydney (Cape Breton), xiv, 11, 12, 36, 39, 71–74, 102, 103, 107, 109, 110, 115, 119, 122, 147, 148, 152, 153, 156–158, 159, 162, 169, 171, 178, 179, 183, 217, 225, 237, 239, 247, 252, 253, 254, 256–257, 261, 262, 264, 267–270, 274, 276, 277, 280–282, 284–292, 295–298, 323, 324
 County of, 50
 Harbour, 10, 11, 153, 157, 306
 coal mines, 122, 148, 162
 settlement, 73
 timber trade, 102

Sydney County (later Antigonish and Guysborough Counties), 50, 309

Syndey Mines, 148, 158

Sympton, William, 48

Tacksmen, 57, 61, 313

Tatamagouche Bay, 92, 128, 134

Tatamagouche (Nova Scotia), 90, 307

Teignmouth (Tinmouth), 35, 310

Telford, Thomas, 315

Theakston, Joseph, 77

Three Rivers (Prince Edward Island), 28, 239, 261

Thurso (Caithness), 140, 141, 170, 172, 174, 214, 226, 239, 241, 244, 247, 260, 264, 266, 269–274, 276, 280, 281, 286, 287, 289–298, 328

Timber trade, xiv, 8, 9, 13, 29, 34, 28, 54, 73, 82–90, 99, 101, 102, 107, 112, 124, 125, 127, 171, 317, 318, 320, 334
 production, 8, 54, 82, 85
 shipping, 8, 29, 38, 86, 320
 tariffs, 87, 318

Times of London, 157

Tobermory (Mull), xiv, 107, 115, 118, 153, 157, 169, 179, 217, 239, 243, 248, 251–256, 259, 261, 262, 264, 267, 268, 270, 280, 281, 283–289, 292, 296, 298, 322

Tongue (Sutherland), 81, 239, 266

Toronto (Ontario), 271

Torridon (Wester Ross), 273

Town Point, see Dorchester

Troon (Ayrshire), 291

Truestate (Truesdale), James, 48

Truro, Nova Scotia, 23, 34, 47, 48, 236, 307

Tucker, Joseph, 308

Typhus (on ship crossings), 113, 140, 172, 181, 270

Tyree, Isle of, 107, 114, 156, 160

Uig (Lewis), 78, 290

Uig (Skye), 258, 269, 270

Ullapool, also see Isle Martin, 63, 76, 110

Ulster (Northern Ireland), 23

Uniacke, Richard John (Att. Gen.), 117, 323

United States of America, 37, 40, 44, 68, 71, 111, 126, 142, 183, 227, 275, 311, 325, 334, 335
Upper Canada, xv, 12, 139, 140, 143, 145, 153, 160, 162, 310, 312, 328, 329
Ure, J. (emigration agent), 237
Urquhart, David, 23, 31
Urquhart (Inverness-shire), 38, 50, 51, 53, 64

Vessel types, 279
Virginia (USA), 310

Wagamatcook, see Middle River, C.B.
Waipu River, New Zealand, 322, 333
Wallace Harbour, 128
Wallace (Nova Scotia), 78, 136, 260, 295, 327, 328
Wallace River, 328
Washabuck (Cape Breton), 103, 147, 152
Waugh River (Nova Scotia), 92, 128
Weavers (from Scottish Borders), 90
Wentworth, John (Sir) (Gov.), 67
West Bay (Cape Breton), 73
West Calder (Mid Lothian), 250
West Indies, 308, 318
West Inverness-shire, 99, 104
West River (Antigonish), 99

West River (Pictou), 18, 27, 29, 31, 32, 51, 75, 76, 79, 80, 111, 125, 127–129, 326
West, William, 47
Western Isles, see Hebridean Islands
Wester Ross (Scotland), 26, 104, 143, 147, 185, 234, 237, 238, 253, 317, 319
Western Shore (Cape Breton), 72, 74, 101, 102, 105, 107, 118, 123, 147, 148, 152, 320
Whitehaven (Cumbria), 234, 290
Whycocomagh (Cape Breton), 114, 115, 147, 155
Wick (Caithness), 110 113, 171, 294
William Liddell & Company (Glasgow), 299, 317
Wilson, Archibald, 47
Wilson, George Washington, 177
Wilson, John, 334
Windsor (Hants County), 23, 31, 40, 41
Witherspoon, John (Rev. Dr.), 24–26, 31, 32, 308
Wolfe, James (Gen.), 313

Young, William, 131
York, Duke of (Augustus Frederick), 126, 325
Yorkshiremen, 305

Zorra (Upper Canada), 154, 328

ABOUT THE AUTHOR

DR. LUCILLE CAMPEY IS A Canadian, living in Britain, with over thirty years of experience as a researcher and author. It was her father's Scottish roots and love of history which first stimulated her interest in the early exodus of people from Scotland to Canada. She is the great-great-granddaughter of William Thomson, who left Morayshire, on the north east coast of Scotland in the early 1800s to begin a new life with his family, first near Digby then in Antigonish, Nova Scotia. He is described in D. Whidden's *History of the Town of Antigonish* simply as "William, Pioneer" and is commemorated in the St. James Church and Cemetery at Antigonish. Lucille was awarded a Ph.D. by Aberdeen University in 1998 for her researches into Scottish emigration to Canada in the period 1770–1850.

This is Lucille's fourth book on the subject of emigrant Scots. Her first book *"A Very Fine Class of Immigrants": Prince Edward Island's Scottish Pioneers, 1770–1850* (Natural Heritage, 2001) was described by the *P.E.I. Guardian* as "indispensable to Islanders of Scottish ancestry."

Her second book, published in 2002 *"Fast Sailing and Copper-Bottomed"*: *Aberdeen Sailing Ships and the Emigrant Scots They Carried to Canada, 1774–1855* was followed in 2003 by *The Silver Chief: Lord Selkirk and the Scottish Pioneers of Belfast, Baldoon and Red River*. According to the distinguished genealogist and author Ryan Taylor "the three titles now stand as a significant contribution to Canadian immigrant literature."

A Chemistry graduate of Ottawa University, Lucille worked initially in the fields of science and computing. After marrying her English husband she moved to the north of England, where she became interested in medieval monasteries and acquired a Master of Philosophy Degree (on the subject of medieval settlement patterns) from Leeds University. Having lived for five years in Easter Ross while she completed her doctoral thesis, she and Geoff returned to England, and now live near Salisbury in Wiltshire. Lucille's is currently working on a fifth book which will cover emigration from Scotland to Upper Canada during the period 1784 to 1855.